Global Pharmaceutical Policy

Global Pharmaceutical Policy

Ensuring Medicines for Tomorrow's World

Frederick M. Abbott

Edward Ball Eminent Scholar Professor of International Law, Florida State University College of Law, USA

Graham Dukes

External Professor of Drug Policy Studies, Institute of General Practice and Community Health (Section for International Health), University of Oslo, Norway

Edward Elgar

Cheltenham, UK • Northampton, MA, USA

Published by
Edward Elgar Publishing Limited
The Lypiatts
15 Lansdown Road
Cheltenham
Glos GL50 2JA
UK

Edward Elgar Publishing, Inc.
William Pratt House
9 Dewey Court
Northampton
Massachusetts 01060
USA

A catalogue record for this book
is available from the British Library

Library of Congress Control Number: 2009930852

Mixed Sources
Product group from well-managed
forests and other controlled sources
www.fsc.org Cert no. SA-COC-1565
© 1996 Forest Stewardship Council
FSC

ISBN 978 1 84844 090 6

Printed and bound by MPG Books Group, UK

Contents

Preface

Two major developments at the outset of 2009 lend a special timeliness to the publication of this book. First, the Democratic administration of President Barack Obama took the reigns of health policy in Washington, DC, promptly signaling a determination to reform the way that health care is provided in the United States. Second, a global financial crisis has sent shockwaves throughout virtually all sectors of economic activity in practically every country of the world. These two developments, taken together, suggest that policymakers will pay increasingly serious attention to the way medicines are developed, distributed and used.

Wealthier societies can no longer afford wasteful and ineffective public health expenditure. Poorer societies face even greater burdens than before. Governments throughout the developing world face extreme difficulty in funding medicines procurement. Under these background conditions, this book analyzes and offers suggestions to improve the global pharmaceutical regulatory system.

The originator pharmaceutical industry confronts its own financial crisis, and is unlikely to greet a critical examination of its role with equanimity. However, our objective is not to question the important role that industry plays in promoting research or manufacturing products of high quality. It is instead to ask whether there are better ways to make use of the vast resources committed in this field, and to improve the level of prevention and treatment available to everyone.

We hope you will find this book a useful contribution to the urgent dialogue.

Frederick Abbott   Graham Dukes
Tallahassee, Florida USA   *Oslo, Norway*

Acknowledgments

Issues surrounding a proper framework for regulation of the global pharmaceutical sector are complex, and have been the subject of analysis and debate for many years. Devising a proper framework is a long-term project, and most likely the approach will be piecemeal. It seemed opportune in the Spring of 2007 to bring together a number of the most creative and forward-looking thinkers on this subject – collectively with a vast experience in medicine, law and technology – to discuss the 'state-of-the-art' in global pharmaceutical regulation and proposals that might be in the works for improving the existing framework. To that end, a three-day open-ended dialogue was held at Florida State University College of Law in Tallahassee Florida, with about 30 participants from across the geographic and subject matter spectrum in pharmaceutical regulation.

This book is in large measure a tangible output of that meeting in Florida but updated to 2009. The text is the 'own work' of the two authors, but to provide additional perspective we have included various brief 'text boxes' on the basis of presentations by meeting participants. In addition, we have solicited input from several other experts, also presented in boxes at various points in the text.

We extend our thanks to all of the participants in the Florida meeting, listed here, and to additional contributors, also listed. We hope that by broadening the intellectual base of the book we provide our audience with a more richly informed perspective.

Florida meeting participants: Frederick Abbott, Ryan Abbott, Tahir Amin, Wilbert Bannenberg, Jorge Bermudez, Timothy Cross, Graham Dukes, Paulo Etcheverry, Carsten Fink, Joseph Fortunak, John Fraser, Marta Gabrieloni, Ellen 't Hoen, Maria Fernanda Hurtado, Elisabet Helsing, M. Fabiana Jorge, Lorelei Ritchie de Larena, David Lee, James Love, Precious Matsoso, Thomas Mays, Priti Radhakrishnan, Jerome Reichman, Pedro Roffe, Dilp Shah, Michael Steffen, Robynn Sturm, Antony Taubman, Yolanda Tayler, Gina Vea, Howard Zucker

Additional contributors: Arthur Daemmerich, Hilbrand Haak, Daniel W. Sigelman

We extend a special note of thanks to Fred's wife, Cathy Abbott, who spent long hours transforming our rough text into a readable end product.

Cross-Atlantic collaborations require reconciliation of different linguistic cultures. Cathy has done a superb job of mediating among our English-language traditions.

Abbreviations

APIs	active pharmaceutical ingredients
ASEAN	Association of South East Asian Nations
CBD	Convention on Biological Diversity
CDER	Center for Drug Evaluation and Research
CPMP	Committee for Proprietary Medicinal Products
DFID	Department for International Development
DNDi	Drugs for Neglected Disease Institute
DTC	direct to consumer
EMEA	European Medicines Evaluation Agency
EC	European Commission
EU	European Union
EURODIS	European Organization for Rare Diseases
FAO	Food and Agriculture Organization
FDA	US Food and Drug Administration
FTA	free trade agreement
GAVI	Global Alliance for Vaccines and Immunization
GMP	Good Manufacturing Practice
HCV	hepatitis C virus
ICH	International Conference on Harmonization
IMPACT	International Medical Products Anti-Counterfeiting Taskforce
INCB	International Narcotics Control Board
IND	Investigation Exemption for a New Drug
LDC	Less Developed Country
MABs	monoclonal antibodies
MHRA	Medicines and Healthcare Products Regulatory Agency
MMV	Medicines for Malaria Venture
NGO	non-governmental organization
NICE	National Institute for Health and Clinical Excellence
NIH	US National Institutes of Health
NSF	National Science Foundation
OGTR	Office of the Gene Technology Regulator
OTC	over-the-counter

PhRMA	Pharmaceutical Research and Manufacturers of America
PPP	public-private partnership
R&D	research and development
TRIPS Agreement	Agreement on Trade-Related Aspects of Intellectual Property Rights
SSRIs	Selective serotonin reuptake inhibitors
TDR	Special Programme for Research and Training in Tropical Diseases
TK	traditional knowledge
UMC	Uppsala Monitoring Center
UNCTAD	United Nations Conference on Trade and Development
UNDP	United Nations Development Programme
UNICEF	United Nations Children's Fund
WHO	World Health Organization
WIPO	World Intellectual Property Organization
WTO	World Trade Organization

1.   The challenges we face

OUR OBJECTIVE

Pharmaceutical products play a central role in the prevention and treatment of disease. Making safe and effective pharmaceutical products available and affordable to individuals around the world is a central challenge to the global governance system. There are however myriad obstacles to achieving and maintaining effective worldwide availability of medicines.

Despite the fact that people around the world face largely similar challenges from disease, the policy framework for promoting innovation and regulating pharmaceutical supply is remarkably disjointed. Innovation policy, insofar as it is implemented at all, is established on a country-to-country basis with minimal attention to coordination of research and development. Regulatory structures are almost equally fragmented. Each country has its own set of approval standards and regulatory procedures that must be dealt with, and only to a limited extent are there cooperative procedures or systems of mutual recognition. Corporate decisions concerning where to concentrate innovative efforts, what to produce, where to supply it and on what terms are based on the likely impact on profits and capital markets.[1]

There are wide disparities in levels of income both among countries and within countries. Prices that are reasonably affordable for individuals covered by health insurance in developed countries are likely to be unaffordable for individuals without health insurance in developed and developing countries. There are compelling needs for new medicines to treat diseases affecting both the rich and poor, such as diabetes, cancer, heart disease and the degenerative disorders of old age. Innovation in these areas is costly, yet even with substantial sums invested in research and development rates of innovation are surprisingly low. There are equally compelling needs for new medicines to treat disease conditions predominantly afflicting tropical regions where poverty rates are typically high. Far less is invested in the diseases of the poor because of a lack of market demand.

Medicines must be safe and effective. Making and keeping them so is a challenge for both private and public sector suppliers, for the regulators charged with promoting and protecting public health and for the policy makers who determine the framework within which regulation operates.

This book examines the state of play of the international system for the development and supply of pharmaceutical products, and offers insights into how some of its challenges might be addressed. This system is enormously complex, with many moving parts, and there is not likely to be a quick fix for the many challenges. There are quite a few good ideas circulating among individuals and groups involved in formulating and implementing public policy in the field of medicines. This book was inspired by a roundtable among such individuals and groups hosted at Florida State University College of Law in the spring of 2007. At that roundtable, a number of the ideas discussed in this book were put forward and debated. The perspectives of some roundtable participants (and others) are incorporated at various points in the book, often in 'boxes'. Certainly new initiatives are needed in this field, and existing initiatives can and should be improved. We try to identify and explain those areas in which present policies are not working, and we offer suggestions regarding ways to improve them. We put forward our own proposals regarding directions that global public policy in the field of medicines should take. We do not claim a monopoly on promising ideas. We hope that this volume will succeed at least in moving the dialogue on these subjects forward.

OVERVIEW

Broadly speaking, there are two main categories of pharmaceutical products available on world markets. The first consists of newer originator medicines that are covered by patent protection (and/or the protection afforded in some instances by regulatory marketing exclusivity) and are typically sold at substantially higher prices than older established medicines. These originator medicines are developed, produced and sold by a handful of large multinational innovator companies, virtually all of which are based in the industrialized countries. The second category comprises generic medicines that are not (or are no longer) subject to patent or marketing exclusivity protection, and that are typically sold at substantially lower prices than originator products – commonly no more than 5 percent or 10 percent of the former price. Generic products are produced by a wide range of companies, ranging from small-scale to major multinational operators, based throughout the world. Generic pharmaceutical products sell in much larger volumes worldwide than originator products but, because of the immense price difference, gross revenues from sales of originator pharmaceuticals far exceed those from generic products. In 2007 total worldwide revenues from sales of pharmaceutical products amounted to approximately $650 billion, of which $550 billion went to the originator companies and $100 billion to the generic companies.

INNOVATION POLICY

Research and development (R&D) aimed at the creation of new medicines is well understood to be necessary for the prevention and treatment of disease, and policies designed to promote innovation are a core component of global public policy in this field. Industry has done much through information campaigns to create the popular impression that major pharmaceutical companies have been consistently successful and efficient in ensuring innovation. In actual fact, as shown in Chapters 2 and 3, the rate of innovation over the past decade has been decidedly low and the medicines developed have not always been well attuned to actual needs. Publicly funded research has made a significant contribution to the progress that has been made, a contribution that is not always sufficiently recognized.

The history of pharmaceutical innovation in modern times has involved periods of ebb and flow. A decade or two of rapid advance across a range of disease targets, generally based on a major technological advance, tends to be followed by a period in which few new treatments are developed, leading to concern as to whether the possibilities for innovation have been exhausted. Today we are in a period of low tide. Few significant new products are being introduced. Most of the products being brought to market by the pharmaceutical originators are minor modifications of earlier products. Perhaps most significantly, the widely proclaimed new era of biotechnology has yet to prove its ability to deliver on the enthusiastic claims that have been made for it.

A number of reasons have been suggested for the present low rate of innovation. First, the originator pharmaceuticals market is influenced by perverse incentives. Innovator companies find they are well rewarded for making minor modifications to previously patented products so as to effectively extend the life of monopolies (so-called 'evergreening'), a low-risk practice that is highly lucrative. Perverse incentives also encourage investment in lifestyle drugs for which there is an ever-present consumer demand. Because capital markets are most concerned about profits, senior management at the originator companies is less inclined to take risks than to pursue relatively safe bets on product line extensions.

Second, it is sometimes suggested that the low-hanging fruit of pharmaceutical innovation already has been plucked. In particular, innovations for which synthetic organic chemistry is capable have largely been identified, and more complex large-molecule and biological materials innovations promised by the biotechnology industry are more costly and difficult than perhaps initially assumed.

It may be – as the industry suggests – that spectacular success in the biotechnology sector is just around the corner. Indeed, looked at from a long-term perspective, the biotech industry is in its infancy. The human organism may be more complicated than biotechnologists expected when they first began to decode the human genome, but patience may be rewarded as more complex biological systems are better understood.

Third, the originator pharmaceutical industry has gone through two decades of consolidation, and the net result of consolidation is a reduction in the targets of opportunity being pursued by R&D laboratories.

Fourth, there is a disconnect – apparent worldwide – between research in university and research institute laboratories and the realities of producing new medicines. There is a shortage of individuals qualified and willing to 'translate' laboratory innovation into products entering the marketplace, and in a position where they can ensure that this happens.

A number of proposals have been made to retool the mechanisms for promoting innovation in the pharmaceutical sector. These include reforming patent laws so as to remove perverse incentives to extend the life of patents through minor modifications, changing the type of remedies that are available to patent holders able to prove infringement, developing alternative quasi-patents that would provide more limited types of exclusivity for minor modifications, shifting the focus of innovation promotion to the use of prizes to address specifically identified disease targets, expanding and improving the use of government (and private foundation) subsidies to channel R&D investment more appropriately, and working to disaggregate the reward for developing innovative products from the prices consumers ultimately pay for medicine.

A critical aspect of the innovation equation involves the lack of attention to diseases primarily affecting individuals in poor and primarily tropical countries, the so-called neglected diseases. These are diseases like sleeping sickness, dengue fever and Chagas disease. Because the individuals who require treatments for these diseases are without financial resources, there is, as noted above, no market-based incentive for investing in R&D on pharmaceutical products to treat them. During the past five or six years a number of public-private partnerships have evolved to pursue research on these treatments, and so far the prognosis is fairly good. But these efforts must be sustained, and this will require continued effort and attention.

There are a significant number of obstacles to overcome when attempting to define and recommend truly global policies on innovation. The financial and human resources available to governments and private sector investors differ widely. The disease profiles of countries vary depending on a variety of factors, including climate, geography and income level. Industrial policy as regards promoting the development and/or maintenance of pharmaceutical manufacturing is an important element affecting innovation policy.

Governments are also limited in the range of innovation policies they may adopt as a consequence of more or less globally applicable rules adopted for countries that are members of the World Trade Organization (WTO) that is now virtually all-embracing. These rules are embodied in the Agreement on Trade-Related Aspects of Intellectual Property Rights (or TRIPS Agreement) that entered into force on 1 January 1995. The TRIPS Agreement requires all WTO member countries to provide protection for pharmaceutical products and processes (with certain exceptions remaining for 'least developed' countries). A ten-year transition period that permitted developing countries like India to avoid granting protection expired on 1 January 2005, so that essentially all countries with advanced pharmaceutical production capacity are today required to provide patent protection.

Patents are not the only form of intellectual property protection available to pharmaceutical originators. Public health regulatory authorities in a substantial number of major jurisdictions grant a period of marketing exclusivity to the first party that obtains approval for a new pharmaceutical product. The theory behind such exclusivity is that it rewards the originator company for investing in clinical trials. In the European Union (EU), there is a ten-year (plus one) marketing exclusivity period. In the United States, there is a five-year period, subject to supplementary clinical data-based extensions. These grants of marketing exclusivity are supplementary to patent protection, and serve to inhibit the introduction of generic versions of originator products. The United States and EU have very actively promoted the adoption of marketing exclusivity grants in other countries, including developing countries. Marketing exclusivity rights strongly enhance the power of the originator pharmaceutical companies, particularly in markets where they have not secured patents, or have secured weak patents. There is presently ongoing in the United States a critical debate in Congress concerning the extent to which originator biotechnology-based pharmaceutical products (so-called 'biosimilars') will be protected against generic competition by marketing exclusivity rules. The outcome of this debate will have an important global effect because complex biotech medicines are typically exported from the major developed countries, and because the United States recently has been successful in causing other countries to emulate its rules.

The TRIPS Agreement allows flexibility in the way governments implement their patent law, and it provides a number of exception mechanisms, such as authority to grant government use and compulsory licenses that bypass the patent holder. It remains, however, arguable whether TRIPS flexibility and exceptions are sufficient to permit developing countries, in particular, sufficient leeway to protect their best interests and to develop their own innovative pharmaceutical sectors. Moreover, the United States has led the way in striking bilateral trade deals with developed and

developing countries that limit even further the options available in innovation policy. (These matters are discussed in Chapter 2.) This is the environment in which government policy makers presently operate.

Economies of scale play an important role in innovation and in the development of successful pharmaceutical manufacturing industries. If it is not
feasible to coordinate innovation policy at a global level, it may be wise to
concentrate efforts at the regional level where similarities among national
capacities and needs are likely to outweigh differences, and where legal
frameworks established by regional economic arrangements may provide
necessary institutional structures. The theme of the potential for enhanced
regional coordination and collaboration is found throughout this book.

The World Health Organization (WHO) was established to promote
global public health. During the past three or four years the WHO has
more actively debated innovation policy and the role that the organization may play in promoting innovation. With the adoption of a Global
Strategy and Plan of Action in 2008, the World Health Assembly (the
senior governing body of the WHO) has taken a significant step toward
proactively encouraging new models of innovation. There is reason to
be cautious about the progress that can be made at the WHO because
of factors that affect governance at all multilateral organizations. With
200 national governments represented and myriad stakeholder interest
groups, with the pharmaceutical industry highly active as one of the nongovernmental organizations (NGOs) in consultation with the agency, it
may be difficult to reach consensus decisions that will exert a meaningful
effect on national governments in the near to medium term. Over the long
term we may expect the WHO to take a larger role in the development and
implementation of innovation policy. For the shorter term we expect that
concrete action will mainly take place at the national and regional levels.

Regardless of the way the structure of innovation policy is determined,
it is essential that all countries and regions have reasonable access to
new technologies that are necessary to develop and produce appropriate
medicines. The international legal structure and international financial
mechanisms must be tailored in a way that promotes rather than inhib-
its dissemination of knowledge. Innovation policy must be designed to
encourage invention by providing suitable reward, but not at the expense
of human suffering.

REGULATION OF SAFETY AND EFFICACY

Regulation of the pharmaceutical sector is aimed primarily at ensuring that
all of the products used to treat patients are safe and effective, regardless

of whether they are originator or generic products. There is a great deal of subject matter under the tent of safety and efficacy. The process of regulation begins in earnest when an originator company seeks approval from regulatory authorities for the introduction of a new product.

Determining whether a new medicine is indeed safe and provides therapeutic benefit (that is, is efficacious) is one of the most difficult areas of pharmaceutical regulation. New products seeking regulatory approval typically must have undergone a series of clinical trials proceeding from a basic test of safety (Phase 1), to a limited test of efficacy (Phase 2), to a wider test of efficacy and safety involving a substantial pool of human subjects (Phase 3). Based on our current state of knowledge, it is perhaps surprising that it remains so difficult to predict whether a medicine that has shown some promise in test tubes (*in vitro*), or in animal testing (*in vivo*), will prove safe and effective when tested on groups of human subjects. Even when the findings in pre-marketing studies in man are positive it remains difficult to extrapolate from these in order to anticipate the effects of medicines taken over longer periods of time. Recent experience with the Cox-2 inhibitors (wherein use for an extended period proved to pose a significantly heightened risk of coronary event) illustrates this point, as well as the absolute necessity for complete openness as regards the results of clinical work.

In principle, medicines should not harm the patients whom they are intended to treat. Yet this is not an absolute standard. Most medicines have some undesirable side effects, at least in certain patients. The objective of regulation is to make sure that these side effects are appropriately proportionate to the benefits the medicines are conferring. We should not put patients at risk in treating common headaches. We may elect to tolerate more significant risk in treating late stage cancer.

In recent years there has been very substantial criticism of a common industrial and regulatory practice of maintaining the confidentiality of the results of clinical trials. This prevents independent researchers from having a close look at the data underlying the conclusions presented to regulators. As a result of this criticism – based on unfortunate real world events – there is now a modest trend toward disclosure of clinical trial results, largely on a voluntary basis in some countries. There are proposals, discussed in this book, to require making all clinical trial results public, or even to shift responsibility for the conduct of clinical trials to the public sector.

It is of some interest that clinical trials in most countries are primarily designed to compare the new medicine with a placebo, and not with existing therapies for the same condition. The regulator approves a new medicine not because it is better than the established medicines, but because it has some benefit in comparison to the placebo. This can naturally lead to confusion in the prescriber marketplace (i.e. doctors, pharmacists and so on), and among consumers. We are accustomed to thinking that a newer product is better than an older product – otherwise, why would we be inclined to buy the newer (and often more expensive) product? This is where pharmaceutical industry marketing exerts an unfortunate influence. Not only does it exploit to the full the instinctive belief that newer is better; it also stresses whatever evidence might be considered to point to advantages of the new product, even where the comparison has not been entirely objective or relates to a matter of no relevance to practice.

There is also a question regarding the extent to which the standards used to judge safety and efficacy should be modified to take into account the circumstances of real life. For example, in light of the extensive threat to sub-Saharan Africa presented by HIV/AIDS, should a potential break-through treatment be subjected to a shortened testing period because delay in introducing the product may result in numerous unnecessary deaths? Such an argument has often enough been advanced, all too easily obscuring the fact that longer term studies are not a mere bureaucratic formality; if a product is released relatively early, critical study will still need to continue in order to confirm (or refute) the earlier evidence that it possesses an acceptable degree of efficacy and safety.

As if this were not enough reason for concern, one must add that even bodies such as the US Food and Drug Administration (FDA) have now begun to experience serious doubt as to some of the evidence of efficacy and safety that they have normally been willing to accept; a very widely used cholesterol-lowering drug accepted by the agency in 2002 has still not been shown to provide any real health benefit and is now suspected of inducing malignancies.[2]

As the technology of medicines changes – broadly moving from synthetic organic chemistry to biotechnology – regulators are finding themselves faced with a host of new challenges, discussed in some detail in Chapter 3. The molecular structure of biotechnology-based medicines is much more complex than the structure of chemistry-based medicines. The potential for longer term effects based upon alterations of human physiology is significantly increased by the introduction of biological medicines. It is a subject of some debate whether the current mechanisms used for evaluating synthetic medicines can be adapted with only minor modification to evaluate biotechnology-based medicines, or whether a new set of regulatory assessment tools is required.

The need to ensure an acceptable level of safety also means that medicines must be produced to the standard of quality needed to ensure that the patient is receiving precisely what is intended, nothing more and nothing less. The production of medicines is typically undertaken in facilities in which environmental factors are carefully controlled, with inputs (that is, active pharmaceutical ingredients (APIs) and excipients) that have been rigorously tested against benchmark standards. It is the job of regulatory authorities to assure that pharmaceutical producers maintain good manufacturing practices (GMP). As will be discussed, however, there are different levels of GMP depending upon the standards of the regulator and upon the type of product being manufactured.

There are major problems in the global supply chain relating to the quality of basic materials used in the manufacture of medicines. A few regulatory authorities in OECD countries – including the US FDA and the EU's European Medicines Evaluation Agency (EMEA) – employ (or have access to the services of) substantial numbers of inspectors undertaking rigorous examinations of production facilities to assure that quality standards are maintained. The work of these inspectors extends to foreign production facilities that export products to the United States and/or the EU. Thus, an Indian API manufacturer exporting to the United States must have its facility inspected and approved by the US FDA. (Of course, experience reported in 2008 with exports of heparin from China illustrate that even this cross-border system has its weaknesses[3].) However, for those products manufactured in China, India and other emerging economy countries that are not destined for the OECD markets, there is a very much weaker regulatory structure. This leads to significant quality problems not only within those countries, but also for importers in regions such as Latin America that rely upon foreign-produced APIs. There is a critical need to improve the regulatory structures in the major API exporting countries – and one must hope that this will be attained before some catastrophic public health failure ensues.

What is striking about the regulation of safety and efficacy from a global standpoint is the fact, already alluded to above, that most countries still maintain their own standards and regulatory approval processes for allowing medicines to be placed on the market. There is doubtless some value in heterogeneity among regulators in that different systems of assessment may yield somewhat different results. Yet, overall, the present system creates significant obstacles to the efficient worldwide supply of necessary medicines as producers are required to pass through regulatory hurdles in each separate jurisdiction. This limits the availability of medicines, and may well increase prices. There is perhaps no better candidate for regional regulation than the field of medicines.

Countries sharing more or less common geography, more or less common disease burdens, and more or less comparable levels of income should be able to cooperate in regulating the introduction of medicines onto their collective markets. By reducing the need for multiple regulators when medicines are introduced, governments could refocus the attention of regulators towards assuring the quality of those medicines that are currently on the market, paying more attention to the quality of medicines at the point-of-sale. A regional approach to the inspection of production facilities – including the dispatch of adequate teams of inspectors to countries of origin – may be effective in terms both of cost and of public health.

The WHO has, despite the fact that it has no regulatory powers of its own, played an increasingly significant advisory role in establishing regulatory standards in the area of GMP compliance. It has now undertaken an important program to pre-qualify manufacturers supplying HIV/AIDS antiretroviral treatments and certain other HIV-related products. By doing so, the WHO is demonstrating its potential capacity as an institution possessing considerable technical abilities, while at the same time highlighting the weaknesses of regulatory capacity in major API producing countries, like India.

Rules governing the safety and efficacy of medicines are only effective if they are enforced. Regrettably, there have been a significant number of notable regulatory failures that have permitted the introduction of dangerous products onto the market. Sometimes this has happened because of oversight by regulators, but it has also happened because of deliberate or negligent failure on the part of the pharmaceutical industry. It is therefore fortunate that private citizens have in such situations been able to play an important corrective role by seeking redress in the courts, thus ensuring that regulators and the industry pay attention to the legal and ethical rules that govern these matters. The courts, for their part, have played an important role by listening to private citizens and, in a good number of cases, providing relief. Unfortunately there are some worrying trends in the United States toward cutting back on the access of private citizens to redress. In 2008 the US Supreme Court had under submission a case in which the industry sought a safe harbor for pharmaceutical products that have been approved by the US FDA. Wisely, in March 2009 the Supreme Court decided against providing such a safe harbor.

REGULATION OF PRICING AND AVAILABILITY, PROMOTION AND EDUCATION

The maintenance of patents and other forms of marketing exclusivity, discussed above, is surely the single most important factor in permitting the originator industry to charge high prices for newer medicines. Nonetheless, governments are not without regulatory mechanisms to control pricing and availability. It is not uncommon for governments to impose price controls on pharmaceutical products. These controls may be based on different factors or benchmarks, including reference to prices in other countries or cost-plus formulas. Direct price controls are not the only method for controlling the price of medicines. Many countries have adopted generic substitution laws that require pharmacists to provide the customer with a low-cost generic version of a patented medicine when that is available.

Pharmaceutical consumers are often not aware of the real price being paid for their medicine. Some public health systems provide medicines free of charge or at purely nominal cost. Many consumers, such as in the United States, receive medicines under a prescription benefit plan that requires the patient to make some co-payment that is small as compared with the actual price paid for the medicine by the health insurance provider. This makes consumers less price-sensitive than they might be if they were paying the actual price of the medicine. There is therefore no strong public lobby to insist on reasonable levels of medicine pricing, such as there would be if the extent of overcharging were more widely known.

Demand for medicines is heavily influenced by advertising and promotion. Such promotion is permitted in most countries with respect to physicians. A very few countries permit direct to consumer (DTC) advertising. The originator industry argues that DTC advertising provides consumers with information they would not otherwise have, and may encourage them to seek advice and treatment from qualified physicians. Critics of DTC argue that it stimulates over-prescribing and over-consumption of medicines. If an individual really needs treatment, he or she is surely likely to find the way independently to a doctor who will provide it, without pushing from the pharmaceutical industry.

One of the most difficult aspects of pharmaceutical policy is the task of encouraging physicians (and other prescribers) to understand the complex effects of the medicines they are recommending to patients, as well as educating patients regarding best practices in the use of medicines. The Internet has been a game changer in this regard, making vast amounts of information about medical conditions and treatments generally available, information that varies considerably as regards its balance and reliability. At the same time, the Internet is a largely unregulated environment that may encourage consumers to pursue courses of treatment that are not in their best interest.

ACCESS AND AFFORDABILITY

Without innovation, new medicines will not become available. But new medicines that are not affordable present a major global problem. This is not a problem confined to poor countries in Africa, or to developing countries in Latin America and Asia. The United States is facing a looming budgetary crisis as health care costs for an aging population weigh on the federal budget. The uninsured and underinsured face enormous difficulties paying for needed pharmaceutical treatments. Even in Western Europe, with its extensive provisions for the social coverage of health costs, the pressure on available budgets has reached the point where expenditure may have to be cut back unless unit prices can be reduced. A recent paper from Britain's National Institute for Health and Clinical Excellence (NICE) on a series of drugs for the treatment of renal cancer concluded that for one of them the cost of providing an extra year of life was no less than £171,300 (approximately $297,000).[4] Even a relatively wealthy nation, before considering whether it can accept such expense, has the right to enquire whether or not it is justified by the sums required for research and production.

While there is general agreement that the cost of researching and developing new medicines is high, the necessary level of investment in R&D is much debated. However the figures are calculated, there is a tremendous difference between the amounts spent globally on R&D and the aggregate amounts paid for new pharmaceutical products.

The major originator pharmaceutical companies claim to spend an aggregate of about $55–60 billion per year worldwide on R&D.[5] The US federal government, mainly through the National Institutes of Health, spends about US$30 billion per year on pharmaceutical-related R&D (predominantly funding basic research), and in various other countries there is also a degree of public funding. Total global R&D on new pharmaceutical products in a given year is claimed to be about $100 billion (giving a generous allowance to the industry estimates).

The cost of producing originator pharmaceuticals represents a significant part of their selling price. Using figures reported by the originator industry, annual total production costs in 2007 can be roughly approximated at about $137.5 billion.[6] The production costs for the originator companies, particularly those manufacturing in the major developed countries, reflect significant investments in compliance with rigorous regulatory standards. One of the major challenges for the global regulatory system is to assure that some countries do not achieve competitive advantage based on inappropriately reduced regulatory compliance levels or costs. At the same time, originator production processes in the major developed countries might well be made more efficient. There is reason to ask whether the price shield these companies have enjoyed based on patents and marketing exclusivity protection has not unduly reduced their incentives to improve production efficiencies. We are not suggesting or advocating that any country outsource its pharmaceutical production to save compliance and/or labor costs. We do, however, suggest that a closer look might be taken at ways to improve production efficiencies based on the successes of the major generic suppliers like Israel-based Teva.

If it is correct that R&D in total is costing $100 billion yearly, while production costs add some $137.5 billion, the remaining $312.5 billion in the price paid for originator products is going to something else. Where is it going?

There are basic supply chain costs (transport, storage, physical distribution and so on). A major element represents amounts expended on marketing and promotion. These marketing and promotion costs, as discussed in Chapter 6, sometimes represent reasonable expenses connected with educating physician and pharmacy professionals as to the profile and proper usage of new medicines. Often and increasingly these expenditures are bypassing medical professionals and going directly to the consumer, with very questionable intent and effect.

There is administrative overhead and employee salaries – including sometimes astonishing sums paid to senior pharmaceutical industry officers. There are dividends paid to investors.

At the end of the day, consumers around the world (including government public health ministries and hospitals) are spending $550 billion for $100 billion in R&D, $137.5 billion in production costs and $312 billion for a very expensive something else. It is hard to escape the conclusion that there is a better way to deliver value to the global consuming public. Somewhere within the $550 billion paid to the originator industry there must be financial room to provide powerful incentives for innovation, and the production and distribution of high-quality medicines, while at the same time providing affordable medicine to people around the world.

CONCLUSION

In this book we examine a range of policies and institutions involved in promoting innovation, developing and implementing regulations, and trying to assure affordable access to high-quality safe and effective medicines. It is difficult to synthesize a set of recommendations in a few short sentences. But we would like to highlight a few that strike us as critical.

First, the system for promoting innovation worldwide must be refocused on the development of new therapeutic classes, with the lesser emphasis on extending product lines through minor modifications. There are various ways to address this objective by retooling the patent system (including to introduce quasi-patents to protect minor modifications), by extending and improving subsidy programs, by the use of targeted prizes and others.

Second, additional transparency must be introduced into the system by which medicines are assessed and approved.

Third, the marketing of prescription pharmaceutical products directly to consumers introduces both direct costs of promotion, and indirect costs from elevated demand. The heavy promotion of new prescription products increases risks that unforeseen injurious effects will be spread more widely. There is good reason to curtail the trend towards DTC advertising of these products.

Fourth, private civil litigants play an important role in increasing transparency and identifying pharmaceutical product risks, in addition to redressing injury. Courts should be very wary of curtailing the role of private litigation (for example, US state causes of action should not be pre-empted by federal law). If the US Supreme Court moves in this direction, Congress should step in to correct the situation.[7]

Fifth, there is a great deal of regulatory cost imposed by country-to-country assessment of pharmaceutical products. While some degree of regulatory heterogeneity is necessary and appropriate to take into account matters such as differences in climate and disease patterns, it is not necessary that every country review and approve every drug. In light of the current state of global political affairs, we recommend increased efforts on a regional basis to cooperate on and coordinate medicines regulatory policy and implementation.

Sixth, it is important that low-income developing countries maintain focus on essential drugs policies that seek to assure wide access to the most needed treatments. This is particularly important as the 2009 global economic climate threatens to reduce even modest levels of support from developed countries. It remains vitally important that developed countries continue to provide support for medicines purchases for countries and populations that are not viable participants in the global pharmaceuticals market.

NOTES

1. The vast part of the world economy is not 'coordinated' by any central authority. The system for development and supply of pharmaceutical products is not so different from that of other types of goods and services. For automobiles, banking, energy, food and entertainment products, decisions are taken primarily by companies operating in the private sector with some degree of control by national government authorities and a lesser degree of oversight or regulation by multilateral institutions.
2. Dr Robert Temple (FDA), as cited by A. Berenson, 'A popular drug with uncertain benefits', *Int Herald Tribune*, 2 September 2008.
3. See, for example, Walt Bogdanich, 'Heparin is Now Suspected in 62 Fatalities Across U.S.', *Times*, 10 April 2008.

4. Anon., 'NICE turns nasty: what lies behind a tiff over drug pricing', *The Economist*, 21 August 2008.

5. According to the website of the Pharmaceutical Research and Manufacturers of America (PhRMA), 'PhRMA members alone invested an estimated $44.5 billion in 2007 in discovering and developing new medicines. Industry-wide research and investment reached a record $58.8 billion in 2007', http://www.phrma.org/about_phrma/ (accessed 26 October 2008).

6. Based on the 2007 annual Form 10K filings with the US Securities and Exchange Commission of Pfizer and Merck, and the Form 20-F filing of Novartis, originator companies claim costs of goods/materials and production of about 25 percent of gross revenues (Pfizer claiming costs of $11.239 billion on revenues of 48.418 (or 23.2 percent), Novartis claiming costs of $11.032 billion on revenues of 38.947 (or 28.3 percent), and Merck claiming costs of $6140 billion on revenues of 24.197 (or 25.4 percent)).

7. In March 2009, the Supreme Court of the United States rendered its decision in *Wyeth v. Levine*, No. 06-1249, decided 4 March 2009 (slip opinion available at http://www.supremecourtus.gov/). The court held that the labeling provisions of the federal Food, Drug and Cosmetic Act do not preempt state law causes of action for mislabeling of pharmaceuticals.

2. Promoting innovation: patents, subsidies, prizes and prices

There are two avenues of inquiry fundamental to the development of policy for the global supply of medicines. One concerns the way in which new medicines are developed and brought to market, including the effects that various innovation mechanisms may have on pricing and access. The other concerns the way in which the medicines sector is regulated in terms of assuring quality, safety and efficacy. The latter system is concerned with the processes by which medicines are developed, approved, manufactured, distributed, used and assessed. The systems of innovation and regulation are integrated at various levels.

We begin by examining global policy with respect to pharmaceutical innovation. Policies with respect to quality, safety and efficacy are no less important. However, throughout the past several years, policy makers, business leaders and public interest groups have expressed the most intense concern with suboptimal rates of medicines innovation, and with whether the mechanisms now used to promote innovation are unduly inhibiting public access to the medicines that are developed.

Chapter 3 provides historical perspective on medicines innovation. It considers whether regulatory approval processes may have contributed to presently low rates of innovation. Chapter 3 delves into future challenges in regulating innovation arising from biotechnology.

With that said, we launch directly into the policies and mechanisms intended to promote innovation, and their potential effect on access to newly developed medicines.

THE BASICS OF PATENTS AND PRICES

The basic idea behind the grant of patents is simple. The inventor of a new product or process is given a reward in the form of a right to exclude others from the market.[1] The inventor can use that reward to attract investment in the plants and equipment necessary to commercialize the invention. Or the inventor can license the invention to someone else who wants to use it, taking a royalty for him or her self. Society provides the patent reward as an encouragement to inventors for acts of creation, as a way to stimulate investment in bringing new products to market and because the patent application discloses the invention to the public.

The cost to society of granting patents is that, during the patent term, only the patent owner (or its licensee) makes and sells the patented product. Without the threat of a direct competitor, the patent owner can charge whatever price the market will bear. What the market will bear depends on a number of factors. How badly do consumers want or need the product? Are there products that can substitute for the patented product, even if imperfectly?

The benefits and costs of patent protection vary depending upon the field of endeavor. Patents promote innovation in the consumer electronics field, but if a patent-owning electronics firm charges too much for a new flat-panel television or DVD player, consumers will stay with older products or find imperfect substitutes. A new flat-panel television is unlikely to be a life or death matter.

Some drugs are different. If a pharmaceutical company develops (and patents) a real breakthrough treatment, doctors and patients will demand that treatment. If the patented product truly is a breakthrough, there may be no substitutes available at any price. If the disease is sufficiently serious, the price the patient may be willing to pay (or to have his insurance company pay) is virtually limitless. Economists refer to this as 'price-inelasticity' of demand (that is, raising the price diminishes demand only weakly). In a life or death situation demand is 'highly price-inelastic'.

For real breakthrough treatments, society wants to provide inventors with suitable rewards. The pharmaceutical company that makes a breakthrough and obtains a patent can earn that reward through charging a high price for the treatment. That makes logical sense, but has an obvious downside. Individuals and public health schemes without substantial resources may be unable to pay. How can the less well off be served? That is one part of the patent and pricing puzzle.

There are not so many real breakthrough pharmaceutical treatments.[2] Most patents are granted for new drugs that are similar to existing drugs. In theory, demand for these 'me too' drugs should be significantly constrained by the availability of substitutes. Demand should be 'price-elastic'. But, the pharmaceutical market does not function very well in terms of the degree to which newly patented drugs are assessed against existing treatments. By stressing whatever advantages a new product might be considered to possess over its predecessors, pharmaceutical companies routinely obtain significant price premiums on new drugs that are similar to existing drugs, essentially short-circuiting the 'substitutability signal' that should make demand price-elastic (that is, normally increased

prices should reduce demand, but here they do not). The way the current
pharmaceutical supply system is designed and operates, market signals are
not properly sent or received.

'Market signal failure' in the case of patented 'incremental' innovation
has serious consequences for new drug development, though separating
cause and effect is not easy. A corporation, the officers of which are constantly assessed by capital markets, needs a certain degree of assurance
that its 'research bets' will pay off. Developing a modification of an existing drug in the hope that it will represent some incremental improvement
is a relatively sure path to success when compared against developing a
truly innovative therapy. More is known about clinical reaction to existing
therapies, and that information can be extrapolated to make educated predictions about the effect of minor modifications (particularly in areas such
as potential toxicity). From the corporate manager's standpoint, a real
breakthrough drug may be the most profitable objective, but developing it
may also be the most risky. The result of corporate cost-benefit assessment
seems to encourage investment in incremental enhancements.

As an aside, it could be that corporate decisions to pursue incremental
innovation are not based on risk aversion. It could be that in some areas
there really are no breakthrough drugs to be discovered, or that it is just
'too damned difficult'. In other words, companies focus on 'me too' innovation because they have 'hit a wall' and can't develop truly breakthrough
therapies.[3] We return to this point later.

Part of the trouble with incrementally enhanced drugs is that doctors
must be persuaded to prescribe them. Pharmaceutical benefits plans must
be persuaded to reimburse for them. Doctors need to hear about the benefits of incremental innovation. This information will not come from newspaper headlines. It will come from pharmaceutical industry advertising
and promotion. And more recently it will in certain countries come from
consumers who have listened to and watched direct to consumer advertising. Ultimately, all of the participants in the chain must be persuaded that
it makes sense to pay a good deal more for the incrementally improved
drug – assuming that it is incrementally improved – than for existing alternatives that have gone off-patent and are available generically.

The persuasion becomes easier when the patient-consumer of the drugs
does not have any meaningful information regarding the cost of filling a
prescription (or of being treated with drugs in a hospital).[4] In many countries drugs are provided 'free' or subject to a small co-payment pursuant
to a public health plan. In some countries private insurance companies
charge premiums to employers that cover prescription drugs, and the
patient-consumer makes a small co-payment at the pharmacy. In either
case the patient-consumer is as a rule not given the choice between two

similar treatments, one costly and one cheap. And even if the consumer is given that choice, most individual consumers have little objective evidence upon which to base a decision regarding the comparative benefits of similar drugs.

While the situation differs among countries, in most cases doctors are not concerned with the financial consequences of prescribing patented as opposed to non-patented drugs. The doctor's compensation is independent of pharmaceutical sales.[5]

These factors result in market signal failures. And, as noted earlier, sometimes there is no real functioning market at all. If a patent holder has exclusive rights in a breakthrough treatment the patient has no real choice. Demand is price-inelastic.

ORIGINATORS AND GENERICS: THE CONSTANT STRUGGLE FOR PROFITS

Technical details regarding the interplay between patented and off-patent medicines differ among countries and regions, but the fundamentals of the relationship are relatively constant.[6] Owners of pharmaceutical patents are typically the 'originators' of the new drugs. The term 'originator' is used to describe the person (including the enterprise) that first receives marketing approval from public health authorities to market a new drug. In the principal developed country markets today the originator typically enjoys both a period of 'marketing exclusivity' granted by public health authorities as a reward for registering the new product and a period of patent protection. The term of patent protection typically (though not always) exceeds the term of marketing exclusivity, particularly as the patent term is subject to 'extension' based upon the duration of the drug regulatory approval process.

The enjoyment of exclusive marketing and patent rights allows the originator to charge a price that is often 10 or 20 times the price that can be charged for the same drug when it goes off-patent.[7] There are a number of government studies that clearly demonstrate the effect of transition from patent to off-patent status on prices. From the standpoint of the originator, it is clearly in its economic best interest to extend the period of exclusivity and thus of higher prices. (Conceptually it might be possible to recoup through increased volume of lower price sales what is lost in higher price sales, but that is not realistic because there is competition in the off-patent/generics market.[8])

Generic producers have interests essentially opposed to those of the originators. They are seeking to produce and market the same products as the originators but at lower prices. To do that, they either need to (1) produce and sell in countries where there is no patent or marketing exclusivity on particular products; (2) wait for the 'natural expiration' of patent and marketing exclusivity terms or (3) do something to hasten expiration of patent terms and marketing exclusivity protection.

Option one (entering markets where there are no patents) is fairly straightforward, provided that the generic producers are able to obtain reliable information about patent status in a given country.[9] That is not always easy. The problem with option one is that there is often a reason why an originator has not secured protection in a particular country, and it is usually because that country is relatively poor and does not provide much of a target market.

Option two (entering markets at the expiration of patent terms) likewise is fairly straightforward. Many countries provide an exception under the local patent law that permits generic producers to seek regulatory approval of 'equivalent' generic drugs prior to expiration of patent terms so they are ready to enter the market promptly upon expiration. Usually the period of marketing exclusivity will also have ended.

In the best case scenario under the current system, pharmaceutical originators would approach the 'natural' loss of patent and marketing exclusivity protection with equanimity. They would be introducing new innovative products that would provide a continuing substitute of high-price revenue streams for those lost through expiration of patent exclusivity.

A variant on option two, however, arises where pharmaceutical originators seek to 'evergreen' their patent and marketing exclusivity by developing incremental innovations to 'old' originator drugs. So, for example, a drug that was formerly taken every four hours may now, as a result of a modification in its pharmaceutical form, be taken once a day. The new version is protected by a renewed patent term. Waiting for the expiration of the patent term may thus not be as straightforward as it initially seemed.

The astute reader will note that there may be nothing to prevent the generic producer from making and selling the old version of the drug on which the patent expires. That is correct, at least in principle. But this is where the marketing team of the originator company comes into play. The additional medical benefit offered by the modified form may be only slight or non-existent, but if persuasive promotion succeeds in conveying the message that the modified product is more convenient or pleasant to use both prescribers and users may prefer it to the original version. Perhaps a generic producer can sell the old version under prescription health insurance plans that look closely at the difference between the old and the new, and perhaps some governments will compare the efficacy of the old and the new. But by and large the originator 'transitions' the prescribers and dispensers from the older to the newer on-patent drug. This is 'standard operating procedure' for the originator industry and should not warrant any particular surprise.

Option three (challenging patents) is what generates most of the 'excitement' in the pharmaceutical industry.[10] This is the option under which generic producers do something to challenge the originators' patents, notwithstanding that they are technically in force. Generic producers may, if they have received marketing approval from the public health authority, undertake what is called an 'at risk' launch of a generic product in the expectation of being sued by the patent holder.[11] More often, generic producers challenge patents before their products are launched. This is less risky because the originator will not have suffered damages in the market (that it may collect in court) if the generic producer guessed wrong when it undertook an 'at risk' launch.

Although the legislative scheme under which patent challenges takes place varies from country to country, generic producers seek to invalidate originators' patents in court (or in administrative proceedings). Generic producers are typically trying to prove that patents should not have been granted in the first place. The pharmaceutical industry involves fairly sophisticated technologies. Experts go back and forth about whether alleged innovations are really new, are sufficiently inventive and/or are actually useful.[12] Allegations are traded as to whether patent holders adequately disclose inventions. Sometimes there are allegations of 'fraud on the patent office' with respect to the suppression of relevant 'prior art'. Judge or juries finally render decisions, usually subject to appeal, regarding the validity of patents. If a generic producer wins, it is free to enter the market.

On top of that, in the United States the first-challenger generic producer is given a 180-day exclusivity period during which it is the only competitor authorized to market a generic version of the subject product.[13] (The question whether the originator may also introduce an 'authorized generic' during the 180-day period is the subject of some debate.) This 180-day exclusivity period may have quite a substantial financial value.

To limit effective use of the patent challenge procedure, the patent owner companies have taken to 'buying out' generics companies that threaten their monopoly position, offering cash payments or other incentives for settlement of the patent invalidity proceedings.[14] Any 'blockbuster' revenue stream may be saved by a substantially smaller 'payoff'. Although the US Federal Trade Commission vigorously opposes these buyouts, the Courts of Appeal have been sympathetic on grounds that companies should be free to settle patent litigation as they see fit.[15] Pretty clearly the buyouts defeat Congress' purpose of encouraging early entry of generic products, but so far Congress has not acted to ban this activity.

The pharmaceutical market thus involves a constant struggle between originators and generic producers. Originators seek 'monopoly rents' based on patents. Generic producers seek to overcome the monopolies and put cheaper versions of the same products on the market. Because the desire for financial gain is a very strong motivator, there is a 'fire' lit under this system. If nothing else, everyone involved is motivated to do something. Because there is tremendous temptation created by the potential for great financial gain, there is an equally compelling need for strong government oversight and regulation. Unfortunately, as detailed elsewhere, the desire for financial gain can motivate otherwise reasonable people to take shortcuts that can wreak havoc with public health. But where there is a strong regulatory presence, the present system has largely avoided catastrophic incident, doing what it does fairly well. If you are fortunate enough to live in an OECD country and, if you are fortunate enough to be covered by a public or private health care plan, the chances are that your access to pharmaceuticals is fairly good, and you can have a pretty high level of confidence in what you are getting from the pharmacist.

PRICES AND INNOVATION

Assuming that originators are operating under the type of patent/marketing exclusivity system described above, in the absence of some other form of government intervention, they are able to charge what the market will bear for their products. It is not so difficult to see the effects on the structure of the market. Worldwide pharmaceutical sales in 2007 were about US$650 billion.[16] Of those sales, about US$550 billion were of patent protected originator products (so-called 'ethical pharmaceuticals'). Market structure data for most countries, developed or developing, is similar. Generic producers dominate markets in the volume of units sold, while originators dominate markets in terms of dollar value of sales.

The prices of originator products vary widely among countries. By far the highest prices are charged in the United States, generally considered the closest to a 'free market' for originator products.[17] Overall pharmaceutical expenditures are far higher in the United States than any other country. (At the same time, the United States has among the lowest generic prices among developed countries.) Most other countries control the prices of originator products in one way or another. This is done in a variety of ways. The government may set maximum prices based on 'cost-plus' or a related formula (generally unsatisfactory since it can be impossible to establish the true level of costs), it may compare prices among countries and set the local price somewhere along the reference spectrum (so-called 'reference pricing'), it may establish a formulary that allows only certain drugs to be reimbursed by insurance schemes, it may adopt a 'generic substitution' law, or it may employ other mechanisms. All of these systems of price control restrain the originators, and there is little evidence that such systems have resulted in any harm to the patient-consumer.[18]

Originator companies, however, vociferously oppose price controls on grounds that this reduces their return on investment and consequently the amount of money they can spend on research and development.[19] They argue that it is the absence of price controls in the United States that has induced a significant bias toward conducting research operations in that country.

The argument concerning the location of R&D facilities is complicated. Obviously a company can conduct its research in one country and its marketing and sales in other countries. There is no direct correlation between the price that can be charged for a drug and where the research on that drug was done. If the only side of the originator argument was that doing research in the United States allows companies to sell more expensive drugs in the United States, the argument would be borderline nonsensical. But it is somewhat more complex than that.

The most obvious reason why originator companies locate R&D facilities in the United States is the high level of basic pharmaceutical R&D funded by the National Institutes of Health (NIH), combined with the first-class university and public hospital research facilities that conduct that research. This NIH-academic research base is a form of US industrial policy that promotes the strength of its pharmaceutical sector. Although there is no direct link between pharmaceutical industry profits and NIH-academic research, the systems are 'synergistic'. The industry provides employment opportunities and an outlet for the results of government-sponsored research. The government in turn views investment in pharmaceutical R&D as a way of strengthening the US economy. Put another way, if the US pharmaceutical industry were not a national profit center, it is doubtful that the government would spend so much money on pharmaceutical R&D.

Needless to say, there is a public health-related motivation behind NIH's investments in pharmaceutical R&D. The social welfare objective is to protect and improve the health of citizens of the United States, and also individuals throughout the world.

Leaving aside cause and effect, the objective facts are fairly clear. The United States has the highest originator drug prices in the world and more pharmaceutical-related R&D dollars by far are spent in the United States than anywhere else.

This might well lead us to conclude that the system is working brilliantly, at least from the standpoint of the United States! Except that we cannot draw that conclusion based on the objective evidence at hand. . . .

GLOBALIZATION AND ONE-SIZE-FITS-ALL SOLUTIONS

A complete exploration of the relationship between pharmaceutical patents and prices requires a discussion of international rules governing pharmaceutical patents and regulatory data. At the highest level of technical detail the international patent system is rather complicated. However, most of the technical detail is not needed for an analysis of the basic policy issues.

Up until 1995 the international rules governing patents were made at the World Intellectual Property Organization (WIPO), based in Geneva. The main treaty governing patents, the Paris Convention on the Protection of Industrial Property, dates back to 1883, although it has been revised several times since then. However, as a result of demands by industrialized country industry groups – among which the US, European and Japanese pharmaceutical industry were leaders – primary responsibility for rule making for the international patent system shifted in 1995 to the World Trade Organization (WTO), also based in Geneva. The Agreement on Trade-Related Aspects of Intellectual Property Rights, commonly referred to as the 'TRIPS Agreement', entered into force on 1 January 1995 as a key component of the WTO legal system.[20] The TRIPS Agreement established new rules governing pharmaceutical patents and regulatory data, required WTO member countries to implement and enforce those rules, and provided a dispute settlement framework that ultimately allows countries to impose trade sanctions against a country-violator of the rules.

The most important change to the international patent system embodied in the TRIPS Agreement was the requirement for all WTO member countries ('Members') to extend patent subject matter protection to pharmaceutical products (and processes).[21] Before the TRIPS Agreement, many countries (especially developing countries) did not provide patent protection for pharmaceutical products (or food-related products). Among those that did so there was wide variation in the scope of protection. The TRIPS Agreement set a common minimum term of patent protection of 20 years from the filing date of the patent application. The extension of pharmaceutical product patent protection to all WTO Members was bound to cause considerable disruption to the economies of developing countries. Negotiators of the TRIPS Agreement took this into account by providing transition periods for developing and least developed Members. Developing Members had until 1 January 2005 to bring their pharmaceutical patent systems into compliance with the new rules, and least developed countries (LDCs) were given until 1 January 2006 (this transition period has now been extended to 1 January 2016).

India was the last major developing country producer of pharmaceuticals to bring its patent system into compliance. This occurred as of 1 January 2005. As a consequence, today every major pharmaceutical producing country in the world grants patents on new pharmaceutical products and processes.[22] In addition, because of complicated TRIPS Agreement transition rules, pharmaceutical products that were patented outside India in the period between 1 January 1995 and 1 January 2005 are subject to patenting within India for the remainder of their patent terms calculated based on the filing date of a so-called 'mailbox' application in India during the ten-year transition. Not all 'mailbox applications' will be approved, based on the specific features of Indian law, but many certainly will be.

Looked at from a broadbrush perspective, the international situation regarding patenting of pharmaceutical products has changed dramatically since 1995. Up until then, countries like India were able to produce and sell generic versions of newer pharmaceutical products patented in the industrialized countries throughout much of the developing world. Producers in other developing countries like Argentina and Brazil were likewise able to produce and sell newer products 'off-patent'. Today the range of 'free production zones' is dramatically limited.[23] This does not mean that the world is suddenly without a supply of lower priced medicines. Much of medicines consumption, particularly in the developing world, is of products that remain available generically. Moreover, because of the comparatively poor recent pharmaceutical industry R&D track record, there are not so many breakthrough patented treatments that are truly essential for treatment in developing countries, although there are several important exceptions to this general rule (such as newer treatments for HIV/AIDS and leukemia). But, as newly patented treatments for epidemics such as diabetes are developed, it will be important to assure access to these treatments among all income classes.

Countries are not without recourse against higher priced patented medicines based upon the implementation of TRIPS Agreement standards.[24] First, while the TRIPS Agreement establishes general rules with respect to patentability, there is considerable flexibility inherent in the implementation and application of those rules. India, for example, took advantage of this flexibility by requiring a demonstration of enhanced efficacy for pharmaceutical products that are based on existing products (as a defense against the practice of 'evergreening'). Second, the TRIPS Agreement authorizes Members to adopt various exceptions and safeguards to patent rights. WTO Members can adopt research exemptions, exceptions regarding regulatory review (that permit the processing of health regulatory approval applications during the patent term), and may authorize 'compulsory' or 'government use' licensing of pharmaceutical patents. Each of the exceptions and safeguards provides a means for redressing the adverse social welfare consequences of restricting access to the market.

Furthermore, nothing in the TRIPS Agreement prevents countries from implementing price controls, as outlined earlier. A government is not required to allow pharmaceutical patent holders to charge the price the market will bear. It is not entirely clear why countries, particularly in the developing world, fail to take greater advantage of the opportunity to control prices of patented pharmaceuticals. Patent holders may refuse to supply if controlled prices are excessively low, but there is little evidence of this circumstance having arisen.

Pharmaceutical originator companies fight the use of flexibilities, exceptions and safeguards at every turn. Novartis sued the government of India for its adoption of the above-mentioned efficacy requirement, though the suit was thrown out by the Indian courts.[25] A decision by the US Supreme Court was required to firmly establish the pharmaceutical research exemption in US law, after that exemption had effectively been eliminated by the Court of Appeals for the Federal Circuit.[26] Thailand's issuance of compulsory licenses for antiretrovirals and a blood thinner (clopidogrel bisulfite) was greeted by intense diplomatic counter-pressure from the EU and the United States.[27] A major element behind the suit by 39 pharmaceutical companies against the government of South Africa regarding its 1997 Medicines Amendments Act was concern over the introduction of a generic substitution requirement and a price control system (the so-called 'single exit price' system).[28] The companies were forced to abandon that lawsuit.

Without going behind the complexity of the various rules, there is a serious problem with relying on safeguards and exceptions as a general solution to public health problems. There is always some economic lever that the economically powerful countries can use to threaten developing countries. The governments of the United States, EU, Japan and other OECD countries use their best efforts to prove that implementation by developing countries of flexibilities, safeguards and exceptions comes at a steep price. This is despite repeated efforts over a period of years by nongovernmental organizations (NGOs) and multilateral organizations to establish the principle that flexibilities, safeguards and exceptions are common instruments of government policy. Of course, we can hope that this situation will change and that the wealthier countries will become more tolerant of the less well-off. But that is not a policy solution. It is a rather speculative 'hope'.

In order to restrain the use of flexibilities, safeguards and exceptions by developing (and developed) countries, the United States (and to a somewhat lesser extent the EU) have been negotiating 'bilateral' trade agreements with third countries that significantly restrict the right to use those legal mechanisms.[29] The Democratic majority in the US Congress recently cut back on the authority of the US Trade Representatives to impose restrictions on developing countries in this area, but the general direction of US policy remains the same.

It should also be recognized that a few 'emerging economy' developing countries, notably Brazil, Russia, India and China (the so-called 'BRIC' countries), are rapidly improving their R&D capacity in the pharmaceutical sector.[30] This is quite positive in the sense that this expands the possibility for breakthrough innovations to occur. At the same time, these countries are likely to follow the same path as the OECD countries in terms of seeking to exploit the maximum price the market will bear for new patented pharmaceuticals. In that sense, patterns of wealth distribution among countries may change, but the extent of access to medicines among the less well-off may not. The increasing attention of the BRIC countries to the global pharmaceutical market is also adding pressure toward harmonization upward of patenting rules, that is, providing greater market power for patent holders.[31]

The rules of the TRIPS Agreement are not limited to 'patents'. Article 39.3 of that agreement addresses unpublished data regarding new chemical entities in the pharmaceutical sector submitted for the purpose of obtaining regulatory approval, typically from public health authorities.[32] That provision requires WTO Members to take measures to prevent the 'unfair commercial use' of such data, as well is to protect against disclosure of such data except where necessary to protect the public (or unless steps are taken to protect against unfair commercial use). Although this is clearly not required by the terms or negotiating history of Article 39.3, a number of Members implement this provision by establishing 'exclusive marketing rights' for a period of years following the approval of a new drug based upon the submission of clinical data. This provides an important exclusionary tool for pharmaceutical originator companies because marketing exclusivity does not depend upon patent protection. Therefore, even if an originator has never secured a patent in a particular country, or if a generic producer succeeds in invalidating the patent in a country, a bioequivalent product cannot be put on the market during the period of marketing exclusivity.

The United States, in particular, has been aggressively promoting marketing exclusivity provisions based upon regulatory submissions in bilateral trade agreements, and has been insisting on the inclusion of such provisions in agreements with countries newly acceding to the WTO. Particularly in the bilateral agreements, the marketing exclusivity requirements have gone well beyond anything contemplated by the TRIPS Agreement, including requirements that marketing exclusivity be granted in a counterpart country on the basis of regulatory submission in the United States. Pedro Roffe discusses the Free Trade Agreements (FTAs) in the context of Latin America in Box 2.1. Changes adopted at the insistence of the Democratic majority in Congress in 2007 have improved the situation somewhat for developing countries, but the general direction remains the same.

A multilateral solution to the problem of patents and pricing must also address the corollary problems presented by marketing exclusivity rules that may exert an independent restrictive effect.

The net result of implementation of the TRIPS Agreement and bilaterally negotiated patent and marketing exclusivity rules is to impose uniform minimum requirements with respect to patenting of pharmaceutical products and processes more or less universally (with the exception for a number of years of least developed countries (LDCs)), combined in some countries with requirements to implement US-level restrictions favoring patent holders. This is a 'one-size-fits-all-plus' regime.

Whatever solutions are considered to address the problems of patents and pricing, those solutions must address individuals in very different income categories and living circumstances. Half of the world's population earns less than two dollars a day. A solution for the OECD countries is not going to solve the problem of providing reasonable access to medicines for half of the world's population.

RIGHTS AND WRONGS OF THE PRESENT PATENT-CENTRIC SYSTEM

The foregoing discussion leads us to summarize some of the main pluses and minuses of the present patent-centric system used for the development of new medicines.

Positive Aspects

On the positive side, the attraction of out-size profit draws a considerable amount of investment capital into the pharmaceutical sector. Although only about 15 percent of that capital is used for R&D, this still amounts to about $50 billion a year in industry contribution. Combined with public sector R&D expenditure (principally from the United States), close to

BOX 2.1   LATIN AMERICAN REGULATORY REGIMES IN THE POST-FTA ENVIRONMENT

Contributed by Pedro Roffe, Senior Fellow, International Centre for Trade and Sustainable Development

While the Free Trade Agreements (FTAs) differ in their details, the main aspects of the agreements with respect to pharmaceutical products are the following:

- Adjustment of the term of a patent to compensate for delays in the granting of it.
- Restoration of the patent term to compensate for curtailment of the effective patent duration resulting from the marketing approval process.
- Regulatory exemption (Bolar exemption) permitted only for purposes related to the generation of information intended to meet requirements for approval to market the product once the patent expires.
- The protection of information concerning safety or efficacy of the product submitted in support of the marketing approval, for a period of at least five years from the date of approval. The parties shall not permit third parties, without the consent of the provider of such information, to market the product based on new chemical entities (the FTAs differ in how they characterize this latter concept).[a]
- Protection of such information, for at least five years from the date of marketing approval of the new product in the territory of the party, based on evidence of prior marketing approval in another territory. The party may require that the person providing the information in the other territory seek approval in the territory of the party within five years of obtaining marketing approval in the other territory.
- When a product is subject to a system of marketing approval and is also covered by a patent, the party shall not alter the term of protection in the event that the patent protection terminates on a date earlier than the end of the term of protection for the undisclosed information (Peru, Colombia).

- The non-granting of marketing approval to any third party prior to the expiration of the patent term, unless by consent or acquiescence of the patent owner (linkage).

The intellectual property (IP) landscape in Latin America has changed radically since the days of the Uruguay Round negotiations. The emerging regulatory framework resulting from the new generation of FTAs is far from the more optimistic scenario at the time of the adoption of TRIPS, in terms of the inbuilt flexibilities of the system and the recognized freedom of implementation of its provisions. The tensions of the past still prevail. This is evident with the recent classification of Chile by the United States as a serious 'non-performing' country in the world of IP, particularly with respect to pharmaceutical products. The emergence of such new tensions calls for a critical reflection on the evolution and shortcomings of the international system.

Note: a. 'For the purposes of this Article, a new pharmaceutical product is one that does not contain a chemical entity that has been previously approved in the territory of the Party', Central America Free Trade Agreement.

$100 billion per year is spent worldwide on pharmaceutical R&D. Without the attraction of out-sized profits, it is fair to assume that investors would not leave the same amount of capital at work in the pharmaceutical sector. The industry, particularly the part involved with new drugs, has a high risk profile, as evidenced by recent collapses in share prices based on semi-catastrophic events (for example, Merck and Vioxx®, Bayer and Baycol® and so on).

Also patents form a kind of 'security instrument' for transactions in innovation. Without that kind of instrument, commercial enterprises (whether private or public) would have difficulty sharing innovation in a way that may ultimately maximize its usefulness. A small biotechnology company with a patent on its innovation can license that technology to a major pharmaceutical producer because the patent allows the small company to define and protect the boundaries of its invention.

By providing the opportunity for great financial reward, the patent system lights a fire under at least some portion of would-be inventors, and certainly encourages the commercialization of the innovations they generate. The step of translating abstract scientific invention into fully formed commercialized products must not be underestimated. Scientific geniuses from the laboratory are not necessarily the right people to turn new molecules into finished products. The whole chain of research through development requires a motive force, and patents help to provide that.

Patents have temporal limits, and usually within a decade or so of a drug's commercialization under patent, it 'goes generic'. The patent monopoly is a limited one. The ability of major pharmaceutical companies to 'evergreen' patents is perhaps as much the fault of regulators, physicians, pharmacists, health plans and the public as it is of the pharmaceutical companies. There is nothing that mandates that a patient who can just as well take one pill every four hours must switch to a 24-hour pill at 20 times the price. Better advantage could be taken of the end of the patent term.

Finally, but certainly not exhaustively, recall that patents are routinely not secured in many developing and least developed countries. There is space for greater use of these patent-free zones of production and distribution.

Negative Aspects

At the moment, the 'innovation yield' from the present patent-based pharmaceutical research system is low.[33] The reasons for this are considered further in Chapter 3, but one major explanation for the low yield appears to be the focus on incremental innovation to evergreen existing patent monopolies. An alternative hypothesis is that the 'low hanging fruit' of small-molecule chemistry-based pharmaceutical innovation already has been picked, and that even the temptation to aim for large financial gains does not materially improve the prospects for new discovery. Large-molecule and/or biotechnological innovation are substantially more complex than small-molecule innovation. We may, as suggested elsewhere in this volume, be at the cusp of reaping rewards from investment in biotechnology. Perhaps we are not as patient as we might be in waiting for new yields from the patent incentive.

Another argument against the patent-based system is that it encourages investment targeted at diseases for which large monetary return can be anticipated. This manifests itself both in the 'blockbuster' phenomenon, and in a reluctance to invest in diseases prevalent among poorer individuals. Pharmaceutical companies are reluctant to 'green light' R&D projects when the potential monetary reward is less than $1 billion per year in revenues. This (and more) is what can be earned from a successful 'blockbuster' product. As a consequence, many leads bearing medicinally significant promise are not followed because the possibility for generating blockbuster returns is not evident.

In the same vein, the patent-based system is profit oriented, not public health oriented. Research and development funds flow to the most potentially profitable markets, whether those markets are in cosmetics, erectile dysfunction or heart disease. Where there is not a sufficient profit potential, for example, in sleeping sickness, there is no appreciable private research despite enormous public health difficulties.

The demand to invest only in blockbuster-potential products is somewhat difficult to understand from an economic perspective. If a company could develop three 300 million dollar per year drugs, why limit itself to one billion dollar per year drug? Are corporate resources so thin that marketing and distribution cannot deal with another dozen medium revenue drugs? The authors of this book have discussed this question with a number of senior executives of major pharmaceutical companies and none have provided a compelling explanation for the blockbuster phenomenon. In fact, there seems to be fairly good recognition that the system is not entirely sensible. But it remains in place at least for now.

In defense of the industry, it is certainly true that companies invest a great deal more in treatments for 'lifestyle' diseases than may be justifiable from a public health standpoint, but a couple of points might be made in defense of the industry. First, the public demands lifestyle drugs! Sad to stereotype, but men want more durable erections and hair restoration, and women want more beautiful skin. The demand for improvement to cosmetic appearance is so strong that it impels (mainly) women to have their faces injected with botulism toxin! Who are we to act as pharmaceutical gods? If the public as a whole is more interested in erections and complexion than in cures for cancer that is the result of some mysterious part of human nature. (No, we cannot attribute the entirety of demand for these products to advertising.) Some significant part of the human population would rather die early 'looking good'. (One need not search too far for 'perversities' involving human nature and public health. By now, nearly every cigarette smoker knows he or she is substantially increasing the risks of developing lung cancer, which is one of the principal burdens on public health systems. But people keep buying and smoking cigarettes.)

The second argument in defense of the industry is that in reality a great deal of money is being spent on research toward cures for 'serious' diseases like cancer, coronary disease, diabetes, HIV/AIDS and leukemia. While more money might be spent on research in these areas if it were not 'frivolously' spent on lifestyle diseases, it is hard to attribute the lack of progress against some of the major causes of morbidity and mortality to a 'lack of trying'.[34]

The Need for Balance

It is certainly true that for-profit pharmaceutical enterprises do not invest materially in finding cures for diseases for which there is no significant paying market. The area of 'neglected diseases' absolutely needs to be addressed, and is being addressed by a number of public-private partnerships and other initiatives. But it is doubtful that the neglected diseases problem can and should be solved with the same set of solutions needed more generally.

It should also be noted that patents and patent laws are capable of being misused, and have been misused. This problem is particularly serious in developing countries where legal systems are less developed, and where those who are the subjects of abuse have less money and sophistication with which to challenge the abusers. The most high visibility instance of this was the case, already noted briefly above, that was brought by 39 pharmaceutical companies against the government of South Africa as it sought to implement its 1996 health reform program. The pharmaceutical companies were eventually forced in 2001 to abandon that case and to pay the legal fees of the government, but not without significant harm to the South African public health system.[35]

The most compelling argument against the current patent-centric pharmaceutical R&D system is that it generally results in high prices for newer drugs, and that these high prices burden individuals and public health systems. Even a decade ago it seemed possible to label this a 'development problem' involving income differentials between North and South. Unfortunately, steadily increasing pharmaceutical prices over the past decade have turned this into a global problem and, as populations in the OECD age, major public health budget pressures are looming. The United States faces enormous increases in Medicare costs over the next two decades, and a good deal of the financial pressure will come from high pharmaceutical prices. The problem of patents and pricing is no longer a 'luxury issue' for people in the North.

OPTIONS FOR REFORM

The foregoing discussion suggests three objectives for reforming the mechanism by which medicines are presently developed and distributed under the current patent system. First, the yield of breakthrough products from expensive R&D efforts must be improved. Second, the prices of new medicines must be moderated, not only for those who have difficulty in affording them, but also in order to bring public health budgets under control. Third, efforts must be made to increase R&D with respect to the so-called neglected diseases.

Patent-based Approaches

Raising the bar on the inventive step

At present, patents for pharmaceutical innovations are granted in key jurisdictions like the EU and United States for virtually anything that is 'different' from what went before. Nominally, an invention must meet criteria of 'novelty', 'inventive step' (or 'non-obviousness') and 'utility' in order to qualify for patent protection.

Novelty means that the invention was not disclosed before or 'anticipated'. In order for novelty to be defeated, an anticipating disclosure must include all of the elements of the claimed invention (or at least all of the elements must be 'inherent' in the single disclosure). It may be difficult to find single prior art references that include each element of claimed inventions, and this ground is not the one most often used to deny patents.

The inventor must have done something that involves an 'inventive step' (or be 'non-obvious') in order to secure a patent. This means there must be something sufficiently different about the claimed invention as compared with previous inventions such that it would not have been 'obvious' to a person 'reasonably skilled in the art practiced by the invention'. This is a substantially more subjective test or inquiry than 'novelty' because it asks the patent examiner (or court) to make a judgment about the intellectual leap necessary to move from Point A to Point B. Here there is considerable flexibility in patent law. A country can set a 'high bar' for this intellectual leap, or it can require only a modest increment. There is nothing inherent in the international rules on patenting that tells us exactly where this bar must be set.

In many of the cases of claimed pharmaceutical innovation, the patent applicant has taken a molecule that it previously developed and patented, and 'tweaked it' to give it some new property that may improve its profile for the patient. As noted above, this may involve a different 'method of delivery', a change in the dosage routine or a change in the 'patient population' on which the drug has been tested. Sometimes the pharmaceutical researcher has figured out a way to make the drug incrementally more pure or stable.[36]

The research-based pharmaceutical industry asserts with some justification that many of these incremental innovations provide some benefit to the patient, even if they are not 'breakthroughs'. There is little reason to argue with this.[37] Without doubt, a patient may be happier and on a better regimen by taking one pill a day rather than three or four. A patient may be better off if he or she avoids the occasional upset stomach. Patients and suppliers are better off if drugs have a longer shelf life, or are more tolerant of changes in temperature.

The question is not whether we want (or do not want) pharmaceutical companies to make incremental improvements to their products. We want them to do that. The question is whether we want to provide such enormous financial incentives for that incremental innovation that companies direct the bulk of their research to incremental innovation in order to preserve out-sized revenue streams, and then spend substantial sums to promote the incremental innovation because the new treatments will not sell themselves. Would we not prefer a situation in which these same companies were encouraged instead to direct their research principally to 'breakthrough' products that provide real changes in the therapeutic environment?

How can this be accomplished through modifications to the patent system? One answer is to raise the 'inventive step' or 'non-obviousness' threshold such that only new drugs that claim a mechanism for targeting a disease in a substantially different way than prior drugs would be entitled to patents. Changes involving 'tweaks' to existing drugs would not qualify for patent protection.

This raises the question whether such a change would so substantially undercut research on incremental innovation that we would be doing patients and public health systems a disservice? The answer to this cannot be stated with certainty. Pharmaceutical companies will however continue to compete for sales of off-patent products in the generics market. Just as with virtually every other kind of product in the world, a pharmaceutical company that makes an improved version of the generic product should presumably be able to increase its share of the market vis-à-vis its competitors. It is hard to understand why pharmaceutical companies would fail to improve their products as against generic competitors just as they seek to improve their products as against patent-protected competitors. Indeed, by 'opening up' this portion of the generics market (that is, that portion which is not evergreened), we might just as well anticipate a flowering of investment and competitive activity in producing improved generic versions of previously patented drugs.

This is not a novel suggestion. The US Federal Trade Commission came to a similar conclusion in an extensive study of US patents with respect to the system as a whole.[38] That is, the 'inventive step' bar should probably be raised. This, then, is one idea for improving the yield of breakthrough products in the pharmaceutical sector.

Require demonstrations of efficacy as condition of patent grant

The third criterion for the grant of a patent is a demonstration of 'utility' or 'usefulness'. This means what it says. An invention should do something of use.

Up until a decade or so ago, the utility requirement rarely played a role in patent decisions because most inventions were of some identifiable use, even if not a very important one. Patent examiners and courts did not concern themselves with just 'how useful' an invention would be. So the utility requirement would not prevent jack-o'-lantern emulating plastic garbage bags from being patented. Advances in chemistry and biotechnology recently vitalized the utility requirement. Why? Because using modern research tools researchers are able to create new molecules and new bioengineered substances without, at least initially, having any idea whether they may be good for anything (that is, useful). In order to prevent a flood of patents on 'speculative' chemical and biotechnological substances, patent offices and courts have required their creators to demonstrate some useful characteristic of those substances in order to secure patents. But still, the 'bar' for utility is not very high. In the United States, for example, the inventor of a new chemical compound does not need to show that the compound will treat or cure a disease. The inventor need only show that it causes some biological activity with respect to the disease target that might have some therapeutic potential. The theory of the US Court of Appeals for the Federal Circuit is that delaying the 'point of patenting' would reduce the incentives for continuing research on these new substances.[39]

This need not be the approach followed with respect to application of the utility criterion. In fact, the US Patent Office attempted to introduce an 'efficacy' standard for pharmaceutical compound claims in the 1980s. In other words, the Patent Office said that a person claiming a pharmaceutical invention should be able to show that the new compound has a therapeutic effect to the extent of demonstration in clinical trials. The Federal Circuit expressly rejected this attempt, saying that the Patent Office was confusing itself with the US FDA.[40]

Another way to limit the number of patents on incremental innovation would be to raise the utility standard so as to require that claimed pharmaceutical inventions prove themselves efficacious in the treatment of disease and, in addition, efficacious in a way distinct (at some level) from comparable existing treatments. To put this another way, the person claiming a pharmaceutical invention would need to show clinical evidence of therapeutic benefit over previously developed compounds for treating the same disease. Or, put more simply, the invention would need to demonstrate something genuinely useful to the public.

Imposing such a utility standard would seem by definition to require pharmaceutical innovators to wait longer to file patent applications. Today applications are filed at the first moment the innovator believes that any evidence of useful activity can be demonstrated. A clinical efficacy requirement could not be realistically fulfilled until (perhaps) Phase 2 (safety and efficacy) clinical trials had been undertaken. That could be six years from the date a compound was first shown to generate potentially useful biological activity.

One complexity from introducing a clinical efficacy requirement is that the differing patentability standards around the world might make it necessary for innovator companies to file patent applications in some countries while they await results of clinical trials as condition precedent to filing in others. This should not ultimately result in patentability problems regarding countries where applications are held back because the results of clinical studies will constitute 'new art' when the applications are filed, but this is a complexity that will require attention from patent applicants.

Assuming the problem of variations among countries could be addressed, adding a clinical efficacy requirement would certainly reduce (fairly dramatically) the number of patents in the pharmaceutical sector. A far lower number of pharmaceutical compounds (or biological materials) clear Phase 2 clinical trials than are covered by patents. If patent offices required a demonstration of improved comparative efficacy over previously known compounds, this would presumably inhibit 'evergreening'.

A major consequence of introducing a clinical efficacy requirement should be to open up the field of R&D. Patents would be granted substantially further downstream and more competitors could remain 'in the race' until a later stage in the process. Only the first innovator to show clinical efficacy would get a patent. Would competitors be willing to remain in the race longer, facing the possibility they might ultimately be shut out from securing any reward? Once the patent was granted to the winner, the losers would presumably not be able to market the 'same product'. (This is an issue that must also be confronted with respect to the 'prize' scenario discussed later on.) Ideally innovators pursuing similar tracks would in fact take different approaches that would lead to more than one successful set of clinical trials using these approaches.

Create a tiered patent system (quasi-patents) with term and/or remedy dependent on the level of innovation

Another potential mechanism to improve the innovation yield as well as to limit price distortions is to establish alternatives to standard 'utility patents' in the form of 'utility models' or 'petty patents'. These quasi-patents or 'not quite patents' might be granted based upon, for example, incremental innovations as described earlier (for example, changes in routes of administration or stability), but providing a lesser form of marketing exclusivity right. The term of the quasi-patent could be limited (for example, eight years instead of 20 or differential terms could be based on innovation/utility criteria), or the rights of the holder could be limited (for example, to collect a royalty from third-party users rather than excluding them from the market).

Innovators would presumably be less willing to commit the same level of investment with respect to securing quasi-patent protection as they are to securing the stronger form of patent protection. But, in terms of redirecting investment toward 'breakthrough' innovation, this may be precisely the result we are seeking! Pharmaceutical companies could choose whether they wanted to invest in lower risk/lower reward R&D projects (that is, incremental innovation) or higher risk/higher reward R&D projects. Presumably companies would elect a mix of such endeavors.

Liability regimes

A patent is a bundle of rights granted to its owner. These rights permit the patent owner to exclude third parties from making and selling equivalent products. As the US Supreme Court recently made clear, the 'rights' granted to patent owners are not the same as the 'remedies' to which patent owners may be entitled.

If a third party infringes a patent, a court (or administrative body) has a number of options for curing the harm. The court may grant an 'injunction' telling the infringing party that it may no longer produce and/or sell the product found to infringe the patent in question. The court may award 'damages' to the patent owner for the harm that it has suffered as a consequence of competition in the marketplace. However, the court may also choose to allow the infringing party to continue producing and/or selling the product upon payment of a royalty (in effect, a licensing fee) to the patent owner. The amount of the licensing fee is not typically preordained (although it may be), but depends upon how the court values the patent and other factors which might include the public interest in access to the patented product. Scholars refer to the royalty option as reflecting a 'liability' regime, as compared with the injunction option that reflects a 'property' regime.[41]

One way to make patented pharmaceutical products more widely (and presumably more cheaply) available would be to move away from granting injunctions against third-party infringers and toward a liability or royalty regime. Prior to the TRIPS Agreement, a number of countries used royalty regimes with respect to pharmaceutical patents, often under the name 'license of right'. In such a regime third parties are automatically entitled to use pharmaceutical patents (perhaps contingent on the occurrence of some precondition), provided they pay a royalty to the patent holder. The government may (or may not) fix the royalty rate as part of the legislative scheme.

International concerns with respect to patents and pricing could be addressed by establishing royalty rates for third-party users of patents that varied depending upon the geographic territory and/or class of purchaser (for example, public or private institution). A generic producer might be required to pay a 25 percent royalty on revenues (gross or net) if it wished to sell the product in an OECD market, and a 5 percent royalty if it wished to sell the product in a developing country market. While a 25 percent royalty may sound high, considering that generic drugs often sell at 10 percent of the price of the equivalent originator patented drugs, a 25 percent royalty would still result in a dramatic lowering of end-user prices. These are illustrative hypothetical royalty rates, but there is a wide range of ways in which royalty rates might be established, including the study of the actual research and development expenditures of the patent holder.

A liability regime could be associated with 'patent pools' that are traditional legal mechanisms used to facilitate sharing of technologies.[42] Consider, for example, a situation in which five or ten companies own patents on technologies used to make a certain class of drugs. All of those companies could contribute their patented technologies into a pool or sharing arrangement. Any person could use the technology from the pool, selecting from among the most useful technologies, and pay a royalty back to the pool for distribution among the technology contributors. Patent pools are sufficiently common as to have become subject to a fairly sophisticated level of regulation, for example, in the European Commission guidelines on technology transfer. Many of the issues surrounding the negotiation and implementation of patent pools already are anticipated by competition authorities.

Another suggestion that has recently been made is to establish funds for the 'buyout' of pharmaceutical patents for specific territories or markets, then licensing (or making available) the technology for use by generic producers. This is a variation on the pooling concept.

The common question with respect to all of the regimes discussed above is whether they will leave adequate incentive for the private sector to invest in the development of new drugs. This is really a nuts and bolts economic question. If the numbers are put together properly there should be a way to exchange royalties from wider markets for high margins in more narrow markets. This does not necessarily mean that the research-based pharmaceutical industry will end up 'just as happy' as it is with the present arrangement, but the objective of these discussions is not to assure the complete happiness of a particular class of investors.

Antony Taubman of the World Trade Organization reflects on the possibilities for maintaining the basic architecture of the present international patent system while re-examining some of its more detailed applications in Box 2.2.

BOX 2.2   REFLECTIONS ON THE CURRENT STATE OF PLAY: THE INTERNATIONAL DIMENSION OF PHARMACEUTICAL PATENT QUALITY AND LINUS'S LAW

Contributed by Antony Taubman

General Observations

- The center of gravity of the international patent system is shifting. This is immediately evident in patterns of use of the patent system – notably, the increased prevalence of patenting by public sector/public interest actors, and the growth in use by some key developing nations, two trends that are conspicuously pronounced in the life sciences. But beyond these empirical observations, it is interesting to reflect on the changing conception or conceptions of the kinds of knowledge and knowledge systems that the patent system recognizes, as it presages broadening cultural perspectives as to what is considered innovative activity.
- This trend is perhaps exemplified by the increasing interaction between the patent system and systems of traditional knowledge (TK), as patent authorities need increasingly to recognize that existing TK systems are legitimate prior art of equal technological value as 'mainstream' Western technologies. But innovation also continues within TK systems, which are living and evolving innovation systems and not inert historical time capsules. This poses questions for the essential tests of patentability: what cultural and intellectual diversity is required, for instance, to acknowledge a traditional healer or medicine person as a 'person skilled in the art', when a claimed invention draws on a traditional knowledge system?
- Yet, even accepting these shifts and tensions, and the more diverse technological, intellectual and cultural contexts of the patent system, it is striking that the core patentability criteria remain essentially legitimate at the level of principle. The fact that the essential tests of patentability have evolved literally through centuries of legal and policy discourse means that they have inherent scope for greater

pluralism. Consideration of greater cultural diversity within the patent system, in particular the recognition of different traditional knowledge systems, was once undertaken by academics on the basis of theoretical scenarios. But these scenarios are now becoming increasingly practical cases, considered by examiners: for instance, the legal and practical recognition of oral forms of disclosure that are often used in traditional knowledge systems, and recognition that practitioners of traditional medicine may either constitute the relevant 'person skilled in the art', or may form part of a composite person skilled in the art developed to apply the test for inventive step or non-obviousness for an invention that draws on different knowledge traditions.

- The very characteristic of patentability criteria as adaptable expressions of public policy responsive to shifts in technology also lends these criteria to evolution, scrutiny, contention and reapplication in new contexts. Even if the general principles remain well established at the broadest level, their practical application will naturally, inevitably require continual reconsideration and debate as the nature of technology and its social context both evolve over time. Much of the jurisprudence of patentability has indeed been generated through adversarial patent cases and the development of judgments over many years.

- However, the current close attention to the social and economic impact of the patent system has led to renewed pressure for more targeted legislative interventions, illustrated by recent legislative changes in India and the current patent law reform debate in the United States Congress. Controversies inevitably – even healthily – swirl around the proper bounds and interpretations of patentability principles. Even so, there is a durable conceptual basis for patent law, in that society marks out certain forms of innovation as meriting the grant of legal exclusions as a conscious means of promoting the production of technological public goods – in the Anglo-American or common law legal tradition this conception reaches back beyond the 1623 Statute of Monopolies.

- Even so, whatever the legal and cultural pluralism that the patent system may need to accommodate, some degree of administrative convergence and 'work sharing' between national patent authorities has become inevitable. This is a consequence of inexorable practical pressures resulting from an ever increasing workload, in an increasing number of active jurisdictions, coupled with the greater complexity and range of technologies covered by patents. Considering practical experience worldwide, it is difficult to imagine a future of individual offices remaining functionally autarchic and wholly uninfluenced by search and examination outcomes elsewhere. De facto or informal convergence will probably occur, even in the absence of any formal or legal structures requiring such convergence, and even in tension with a more abstract conception of idealized policy settings uniquely tailored for individual nations' economic and technological context.

- An overarching challenge is to define the kind of policy and legal framework that is required to respond to this development: centrifugal forces towards regulatory diversity; centripedal forces towards practical convergence. These forces are not necessarily contradictory, and more systematic practical cooperation need not exclude necessary regulatory diversity. Administrative cooperation may indeed be essential for better policy outcomes, especially patent quality, construed here as the greater conformity in practice between actual patent grant outcomes and the public interest as expressed in the patentability criteria. Work sharing has a strong qualitative component, and is not merely a matter of more efficient processing of files: it concerns the better application of resources to achieve more consistent outcomes in the public interest. This means patent search and examination needs to be both broader and deeper.

- Appropriating Linus's law from the domain of collaborative software development – 'given enough eyeballs, all bugs are shallow' – and applying it to patent procedures, a broader, open pool of expertise in the identification of prior art would be helpful in strengthening the information basis for the scrutiny of novelty and obviousness. Peer to patent initiatives are exploring the logic and effectiveness of such collaborative search and examination. But deep and diverse focused expertise – and the expenditure of more expert time per patent application – are also needed to ensure a full assessment of non-obviousness, utility/industrial applicability and adequacy of disclosure. Logically, instead of 20 functionally discrete patent offices, each undertaking a relatively brief review of the same application for one working day, one highly specialized examiner in one office could devote a full month to the same application, using the same level of resources. Such a mechanism could be achieved by establishing concentrations of expertise in distinct offices. Nor need this be an effective ceding of patent grant questions to authorities in the major developed economies. For example, consideration of patents drawing on traditional knowledge systems could well be handled by those patent offices in the countries where those systems are indigenous. Developing country patent offices could concentrate on those areas that are most important to their development needs – such as infectious diseases or tropical agriculture. Practical options include de facto or informal arrangements, whereby offices are effectively guided by outcomes elsewhere; formal consortia or work sharing agreements; and the strengthening of the multilateral legal/administrative platform as a common basis. Driven by pragmatic need rather than ideology, offices are already exploring a range of such mechanisms.

- These observations contain the seeds of a sufficiently democratic and diverse notion of 'patent quality' that still provides a common basis for confidence in the capacity of patent grant decisions to serve general public welfare. Over 150 countries and separate customs territories are bound by a treaty establishing that the objective of the protection of IP is to: 'contribute to the promotion of technological innovation and to the transfer and dissemination of technology, to the mutual advantage of producers and users of technological knowledge and in a manner conducive to social and economic welfare, and to a balance of rights and obligations'. (WTO TRIPS Agreement, art. 7) These obligations have significant legal and theoretical implications, but in reality they can only be delivered in practice by effective, well functioning national legal systems and administration. These desiderata cannot be achieved in the multilateral sphere alone.

A challenge therefore remains to clarify what contribution is required from the multilateral level to buttress more wide-ranging efforts to (1) promote patent quality, construed as working to ensure that actual patenting outcomes accord in practice with public interest as defined in 'technical' patentability criteria – within a globalizing patent system, but one that will be called on to draw on distinct knowledge systems; (2) while meeting expectations of equity – both in access to the fruits of the system, and in access to the system (considering the de facto discriminatory effect created by current price structures); and (3) with resources that are inherently scarce, both in terms of quantity and the qualitative dimension of specialized expertise, creating the practical need and arguably the inevitability of forms of work sharing and collaboration on patent search and examination.

These demands may be dealt with in a contradictory or ad hoc manner – inadequate and inexpert resources dedicated to duplicative work, yielding outcomes of limited and uneven quality and thus sowing unpredictability, and creating regulatory costs and costs of access to the system that effectively discriminate against small and medium enterprises, developing country firms, and public sector applicants; or they may be resolved in a more harmonious way that recognizes the need for patent quality, more open and efficient peer review (Linus again), work sharing and collective benefit from pockets of deep expertise in specific technological areas and potentially in diverse knowledge systems.

Subsidies

The present situation

The classical description of mechanisms to promote innovation distinguishes between patents, 'subsidies' and prizes. The patent system provides a speculative reward in the form of marketing exclusivity for the first successful innovator. A 'subsidy' is a grant or benefit paid by the government. A prize is a speculative reward paid to the first (usually) successful innovator upon the meeting of a defined objective.

The way the patent system presently operates, it is the innovator that defines his or her objective. A patent may just as well be granted for a mousetrap as a drug. It is innovators and markets that determine the direction of research. By establishing this type of 'open-ended' reward system we impose the risk of research on the innovator, but at the same time the innovator is free to deliver what he or she wishes. This has significant implications in the field of pharmaceutical research. A patent may just as well be granted for a new hair restoration ointment as for a sleeping sickness cure. Researchers choose where they will invest their research funds and bear the risk of those decisions.

When the government, foundation or other funding source provides a research subsidy, it typically defines the objective of the research. Research subsidies are quite typical for the development of military technologies. The US Air Force decides that it wants or needs a new type of jet fighter with particular technological features. It pays research firms to develop the technology that it needs, defining the parameters of the 'outcome' technology in advance.

In the field of public health governments and foundations know the target diseases that need to be addressed. In principle, it seems most sensible for public health authorities to define research targets and to subsidize researchers to address those targets. That way, research funds would be addressed to public health priorities.

Governments indeed already do this. The US NIH, for example, provide research subsidies for addressing particular disease targets. US bio-weapons defense initiatives are almost wholly subsidized.

If societies are going to spend money either in the form of high prices for patented pharmaceuticals or on subsidies, why not spend the money on specifically targeted public health priorities? Why leave questions about the direction of R&D to the market? Intuitively, subsidies would appear to be the most efficient way to address 'priority diseases'.

Reliance on patents rather than subsidies in the pharmaceutical sector evidences the belief that government policy makers do not necessarily make the best decisions about the direction of research, and that the recipients of subsidies may be inefficient (or 'lazy') with respect to accomplishing their objectives.

The reward of subsidies requires government officials to evaluate proposals and make determinations about what may be the most promising research leads. It is not clear that government officials are particularly good at making these choices. And giving discretionary authority to government officials can lead to favoritism, corruption and other negative influences on decision making.

If payment to the recipient of a subsidy is not made contingent on his achieving a particular objective, the recipient may not work as hard as an alternative researcher who will not be paid unless he or she succeeds. Because a patent (or prize) is awarded only to the 'first' innovator to cross the finish line, there is a premium on working quickly in developing a practical application that can be presented to the patent (or prize) office.

Moreover, even if subsidies are a good tool for promoting basic pharmaceutical research, they may not be as effective in stimulating movement of products into the hands of patients.

Should the general public insist that a larger percentage of pharmaceutical research and development funds be channeled through government subsidies rather than through speculative expenditure by the private sector seeking patents? If the public wants the government to control the direction of research, the answer may be 'yes'. But we do not have very good tools for predicting whether increasing subsidized research would lead to more innovation than occurs under the patent-centric system. It is difficult to predict which system will be more cost-effective from the public's standpoint.

Under the approach of the NIH, subsidies do not usually cover the entire R&D chain from basic research to refinement of production processes. Using the Bayh-Dole legislative mechanism, private sector companies are able to obtain patents for innovations developed through public subsidy, and take these innovations into the marketplace. There is argument to be made that this harnesses the 'best of both worlds': subsidized targeting of initial research with encouragement of rapid translation into usable products. But the Bayh-Dole legislative mechanism is open to criticism because NIH has not exercised any control over the prices which are ultimately charged by private sector companies. NIH has taken the position that this is an issue for Congress, should it choose to address it.

A better subsidy system?

Criticism of subsidization as a mechanism for inducing innovation tends, as noted above, to focus on doubts as to the capacity of government officials to make 'good decisions' and on a lack of market-based incentives to push products forward through the pipeline to patients.

The history of 'centrally planned' economies indeed supports the hypothesis that 'bureaucrats' isolated from external performance pressures may not be the best decision makers. But it may be wrong to extrapolate from the planned economy of the Soviet Union to the world of pharmaceutical R&D. Some of the great scientific successes of the Western world have resulted from government subsidized research projects, including the NASA space program (for example, the International Space Station, Mars Landrover and Hubble Telescope), development of Internet technologies by DARPA, and various military technologies adapted to civilian use, such as Global Positioning Systems. Moreover, subsidized technological programs intended for commercial implementation, such as Europe's Airbus, have proven remarkably successful. More work is needed to identify the elements of successful subsidized research programs, a number of which may be broadly defined as 'Large Science'. Some of these cases may appear, at least initially, to involve substantial economic inefficiency as 'cost overruns' are not uncommon. Yet it would be interesting to compare the extent of these cost overruns with the social cost, for example, of obligating the public to pay the price of 'patented' drugs as compared with more directly absorbing the costs of inefficiency in subsidized R&D programs. In other words, the world community as a whole today is paying $550 billion to purchase patented pharmaceuticals, but only $100 billion to purchase a far greater quantity of generic drugs. If all drugs were produced generically there would be a tremendous financial saving, with a very large sum remaining to invest in research and development, even if that R&D were to be less efficient than private sector R&D.[43]

In addition to the general question of inefficiency, there is the question of the capacity and/or willingness of government officials to make 'good decisions' about the direction of research. Assuming for the sake of argument that there are influences affecting bureaucratic decision makers that result in 'suboptimal' performance, there are mechanisms that could be used to improve decision making with respect to subsidized R&D programs. One mechanism would involve establishing 'independent' panels of experts to assess proposals. Those experts could be drawn from various fields that would typically be involved in research programs, whether private or public, and might include public interest advocates. This is not to suggest that current NIH or other agency practices do not include external reviewers, but rather to indicate that it is not necessary to build a system that relies on 'bureaucrats' for substantive decisions.

A very significant part of pharmaceutical R&D costs are accounted for by 'clinical trials'. Perhaps the single most important set of decisions made by Pharma companies involves selection of drug candidates for clinical testing. Once those decisions are made, companies are committed to large-scale expenditure and market feedback regarding outcomes. There is no obvious reason why panels of 'independent' public health and science experts could not make decisions about which drug candidates to take into clinical trials just as competently as private sector decision makers. It might indeed be that independent experts who are not subject to 'market discipline' would be more willing to take risks to find breakthrough treatments. It is almost certain that independent experts would be less inclined to focus on lifestyle drugs or treatments than are private sector decision makers. Government subsidization of clinical trials is not so difficult to contemplate.[44] One important benefit from government subsidized clinical trials is that such trials would presumably be far more 'transparent' than the trials presently conducted by the private sector. There are a number of recent episodes of private sector companies shielding negative clinical trial data. It is by now well accepted that increasing external oversight and review of clinical trials is bound to bring to the surface problems that might not be disclosed by private companies.

Finally, there are ways to address the argument that the private sector is better than the public sector at translating basic research into products eligible for commercialization. Some of the best pharmaceutical production processes have been developed and implemented by generic producers in India. These companies were (and are) competing to supply OECD originator companies with active pharmaceutical ingredients, as well as competing in the international market for generics. In principle, if new pharmaceutical products are developed under a government subsidized research program that includes clinical trials, there is no reason why the work of moving the products into production cannot be undertaken by generics producers.

The foregoing suggests that there may be ways to move toward increased reliance on government subsidization of pharmaceutical R&D as a mechanism for developing and placing medicines into the hands of physicians and patients. There is not enough historical precedent to assess/predict whether a subsidization-based system may perform better than the present patent-centric system. It certainly seems as though it would be possible to reduce aggregate global pharmaceutical expenditures through a subsidization system because the 'patent premium' would be removed from the system. That may result in some less efficient R&D processes, but probably not so inefficient as to swallow the rather enormous potential savings from the current $550 billion originator pharmaceutical bill.

The need for savings becomes particularly important when looking at the not so distant future in OECD countries, and particularly the USA, as average population ages increase. The US Medicare system is facing a tremendous budget shortfall. Yet the response of the Congress was to turn the administration of the US Medicare pharmaceutical system over to private insurance companies purchasing expensive patented products from major Pharma companies, with all parts of that supply chain standing to make enormous profits. At some point achieving cost savings will become a necessity rather than a luxury, and the federal government will need to consider how to develop and distribute medicines at prices that can be absorbed by the federal budget. Whether Congress can be persuaded to act before the money runs out is not at all clear. But, if and when Congress does begin to confront necessity, there are options for rationalizing the medicines supply system.

Governments, Universities and Research Institutions

As noted above, industrial research has at various times relied heavily on basic discoveries made in the academic and institutional environment, selecting and reducing to practice those which could form the basis for new treatments. Even with respect to products developed within its own walls, industry has relied heavily on academic circles for expert advice and guidance, and particular projects have been farmed out for study in the specialized laboratories of universities and government-funded scientific institutions. It therefore makes eminent sense to consider whether, at a time when industrial research seems to be functioning less than optimally, this type of non-industrial institution could play a greater role in one way or another in ensuring ongoing innovation (see Box 2.3).

At this point one must however recognize that the creation and development of new products is not the generally accepted task of universities and colleges. That role is to create new knowledge (particularly through basic research) and to impart it. That new knowledge may have practical application, but it will generally be up to others to explore that possibility. The role of the NIH and similar bodies in other countries is rather different, and some such institutes have indeed been officially charged with product development (for example, the creation and even the manufacture of vaccines). Neither these institutes nor the universities possess, however, the sort of project structure that has proved so successful in the pharmaceutical industry, with potential new products moving smoothly from their point of creation by the chemist to their testing by the pharmacologist and toxicologist, their formulation as usable entities by the pharmacist and their testing by the clinician. Nor do these institutions as a rule possess the apparatus needed to ensure that large-scale trials are carried out and products submitted for regulatory approval. Primarily, therefore, universities and institutions will be likely to contribute most in the form of basic discoveries and ideas, and at a later stage specialized advice when it is sought.

On occasion, national authorities have indeed urged, supported and even initiated particular types of research effort. The fact is, for example, often cited that the urgent need to avoid travel-sickness among allied troops destined for the invasion of Nazi-controlled Europe in 1944 led to successful research underlying the creation of the antihistamines. In more recent times multi-government support has been provided for WHO's development of an artemesin preparation for acute malaria and for the innovative work sponsored by global funds and alliances working in the areas of malaria, tuberculosis and vaccine development (see Chapter 5). Less directly, governments and taxpayers have made an immense financial contribution over the years to the type of basic research in universities and institutions that usually underlies, fertilizes and complements the research efforts of the industry.

Quite apart from the public funding of universities, there are numerous state institutions carrying out exploratory studies in this area. They range from the Medical Research Councils of the United Kingdom and South Africa to the Pasteur Institute of France and the NIH in the United States. One classic example is the manner in which the work of Sir Bernard Katz at the University of Liverpool in the 1960s in identifying the role of neural transmitter substances, complemented by other academic studies, provided the basis on which Sir James Black and others were inspired to develop the theory that enabled them to create the beta-blocking agents and the H2 antagonists.[45] Another is the manner in which Taxol® (paclitaxel), used in female cancers, was developed by Bristol-Myers Squibb in the United States, using research on synthesizing the molecule developed at Florida State University, after the active substance had been isolated and its medical uses defined in a National Cancer Institute Program at the Research Triangle Institute. There are many other examples.

One real risk in this connection is the manner in which governments are prone, at times of economic downturn or as a form of market liberalization, to reduce university and institutional funding, leading these bodies to turn to industry to maintain their income. As Derek Bok of Harvard has pointed out:

> The last line of defence for basic academic standards is an adequate and stable level of support. As a practical matter, survival will almost always take precedence over institutional values. . . . If federal support for science is cut severely, the balance will shift too far from basic inquiry toward applied, commercially funded research.[46]

Such a trend all too readily develops where pharmaceuticals are concerned since the industry already contracts out a great deal of its applied development work to academic institutions. For the corporation this renders its work program more flexible, reduces its own overheads and gives it access to a pool of experience far wider than that available within its own walls. For the public institution, however, it entails a series of dangers. One is aware of serious instances of conflict of interest[47] and to well-documented instances in which an industrial firm has pressured an investigator to produce findings that are favorable rather than reliable[48] or has even sought to suppress unfavorable results.[49] Such practices certainly pollute the academic environment and distort the innovative process, but in the present connection the most serious danger in the entire process is the likelihood that intellectual resources will be shifted

BOX 2.3 THE ROLE OF UNIVERSITY RESEARCH
IN THE DEVELOPMENT OF GLOBAL
PHARMACEUTICALS

Contributed by Lorelei Ritchie de Larena, Administrative Judge, Trademark Trial and Appeal Board, US Patent and Trademark Office

Universities are largely educators, primarily to their students and secondarily to their communities, but of equal importance is their role as innovators. Professors know that they are judged as much by measures of innovation (that is, publications) as by education. Where drugs are concerned, universities participate typically only in the first phase of research (drug discovery) and occasionally in pre-clinical or clinical studies (if prompted and funded by 'Pharma' partners).

A translational gap can however exist between the 'R' contributed by universities, and the 'D' undertaken by industry. Industries are typically not interested in investing in, licensing or funding university pharmaceutical research that is still at too early a stage while university researchers are not motivated to undertake translational research (which is undervalued both in the tenure and promotion process and by scientific publishers). In addition, 70 percent of NIH grants are for basic (early-stage) research only.

As innovators, universities struggle to maintain sufficient resources for their researchers. A battle over patent rights has added to the possible costs to universities. In *Madey* v. *Duke* in 2002[a] the Federal Circuit Court of Appeals took the view that universities could no longer trust a non-existent research exemption for their use of patents held by others. On the other hand, in *Merck* v. *Integra* in 2005[b] the Supreme Court granted a 'wide berth' to drug development research that would otherwise be subject to patent infringement suits.

Increasingly, universities have come to see themselves as patent owners, developing income from their innovative work. This commercialization of universities has been criticized[c], for example, for tying up technology by over-patenting or for encouraging excessively 'cozy' links with industry, and some researchers believe it pulls them away from their core missions. On the other

hand, universities have argued that the increased commercialization fuels the national economy and has positive repercussions
for drug access internationally.

In 2006 the US Government Accountability Office proposed
that measures to shorten the drug development process and
reduce its cost should include the development of more staff with
translational skills;[d] since then, various universities have sought
to fill the gap by providing special funds to faculty members no
longer eligible for NIH grants. A more radical proposal would
create a national technology transfer center to manage licensing of all federally funded inventions. Meanwhile, grant-back and
march-in rights under the Bayh-Dole Act can be used to promote
innovation and access to safe and inexpensive pharmaceuticals.

Notes:
a. 307 F.3d 1351 (Fed. Cir. 2002).
b. 125 S.Ct. 2372 (2005).
c. Jennifer Washburn (2005) *University, Inc.: The Corporate Corruption of
    American Higher Education.*
d. GAO-07-409, p. 36.

Source: This brief account draws on two recent law-review articles by the
author: 'The price of progress: are universities adding to the cost?' 43, *Hous L
Rev*, 1373 (2007) and 'What copyright teaches patent law about "fair use" and why
universities are ignoring the lesson', 84, *Or L Rev*, 779 (2005).

from fundamental investigation to what is commonly no more than a
routine but financially more rewarding chore. One can impose rules on
teaching institutions and state bodies as regards the conditions which
they must respect when accepting commercial funding, but making regulations is no substitute for positive action. Poverty, like hunger, is one
of the most potent reasons for brushing rules aside. The maintenance
of adequate public funding for basic research in areas relating to public
health is surely one of the essential tools to ensure that innovation continues to be soundly based.

It is also important to consider the financial aspects of the contribution that these institutions can or should make. Often they are funded
largely by the state, and when an important discovery is made within
their walls, it will essentially have been at the taxpayer's expense. If that
discovery subsequently provides the essential basis for the development
of a highly profitable industrial product, it would seem reasonable to
require that an appropriate part of the resulting income should flow
back to the institutions concerned in order to fund their work, or even to

the government. As recent discussions have shown, that has not always been the case. Large pharmaceutical firms have in some cases appeared to regard universities as 'cheap' sources of new products, concluding license agreements that provide only a meager reward for their achievement. When that happens a university may rightly regard itself as having been short-changed, and the community that has both financed the initial discovery and then found itself charged substantial sums for the drug that ultimately emerges may well consider that it is being required to pay doubly for its contribution.

All the above considerations seem universally applicable, though the balance of interest may vary from country to country. In the United States, and to some extent in parts of Europe, universities find themselves in a situation where community funding falls seriously short, and they are both encouraged and indeed obliged to develop their own sources of income, for example, by aggressively licensing the products of their research. These movements are in a state of flux; but it would be unfortunate if, in the case of universities, financial penury were to result in their moving on a large scale into applied product research, to the neglect of the process of creating new basic knowledge.

Prices
Government authorities have been able to exert a major influence through their pricing policies that may be designed to favor highly innovative products.

Prizes

Among the earliest forms of incentive for innovation is the 'prize'.[50] The prize is a reward granted to a person(s) who achieves a defined goal. There is no single type of prize mechanism. It can be defined in accordance with the wishes of the person establishing it. It need not go to the 'first' person that achieves a particular goal, or to only one 'winner'. It could go to the person who 'best' achieves the goal within some defined timeframe, or it might be divided among persons that achieve the goal. There is nothing to prevent a prize mechanism from allowing the innovator to patent whatever invention secures the prize (or to prevent those who try and fail from patenting their efforts). Though, certainly, the person establishing the prize could impose a condition not to patent the invention, or to patent and license it under prescribed conditions.

Prizes, like subsidies, channel innovation efforts toward pre-established goals. The main difference is that the prize system generally (though not necessarily) relies on the prize seekers to expend their own resources to reach the goal(s). The unsuccessful participants in the race for a prize lose their investment (or at least the portion that cannot be turned to other uses). Conceptually, there would be less upfront government investment in a prize system than in a subsidy system.

'Bureaucrats' would not be seeking to determine how the objectives should be accomplished. Because the prize system typically has the characteristics of a 'race', there is an incentive to work rapidly.

In the past three or four years considerable attention has been turned to the potential use of prizes to encourage innovation in the pharmaceutical sector, and some prize mechanisms already have been established. James Love and Tim Hubbard have been notable proponents of the prize system for medicines. One of the major advantages of the prize system is that, assuming the prize winner is suitably rewarded by a payment, the production and distribution of 'prize-winning' medicines could be undertaken without extracting additional 'innovation rent' from consumers. Generic producers could be licensed with the innovation and encouraged to compete on price.

As Love and Hubbard have observed, however, the allocation of prizes for medicines innovation may be a more complex business than simply establishing a one-time endpoint and awarding a fixed amount to the 'winner'. The extent to which a medicine succeeds in treating a disease may not be immediately known, and 'future treatments' may render the initial prize winner less attractive than alternatives. It might be desirable, in their view, to set up a mechanism under which the level of prizes is determined 'after the fact' by assessing the success of prize winners. They discuss their proposal in Box 2.4.

The proposals outlined in Box 2.4 are not merely theoretical. The United States has recently established a 'prize voucher' system to reward innovation on 16 'neglected diseases'.[51] Prizes will be awarded to persons who successfully register new treatments (or vaccines) for these diseases. Prize winners will be entitled to accelerated FDA assessment of drugs other than treatments for neglected diseases, and may sell that 'priority'. Prize winners will be permitted to patent their innovations. Prize mechanisms are today also being used in various other fields, including private space exploration and mathematics.

Whether prize mechanisms will successfully provide real incentives to R&D on new medicines is difficult to predict. This will obviously depend, at least in part, on how valuable the prize is. It will also depend on whether pharmaceutical companies are willing to participate in a race in which they may 'not win', being left without a viable means to recover their investments. Love and Hubbard take this risk into account in their proposals that do not involve a 'first winner takes all' solution.[52]

BOX 2.4   THE BIG IDEA: PRIZES TO STIMULATE R&D FOR NEW MEDICINES

Contributed by James Love (Knowledge Ecology International) and Tim Hubbard (Wellcome Trust Sanger Institution)

It is possible to construct a viable new system to finance innovation in a way that maximizes access to new inventions while continuing to exploit commercial competitive market incentive mechanisms.

1. The prize mechanisms should be thought of as part of a larger ecosystem of financing of medical R&D, and should be implemented in combination with other instruments, such as direct or indirect government funding of basic research, non-profit product development partnerships (PDPs), clinical trials, and other traditional and non-traditional types of funding R&D. What the prizes offer uniquely is an alternative to the marketing monopoly as an incentive for private investment.
2. When implemented properly, prize-based models can directly reward successful R&D projects, while permitting marginal cost pricing of products, and avoiding the trap of overly bureaucratic and centralized decision making.
3. By decoupling the rewards for successful R&D investment from the sales of products, the new model will permit governments to create more efficient and useful incentives for R&D that focus on inventions that improve health outcomes.
4. Prize mechanisms can be implemented in ways that are consistent with a robust patent system, but are best implemented in systems where the patent system is used to establish ownership of inventions and thus claims on the prize rewards, rather than through exclusive rights to market products.
5. It is important that those incentives are linked to broad research priorities, and not be overly prescriptive in terms of diseases, mechanisms or technologies.
6. By eliminating marketing monopolies on products, there is an opportunity for much greater efficiency through unrestricted

competition to manufacture the resulting medical products.

7. The elimination of marketing monopolies, the decoupling of R&D incentives from prices and the creation of an evidence-based reward system linked to changes in health outcomes will lead to significant reductions in expenditures to market products, the area of the largest waste in the current system.

8. It is important that the total obligations to finance the reward payment are not directly tied to utilization, but rather measures of a country's ability to contribute to global R&D costs, so that countries do not have incentives to limit access to products in order to control budget outlays on innovation rewards.

9. Prize mechanisms can be introduced in areas where the markets are functioning the poorest, such as for diseases that primarily affect poor people living in poor countries. But the largest benefit will come from the adoption of prize mechanisms in higher income markets, such as the United States, both because improvements in the efficiency of R&D incentives in high-income countries are important for the development of medicines used everywhere, and also because pricing norms in high-income countries are forcefully exported to developing countries, creating enormous hardships.

10. Whilst additional detailed modeling will be required to improve reward structures and evaluation criteria, these efforts are feasible, and not materially different from efforts by governments or insurance companies to determine acceptable reimbursements for insured products.

11. A significant shift to a new system of incentives that relies upon prizes rather than prices will also require a shift to a new global trade framework that focuses less on intellectual property rights and more on country contributions to mechanisms that support R&D, including but not limited to prize incentive mechanisms.

The major challenge to switching financing systems for medical innovation on a global scale depends on whether there is sufficient political leadership.

Source: Based on The Ruby Hutchison Memorial Address, KEI Research Paper 2007, p. 1, Presented 14 November 2006, Revised 26 March 2007.

Philanthropy

Private philanthropy is playing an increasingly large role in R&D of new medicines. This is in particular due to the contributions of the Gates Foundation, although of course there are a number of other major contributors.

Private foundations, such as the Gates Foundation, work principally through subsidized research. The Gates Foundation targets certain disease conditions and allocates funding among individuals or groups submitting promising research proposals for addressing those targets. That funding may be quite substantial. There is no obvious reason to distinguish government subsidies and private philanthropic subsidies as mechanisms to promote innovation, other than in terms of 'who decides' on the direction of research.

It is for this distinguishing reason that private philanthropy is somewhat controversial. The global community relies on the judgment essentially of one person – Bill Gates – with respect to what disease targets and what methods of research are going to be used. Mr. Gates may today have more to say about the direction of research on medicines than the WHO. There is an advantage to this. Since Bill Gates need only persuade himself as to the benefits of a particular direction, decisions can be made and implemented quickly. Governments, including multilateral organizations, almost by definition move more slowly. At the same time, it is not unreasonable to be concerned that a great deal of power in this area has been concentrated in one individual, and equally well to be concerned that international institutions are so lacking in capacity that they can be marginalized by one or two wealthy individuals.

The Gates Foundation and other philanthropic organizations tend to channel their money into public-private partnerships (PPPs) that involve collaborations between non-profit institutions and private sector research companies. Through cross-licensing of patented technologies with public and private institutions, they can allocate the results of research among different geographic territories, types of purchasers (for example, public sector and private sector health providers) and income classes.

While there is not enough experience of the Gates Foundation or other PPPs to determine the extent to which subsidized funding of this nature is a practical approach to addressing disease conditions, certainly PPPs like the Drugs for Neglected Diseases initiative (DNDi) have already developed, sometimes in cooperation with private sector partners, novel therapies and/or delivery systems in areas such as the treatment of malaria.

ACHIEVING GLOBAL EQUITY

Dramatic steps must be taken to assure a degree of equity in the distribution of pharmaceutical products among the world's population. As noted in Chapters 5 and 9, dramatic steps must also be taken to increase the level of R&D funding with respect to 'neglected diseases'.

The patent system as it is currently implemented in the OECD countries channels considerable private investment into the pharmaceutical sector through the promise of large returns (at some substantial risk). If we assume for the sake of argument that the present system encourages innovation at an acceptable level, the problems of price and availability remain. Mechanisms such as differential pricing along territorial and/or income level lines can be used to ameliorate the access problem, though such mechanisms are not today widely employed. There are serious risks with such mechanisms, particularly that they are likely to entrench the position of major suppliers by diminishing price incentives for new market entrants. Such risks will need to be addressed if differential pricing mechanisms take on a greater role.

A more fundamental question is whether the present patent-centric system is working quasi-optimally to generate innovation. It is suggested above that 'perverse incentives' channel research into evergreening of patent monopolies at the expense of investment in breakthrough products. It would be advisable to retool current patent rules to diminish the evergreening incentives, such as by modifying the patentability requirements or creating a subclass of quasi-patents that would reward minor modifications differently.

Governments should well consider whether public health budgets would be better served by investing in subsidized research and generic production of the resulting products. There are ways to address some of the objections traditionally aimed at government subsidies, including establishment of independent decision-making expert bodies and government-sponsored clinical trials.

There is a place for 'prizes' in the mix of research incentives, particularly when the prize will act as a substitute for exclusive marketing rights. The key to a prize system will be creating a sufficient incentive structure. None of the foregoing suggestions is a radical departure from ideas already in the public arena.

The medicines problems of people earning less than two dollars per day – more than half of the world's population – will not be solved by tinkering with the criteria of patentability. These are problems that need to be solved by focused attention at the multilateral level, with funding agencies, suppliers and public health providers cooperating to make the best use of available resources. There is a good deal of activity today, such as at UNITAID, but certainly more needs to be done – and at a fairly large scale. Market-based solutions cannot be used to address the needs of people who have no meaningful basis for market participation.

NOTES

1. A detailed description of the international patent system can be found in Frederick M. Abbott, Thomas Cottier and Francis Gurry, *International Intellectual Property in an Integrated World Economy*, (2007 Aspen, USA), ch. 2. The 'patent' is an intellectual property right granted to the inventor of a new, inventive and useful product or process. The owner of a patent may prevent others from making or placing on the market the same product (or from using the same process) for the term of the patent. The minimum patent term prescribed by international rules is 20 years from the filing of the patent application, but this term may be extended in some countries for pharmaceutical products that undergo regulatory approval. National patent office authorities grant patents 'independently' from country to country. The same drug may be 'on patent' in some countries and 'off patent' in others.
2. See, for example, US Government Accountability Office, 'New drug development: science, business, regulatory, and intellectual property issues cited as hampering drug development efforts', GAO-07-49, November 2006.
3. If that is true, fixing the patent system will not lead to new and better drugs. What it might do, however, is reduce the incentive to spend wastefully on products that society does not really need.
4. See, for example, M.N.G. Dukes, F.M. Haaijer-Ruskamp, C.P. de Joncheere and A.H. Rietveld (eds) (2003), *Drugs and Money: Prices, Affordability and Cost Containment* 7th edn, WHO, IOS Press, The Netherlands.
5. An exception exists in those countries where, especially in a situation where there is a shortage of health professionals, the doctor both prescribes and dispenses drugs. This may in some instances be a necessary solution in the short term, but there are obvious objections to an arrangement under which the physician has a financial motive to prescribe generously.
6. See generally US Federal Trade Commission, 'Generic drug entry prior to patent expiration: an FTC study', July 2002.
7. See, for example, 'Canada Patented Medicine Price Review Board', http://www.pmprb-cepmb.gc.ca/english/home.asp?x=1, including reports on both patented and non-patented medicines; and US Government Accountability Office, 'Prescription drugs: price trends for frequently used brand and generic drugs from 2000 through 2004', GAO-05-779, August 2005, http://www.gao.gov/new.items/d05779.pdf, last accessed 3 November 2008.
8. In fact, today most major pharmaceutical originator companies also operate generics affiliates, no longer being content to leave the generics markets to third parties.
9. See, for example, Frederick M. Abbott, 'Patent landscaping in the field of medicines: policy and technical options', Presentation for Life Sciences Symposium: Public Policy Patent Landscaping in the Life Sciences, WIPO in cooperation with FAO, Geneva, 7–8 April 2008, available at http://www.wipo.int (Life Sciences), last accessed 3 November 2008.
10. See US Federal Trade Commission, FTC Orange Book Study.
11. A generic producer will typically respond to the lawsuit by the patent holder with a counterclaim of invalidity of the patent. See, for example, Gauri Kamath, 'Launch first fight later: Cipla and Roche fight a patents battle that can set a precedent', *BusinessWorld* (India), 4 February, 2008, p. 24.

12. See, for example, *Sanofi v. Apotex*, SDNY 02 Civ. 2255 (SHS), 19 June 2007.
13. See US Federal Trade Commissions FTC Orange Book Study.
14. Jon Leibowitz, Commissioner, Federal Trade Commission, 'Exclusion payments to settle pharmaceutical patent cases: they're b-a-a-a-ck! (the role of the Commission, Congress, and the courts)', Second Annual In-House Counsel's Forum on Pharmaceutical Antitrust, Philadelphia, 24 April, 2006.
15. See, for example, *Sanofi-Synthelabo v. Apotex* (Fed. Cir. 2006), 2006 US App. LEXIS 30090.
16. Frederick M. Abbott, 'Comparative study of selected government policies for promoting transfer of technology and competitiveness in the Colombian pharmaceutical sector', USAID-MIDAS, 12 September, 2007.
17. US Government Accountability Office, 'Prescription drugs: price trends for frequently used brand and generic drugs from 2000 through 2004', GAO-05-779, August 2005, http://www.gao.gov/new.items/d05779.pdf, last accessed 3 November 2008.
18. See Dukes et al., *Drugs and Money*.
19. US Department of Commerce, International Trade Administration, 'Pharmaceutical price controls in OECD countries: implications for U.S. consumers, pricing, research and development and innovation', December 2004.
20. See generally UNCTAD-ICTSD, *Resource Book on TRIPS and Development* (Cambridge University Press, 2005 Cambridge).
21. See generally Frederick M. Abbott (2005), 'The WTO medicines decision: the political economy of world pharmaceutical trade and the protection of public health', *Am J Int L* 99, 317–58.
22. Russia is in the process of joining the WTO. While it is not technically bound by TRIPS Agreement rules, Russia provides patent protection for pharmaceutical products and processes.
23. Because of their continuing exemption from TRIPS requirements it is possible for LDCs to step into the breach left by India and to produce drugs off-patent, including for export. Although countries like Bangladesh have been building up their production capacity, the LDCs as a general rule face substantial obstacles to becoming major global medicines suppliers. Recall also that products cannot be exported to markets where they are covered by patents.
24. See generally Frederick M. Abbott and Jerome H. Reichman (2007), 'The Doha Round's public health legacy: strategies for the production and diffusion of Patented medicines under the Amended TRIPS Provisions', *J Int Econ L,* 10 (4), 921–87.
25. *Novartis v. India*, WP Nos. 24759 of 2006 and 24760 of 2006, decided 6 August, 2007.
26. *Merck v. Integra Lifesciences*, 545 US 193 (2005).
27. See Abbott and Reichman, 'Doha Round's public health legacy'.
28. Pharmaceutical benefits providers engage in price negotiations with industry suppliers, resulting in price reductions. Uninsured individual pharmaceutical purchasers do not benefit from such price negotiations. The objective of the 'single exit price' system was to assure that uninsured individual purchasers obtained the same low prices as pharmaceutical benefits providers. It was not clear that this conceptual framework would work in practice because industry suppliers might choose to raise prices to all purchasers rather than maintain low 'single exit prices'. See Frederick M. Abbott, 'WTO TRIPS Agreement and its implications for access to medicines in developing countries', Study Paper 2a, Commission on Intellectual Property Rights, UK, November 2001, Section IV.B.
29. See Abbott, 'WTO medicines decision'.
30. See Dilip G. Shah, Secretary General, Indian Pharmaceutical Alliance, 'Evolution and Challenges of The Asian Pharmaceutical Market', Global Pharmaceutical Regulation 2007, FSU College of Law, Tallahassee, April 2007.
31. This is not inconsistent with the earlier observation that India has taken steps to make it more difficult to 'evergreen' patents. There are competing forces within India pushing in different directions.

32. See Abbott and Reichman, 'Doha Round's public health legacy'.
33. See generally US Government Accountability Office, *supra* n. 2.
34. The US NIH annual budget of $28 billion is not devoted to lifestyle diseases.
35. See Abbott, 'WTO TRIPS Agreement'.
36. See, for example, *Altana Pharma v. Teva*, 532 F. Supp. 2d 666 (DNJ 2007).
37. For example, heat stabilized versions of antiretroviral drugs are quite important from a public health standpoint.
38. See US Federal Trade Commission (2003), *To Promote Innovation: The Proper Balance of Competition and Patent Law and Policy, a Report by the Federal Trade Commission*, Federal Trade Commission, Washington, DC, October.
39. In *re Brana*, 51 F.3d 1560 (Fed. Cir. 1995).
40. Ibid.
41. See generally J.H. Reichman, (1995), 'Charting the collapse of the patent-copyright dichotomy: premises for a restructured international intellectual property system', *Cardoza Arts & Ent. L. J.*, 13, 475. Real property is generally considered 'unique' in the sense that an owner deprived of such property can be put back in 'just as good' a position only by having the property restored. In some movable property cases, typically involving unique goods, restoration of the 'thing itself' is considered the appropriate remedy for an unauthorized taking. An injunction against a third party continuing to produce or sell a patent-infringing product is considered the equivalent of restoring the real property owner to its 'just as good' position, and therefore a 'property' rule.
42. See, for example, discussion in European Commission, Guidelines on the application of Article 81 of the EC Treaty to technology transfer agreements (2004/C 101/02), 27 April 2004.
43. Love and Hubbard also make this point in James Love and Tim Hubbard, 'The big idea: prizes to stimulate R&D for new medicines', The Ruby Hutchison Memorial Address, KEI Research Paper 2007, p. 1, Presented 14 November 2006, Revised 26 March 2007.
44. Tracy R. Lewis, Jerome H. Reichman and Anthony D. So (2007), 'The case for public funding and public oversight of clinical trials', *Economists Voice*, January.
45. B. Katz (1969), *The Release of Neural Transmitter Substances*, University Press, Liverpool.
46. D.C. Bok (2003), *Universities in the Marketplace*, Princeton University Press, Princeton and Oxford, pp. 196–7.
47. D. Blumenthal (2003), 'Academic-industrial relationships in the life sciences', *N Eng J Med*, 349, 2452–9.
48. D. Shenk (1999), 'Money science = ethics problems on campus', *The Nation*, 22 March.
49. J. Thompson, P. Baird and J. Downie (2001), *The Olivieri Report: The Complete Text of the Report of the Independent Inquiry Commissioned by the Canadian Association of University Teachers*, James Lorimer, Toronto.
50. See generally Love and Hubbard, 'The big idea'.
51. See Tatum Anderson, 'New US voucher prize system for neglected diseases launches amid doubts', *IP-Watch*, 6 August 2008.
52. This is also an issue in the patent arena, where the first inventor can prevent any second comers from selling the same product. But often times on the patent side the originators are working on molecules that are sufficiently different that there is room for more than one patented therapy on the market.

3.   Policies on innovation: past, present and future

POLICY AND INNOVATION

Innovation – in the sense of the discovery or development of new and better medicines – is critical to addressing present and future public health needs. Official policies have sometimes sought to encourage or facilitate such innovation, or have done so incidentally. Governments have also been accused of discouraging innovation, especially by imposing excessive regulatory requirements, either on the process itself or on the products that emerge from it. In considering the various options for policy, it is important to consider the manner in which drug innovation comes about and the means by which it is likely to be attained in the future.

ERAS OF INNOVATION

Until early in the twentieth century, professional medicine was almost entirely reliant on an armory of relatively old medicines that had been in use for generations, and in some cases for centuries. The great bulk of these – such as opium as an analgesic, senna as a laxative and plant extracts containing tannin for use as astringents – were of herbal origin. As a rule, each was prepared by the local apothecary from the plants with which he was familiar. Much the same applied to the inorganic materials and substances of animal origin that were in use. Knowledge was largely passed on from one generation to the next through apprenticeship. Yet there was some formalized teaching of *materia medica*. And, since antiquity, a number of standard works on the subject had appeared, the oldest being that of the Greek Pedanius Discorides (AD 54–68). Over the years there was a measure of innovation, but it was largely haphazard and limited to modified extraction techniques and the preparation of supposedly more effective mixtures. While in many places practice was modified to benefit from the ready availability of indigenous plants, basic knowledge and beliefs did not fundamentally change. It is striking that standard teachings on herbal remedies dating from ancient Greece or from the Middle Ages continued to be regarded as authoritative, both in pharmaceutical and in medical practice, for generations or even centuries after they first appeared.

Very occasionally a critical scientific approach to traditional herbal practice emerged, as when Anton Stoerck of the Vienna School of Medicine between 1760 and 1777 examined the pharmacology and toxicology of a range of preparations including colchicum and hyoscyamus, thus laying the basis for their more rational use.[1] Almost simultaneously, in Britain, William Withering (1741–99) examined the components of an old family remedy for cardiac edema and succeeded in identifying the active principle as the leaf of the foxglove (digitalis). He went on to develop it in a more or less standardized form for the treatment of heart failure.[2] Even such advances, however, hardly altered the fact that the bulk of the accepted wisdom in pharmacological medicine was still based on long and largely unquestioned experience. The remedies were familiar; there was some understanding of their uses and risks, and while the individual physician might have to adapt his treatment in the light of a patient's reaction, he was unlikely to be faced with any entirely unanticipated surprises.

One type of innovation that came to the fore at various times concerned the attempt to introduce the use of various inorganic compounds into treatment. Mercury had been used by the Arabian physician Rhazes (AD 860–932), but it was the eighteenth century that saw a move in Europe to propagate the salts of both this and various other metals, including arsenic and lead, as remedies. While mercurial diuretics were to remain in use for two more centuries until safer alternatives were developed, the eighteenth century may be recalled as one in which the risks of unfamiliar medicines came sharply to the fore.[3] The risks of poisoning by salts of lead and arsenic led to their rejection in orthodox medical practice.

By contrast, the rise of the organic chemical industry in the nineteenth century – beginning primarily with ventures in Germany to develop new dyes – was destined to bring about the first major breakthrough in medicinal innovation. The analgesic acetylsalicylic acid (better known as aspirin after its earliest brand name) was synthesized in a university chemical laboratory in Germany in 1853, but its value as a relatively non-irritating compound to relieve pain and inflammation was first confirmed much later by Heinrich Dreser of the Bayer company. It was introduced into medicine in 1899.[4] The earliest organic arsenicals became available as chemotherapeutic agents, notably for venereal disease, by 1911.[5] The value of the first sulfonamide for the treatment of a wide range of infections was demonstrated by 1938.[6] The arrival of penicillin, based on the observations of Fleming,[7] opened the antibiotic era by 1940. While in these instances the pharmaceutical industry had largely continued to benefit from basic innovations made in university laboratories, many firms took steps, particularly after 1945, to establish their own units for innovative research, and three decades of massive drug discovery followed. Chemists synthesized new substances, pharmacologists tested them in animal studies, pharmacists developed formulations and clinicians conducted investigations in human subjects. The result was the creation of entirely new classes of effective and relatively safe drugs, such as the modern diuretics, the benzodiazepine tranquilizers and treatments for psychosis and depression. Modifications of natural bodily agents, such as the corticosteroids and sex hormones, produced equally valuable therapeutic tools.

THE EMERGENCE OF CONCERN

While the prospects for unending progress appeared bright, as the twentieth century progressed the rate of achievement was uneven. Quite apart from the occurrence of a number of drug-induced disasters which served as warning signals that all might not be well (see Chapters 4 and 7), the Organisation for Economic Co-operation and Development (OECD) in 1969 expressed grave concern that the rate of innovation in Europe was falling behind that of the United States.[8] Its report issued in that year ventured the belief that much innovation during the previous two decades had been due to discoveries made in scientific programs associated with military activity during the Second World War, and that this source of inspiration had now largely been exhausted.

The pessimism inherent in that conclusion was soon discounted as a new wave of drug discovery followed during the 1970s. Innovation seemed to be erupting once more on both sides of the Atlantic, marked by the appearance of the beta-blockers, new oral contraceptives and enzyme inhibitors. Predictions, however, varied as to whether such progress could continue indefinitely. Certainly towards the end of the twentieth century, wide concern was arising as regards what appeared to be an era of rapidly diminishing returns in drug research in the world as a whole. A graph published by Achilladelis and Antonakis in 2001 (Figure 3.1) pointed to what appeared to be a rapid collapse of industrial innovation during the decade that had just ended.

No less striking than the absolute figures reflected in such a graph are the details regarding the degree of innovation delivered. The bulk of new drugs introduced from 1970 onwards are seen to be closely related to those already existing, sometimes representing merely alternatives rather than further improvements; the term 'semi-innovative' was used by some to characterize them.[9] Only a very small proportion of new drugs entering the market could be considered radical innovations, that is, items adding

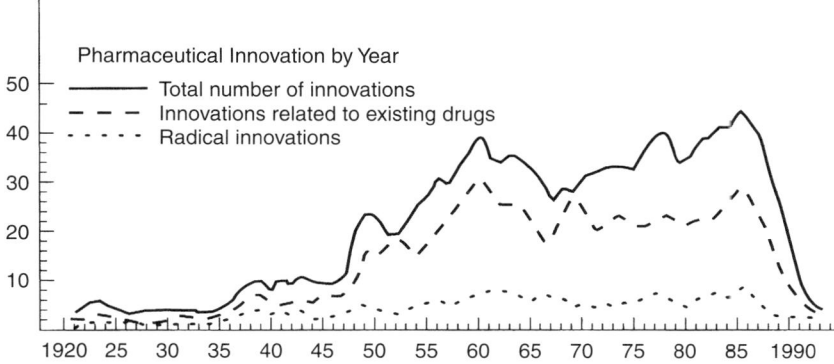

Source: B. Achilladelis and N. Antonakis (2001), 'The dynamics of technical innovation; the case of the pharmaceutical industry' *Res. Policy*, 30, 535–8.

Figure 3.1   Drug Innovation 1920–90

something of significance to the quality and breadth of medical care. The industry was often criticized for poor planning and the direction of some of its research, with too great an emphasis on rapid results in terms of new molecules. Within industry the outcome of many projects was considered to be as disappointing to their sponsors as to the medical world. Many 'me too' preparations were little more than imitations of what already existed, representing the pathetic outcome of a project that had originally been designed to deliver a breakthrough in treatment.

A parallel concern in recent decades is that so many of the new products emerging from industrial laboratories are intended, not for the treatment of the world's most challenging diseases (cancer, malaria, tuberculosis, atherosclerosis), but for the disorders of Western affluence. Numerous products have, for example, been developed to treat obesity or high blood lipid levels, or for 'lifestyle' purposes.

Some experts such as Joseph Fortunak (Box 3.1) subscribe to the pessimistic view of the new drug scene during the last two decades, and have sought to explain it. Spokesmen for the pharmaceutical industry and those closely associated with it have, not surprisingly, attempted to promote a more positive interpretation. They stress the fact that new drugs are still introduced every year, and argue that some of those which have been criticized as merely semi-innovative, or even non-innovative, represent at least minor improvements on what has gone before, with progress sometimes resulting from a succession of such small steps rather than from dramatic breakthroughs.

BOX 3.1   THE CHALLENGE OF RESEARCH AND DEVELOPMENT (RRD)

Contributed by Joseph Fortunak

Discussion is widespread around the common perception that R&D in the pharmaceutical industry is 'failing'. New product approvals are down from prior decades and the number of priority drug approvals for truly innovative, new medicines with widespread impact are very few. Inadequate access to medicines is also troubling; even in the USA up to 90 million people do not have adequate access to prescription drugs, while globally the richest 15 percent of the world's population consumes 91 percent of medicines (mid-2005 estimate from the WHO's report on progress towards achieving the UN's Millennium Goals).

A fundamental difficulty associated with increasing the number and impact of new medicines is the staggeringly high associated cost. The R&D investment to discover, develop and launch a new medicinal product has been claimed to be roughly $1.7billion [a] while only one in three new products recovers its investment costs.[b] The industry's rule of thumb is that projected annual sales for a new drug must minimally be between $500 million and $1 billion to justify development. It may well be that in the foreseeable future the only companies which can afford new product innovation are the ones who find effective means of reducing overall cost to the consumer. The US Pharmaceutical Research and Manufacturers Association of America (PhRMA) has estimated that every dollar spent on medicines avoids roughly $6 in otherwise associated costs. This is not, however, a reason to avoid a critical, unbiased analysis of how innovation might be more efficient to better serve the public good. The public – through tax dollars spent by the US NIH and National Science Foundation (NSF) – is a major contributor to the overall process. It seems clear that:

- Access is at least as important as innovation. The cost model developed by PhRMA, based on high prices, cannot substantially meet the needs of lowest- to middle-income populations. It is notable that the Indian generic industry has been carrying the burden of access for low-income markets. The success of this industry shows that it is entirely possible to improve global access without increasing cost.

- Manufacturing is a major contributor to the cost of drugs. Since R&D investment in process development is delayed until after therapeutic proof-of-concept is shown most new entities are launched with suboptimal manufacturing. Manufacturing is the largest single element of PhRMA expense (roughly 36 percent). Surprisingly, this figure is higher than marketing (24 percent) and over twice the cost of R&D (16 percent). Later efficiencies are rarely introduced since this involves regulatory hurdles and, in the high-cost PhRMA operational model, they would have little effect on overall profitability.

- Genomics is a relatively new, permanent and very expensive feature of pharmaceutical R&D. The sub-domains of toxicogenomics, metabonomics and pharmacogenomics are powerful new forces in drug discovery. The promise of genomics is two-fold. Patients can receive 'personalized medicine' by the matching of their genetic profile with the actions and potential benefits of available medicines. In addition, genomics can potentially identify reasons why new drug candidates would fail in clinical trials, thereby increasing the success rate of new drug candidates in very expensive human trials. While genomics is a large, new contributor to R&D expense, the promise of increasing success rates in clinical trials has not yet substantially materialized. Indeed, the timing of R&D investment is such that this may take a decade to fully realize.

- Improving R&D efficiency will largely translate into more drugs coming out of the pipeline. It is feasible to improve efficiency. There is, for example, a wasteful duplication of effort, because so much of the knowledge generated by firms is externally unavailable.

- Intellectual property protection coverage should be modified to require release of more data, notably on toxicology, clinical trials and optimal manufacturing processes.

- Emergent patterns of collaboration with generic drug providers in developing countries, such as those developed by Howard University in Washington, DC, promise to reduce the cost of essential medicines for some major diseases.

- A series of praiseworthy international activities are now underway to enhance global supply chain management and align demand with supply, so as to maximize the availability of access to drugs. The William J. Clinton Healthcare Access Initiative has negotiated huge cost reductions for HIV/AIDS drugs in the developing world, largely by aligning the supply and demand sides of the equation, and by providing technical assistance to partners involved in the process. Other worthy activities include the Drugs for Neglected Diseases Initiative (DNDi), moves to induce innovator companies to test new chemical entities entering clinical development for their applicability to neglected diseases, and a global treaty to provide early access with generic pricing to new drugs in the R&D pipeline (for example, for HIV/AIDS).

Notes
a. Estimate by Accenture (2002).
b. Data provided by the PhRMA, Washington, DC.

That argument is, in turn, countered by critics observing that a fair proportion of the new drugs that therapeutically bear little promise nevertheless introduce significant new risks and have to be withdrawn shortly after they have been launched.[10] The field of anti-inflammatory therapy starkly illustrates the risks. A significant number of new compounds were introduced over five decades, too many proving injurious, with a lack of therapeutic progress. The cases of the anti-inflammatory drugs Opren® (benoxaprofen) that damaged the liver in many elderly patients,[11] and Vioxx® (rofecoxib) that produced serious cardiovascular complications[12] are often cited, though they are far from being the only examples. Many physicians still choose to treat rheumatism with drugs that were available in 1960 or earlier. As Sigelman has pointed out,[13] not one of 13 relatively new medicinal products which had to be withdrawn for safety reasons from the US market over a decade left a significant gap in therapy.

THE REASONS FOR DECLINING PROGRESS; DID POLICY PLAY A ROLE?

Sometimes the rise and continuing prosperity of a pharmaceutical company has been almost entirely attributable to successful innovation within its walls. The success over a long period of Merck in the United States[14] has been explained in this way, as has the international rise of the much smaller and younger Janssen company in Belgium.[15] A study of Genentech, a biotechnological firm with a remarkable innovative record, has concluded that innovation has proved to be considerably more rewarding than investments in marketing, patent policies or aggressive mergers.[16] In theory, the foregoing examples may suggest that firms should concentrate their efforts to achieve growth on achieving innovation rather than in other directions. However, conclusions such as these have been drawn on the basis of successes achieved only in selected firms. Even in these firms there have been ups and downs in research output. In many other pharmaceutical companies it is precisely the failure of massive innovative efforts to deliver results that have driven them to put greater weight on marketing, patent policies and mergers, which are considered to involve less risk.

Fortunak's analysis (Box 3.1) is only one of many documentary attempts to explain the decline in overall industrial innovation in the pharmaceutical field. It is likely that each of the many reasons that have been adduced have played some role, though it is difficult to evaluate their relative importance.

- *It is argued that many of the more straightforward approaches to therapeutic advance have already been fully exploited and that the challenges that remain are much more daunting.* This argument is reminiscent of the OECD analysis of a similarly perceived crisis in 1969 (see above), but it is not entirely without foundation. It is true, for example, that the treatment of most cases of elevated blood pressure was rendered simple and satisfactory with the arrival of the thiazide diuretics, beta-blockers and the angiotensin converting enzyme inhibitors, but it is probably not correct to categorize these advantages as having been straightforward in their day. The beta-blockers, for example, were based on an entirely novel concept of pharmacology developed by James Black[17] and his colleagues that had been far from obvious before their time. It is, however, fair to describe the challenge of malignant disease as one that still defies the innovators. A great deal more basic knowledge is likely to be needed before substantial progress is made.
- *It has at times been suggested, particularly from the side of the pharmaceutical industry, that the stringency and slowness of national drug regulation has discouraged innovation and perhaps also deprived the public of medicines that do in fact exist but have been refused access to the market.* The proper role of regulation is discussed in Chapter 4, and the view that it has done harm to innovation is discussed more

fully towards the end of the present chapter. Many of the requirements set regarding the admission of drugs to the market, especially
those relating to the need to demonstrate efficacy and safety, have
been necessary in public health terms. They could be and were overcome by those firms and products achieving sufficient standards. In
certain instances, nonetheless, regulation over-reached itself. Well-
founded opposition led to the correction of some excesses.

- *The progressive concentration of industry into ever-larger units has
  been considered to reduce the number of centers capable of innovation.* Particularly since 1990, there has been a rapid concentration
  of the pharmaceutical industry, with a small number of global
  firms acquiring other entities. When this happens, there is often a
  reduction in research capacity, with smaller units and projects being
  closed down. There also seems to have been a tendency for the new
  entities to concentrate their efforts on developing 'blockbusters'
  – breakthrough drugs that will be capable of dominating large
  existing markets or creating new ones. Insofar as this will mean a
  lessening of the effort to produce insignificant variants on existing
  products it may be welcomed. However, it may also lessen interest
  in embarking on innovation to serve smaller or less affluent markets
  (for example, rare diseases). Since 'blockbusters' are achieved only
  rarely, it is likely that there will still be a flow of marketable, if unex-
  citing, products into the medical world.

- *The costs of fully innovative research are, it is argued, now almost
  prohibitive.* The expenses of developing a new drug and bringing it
  to market are claimed to have risen to the level of a billion dollars
  or more, though the figures are heavily contested.[18] This issue was
  considered in Chapter 2 in connection with drug pricing. Whatever
  the true cost of innovation, it is sufficiently high to deter an under-
  capitalized player.

- *The costs of marketing have risen disproportionately.* This matter
  is considered in Chapter 2. The pharmaceutical market is a highly
  competitive one. The rewards of success are considerable. Firms
  that doubt their ability to win global commercial battles may choose
  to move into the production of non-innovative generic equivalents
  or retreat into less demanding areas of business. Within firms that
  remain in the pharmaceutical field it may be tempting to divert
  funding from innovation into marketing, seeking to assure a good
  financial return.

- *The world may be experiencing nothing more than a lull before the
  next era of achievement.* It is tempting to adopt this explanation,
  especially when one recalls the ups and downs of the innovative

process over the last seven decades. Repeatedly one encounters suggestions as to the promise borne by initiatives in novel quarters. Advances in biotechnology may well provide the principal advances of the next generation. Reorientation of academic and institutional research toward biotechnology already is occurring.

- *Regulation and innovation.* Governments do not ordinarily engage directly in the process of discovering or developing new medicines, though through subsidization of research and other policies they indirectly exert an important influence on the process. National governments and international organizations should refrain from creating avoidable obstacles to innovation in this field. Where possible, they should encourage processes likely to lead to genuine advances that could serve the public interest.

The allegation that governmental controls, especially in the form of drug regulation, have ever significantly *discouraged* real innovation seems very poorly based. Cromie's description in 1979 of what he termed the 'mass murder activities of regulatory authorities'[19] reflected the view, repeatedly advanced by some industrial spokesmen at the time, that drug regulation would discourage innovation and ultimately might stifle the pharmaceutical industry in its entirety.[20] It was variously argued that the costs of extensive toxicological and clinical studies would render innovation uneconomic, that the delays sometimes incurred in approving new products or indications would deprive the industry of essential income prior to patent expiry, and even that reluctance to accept 'me too' drugs (that is, minor modifications of existing products) would impede progress since any or all of these could represent steps in the process of incremental improvement. With hindsight there appears to have been little basis for the somber predictions of a generation ago.[21] The frequency of major breakthroughs has indeed declined, but there are more credible explanations for this than the growth of restrictive regulation. Nor would it seem at all likely that stringent inspection and quality control, imposed by the authorities, have seriously impeded worthwhile innovation.

While one can indeed cite instances in which both regulation and inspection have made excessive demands, the very fact that these forms of over-restrictive control have generally been exercised purely at the national or regional level means that they have exerted relatively little effect on any global corporation, and where they have been truly excessive they have soon been corrected. In addition, regulatory agencies have introduced accelerated assessment procedures for drugs that bear exceptional promise, for example in the treatment of rare and hitherto incurable diseases.[22] Particularly bearing in mind the existence of other causes for the rapid decline in drug innovation during the closing years of the twentieth century, at a time when mutual understanding between governments and responsible companies had grown significantly, it would be hard to hold either regulation or inspection liable for these events.

THE CHANGING FACE OF INNOVATION

There is a dynamic need to develop new policies with respect to medicines because of the simple fact that the field is constantly changing. New innovative techniques are all the time being introduced, and new products are emerging. Both the techniques themselves and the products that they help to create can bring with them fresh promises, but also fresh problems. Society needs to keep a careful watch on older medicines, since new knowledge may reveal the need to prepare or use them differently, modify or discard them. The greater challenge, however, is presented by new substances or preparations that arrive claiming – often very forcefully, though not necessarily correctly – a place in the practice of medicine. The claims made for any new product, whether by an enthusiastic investigator or by the marketing organization that hopes to profit from it, may well prove over-ambitious. Society will have to examine them critically and in the light of the best evidence available in order to determine whether the drug in question is reasonably safe and efficacious, of adequate quality, and whether the information to be provided to the user can be considered reliable. The manner in which that examination is conducted is considered in Chapter 4.

The more novel an investigational technique or a new drug is, the greater the likelihood that it will deliver surprises, welcome or unwelcome. The process of reviewing a drug emerging from the biotechnology of the twenty-first century will need to differ in some respects from that developed to assess one created in an organic chemical laboratory.

THE PROMISE – AND PROBLEMS – OF BIOTECHNOLOGY

The relevance of biotechnology to medicinal care: natural biological products of animal and even human origin came into use early in the twentieth century. Insulin became available from slaughterhouse material from 1923 onwards,[23] while the first sex hormones to be marketed were similarly derived, and the initial generation of antibiotics was again entirely natural substances of microbial origin; substances of human origin included growth hormone taken from cadaver material and gonadotrophins extracted from urine. Biological technology, a term soon contracted into 'biotechnology', and the related field of genetic engineering followed in due course, particularly developing on the work of Paul Berg and others in the 1970s who developed recombinant DNA technology. The new techniques involve modifications in the manner in which a living organism functions.[24]

One direct application of this, already in use for a generation, is to cause an animal or plant to secrete modified substances, which can be used in medicine or health care ('pharming'). As early as 1982, approval was given to the therapeutic use of human insulin produced by a strain of the bacterium *Eschericia coli* which had been altered by inserting a gene for a human protein into the microorganism's genome. In an analogous manner cultures of animal cells have been modified, causing them to secrete pure Human Factor VIII, used to treat hemophilia. Recombinant erythropoetin used for the treatment of anemia is now produced in a similar manner.

Another very promising field is that of pharmacogenomics, that is, the examination of all the genes in an individual patient in order to determine whether or how adequately he or she will react to a particular drug. It is thought that if this approach succeeds it will be possible to produce several variants on a given drug, each being best suited to patients having a particular genetic constitution ('personalized therapy'). It will also be possible to classify the subjects entering clinical trials in order to define which groups of individuals will react adequately to a given drug or will tolerate it best. Since 2002 it has been possible to determine genetically, using a commercialized test, which subjects suffering from breast cancer can be expected to react well to the drug trastuzumab (Herceptin®).

The two approaches outlined above are clearly of direct interest to the pharmaceutical industry; they will enable it to produce drugs more efficiently by 'pharming' and to develop more specific medicines and diagnostic tests so that treatment can be rendered more efficient. The industry is, however, clearly anxious to develop beyond the provision of packaged products, hoping to provide commercialized backing to medical practice in other ways; here too biotechnology may offer important opportunities. Gene therapy is one such field; it involves the transfer of a normal human gene into a diseased subject so as to induce normal function. This could revolutionize the treatment of hereditary diseases and perhaps also of cancers. Unlike other biotechnological approaches it does not involve the sale of a product, but there is no doubt that where a pharmaceutical firm has contributed to the development of such a method, or has acquired rights to it, it will find ways of reaping financial benefit from its use. In doing so, however, it will inevitably assume responsibility for its employment, and will be likely to find itself called upon to meet appropriate regulatory requirements and held liable for any inexcusable failings.

There is no doubt that the impact of biotechnology on health care will in the coming years go far beyond the areas sketched above. A draft report from the OECD in 2007,[25] while specifically excluding traditional biotechnological techniques of some relevance to health (such as grafting of crop plants and selective breeding of farm animals), listed at various points some 150 very diverse areas that would need to be considered when defining for the future official policies on biotechnology bearing on medical care. Not all these areas demonstrate such relevance at present, but many may prove to in the near future, and it is instructive to provide that listing in a somewhat simplified form (Box 3.2).

The mere citation of the listing in Box 3.2, with its wide variety of topics, illustrates the need for flexibility in policy development, particularly since the list is likely to develop considerably in coming years. That flexibility will necessarily relate, not merely to the content of policy, but to the entities to which policy is directed. In recent decades policies have been concerned primarily with the regulation of large pharmaceutical companies. Many of these companies have, however, played only a minor role to date in advancing biotechnology. Advances have been achieved in many academic institutions, but to a much larger extent, they have been achieved in very small private research groups – many of these being spin-off companies founded by scientists who have left larger concerns on both sides of the Atlantic (and elsewhere). The major pharmaceutical corporations for their part, having since 1990 suffered such a dramatic fall in their own innovative output of the more traditional type, increasingly seek to benefit from this activity, either by licensing agreements or by outright acquisition of biotechnological units.

How are situations like this to be dealt with in policy, law and regulation? The question is by no means unprecedented. In a competitive society there is a tendency to legislate parsimoniously, particularly where commerce is concerned, introducing new rules only where old rules cannot be applied. Most forms of law and regulation, whether civil, administrative or criminal, are necessarily formulated so as to allow for a degree of change and development. Only when a fundamentally new element appears in society will there have to be new law; most other changes can be dealt with by judicial interpretation of existing law, or occasionally by regulation within the law. Donald Black, in a classic sociolegal study, explains this process very well with respect to the laws of economic life.[26] In principle, then, one needs to consider to what extent existing drug regulation and policy can be interpreted to handle developments in the era of biotechnology. That era

BOX 3.2   FIELDS OF BIOTECHNOLOGICAL
EXPLORATION OF KNOWN OR
POSSIBLE RELEVANCE TO MEDICAL
TREATMENT

Products produced using one of the following technologies:

1. DNA/RNA: genomics, pharmacogenomics, gene probes, genetic engineering, DNA/RNA sequencing/synthesis/ amplification, gene expression profiling, and use of anti- sense technology.
2. Proteins and so on: sequencing/synthesis/engineering of proteins and peptides (including large-molecule hormones); improved delivery methods for large-molecule drugs; pro- teomics, protein isolation and purification, signaling identifi- cation of cell receptors.
3. Cell and tissue culture and engineering: cell/tissue culture, tissue engineering (including tissue scaffolds and biomedi- cal engineering), cellular fusion, vaccine/immune stimu- lants, embryo manipulation.
4. Gene and RNA vectors: gene therapy, viral vectors.
5. Bioinformatics: construction of databases on genomes, protein sequences; modeling complex biological processes, including systems biology.
6. Nanobiotechnology: applying the tools and processes of nano/microfabrication to build devices for studying biosys- tems and applications in drug delivery, diagnostics and so on.
7. The use of any of the above technologies in research for health applications.
8. Development of large molecular recombinant therapeutic agents, including monoclonal antibodies (MABs), recom- binant vaccines, enzymes and hormones.
9. Diagnostic tests (including DNA testing) for genetic con- ditions and molecular diagnostics for infections, cancer screening, other diseases and tissue rejection; protein testing using micro-arrays and immunoassays of blood and so on.
10. Molecular imaging (using peptides to bind to receptors) to identify diseases or tumors.

11. Products produced using stem cells, or research into stem cells.
12. Small-molecule therapeutics developed through a significant contribution of biotechnology. Examples include the use of DNA-based molecular methods to identify new active molecules produced by microorganisms, using comparative genomics to identify new drug targets (as with comparing metabolic pathways between hosts and parasites), or using other genetic information to identify drug targets.
13. 'Neutraceuticals' (food products with health benefits) produced using biotechnology.
14. Application of pharmacogenomics, based on knowledge of a patient's genetic status, to develop personalized medicine.
15. Use of new methods of producing tissues or organs, including xenotransplantation, tissue engineering to construct *in vitro* organs and tissues, and new tissues produced through stem cells.
16. Bioprospecting to identify novel therapeutic compounds and/or the gene sequences that produce them.

In addition, the OECD report notes the relevance of a number of fields in agriculture, forestry and marine biology where use of biotechnological methods could have effects on the human population.

Source: Based on OECD (2007).

brings with it new developments both in the innovative process itself and in the nature of the products that emerge from that process. Over the last 50 years, public drug policy has hardly touched the developmental process itself, except where some form of risk appears to be present, as is the case for example with the rules regarding the safety of the subject in clinical trials,[27] the need to avoid suffering to animals in laboratory studies,[28] the use, control and safe disposal of materials, or the need for transparency. There has been much more concern with the fruits of that process, that is, the drugs emerging from it, because of the perceived need to ensure adequate standards of quality, safety and efficacy and in some instances to check irresponsible commercialization or use.

As regards the innovative process itself, biotechnology does introduce a number of new elements that need to be the subject of adapted or entirely new public policies. There is, for example a wide consensus that, while human experimentation is necessary to medical progress, the risks to the trial subject must not be disproportionate to the goal. The possible risks must have been defined as far as possible in advance and the trial subject must, after adequate explanation, have acquiesced to them. An independent and expert body must have approved the study and must monitor its progress, and there must be criteria for ending the study where this appears advisable. These general rules have been formulated with medicines of the type currently employed in mind, but the manner in which they are formulated renders them applicable to almost any conceivable form of human experimentation, clearly including novel biotechnological techniques or products.

What will have to be determined from one product or class to another is the nature of the measures that will need to be used to detect both wanted and unwanted effects. For medicines of a familiar type this is generally not too difficult since one may anticipate many effects from what one knows of the properties of earlier products that are chemically or pharmacologically similar, but for novel biotechnological products and especially for techniques involving human genetics one will need to spread the net more widely, having regard to the acute or permanent changes in bodily function that they might be expected to bring about.

Similarly with animal studies, the principles developed for drug research[29] are broadly applicable in biotechnology. They include the principle that animal experiments may be conducted only by a qualified licensee and that 'A licence shall permit experiments . . . .. only insofar as the experiments are intended to benefit, either directly or indirectly, the health or nutrition of human beings or animals'. Again, experiments shall not be conducted where the required knowledge can be attained in other ways. Measures to avoid undue suffering are imposed, and (as in the case of human experimentation) an ethics review committee must give its approval to the experiment. The only reservation that one might advance when applying existing ethical rules to this new field of experimentation is that the more novel the area of study, the greater the difficulty of foreseeing and perhaps even recognizing risk, and the importance of keeping a close watch on the animal to detect any unusual form of suffering or other concomitant effect.

This being said, however, an adverse effect on a test subject – animal or human – may not become apparent for an extended period of time. When effects are discovered months or years later it may be difficult to prove a linkage between the administration of experimental substances and the adverse event. For example, a negative effect may take the form of a weakened immune system that allows the introduction of an opportunistic disease that might vary among test subjects. Given the enormous complexity of animal and human organisms, predicting the longer term effects of introducing changes to biological mechanisms presents new challenges.

As regards the use, control and safe disposal of materials, biotechnological work again demands an appropriate approach to rule making. In the medicines field special rules and controls have been applied where narcotics or other controlled substances are used in research laboratories, as has been the case with radioactive preparations. The narcotics rules seek to prevent the wider dissemination of dangerous or addictive substances through carelessness or theft, while the rules on radioactive substances are concerned primarily with prevention of environmental contamination (for example, through pollution of effluents). There are also rules regarding the disposal of research materials, for example, the destruction of cadavers. Again it is not difficult to envisage closely parallel rules being applied to certain biotechnological materials, particularly where these might prove dangerous to the community, for example by entering the food chain or water supply. Both the end-products and intermediaries may in some cases prove to be extremely potent. To take a slightly more distant analogy: society has for half a century succeeded in keeping the surviving samples of the smallpox virus under strict control in a mere two centers,[30] and it should surely be capable of guaranteeing that any dangerous biotechnological vector or form of life is maintained under strict supervision and prevented from escaping into the community.

As noted earlier in this chapter, there has been considerable controversy regarding the issue of transparency in R&D and the sometimes excessive confidentiality that commonly surrounds innovation, particularly where it has a pronounced market potential. This issue could well become of even greater significance with biotechnology, especially since the field is fiercely competitive. Since biotechnology may well become the key to major therapeutic progress, it is particularly important to avoid advances being blocked as a result of exaggerated secrecy surrounding basic discoveries.

The products of biotechnological innovation, irrespective of whether they involve new medicines, novel diagnostic aids or new methods of non-drug treatment, will obviously need to attain adequate and proven standards of quality, safety and efficacy prior to marketing and, as for more familiar types of drug, there will be a need for mechanisms to recognize and deal with whatever new evidence emerges subsequently in the field, for example, unanticipated or delayed adverse effects. With medicines as they have existed hitherto these regulatory approaches have by no means eliminated risks and abuses, but they have certainly done much to diminish their incidence. One cannot expect more where biotechnological products are concerned. Absolute purity, guaranteed efficacy and complete safety will generally remain ideals that are just out of reach.

One issue that needs particular attention is that of the products which in European legislation are termed 'biosimilars'. Where the originator's patent on a biotechnological product expires, other firms will be able to seek regulatory approval for a product having precisely the same characteristics and indications. Being prepared in all probability by a process differing from that used by the originator firm, it may show some structural difference from the original version, but provided it is to all intents and purposes capable of replacing the original product in clinical use it will be acceptable for marketing. Biosimilars accepted and marketed to date include versions of human growth hormone and of erythropoietin.[31]

The issue of the appropriate regulatory track for the approval of biosimilars is presently before the US Congress. Biotechnology industry lobbyists are pressing for a long period of marketing exclusivity (for example, 14 years) so as to provide greater access to monopoly profits, ostensibly to fund continuing R&D projects. The generics industry is lobbying for a substantially more expedited pathway (for example, keeping the marketing exclusivity term in line with the five-year period applicable to new chemical entities). Because of the tremendous budgetary strain posed by Medicare Part D (prescription drugs for the elderly) and similar strains facing corporate prescription drug benefits for employees, it will be of some interest how Congress balances the interests of biotechnology industry profits with the challenges facing consumers. For its part, the FDA has indicated that the challenge of assessing biosimilarity can be dealt with, recognizing that European regulators have led the way on this issue.

The International Conference on Harmonization (ICH), involving the EU, Japan and the United States, but providing for consultation with industry, developed in 1997 a series of policy documents relating to biotechnological and biological products. Its guideline on the safety evaluation of such products is helpful but very general in its formulation. It must clearly be further developed as the field expands.[32] It is notable that the role of animal studies is defined much more restrictively than has been the case where the development of more familiar types of drugs is concerned. Like other bodies, the ICH seems to shift the main burden of proving safety onto studies in man, though it suggests that the animal work can still serve to indicate what needs to be studied in humans and how. The ICH Guidelines also points to the possibility that materials derived from living tissue may be contaminated with noxious substances and stresses the need for progressive purification. The need to exclude viral contamination also is stressed. There is further a welcome reference to studies on isolated materials (notably *in vitro* work) rather than in living animals. On the other hand, when any of the evidence obtained suggests a possible form of toxicity or noxious effect, the ICH document hastens to point toward the need to follow up with more traditional studies, including long-term toxicity or carcinogenicity studies as appropriate. By and large, however, the ICH Guidelines do not succeed in providing very specific guidance as to what needs to be done, but stresses throughout the need for caution and flexibility and for adapting one's methods from one type of substance to the next. Overall, the ICH documents, drawn up by regulators of varying plumage and with input from industrial scientists and policy makers, do breathe the spirit of compromise.

Taking into account the ICH Guidelines, as well as the lines of policy emerging to date in the practice of various regulatory agencies, one can, however, propose a series of principles that seem applicable to policy development in this field.

First, while many provisions of existing law and policy can undoubtedly be interpreted adequately to deal with biotechnology issues, the growing importance of biotechnology in the health field does seem to create a need for some *supplementary provisions* in law, sometimes entailing modifications of practice or the creation of specialized institutions. The latter point is well exemplified in regulations in force in Australia, which have involved the establishment of an 'Office of the Gene Technology Regulator' (OGTR). Such complementary provisions are required in fields that demand specialized knowledge and experience in order to assess and decide relevant issues. These new institutions will need to work in close collaboration with existing regulatory bodies (for example, those handling drugs) in order to gain from their practical experience, and to assure proper coordination of policies and enforcement.

Second, existing regulatory institutions will also need to be somewhat differently constituted if they are to deal optimally with biotechnological issues. This applies to drug regulatory authorities but also to bodies such as an Ethical Review Committee charged with assessing the acceptability of a proposed human experiment. Again the regulatory arrangements (including inspection) designed to prevent excessive suffering in animal experiments may need some rethinking where genetic experiments rather than toxic chemicals are concerned.

Finally, bearing in mind the limited availability of expertise, the fact that some national institutions in the area of drug regulation are entitled to delegate certain decision-making powers to provisional or local bodies raises questions. The latter may lack the experience needed to pass judgment on biotechnologically novel issues, and this could jeopardize the establishment of a reasonably watertight system with consistent operation.

Similarly, *small and developing countries* may not possess the resources and experience needed to deal with these new technical issues on behalf of their own populations. This could provide a further argument for global or at least regional decision making or for mutual recognition of decisions under a global convention.

When dealing with various types of biotechnological product, policy makers and regulators may indeed, as the ICH Guideline notes, need to reconsider their traditional views on the *role of animal studies*. Most drugs of the hitherto familiar type have emerged from the pharmacological laboratory. Studies in animals have served to predict (though not always reliably) both their efficacy and safety in human subjects. Where biotechnology has led to the emergence of agents that are entirely identical to substances involved in human physiology, however, the effects of these compounds may be entirely specific to man, and animal studies may prove misleading. Again a novel agent administered on a single occasion to exert an acute effect, for example, modifying the genetic constitution or the functioning of a biological system, will probably not need to be the subject of chronic toxicity studies in animals. On the other hand, very long-term follow-up of human subjects will be called for to detect any delayed consequence of the change.

Under some circumstances, the novelty of biotechnological products may be such as to justify *priority in the review process*. Such a system for prioritizing particular applications has been applied informally by many drug regulatory agencies and formally in others, such as the US FDA. It has now been suggested that a system of priorities should be introduced for new therapeutic and other products of biotechnological origin because of their potential importance. It is not unlikely that some highly novel products of this type might be subject to considerable regulatory delay because of general overburdening of the system, or because of their unfamiliar character and potential. Should this occur it could be necessary to institute a priority grading system in all agencies to ensure that sufficient capacity is mobilized to deal promptly with those products bearing particular promise in terms of public health.

For some types of novel biotechnological innovation the need for policy definition may relate not so much to the products themselves as to the *special knowledge and conditions required in order to use them responsibly and safely*. Some, though not all, regulatory agencies have the authority to license particular drugs exclusively for use in hospital or by specialists who have undergone a particular form of training. One emergent biotechnological procedure for which this could be very necessary is the use of gene therapy as defined above. Another would be the still emergent technique of tissue engineering, that is, the use of a combination of cells, materials and methods alongside appropriate and biochemical or physico-chemical factors to improve or replace biological functions. This has become an important research field but has not yet reached the point of practical application. Matters such as these need to be the subject of policy definition. They fall on the borderline between the regulation of drugs and the regulation of the medical profession, but from either or both of these directions they demand action.

The extent to which the possible *environmental risks* of biotechnological activities have been appreciated and have been reflected in the creation of appropriate regulatory standards still varies markedly from country to country. Since whatever problems arise are likely to be of global significance, broad international consensus should be sought on the steps necessary to avoid unnecessary risks to human health.

It would seem necessary to ensure the availability of reliable *public information* and where necessary provide for *public consultation* on some matters involving biotechnological innovations. It may be noted that the international agreement on biosafety known as the Cartagena Protocol requires public involvement in the decision-making process where safety issues in biotechnology are concerned.[33] This is another issue that has been tackled well in Australia. Elsewhere, the general public has been alternately reassured and alarmed by information regarding biotechnological progress. Newspaper headlines regarding reported attempts by the Rowatt Institute in Scotland in 1999 to suppress the results of a study apparently showing adverse effects of genetically modified potatoes administered to experimental rats gave rise to much controversy. Rightly or wrongly, this was one of the incidents underlying public rejection of biotechnology-inspired foods in Europe.[34] Conversely, considerable commercial pressures on public opinion can be exerted in such a field (as has been the case with genetically modified crops in the United States), particularly when there is a degree of mistrust of scientific institutions and their statements. Not entirely unrelated to this is the issue of public advertising of prescription medicines. Even for medicines of the existing type this is a disputed issue; such advertising is permitted in the United States and New Zealand and tolerated in some developing countries, but is explicitly prohibited elsewhere. Whatever the outcome of the current debate on the matter, one might suggest that the more novel a new therapy, the greater the reason to restrict commercial promotion of it to the professions. Even for certain existing medicines some agencies insist (as a condition of marketing) on the performance of supplementary studies in the field in order to settle particular issues, and this type of 'Phase IV' investigation may well be considered particularly necessary where novel biotechnological products are concerned; where this is the case, it would seem unwise to allow public advertising until the transitional phase had passed.

It is only fair to point out that the view advanced here as regards the need for a prospective (that is, anticipatory) approach to the regulation of bio-technology has been challenged. In a series of recent papers on the regulation of biotechnology, though they relate more particularly to the genetic modification of food sources, J. Kinderlerer from Sheffield has argued that:

> In most circumstances the introduction of safety legislation within a country has followed a major accident or incident. Regulation has been reactive whereas for modern biotechnology the system of regulation has been proac-tive. There are no documented cases of harm resulting directly from the use of recombinant techniques, whether in the research environment or for com-mercial applications. There are many who ask whether a proactive approach to biotechnology regulation is sensible, for it places in the public domain a concern that has been translated into a fear of the new technology, particularly in Europe. Would most of the innovations that have so fundamentally modi-fied our way of life during the twentieth century have happened had a full risk evaluation been required? Policy indeed involves making and implementing laws and regulations but it also involves education, allocation of resources provision of information, and where appropriate a degree of persuasion and attempts to attain consensus . . . .[35]

In this connection one might express the hope that progress in the develop-ment of policies with respect to new biotechnological tools in medicine will be attainable on the basis of consensus rather than controversy. It is encour-aging to observe how, in a number of countries but also at the international level, standards in the fields of food, medicines and other products have not only been the subject of consultation between the authorities and industry but have also been formulated by both parties as legal norms and as vol-untary codes of behavior respectively, the two types of instrument comple-menting one another. This example should be widely emulated in the field of biotechnological products. The active involvement of trade and industry in the development of standards enriches the input to the debate, and it may also facilitate adherence by industry to the standards that emerge.

All in all, the pattern of innovation over the years appears to have been determined by multiple factors. In Chapter 2 the types of policy instru-ment used to promote innovation were assessed in depth, with a view toward improving on the present record. The particular issues of creating drugs for developing countries will be considered in Chapter 5 and the matter of drugs for neglected diseases and populations in Chapter 9.

NOTES

1. R.D. Mann (1984), *Modern Drug Use; An Enquiry on Historical Principles*, MTP Press, London, p. 351.

2. W. Withering (1785), *An Account of the Foxglove, and Some of its Medical Uses: With Practical Remarks on Dropsy, and Other Diseases*, Robinson, Birmingham. Facsimile: London 1949.
3. As early as 1563, warnings had been published regarding the toxicity of mercury when used to treat syphilis. G. Falloppio (1563), *De morbo gallico*, Laurentino, Venezia.
4. Mann, *Modern Drug Use*, p. 481.
5. P. Ehrlich and S. Hata (1910), *Die experimentelle Chemotherapie der Spirillosen*, Springer, Berlin.
6. L.E.H. Whitby (1938), 'Chemotherapy of pneumococcal and other infections with 2-(*p*-aminobenzenesulphonamido) pyridine', *Lancet*, 1, 1210–12.
7. A. Fleming (1929), 'On the antibacterial action of cultures of a penicillium, with special reference to their use in the isolation of *B.influenzae*', *Br J Exp Pathol*, 10, 226–36.
8. OECD (1969), *Gaps in Technology: Pharmaceuticals*, Organisation for Economic Co-operation and Development, Paris.
9. M.N.G. Dukes and I. Lunde (1981), 'The regulatory control of non-steroidal anti-inflammatory agents', *Eur J Clin Pharmacol*, 19, 3–10.
10. For figures on this issue see 'Safety-based drug withdrawals (1997–2001)', *FDA Consumer Magazine*, January–February 2002.
11. Department of Health and Social Security (1982), '*On the State of the Public Health. The Annual Report of the Chief Medical Officer*, HMSO, London.
12. Statement by Raymond V. Gilmartin, President of Merck Inc., 'Merck voluntarily withdraws Vioxx', Press Release, 30 September 2004.
13. D.W. Sigelman (2002), 'Dangerous Medicine', *American Prospect* (Online edition), 13 (17).
14. F. Hawthorne (2003), *The Merck Druggernaut*, John Wiley and Sons, Hoboken, NJ, Ch. 2.
15. P.J. Lewi (2007), 'Successful pharmaceutical discovery: Paul Janssen's concept of drug research', *R&D Management*, 37 (4), 355–62.
16. M. Rosen (2005), 'Drug innovation beats marketing, patents and mergers', WTN News, Wisconsin Technology Network (accessed September 2008).
17. J.W. Black et al. (1964), 'A new adrenergic beta-receptor antagonist'. *Lancet*, 1, 1080–1.
18. M. Goozner (2004), *The $800 Million Pill; The Truth Behind the Cost of New Drugs*, University of California Press, Berkeley and Los Angeles, CA; J. Robinson (2001), *Prescription Games: Money, Ego and Power Inside the Global Pharmaceutical Industry*, Simon and Schuster UK, London, pp. 85 ff.
19. B. Cromie (1979), 'Present problems: the effects of British regulations', in: *Medicines for the Year 2000*, Office of Health Economics, London.
20. Anon. (1984), 'Aleotti on "death" of Italian industry', *Scrip*, 905, 1.
21. CRA (2004), *Innovation in the Pharmaceutical Sector; A Study Undertaken for the European Commission*, Charles River Associates, London.
22. B.E.G. Rothberg and J.M. Rothberg (2007), *Drug Innovation 2000: Orphan Diseases and Global Health Project*, Rothberg Institute for Childhood Diseases, Guilford, CT.
23. F.G. Banting and C.H. Best (1922), 'The internal secretion of the pancreas', *J Lab Clin Med*, 7, 251–66.
24. S.P. Barnum (1998), *Biotechnology: An Introduction*, Wadsworth Publishing Co., CA.
25. OECD (2007), *Definition of Biotechnology for the Bioeconomy to 2030*, Draft June, Organisation for Economic Co-operation and Development, Paris.
26. D. Black (1976), *The Nature of Law*, Academic Press, Orlando and San Diego, pp. 39 ff.
27. World Medical Association (revised 1996), *Declaration of Helsinki on Biomedical Research Involving Human Subjects* (subject to continuous revision).
28. The Netherlands (1997), *The Experiments on Animals Act* (Entry into force 5 February).

29. J. Lexchin and B. Mintzes (2004), 'Transparency in drug regulation: mirage or oasis?' *CMAJ*, **171**, (11). doi:10.1503/cmaj.1041446.
30. Center for Disease Control, Atlanta, USA and the Vector Institute, Siberia, Russia.
31. EGA (2008), *EGA Handbook on Biosimilar Medicines*, European Generic Medicines Association, Brussels.
32. ICH (1997), *ICH Harmonised Tripartite Guideline. Preclinical Safety Evaluation of Biotechnology-derived Pharmaceuticals*, International Conference on Harmonization of Technical Requirements for Registration of Pharmaceuticals for Human Use, Geneva.
33. The Cartagena Protocol on Biosafety, Press release from the US Department of State, Bureau of Oceans and International Environmental and Scientific Affairs, Washington, DC, 21 July 2003.
34. Anon. (1999), 'Potatoes genetically modified to produce *Galanthus nivalis* lectin', in 1999 *Annual Report of the Committees on Toxicity, Mutagenicity, Carcinogenicity of Chemicals in Food, Consumer Products and the Environment.* Department of Health, London.
35. J. Kinderlerer (2002), 'Regulation of biotechnology; needs and burdens for developing countries', http://www.unep.org/Biosafety/Documents/BTregulationJK.pdf

4. The global regulatory environment: quality, safety and efficacy

The term 'regulation', as it relates to the drug field, has commonly been used in a relatively narrow sense, relating only to the process by which new drugs are evaluated to determine their eligibility for admission to the market. In fact the broad field of drug regulation involves many more layers of policy. In order to ensure that the way medicines are created and used serves society as well as possible, a series of mechanisms must be deployed, some of them regulatory in the narrow sense of assessing safety and efficacy, but also involving provision of information, education, persuasion and financial resources.

The term 'regulation', with overtones of bureaucracy and deprivation of freedom, tends to arouse protest and opposition, and this reaction can serve a useful purpose. The more that can be achieved by developing a broad consensus in society regarding an optimal pattern of behavior rather than by imposing intrusive rules, the better. In practice, it has been possible in many cases to formulate rules on which there is such a broad measure of agreement that they do not have to be imposed upon the unwilling. That, after all, is precisely the way in which the community of nations, having no superior authority, has at its best always functioned, and that is the way in which a rational society can hope to function. Yet it must be recognized that large economic interests are at stake in the field of medicines, and that from an historical standpoint, there is a demonstrated need for governments to adopt and implement mandatory rules to regulate economic behavior.

The fundamental reason the law needs to protect the individual where medicines are concerned is very evident, but it deserves to be emphasized. *Where medicines are concerned, the old rule of consumer protection* – caveat emptor – *let the buyer beware! – is likely to be of small value.* The patient is entirely unable to judge for him or herself the quality of the drug offered, unable to determine of his or her own accord whether it will be safe or not, and poorly equipped to decide whether it is effective – even after taking it. In all these matters he or she will be dependent on others, acting in effect on his or her behalf.

The following discussion will examine in turn the development and form of public policies regarding the quality, safety and efficacy of medicines, restrictions on the availability of products, confidentiality issues, appeal procedures and finally the available evidence on the effects of regulation as a whole. A number of specialized regulatory areas will be examined separately in Chapter 8.

Something of the complexity of drug policy, and the place of regulation in that field, is illustrated in Figure 4.1. The aim of such a policy is to achieve a series of related purposes: the community must ensure that efficacious and safe drugs of good quality are accessible and affordable to the entire population and that they are rationally used. The patient is the central player on the scene, but there are a series of others including the health professionals, the creators, makers and sellers of drugs, the educators and the media, as well as the government and the regulators. If all parties understand their proper role and play it ideally, the policy apparatus will simply have the function of the conductor in an orchestra, ensuring harmony and applying a little instruction, encouragement and correction where needed. Bearing in mind the occasions in which drug problems or disputes reach the newspaper headlines, one might be inclined to doubt the analogy. But it is a fact that to a large extent and in many countries the drug scene is well managed and that consensus on many issues exists. Malpractice, misjudgment, excessive enrichment and dishonest behavior all occur, but the system accommodates and corrects the individual fault, and policies are progressively adjusted to counter undesirable trends. It is striking how seldom fundamental disputes reach the courts of law, though there can on occasion be a great deal of sabre-rattling.

A policy scheme such as that illustrated in Figure 4.1 is also helpful in understanding the need for policies to be comprehensive and balanced. A one-sided measure, intended to correct a problem but taking insufficient account of all the factors involved, can aggravate the situation that it was intended to relieve:

> In a European country, simple antacids for the relief of stomach disorders were eligible for full reimbursement under the public insurance system. There was reason to believe that they were often unnecessarily used and constituted an avoidable expense. Rather than seeking to correct this excessive prescribing, the authorities cancelled their eligibility for insurance coverage. The immediate effect was to cause physicians to prescribe instead an H-2 blocking drug at considerably greater expense to the system.[1]

THE QUALITY OF MEDICINES

By far the earliest regulatory measures to be introduced with respect to medicines reflected concerns regarding their quality. Throughout much of

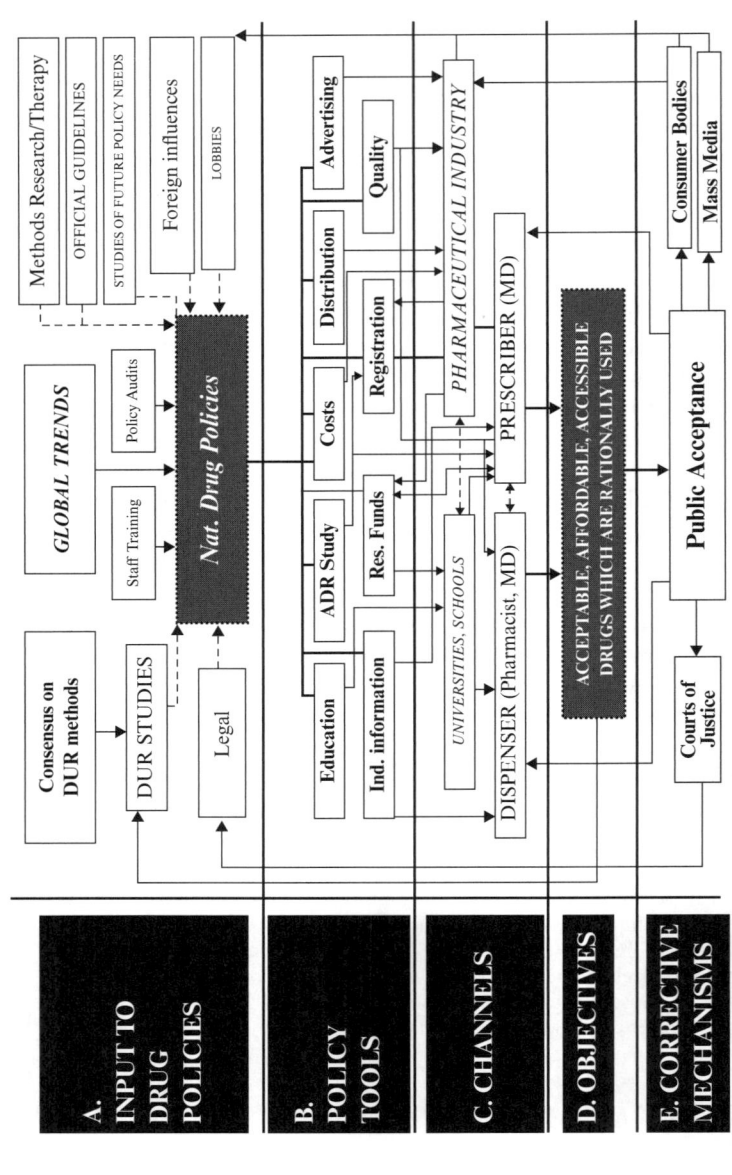

Note:
As used at the Universities of Groningen and Oslo.
DUR = Drug Utilization Research.

Figure 4.1   Drug policy matrix

history medical treatment was based on the herbal tradition (see Chapter 8), and while there was widespread trust in the merits of plant remedies there was sometimes concern regarding the manner in which they were prepared for use, whether by a qualified apothecary or an individual offering medicines for sale.

The Pharmacy Profession[2]

In some cases the health professions took the necessary action; as early as 1423 the 'Commonalty of Physicians and Surgeons of London' appointed two apothecaries to inspect the premises of their colleagues and to bring all who were supplying wares of insufficient quality before the Mayor and Aldermen of the City. In that same century in Vienna a decree was issued commanding that false and improper apothecaries should be cast out onto the street and their wares with them. More structured official measures followed in London in 1540 when a Statute signed by Henry VIII empowered the College of Physicians to search apothecaries' shops for wares that were 'defective, corrupted and not meet nor convenient to be ministered in any medicines for the health of man's body'. Such products were to be burnt or otherwise destroyed. A further major step was taken in 1614 when the English Crown, acting explicitly in the interests of public health, granted a Royal Charter to establish a Society of Apothecaries as a means of distinguishing the skilled men from the unskilled, since

> very many Empiricks and unskilful and ignorant men do abide in the City of London which are not well instructed in the Art or Mystery of Apothecaries, and do make and compound many unwholesome, hurtful, dangerous and corrupt medicines and the same do sell . . . to the great peril and daily hazard of the lives of the King's subjects.

By 1617 the Society had established a production laboratory, while a generation later it found it necessary to create in addition a chemical laboratory to test the remedies of chemical (generally mineral) origin which were then coming into favor.[3,4]

Many other countries in Europe followed a similar course, allocating the task of ensuring drug quality to an officially licensed pharmaceutical profession. Not until the nineteenth century did it become usual for the state to assume this responsibility directly through the establishment of publicly funded institutes in which the pharmacy profession continued to play a leading role. Notable statutes in Great Britain were the Arsenic Act of 1851, the Pharmacy Act of 1868 and the Adulteration of Food and Drugs Act of 1872, the latter establishing a network of inspectors and analysts working under the authority of local government.[5] Quality control was also a central motive for the passage in the United States of the Federal Food and Drugs Act of 1906.[6]

In all these matters the existence of a pharmaceutical profession provided the backbone of the state's quality assurance and control system, though its point of input shifted progressively from the individual pharmacy to the multidisciplinary state institutions which emerged as the principal instruments of medicinal policy in the mid twentieth century. In recent decades the profession has become increasingly engaged in matters of drug information and education (see Chapter 6).

Pharmacopoeias

The pharmacopoeia, as a standard work of reference providing specifications for the preparation and testing of individual drugs, is similarly of ancient origin. The first such volume, intended as an official and obligatory guide for the apothecaries of Florence, appeared in 1498. Others followed in Spain, Germany and Italy. By 1900 every developed country had its own national pharmacopoeia, generally produced under state auspices and setting legally binding standards. In more recent years the number of national pharmacopoeias has declined, as communities of nations have jointly developed common standards. The *European Pharmacopoeia* was first published in 1967 under a Convention signed in 1964.[7] Both this and the *US Pharmacopeia*, published since 1820, enjoy wide international recognition and influence. The *International Pharmacopoeia*, compiled under the auspices of the WHO has only an advisory role, but member states can and do adopt monographs from its pages as a basis for legally binding standards within their own borders.

Quality Standards for New Drugs

It is obvious that for a newly developed drug there will at the time of its introduction be no published pharmacopeal quality standard. The standards applicable to its preparation and analysis will therefore ordinarily be developed by the research-based manufacturer and will be included in the file submitted to the regulatory authority for approval; the latter may insist on modifications or additions before the drug is approved for marketing. At that time an important part of the data is likely to be regarded as confidential by the manufacturer, but in a later phase, if the drug has come into widespread use and certainly as the date of patent expiry approaches, the firm will as a rule seek the inclusion of its standards and methods in the form of a monograph in one or more of the major pharmacopoeias.

Relativity of Quality Standards

Whether one is concerned with quality, safety or efficacy, it must be recognized that no drug is likely to be perfect. In matters of quality the standards that need to be set, whether in a pharmacopoeia or in approving a new drug application, are those which are considered necessary, but also reasonable to attain. Three examples may be given:

- Purity: The minimum level of purity may, for example, be set at 95 percent or 99 percent. A relatively low level may be acceptable where there is sufficient reason to consider that the contaminants are not toxic, do not have a significant allergenic potential and will not interfere with the principal effect of the drug. Insistence on a very high level of purity may drastically raise the costs of purification and hence the cost of the product as a whole.
- Content variability: The degree of variation that is permissible in the percentage of active substance (for example, in a tablet) will depend on the nature of the product. In the case of a benzodiazepine tranquillizer, where the toxic dose is vastly higher than the normal therapeutic dose, a substantial variation in content may be entirely acceptable. With digitalis, where the toxic dose is only very slightly higher than the therapeutic level, tight limits on content variation will be required, whatever the expense.
- Shelf life: To secure approval in a typical regulatory system it must be demonstrated that the product will remain stable and usable for a sufficient period, taking into account the conditions under which it is likely to be distributed and used. These may include global distribution with its attendant delays and the possibility of exposure to heat, cold or damp. Where necessary, storage conditions may need to be imposed, for example, 'continuous refrigeration is necessary' or 'store in a dark place'. In some instances a sufficient shelf life may be attainable only if a specific type of packaging is employed, for example, dark glass.

Good Manufacturing Practice

To an increasing extent, national authorities are adopting the requirement that pharmaceuticals be manufactured according to the conditions of 'Good Manufacturing Practice' as laid down, for example, by the WHO,[8] the US FDA or the ICH.[9] The extremely high standards set by these bodies demand substantial investment in facilities, well-trained staff and meticulous record-keeping, and the manufacturing plant is subject to strict

BOX 4.1   A SHORT HISTORY OF THE US FOOD
            AND DRUG ADMINISTRATION (FDA)

With Acknowledgments to Arthur Daemmerich

Around 1900, a movement comprising farmers, state agricultural officials and federal officials pressed for greater federal oversight of food manufacturing. As public and presidential opinion in support of this view developed, the need to deal similarly with drugs was recognized. The 1906 Pure Food and Drug Law resulted, banning 'the manufacture, sale or transportation of adulterated or misbranded or poisonous or deleterious foods, drugs, medicine and liquors'. The FDA was formed, and government agents were now able to seize mislabeled products and prosecute firms selling tainted food or drugs. The Law also codified an earlier arrangement under which physicians and pharmacists at the US Pharmacopoeia and National Formulary set standards for the strength, quality and purity of medicines which firms were obliged to follow.

By the 1930s the FDA was finding it difficult to prevent mislabeling or misbranding since they had no authority to perform or demand scientific studies. Heavy industrial lobbying prevented an expansion of the law in this direction until the Elixir of Sulfanilamide disaster of 1938 (involving the use of an untested and toxic solvent) led in that year to the new Federal Food, Drug and Cosmetic Act. In the years that followed, armed with improved methods for animal and clinical testing, the FDA developed increasingly sophisticated criteria for drug approval, paying special attention to the efficacy/safety balance of a medicine and issuing detailed recommendations on study methods. A further strengthening of the FDA to formalize drug approval procedures, proposed by Senator Kefauver in 1961, was delayed by vigorous lobbying of the Congress by industry. It was passed in 1962 after the thalidomide disaster (see Box 4.3) had shown the agency's ability to prevent serious harm by a dangerous new drug.

At times, industry pressure has led to some reduction in the FDA's powers. Its ability to demand explicit and prominent correction of misleading advertisements was withdrawn. In 1994 a large number of products were reclassified as 'dietary supplements' rather than medicines, removing them from pre-marketing control by the FDA. It is also widely considered that heavy industry pressure to speed the evaluation of new drugs has led to the ill-advised approval of a number of products that were subsequently withdrawn shortly after entering the market because of adverse effects.

Since 1990 the FDA has participated together with the European and Japanese agencies in the ICH that formulates joint standards for drug investigation.

Source: Based on A. Daemmerich (2003), 'Regulatory laws and political culture in the United States and Germany', in J. Abraham and H. Lawton Smith, (eds), *Regulation of the Pharmaceutical Industry.* Palgrave Macmillan, London.

and repeated inspection. Much of the world's pharmaceutical manufacturing does not yet attain these standards. As is the case for quality standards, not every drug demands approximation to perfection, and the costs involved in meeting the most severe demands can be formidable.

THE SAFETY AND EFFICACY OF MEDICINES

If, in terms of history, quality was society's earliest concern regarding medicines, safety issues followed in due course. The rapid growth of drug regulation during the mid twentieth century was largely due to the occurrence of a series of tragedies involving the serious adverse effects of new drugs. They have been documented extensively and will not be reviewed here, but Boxes 4.2 and 4.3 provide a number of notorious examples of events that deserve to be characterized as 'disasters' because of their extent, their severity or both. It goes without saying that these examples relate only to a small selection of extreme cases. Less dramatic outbreaks and incidental complications are very frequent. Estimates of the frequency of severe adverse drug reaction vary, but in the United States, such reactions have been found to be one of the leading causes of death in the population.[10] An extensive study in Britain[11] concluded that in 2004 there were 10,396 hospital admissions in which an adverse drug reaction was the primary diagnosis while in 66,296 other cases such reactions were a secondary factor. Combined, these cases accounted for 0.56 percent of hospital episodes. The three most common classes of adverse drug reaction resulting in hospital admission involved analgesics, the group of antipyretics and anti-inflammatory drugs, and the injected antibiotics. 'Mental disorders' secondary to opioids and psychoactive drugs accounted for 63 percent of all primary diagnoses of such adverse reactions. Most episodes demanding hospitalization because of adverse drug reactions occurred in the elderly. Taking into account the many other adverse reactions which, while not leading to hospital admission, cause suffering and loss of time at work, this is clearly an issue calling for a public policy approach. In the majority of countries some measures have been taken to assess and tackle the problem. The six examples of severe adverse effects presented in Box 4.2 do, however, underline the difficulty in eradicating such problems, four of these disasters having occurred at a time and place where reasonably comprehensive systems of drug regulation were in operation.

In view of the fact that modern drug legislation was sparked primarily by disasters, it is understandable that during its initial development considerations of safety were more prominent in policy and planning than were issues of efficacy. Indeed, when the United Kingdom moved to introduce a drug policy regime, its first step in 1963 was to create a private-law Committee on Safety of Drugs which had no authority to assess efficacy. This was followed in 1968 by an official Committee on Safety of Medicines (which as originally constituted could assess efficacy only as a tool to determine whether safety was sufficient).

The delay in introducing clear efficacy requirements as an element of policy reflected the relatively late development of clinical pharmacology as a science. Medicine had long been practiced on the assumption that any experienced physician could readily recognize efficacy in a medicine, a belief that only slowly faded as evidence from well-designed clinical trials demonstrated its fallibility.[12]

Means of Demonstrating Safety and Efficacy

To a large extent both drug researchers and regulatory authorities have relied from the outset on animal studies as the principal means of anticipating wanted and unwanted drug effects in human subjects. The basic pharmacological tests carried out to determine the properties of a new substance may throw some light on its potential to do good or harm. Where a substance is further developed, toxicity testing in various species of animals will follow, progressing from the crude LD50 technique (determining the dose required to kill 50 percent of experimental animals) to sub-chronic and chronic toxicity testing in a range of animal species, with the most extensive studies involving exposure to high doses for two years or more. Such experiments, culminating in the sacrifice of the animals and post-mortem examination, have proved helpful in detecting frank toxicity to organ systems and physiological function; they have rendered it possible to discard those substances that are excessively toxic to the mammalian

BOX 4.2   SOME EXAMPLES OF DRUG
            DISASTERS

Drug: Elixir of Sulfanilamide
Period: ±1937
Field of Use: Anti-infective
Complication: Fatal poisoning due to use of an untested solvent

Drug: Thalidomide
Period: 1960
Field of Use: Hypnotic
Complication: Severe fetal deformities when used in pregrancy

Drug: Clioquinol
Period: 1974
Field of Use: Anti-diarrheal
Complication: Neurotoxicity (paralyses, blindness)

Drug: Triazolam
Period: 1979
Field of Use: Hypnotic
Complication: Severe psychiatric derangement

Drug: Benoxaprofen
Period: 1980
Field of Use: Anti-inflammatory
Complication: Fatal liver disorder in the elderly

Drug: Rofecoxib
Period: 2002
Field of Use: Anti-inflammatory
Complication: Cardiac disorders

system and to identify possible wanted and unwanted effects that should be looked for specifically when a substance merits subsequent study in humans.

There are unfortunately few situations in which the efficacy of a drug in man can be predicted accurately from animal work. Though a number of animal models for human disease do exist, the bulk of laboratory work will inevitably be performed in entirely healthy animals. The shortcomings

---

BOX 4.3   THALIDOMIDE – THE ESSENTIAL FACTS

In 1958 the German drug manufacturer Chemie Grunenthal introduced a hypnotic having a novel chemical structure that it claimed
was extremely well tolerated. Outside Scandinavia many European
countries did not at the time have modern drug regulatory systems,
and the drug was marketed in several of them. It was also licensed
to Richardson-Merrell for sale in the United States. By 1960 a
number of reports of phocomelia (absence or defects of limbs)
in newborn infants were made, and the German physician Lenz
found that in several of these cases known to him the mother had
taken thalidomide during pregnancy. Evidence of neurotoxicity in
users was also advanced. The firm ridiculed the evidence on both
counts and maintained marketing for a further period until the connection was so clear that it could not be denied and the drug was
withdrawn. In the United States, the FDA assessor (Dr Frances
Kelsey) had been dissatisfied with the evidence of safety and
delayed approval repeatedly despite extreme company pressure.
As a result, thalidomide was never marketed in the United States,
and Dr Kelsey is widely considered to have prevented a public
health disaster there. Elsewhere some 5000 cases of birth defects
are believed to have occurred. As noted in Box 4.1, these events
precipitated the legislative strengthening of the FDA in 1962.

Note: Based on H. Sjöstrom and R. Nilsson (1972), *Thalidomide and the Power
of the Drug Companies*, Harmondsworth, UK: Penguin Books.

---

of animal experiments have thus become increasingly clear. Findings
involving various species of laboratory animals do not necessarily cor-
relate at all well with the effects of a substance in human volunteers, let
alone human patients, and in some respects (for example, where effects on
mental function are concerned) they provide very little helpful evidence
indeed. In addition, ethical and moral objections to the use of test animals
are today forcefully advanced, as are objections to the mounting costs
of animal testing, and such arguments have to be taken into account in
determining policy, particularly where the limitations of these studies are
considered. *In vitro* techniques involving the use of isolated tissues and
materials rather than entire animals have increasingly been developed, but
these too have their limitations.

Studies in human subjects can clearly be undertaken only where there is a strong reason to believe that a new substance bears real promise in terms of both efficacy and safety. In the United States and a number of other countries human studies may be undertaken only if a fully documented 'Notice of Claimed Investigational Exemption for a New Drug' (IND) has been filed in advance with the FDA and a number of associated conditions are met. Similar requirements that the authorities be notified in advance of clinical studies are being introduced in a number of other countries. Most countries, however, have not chosen to require official approval for such studies, considering that the responsibility for this work must lie fully with the firm or sponsor concerned. Nevertheless there is an increasing tendency to require that the results of the studies be notified to the authorities as the work proceeds, enabling the latter to exercise a degree of surveillance and to intervene if necessary.

Human studies proceed cautiously and in well-defined stages from single-dose investigations in healthy volunteers (Phase I) to the ultimate long-term investigations needed in actual patients (Phase III). Policy concerns at this juncture relate primarily to the means of ensuring the well-being of the test subject. The latter must be involved only after having been fully informed as to the nature of the experiment and its possible benefits and risks, and at all stages the effects of the treatment must be closely studied so that the experiment can be adjusted and if necessary stopped. The entire experiment must also, if it is to be justifiable, be conducted in a scientifically defensible manner so that valid results can be obtained.[13] On all these and related matters states have tended to ensure that adequate rules are recognized and respected at the most appropriate level (for example, by hospital ethical committees) and not necessarily imposed in national law. The applicable ethical principles are well recognized, having been formulated by the World Medical Association as early as 1964 and repeatedly updated.[14]

All in all, it remains an unfortunate fact that neither animal studies nor pre-marketing experiments in man provide a definitive efficacy and safety profile for a new medicine. Once it enters the market it is likely to be used by a vastly larger population than that involved in the clinical investigations, and employed under a range of circumstances in which its effects have not previously been studied. It may, for example, be taken by the elderly or the very young, by women who are not aware that they are in the early stages of pregnancy, by subjects suffering from various allergies, by persons with metabolic disorders that affect drug metabolism or by patients who at the same time are taking one or more other drugs with which the new product may interact in an unexpected manner. Some of these situations may provide welcome new evidence of a product's value, but others may profile unexpected problems. In the light of these findings in the field, warnings or contraindications may need to be imposed (for example, against use in children), or specific studies may be required to identify or exclude particular uses on the one hand or risks on the other. So long as a product remains on the market, surprises may prove to be in store; the fact that the use of aspirin in children and young people with fever might precipitate the permanently incapacitating condition known as Reye's syndrome was recognized only six decades after the drug had been marketed.[15] The fact that some of those surprises may be disagreeable is the reason for the creation in many countries of official adverse reaction monitoring systems, some of which have now functioned for five decades.

The principle of an adverse reaction monitoring system is that prescribers (and in some systems pharmacists and patients as well) are encouraged to voluntarily submit reports on suspected adverse reactions or interactions that they have encountered. These reports can then be studied and collated at a central point (generally a monitoring office linked to the national drug regulatory agency) in order to detect as early as possible the occurrence of unexpected reactions. Significant findings are then communicated to the medical profession and/or to the regulatory agency so that any necessary action can be taken or warnings issued. Even in small countries with a limited population, national systems of this type have repeatedly proven effective in detecting adverse effects and interactions, thereby contributing to the protection and maintenance of public health.[16] An international system using information derived from Member States was established by the WHO in 1971. Operational responsibility for the program rests with the WHO Collaborating Center for International Drug Monitoring, Uppsala Monitoring Center (UMC), in Sweden. A common reporting form has been developed, agreed guidelines for entering information formulated, common terminologies and classifications prepared, and compatible systems for transmitting, storing and retrieving and disseminating data have been created. The adverse drug reactions database in Uppsala currently contains over three million reports of suspected adverse drug reactions.[17] The fact that it is accessible to the national agencies greatly augments its value.

It may be noted that in most of the countries involved the adverse reaction reporting system depends upon the voluntary input of those contributing information on suspected effects. A number of countries have sought to create a legal obligation to report, but it is doubtful whether this is legally enforceable. The system depends for its success on the early detection of problems and on the reporter's communicating a suspicion that has been aroused in his or her mind. This cannot realistically be regarded as the subject of legal obligation. Although it would be possible to require in law the reporting of a known and proven effect, this would not serve the essential purposes of the system.

Relativity of Safety and Efficacy as Standards

Just as quality is not an absolute concept, so safety and efficacy are relative matters. It has often enough been said that no medicine is entirely safe, and it is evident that no medicine proves to be effective in every case in which it is used. From the viewpoint of public health law it is sufficient that it be 'sufficiently' or 'reasonably' safe and effective, bearing in mind the conditions in which it is indicated, and that the degree of risk, whatever it may be, is not disproportionate to its efficacy. These common-sense standards are not exact, but they are defensible, and most effective drug regulatory agencies will employ them. The fact that a drug has a degree of efficacy that is only slightly greater than that of a dummy or placebo, even if the difference is statistically demonstrable, is today unlikely to suffice to earn it a place on most registers of approved drugs.

Conditional Approval

Standards dictated by common sense are also likely to be applied when a regulatory agency determines the proper place of a drug in the community. No drug is approved unconditionally. In all cases the labeling will have to meet a series of requirements relating to its completeness and accuracy since the text is likely to have a considerable effect on the manner in which the product is perceived and used. The same applies to the more extensive text that is generally assessed at the same time and that will serve as a basis for information provided to physicians. Many agencies today also require the inclusion in packaging materials of symbols or emphatic texts drawing attention to particular risks, for example, the fact that a medicine may impair the ability to drive a vehicle or operate machinery safely. Other conditions will relate to the manner in which a drug is sold. An entirely new drug will be approved for sale only on a physician's prescription, and in countries where medicines are sold both in pharmacies and drug shops, it is likely to be restricted to the former. Release for entirely free sale (that is, for self-medication/over-the-counter) will be given only for older drugs which have been shown to be safe by long experience or for newer products that are entirely identical to existing products.

A point on which national laws differ is whether at the time of licensing a requirement can be imposed to carry out further studies. In the United States, Phase IV studies can be required in order to obtain further information that is considered desirable but not so essential that its absence is a reason to delay marketing approval. In many other administrations there is no such legal provision, but an agency may agree with an applicant that the work be performed in due course. Adherence to such a 'gentlemen's agreement' and provision of the results as soon as these are available will be conducive to the maintenance of trust between the agency and the firm concerned.

Narcotics and Controlled Medicines

Controls on the trade in opiates and other drugs of addiction represent one of the oldest areas in which international public health law has grown up, motivated by a realization of the serious social dangers presented by an unregulated trade in such substances. Following the deliberations of an international conference convened at Shanghai in 1909, the first International Opium Convention was signed at The Hague in January of 1912.[18] It provided that

> The contracting Powers shall use their best endeavors to control, or to cause to be controlled, all persons manufacturing, importing, selling, distributing, and exporting morphine, cocaine, and their respective salts, as well as the buildings in which these persons carry on such an industry or trade.

In 1919 this convention was incorporated into the Treaty of Versailles. Its text, and those of a number of subsequent Conventions, was consolidated into the International Opium Convention of July 1931.[19] Following the establishment of the United Nations, the existing instruments were incorporated into the Single Convention on Narcotic Drugs of 1961. The International Narcotics Control Board (INCB) was created at that time to ensure the implementation of the Convention, and subsequently to handle complementary agreements bearing on a wider range of psychotropic drugs.[20] As regards the lawful manufacture of, trade in and use of drugs, INCB would endeavor, in cooperation with governments, to ensure that adequate supplies of drugs were available for medical and scientific uses and that the diversion of drugs from lawful sources to illicit channels did not occur. INCB would also monitor governments' control over chemicals used in the illicit manufacture of drugs and assist these governments in preventing the diversion of these chemicals into the illicit traffic. As regards the illicit manufacture of, trafficking in and use of drugs, INCB would identify weaknesses in national and international control systems and contribute to correcting such situations. INCB would also be responsible for assessing chemicals used in the illicit manufacture of drugs, in order to determine whether they should be placed under international control.

While the control regime has now performed its duties for half a century and its creation has been widely regarded as representing a notable success in international public health, the existing system has in recent years been criticized on two grounds.[21] On the one hand, there is an illegal but burgeoning international trade in raw opium, and the control system appears unable to suppress it. On the other hand, the control system as it currently operates exerts such rigid restrictions on the medical use of controlled substances that these are sometimes insufficiently accessible. The WHO Model List of Essential Drugs includes morphine, codeine and pethidine.[22] The WHO recommends their use for severe pain (for example, in malignant conditions[23]) but has experienced problems with what may be excessively strict conditions on their supply.[24] Such problems have not been limited to the opiates. In 2004 the UN Commission on Narcotic Drugs proposed the scheduling of buprenorphine (widely used in the treatment of drug dependence) as a narcotic. The rules are also on occasion so interpreted that access to essential drugs such as ephedrine and ergometrine is impeded, since ephedrine can be used illegally to synthesize the drug of addiction methamphetamine while ergometrine can be used to prepare the illegal hallucinogen LSD (lysergic acid diethylamide). Problems such as these, and the apparent need for a revision of the control system, were considered at an international conference called for 2008.

Political and Other Interference with Regulation

While drug regulatory agencies have as a rule been endowed with considerable autonomy, many are ultimately subject to a superior authority, for example, a Minister of Health. It is not unknown for their decisions to be overruled on grounds that are not necessarily technical.

> In *South Africa* in the mid-nineties the drug Virodene was developed by researchers closely associated with the ruling party and was claimed to be a cure for HIV infection and AIDS. The Medicines Control Council, as the regulatory agency, found that clinical trials with the drug were designed in an unethical manner and insisted that they be stopped. The MCC subsequently refused approval for the drug, regarding it as ineffective and potentially dangerous ('the product is made from an industrial solvent with unknown impurities, and is known to be toxic'). Both the Minister of Health and the Vice-President exerted considerable pressure on the Chairman of the MCC to induce it to change its decision but without success. Some years later the product appears to have been abandoned by its promoters.[25]

In the United States each of the main political parties has at various times brought accusations against a President for supposed interference with the decision-making process of the FDA, sometimes in order to ensure compliance with the views of particular religious groups. Among the issues that have been the subject of such controversies was the approval of RU-486 (mifepristone) for the termination of early pregnancy, the licensing of the so-called 'morning after pill' (and its subsequent release for sale without prescription) and the long-term refusal to permit the marketing of low-cost generic equivalents of the 'equine' estrogen Premarin® for treatment of post-menopausal women.

Much more criticism has related to the considerable influence that the pharmaceutical industry exerts at the political level through its lobbying process, and economic or other arguments may well play a role in securing interference with decisions taken in good faith and conceived to be in the public interest. Public interest organizations in a range of countries have also become increasingly critical of the attitude of those regulators who have come to regard the industry as their principal client whose interests they are in a sense obliged to serve. The latter problem has also been acknowledged by some regulators: Dr. David Graham, a physician with the US FDA who had been critical of the Administration, has been quoted as stating in an interview:

> The FDA has a very peculiar culture. It runs like the army so it's very hierarchical. . . The culture also views industry as the client. They're serving industry rather than the public. In fact, when a former office director for the Office of Drug Safety criticized me and tried to get me to change a report I'd written on another drug . . . he said to me and to a colleague who was a coauthor on this report that 'industry is our client.' I begged to differ with him. I said, 'No, industry is not the client, it's the American people, the people who pay our taxes. That's who we're here to serve.'[26]

At the present time, it seems likely that there will be an ongoing effort in coming years to redress what is seen as an imbalance between commercial interests and those of the public at large.

It is clearly impossible to obtain a reliable picture of the extent to which corruption plays a role in regulatory decisions, though extreme cases have been reported. In 2007 the principal Chinese drug regulator, Zheng Xiaoyu, was tried and executed on corruption charges, after the court heard evidence that a large number of ineffective and dangerous products had entered the market as a direct consequence of improper practices on his part.[27] More common are allegations that many of those involved in drug regulation have some sort of financial association with major manufacturers, which may induce them to favor the interests of a particular firm. To some extent, links are inevitable. A senior medical scientist sitting on a part-time basis on a government committee charged with drug approvals is likely to spend a portion of his professional time participating actively in drug research. The latter activity will ensure his or her ongoing contact with scientific progress in the field and further it. But it is in the nature of the research work that a pharmaceutical firm generally will have sponsored it. The principal rule that needs to be respected here, and one maintained in many agencies, is that any individual maintaining such contacts should declare his or her interest, and refrain from participating in any discussion or decision bearing on the firm or product with which he or she is or has been associated.

Confidentiality of Data

The staff of national regulatory agencies will normally be bound by the provisions regarding confidentiality incumbent on civil servants (for example, in the United Kingdom, the Official Secrets Act of 1911), and both the staff and its external consultants will be bound by corresponding provisions in the special legislation relating to the regulation of medicines.[28] In the United Kingdom, the relevant provisions were incorporated in Section 118 of the 1968 Medicines Act. In part, provisions of this type were typical of those applicable to any type of quasi-judicial process, where the parties involved might be obliged to present confidential data (for example, manufacturing secrets) for examination within the ambit of a case but could rightfully consider themselves injured if these data were to reach a wider audience. The original reason for this provision was simply to protect a firm's commercial secrets from being viewed by potential competitors. In the case of pharmaceuticals the industry pointed out on numerous occasions prior to the passage of such national regulations that the approval process would necessarily involve the release by the applicant of highly sensitive research findings that had been created at great expense, were not protected by patent and that must not in the course of this process be allowed to pass to any other party.

In some instances the scope of the data to which the confidentiality principle applied was defined quite narrowly in law. The Netherlands Law on Medicaments of 1958 decreed that: 'The members and secretary of the Board (for the Evaluation of Medicines) are obliged to regard as confidential all information regarding the composition or preparation of marketed medicines which becomes known to them by virtue of their tasks . . .'[29]

There was at first some uncertainty regarding the exact scope of such limited confidentiality rules. The composition of a medicine could not literally be regarded as secret, since it was to be listed on the package, at least with respect to the active components. The term 'preparation' could, however, relate to all stages of manufacturing, whether patented or not. Over a very short period it became clear that the board chose to regard the entire contents of the regulatory file as comprising company secrets, and that all those who were members or servants of the board would similarly be bound to secrecy by virtue of their professional oath. This principle has since been applied, in one form or another, in the practice of all other major regulatory authorities.

One of the consequences of broadly interpreting such confidentiality provisions proved to be the creation of a type of monopoly – market exclusivity (discussed below). A more general and fundamental objection to the strict maintenance of confidentiality was soon raised from the professional and public interest points of view. It was pointed out that where serious adverse effects or other problems arose after a drug had entered the market, there would be a need for all conceivably relevant data (for example, the findings from toxicological and clinical studies) to be available at once for scientific and public scrutiny. When in 1959–60, to take an early example, evidence began to emerge from the field that thalidomide might cause serious congenital malformations when administered in pregnancy (see Box 4.3), it was clearly a matter of urgency to know whether any experimental data existed that might shed light on such a complication. The manufacturer exhibited some reluctance to release its internal data, and had the drug been approved by any major agency (which in fact was not the case), it would have been important to open the regulatory files to public scrutiny at once. Even more generally, Lexchin and Mintzes in Canada have pointed out that the confidentiality provisions imposed on the Therapeutic Products Directorate (TPD),[30] which cannot release information from regulatory files without the manufacturer's approval, can impede the rational use of drugs.[31]

The issue of confidentiality of scientific data entering the regulatory files is naturally only part of the broader discussion of confidentiality of such data in any connection. While the scientific desire to publish one's findings and the ability to protect intellectual property tend to counter excessive secrecy, there has been mounting concern as regards the concealment of known risks, for example, in the course of clinical trials. So long as the emergence of such risks remains known only to the scientists directly involved, the sponsoring corporation and perhaps a single regulatory agency (that is bound to its own confidentiality rules), others may unknowingly be exposed to those risks. Particularly in the United Kingdom and Canada, but also in the United States, important initiatives have recently been undertaken both to promote the release of all data from clinical trials[32] and to ensure greater transparency in health research generally.[33]

As regards the specific matter of data present in regulatory files, some participants to early discussions of the question favored strict maintenance of the confidentiality principle. At most, in their view, the firm concerned might be requested to release the data voluntarily. Others proposed a compromise. In issuing a license for a drug, an agency might impose a condition that data could be released in particular circumstances. Here too, however, one would be departing from the original intention of the legislator. It would be fair to say that this vexing issue has not yet been satisfactorily settled in any consistent manner. But some agencies (including those in the United States, Europe and Sweden) have found it possible to release information where the public interest so requires. Release may be on a website or in a printed 'Summary Basis of Approval', outlining the grounds on which a marketing license has been issued. Lexchin and Mintzes[34] have presented evidence strongly suggesting that release in sufficient detail of certain data held in regulatory files can provide a more reliable picture of a drug's properties and risks than do published papers by authors who have not enjoyed access to these data. Below are two of their examples.

A paper published in the *Journal of the American Medical Association* concluded that the COX-2 celecoxib caused fewer serious gastrointestinal side effects than older anti-inflammatory agents.[35] However, reference to data released by the US FDA on its website made it clear that the published paper was only an interim report, and that the full study showed no difference in gastrointestinal adverse effects between celecoxib and traditional products.

The Women's Health Initiative study of hormone replacement therapy, as published in 2002, showed that use of estrogen and progestin in healthy post-menopausal women led to increased cardiovascular risks.[36] However, a subsequent comparison by McPherson and Hemminki of published and unpublished data submitted only to regulatory authorities, but to which they had been given access, appeared to show that these risks could have been uncovered well prior to 2002, potentially sparing women adverse health outcomes.[37]

Market and Data Exclusivity

Since the broad acceptance of the free market principle in Western society, there has been a marked reluctance on the part of states to grant monopolies. They may be conferred for certain specific purposes, and the main generally accepted form of industrial monopoly is that provided for a limited period under the patent system as a means of providing a due reward to inventors and innovators (see Chapter 2). In the pharmaceutical field, however, the research-based industry has on many occasions sought to obtain monopoly rights through the drug regulatory system as a means of extending a firm's exclusive right to a particular section of the market in the absence of patent rights or beyond the point of patent expiry. It is claimed that the scientific data provided by an originator firm as a basis for its new drug application comprise its unique property, and that any other company submitting an application to market a similar or identical drug cannot rely upon the fact that the regulatory agency is already in possession of the necessary data. If accepted, this principle will mean that the second firm will need to repeat experimental work, including toxicological and clinical studies, that has already been performed successfully by the original innovator.

It is clear that, during the period which followed the establishment of modern regulatory systems, many agencies did use data from their files in order to assess equivalent generic products submitted at a later date, and some may continue to do so. The issue is, however, clearly not settled. With the current and impending expiry of many important patents, originator firms are now increasingly taking up once more their initial position that generic firms seeking to market their own versions of these drugs have no right to rely at any time on the scientific work submitted to obtain the original registration. It is also evident in the European Community (EC), where in 1965 the basic Directive 65/65 initiated the harmonization of drug regulatory activities in Europe, which has over the years shown considerable support for the innovation role played by research-based firms, and the promise of similar innovation from the more recently arrived biotechnology industry. It has, therefore, favored the view that some degree of protection of the data deposited with regulatory authorities is 'advisable'. It has also considered that patent procedures alone might provide insufficient protection, for example, where new uses had been developed for an older substance or for an entirely unpatentable natural substance.

It is not known how the Commission came to regard this approach as 'advisable', but the research-based industry had pressed heavily for a move in this direction, whereas parties concerned with the pricing of products to the public and to health systems have contested the Commission's view. One argument that appears to have played a role with the Commission was that in the 1960s there were no patents on pharmaceuticals in Spain or Portugal (which were not in the EU at the time), so that additional means for protecting the EU market were sought.[38] When in 1986 revised legislation was enacted, note was taken of the Commission's position, although it was not precisely followed. Article 4.8 of Directive 65/65/EEC was amended to provide three possibilities for submitting an abridged application: the original provider of the test data could consent to 'follow-on' registration being granted on the base of the original data; the follow-on registration could be based (where appropriate) on the published scientific literature; or it could be decided that the new product was 'essentially similar' to a product already registered, and which had been registered for six years or more. A period of ten years would apply where 'high technology medicinal products' were concerned or where a member state considered that the ten-year period was required in the interests of public health. The period was not to be extended beyond six years if this would carry protection beyond the validity of the patent unless the new item was to be used for a new indication, documented by new evidence.

Most of the larger Member States, with substantial levels of manufacturing, in fact chose the ten-year option. However, the Community also ruled that the period from which the maximum period of protection was to run began for all countries with the first registration granted within the Community. The situation created in this way went some way towards meeting the wishes of the originator industry, although it was clear that industry would have preferred long-term or permanent retention of their exclusive rights to their data. The issue has been tested in court in the United Kingdom.

In Britain Smith Kline & French Laboratories Ltd (SKF) took legal action to prevent the authorities from allowing others to use their data even after expiry of the ten-year period. The case revolved around cimetidine, which had been marketed in 1976 and enjoyed a patent dating from 1972. Cimetidine was to be protected by patent for 20 years, that is, until 1992, though with allowance for licensing to other parties after 1988. In 1987 SKF sought to restrain the agency from registering generic versions of the drug on the basis of SKF data. The court of first instance granted a restraining order but that judgment was overturned on appeal to the House of Lords. In the view of the Lords:

> It is essential for the licensing authority to compare the applications of the first and subsequent applicants in order to satisfy themselves that both products are similar, safe, effective and reliable. The licensing authority cannot discharge its duty to safeguard the health of the nation and its duty to act fairly and equally between the applicants without having recourse to all the information available to the licensing authority, confidential or otherwise . . .[39]

Although it is perhaps true to say that there is some considerable debate as to whether the sort of activity contemplated by the legislation amounts to 'making use' of the data, the Lords were clear in any case as to the resulting regime. If a pharmaceutical company wants to market a new medicinal product in the United Kingdom it has to comply with mechanisms created under the legislation, which allow (only) a limited period of exclusivity. If they do not like this, then, in the view of the Lords, they need not apply to market their medicine in the United Kingdom. The House of Lords indeed went on to suggest that use of regulatory procedures to obtain protection from imitation amounted to misuse of the system. The ultimate consequence was therefore that the generics producers involved in the case were allowed to rely for their application on the evidence originally submitted by SKF in order to obtain a product license for its own original version of cimetidine (Tagamet®).

The notion that it would be inhumane, in the interests of data protection, to demand repetition of experiments on animals was not raised, but it may be noted that in the UK this issue has been brought up in connection with regulatory practice in the field of agricultural chemicals. In that field repetition of studies in 'vertebrate animals ' has been expressly excluded. The parties are 'encouraged' to come to an agreement (with compensation) on the sharing of data and can even be obliged to do so.[40]

An interesting compromise on this issue is to be found in the area of 'orphan drugs', that is, medicines developed to treat rare conditions or serve a market that is unlikely to provide a fair return on investment. As discussed in Chapter 9, both the EU and the United States have chosen to award data exclusivity for a limited period to firms engaging in this field with its high risks and sometimes low rewards.

Outside the United States and the EU, the issue of data exclusivity only came into focus in negotiations under the auspices of the WTO for what ultimately became the TRIPS Agreement of 1995, discussed in Chapter 2.

CONSIDERATIONS OF MEDICAL NEED

A final issue closely related to that of market exclusivity is that of considerations of need in the practice of drug licensing.

In Norway the drug approval system for many years incorporated a 'need paragraph' according to which a product would be registered for sale only if there was a medical need for it.[41] The consequence was that many new products were refused admission to the market since they did not represent any useful alternative to (or advance upon) those already available. When the market situation of non-steroidal anti-inflammatory drugs was examined in 1980, it was found that only 7 products of this type were on sale in Norway as compared with 11 in Czechoslovakia, 22 in the Netherlands, 27 in Britain, 31 in Germany and 50 in Italy.[42] There appeared to be no question of therapeutic deprivation; most Norwegian physicians were in fact using only five of the drugs available to them. In a later study[43] it was noted that between 1985 and 1992 between 29 percent and 47 percent of all new drug applications in Norway were rejected because of 'lack of need'.

Norway was later obliged to abandon its 'need paragraph' on entering the European Economic Area since in the European Community the approach had been excluded under strong commercial pressure. In fact, however, the 'need clause' approach is now widely used throughout the world, though not as a rule at the level of national regulation. In the developing world it exists in the form of the 'essential drug lists' for public health supply systems (see Chapter 5) while in industrialized countries a parallel concept operates in the form of 'hospital formularies' and the limited lists of drugs eligible for reimbursement under health insurance systems.

RIGHT OF APPEAL

In any quasi-judicial process there should normally be a right of appeal, and this has been provided for in most forms of national drug regulation. As a rule, however, there is no clear definition of the grounds on which appeal may be lodged. Appeal will as a rule lie to a government body, to the Minister of Health, or to the courts. This may be entirely adequate where an appeal against a negative decision is lodged on procedural grounds, but the reality of drug regulation is that a firm may be most tempted to base such an appeal on a technical issue, for example, the rejection by an agency of the results of a clinical trial or a toxicological experiment. Not only is the appellate body unlikely to have the technical expertise at its disposal to assess such an issue, but in many of the world's countries the pool of specialized medical and pharmacological knowledge is extremely limited. This type of problem appears to occur repeatedly; the most acceptable solution to date may lie in cross-border collaboration, rendering it possible to call upon one or more foreign experts to advise in the matter.

In the United States, a Formal Dispute Resolution process at various levels is maintained, principally within the FDA Center for Drug Evaluation and Research (CDER) and with final appeal to the Commissioner of Food and Drugs. Responses to appeals at the CDER level are typically made within 30 to 60 days. Under the European procedure, appeal is possible to the Court of Justice of the European Communities at Luxemburg.

An aspect that has received very little attention is the possibility of lodging an appeal in the public interest against a positive regulatory decision.

Dr. Nancy Olivieri, a specialist in the treatment of hereditary blood disorders at the Hospital for Sick Children in Toronto, Canada, undertook in 1993 to study the use in children with thalassemia of the drug deferiprone on which the Apotex company held a license. Early in 1996 her findings led her to conclude that after a period of use, the efficacy of the drug declined. By early 1997 she had also concluded that the drug caused progression of liver fibrosis. Apotex challenged both her findings and her decision to inform the patients of these risks, and it terminated her studies. Thereafter the company continued to perform clinical studies with deferiprone in various countries and in due course applied for marketing approval in the European Union, where a limited sales license was granted in August 1999. Dr Olivieri subsequently discovered that Apotex had not provided the European authorities with her results and the risks that she had identified, asserting that they were invalid since she had violated the study protocol. She also had reason to believe that the studies on which the European license was based were invalid. She therefore applied to the Court of Justice of the European Communities for a judicial review of the European license, arguing that it should be quashed since the drug was neither effective nor safe. The Court refused to issue an injunction to quash the license but allowed the case to proceed on its merits. However in 2003 it ruled against her claim, concluding that the European regulatory body had taken a correct decision on the basis of sufficient evidence.[44]

A related issue concerns the possibility of bringing a legal action against a regulatory agency for dereliction of duty, for example, failure to remove a toxic agent from the market or otherwise act in the public interest. A case heard by the High Court in London may be cited.

In 2002 a case was brought against Britain's Secretary for Health (to whom the Committee on Safety of Medicines is answerable) on behalf of Amanda Smith who as a child had been treated for chickenpox with acetylsalicylic acid ('aspirin'). In March 1986 the Committee had determined in the light of the literature that a child treated with aspirin for fever could develop Reye's syndrome, involving severe damage to the nervous system. It delayed issuing a public warning on the matter until June 1986 because of the need to secure industry support for the move. Amanda had been treated in the intervening period and had in consequence been severely injured, with epilepsy, quadriplegia and a much-reduced expectation of life. The High Court in London tried the case but rejected the claim on its merits, concluding that the delay in issuing the warning was reasonably justifiable ('Without that postponement the prospect of full positive cooperation from the industry, which in the event achieved so much, might be lost.').[45]

A highly unusual but significant case was decided in Japan by the Tokyo District Court in 1975. Clioquinol, developed at the beginning of the twentieth century, was originally sold as an antiseptic for use on the skin. Around 1930 it was additionally introduced in tablet form in the belief that it could be used to treat diarrhea. Beginning in 1935, incidental case reports and animal studies suggested that it could exert toxic effects on the nervous system. In Japan after 1955 a condition involving paralyses and blindness was increasingly encountered and termed subacute myeloneuropathy (SMON). Initially the cause was unknown, but evidence emerged that it was induced by clioquinol, which was widely used in the Japanese population. After the incidence of SMON in 1969 reached 1240 reported cases in a year, the Japanese authorities prohibited further use of the product.

Victims of SMON sued the companies concerned for damages, but also sought damages from the government of Japan for its delay in prohibiting the product. The Tokyo District Court found that the toxicological case against clioquinol had been established by 1967 and held the manufacturers and the government severally and jointly liable for the injury suffered after that date. With respect to the government, the Court stated inter alia:

> the authority of the Minister of Health and Welfare to approve or revoke approval of the manufacture etc. of pharmaceutical products is none other than an administrative supervisory authority. Accordingly, in the event harm is caused to users of such pharmaceutical products by inherent defects, the entire liability for compensating such damage naturally lies with the manufacturers or importers . . . However, in cases where the administrative authorities are found to have been legally at fault with respect to the exercise or nonexercise of such authority, the companies . . . and the administrative authorities (the national or local governments) can be considered to stand in a position of quasi joint-and-several liability with respect to their respective liabilities in that both can be held liable to make compensation for the same damage. . . The Minister of Health and Welfare has been found to have been at fault in not exercising his regulatory authority . . . after the aforementioned standard date. . . Accordingly . . . in the opinion of this Court the Government as one of the defendants in this case is liable for damages to the extent of one-third of the total liability of the other Defendants, who are directly responsible for inflicting the damage. . .[46]

Although only one of these public interest challenges to regulatory policies succeeded, it is clear that, at least in British, European and Japanese law, they can validly be raised in the courts. One important aspect of such public interest cases, whether they relate to alleged misjudgment or dereliction of duty, is the fact that drug regulatory matters have often been viewed as processes involving only the commercial applicant and the company, and are defended as such. As noted when discussing issues of confidentiality above, this structure is now open to challenge, with certain other parties or the public as a whole demanding access to the material or some part of it and seeking correction where this appears necessary. There is little doubt that the challenge will develop further, and this could have a substantial influence on future drug regulation.

DOWNSTREAM EFFECTS – SOME PRELIMINARY QUESTIONS ABOUT WATER SUPPLY

Over the past several years, a number of studies have identified trace amounts of a wide range of pharmaceutical products in water supplies, both pre-and post-purification for use as drinking water.[47] The presence of such trace amounts appears to result from disposal in the home of medicines by the general public, such as through flushing in toilets, as well as from routine excretion of human waste. Since ingested medicines are not completely absorbed by the human body, they will typically be present at some level in human waste. Today there is little that can be said with assurance concerning the potential impact of trace amounts of pharmaceuticals in water supplies. The identified trace amounts are far below levels that would ordinarily be ingested in the course of pharmaceutical treatment. Experts in risk assessment, largely adopting a measured attitude, suggest that considerable work must be done to determine the potential long-term impact of ingesting minute amounts of pharmaceutical products, and/or the potential long-term impact of such pharmaceuticals on ecosystems (including on wildlife). The trace levels identified in some samples involve a large number of products not often ingested in combination by an individual medicines user. It is not inconceivable that unusual combinations of trace amounts could produce surprising effects. At this stage, what can prudently be recommended is further study of this phenomenon with a view toward identifying the extent of pharmaceutical presence in water supplies, and perhaps developing improved cost-effective methods for treating drinking water that will better eliminate the presence of trace pharmaceuticals. It may also be prudent to include information on pharmaceutical packaging that will recommend best methods for disposal. Some municipalities have already adopted programs intended to facilitate prudent public disposal of medicines.

THE EFFECTS OF REGULATION

In 1983 the European Office of the WHO undertook a project to examine the effects of drug regulation. The work was undertaken in view of controversy that had arisen, particularly in view of industrial accusations that regulation was unjustifiably delaying the introduction of new drugs and raising the costs of development. A series of approaches was proposed to determine whether or to what extent the regulation of medicines was having its intended effect in advancing public health and in reducing risk.[48] Although strict national provisions on the confidentiality of regulatory data prevented access to much relevant information, sufficient work was performed to provide clear indications that national regulation at its best was capable of reducing risk, apparently without having serious adverse consequences in other respects. A number of restrictive decisions taken in Australia had, for example, protected the population from serious adverse effects that had been experienced elsewhere. In the United States the refusal of the FDA to license thalidomide has for many years been cited as the best example of the ability of such an agency to protect the public from dangerous medicinal products.

A largely undocumented but very relevant role commonly played by drug regulatory agencies lies in their ability to provide scientific guidance to research-based firms in matters of methodology. Many new drug applications that were deficient at the time of their initial submission have been upgraded with new and valid evidence as a result of methodological advice provided by experienced regulators during the review process.

Any overall consideration of the effects of regulation must, however, pay due attention to its weaknesses and its sometimes spectacular failures, some of which have related to disasters such as those listed as examples in Box 4.2. A number of these occurred at a time when regulatory systems were still immature and in some countries non-existent. In other instances it has been argued that agencies were insufficiently diligent or tended to place the interests of industry above those of public health. In some instances (as in the cases of triazolam and rofecoxib) the policy failure appears to have been due to a lack of openness or frank concealment of data on the part of the applicant. Even in the latter case, however, one must recognize a deficiency in the system in that it failed to detect deceit.

Although further work is needed in order to assess the repercussions of drug policies and regulation, it is important to realize that the effects of these measures are not limited to the evaluation of individual drugs. The fact that drug control agencies have come into being and operate to an increasing extent as a global (though not entirely homogenous) network means that the public health interest in this field has for the first time in history been given institutional form in which it is, in principle, capable of exercising a broad influence on scientific and medical developments. As noted earlier, however, there is currently a conviction that some drug regulatory agencies have in their day to day dealings tended to place the interests of industry before those of public health. It is clear that any such imbalance that is found to exist will need to be redressed.

NOTES

1. E. Pedersen (1988), Personal communication.
2. W.S.C. Copeman (1967), *The Worshipful Society of Apothecaries of London: A History 1617–1967*, Pergamon Press, Oxford.
3. R.G. Penn (1979), 'The state control of medicines: the first 3,000 years', *Brit J Clin Pharmacy*, 8, 293–305.
4. J.P. Griffin (1992), 'Medicines control within the United Kingdom', in J.P. Griffin (ed.), *Medicines: Regulation, Research and Risk*, Queen's University of Belfast, pp. 1–3.
5. I.H. Harrison (1986), *The Law on Medicines. Vol. I: A Comprehensive Guide*, MTP Press, Lancaster and Boston, pp. 1–3.
6. J.R. Nielsen (1986), *Handbook of Federal Drug Law*, Lea and Febriger, Philadelphia, p. 3.
7. http://conventions.coe.int/Treaty/Commun/QueVoulezVous.asp?NT=050&CL=ENG.
8. WHO (2003), *Good Manufacturing Practices for Pharmaceutical Products: Main Principle*, Annex 4, WHO Technical Report Series 908, World Health Organization, Geneva.
9. ICH (2000), *ICH Harmonised Tripartite Guideline. Good Manufacturing Practice Guideline for Active Pharmaceutical Ingredients*, Current Step IV version, 10 November International Conference on Harmonization.
10. J. Lazarou, B. Pomeranz and P. Corey (1998), 'Incidence of adverse drug reactions in hospitalised patients. A meta-analysis of prospective studies, *JAMA*, 279 (15), 1200–05.
11. H. Patel, D. Bell, M. Molokhia et al. (2007), 'Trends in hospital admissions for adverse drug reactions in England: analysis of national hospital episode statistics 1998–2005', *BMC Clinical Pharmacol.*
12. A. Bradford Hill (1960), 'Aims and ethics', in *Controlled Clinical Trials*, Blackwell Scientific Publications, Oxford, pp. 3–7.
13. S.C. Chow and J.P. Liu (2004), *Design and Analysis of Clinical Trials: Concepts and Methodologies*, Wiley-VCH, Berlin, S.J. Pocock (2004), *Clinical Trials: A Practical Approach*, John Wiley & Sons, Bristol.
14. WMA (1996), *Declaration of Helsinki 1964* (and updates: 1975, 1983, 1989, 1996 and continuing), World Medical Association, Ferney-Voltaire, France.
15. K.M. Starko, C.G. Ray and L.B. Dominguez (1980), 'Reye's syndrome and salicylate use', *Pediatrics*, 66, 859–64.
16. R.H.B. Meyboom (1998), 'Detecting adverse drug reactions: pharmacovigilance in the Netherlands', Thesis, Catholic University of Nijmegen, the Netherlands.
17. Anon. (2002), 'Profile: the Uppsala Monitoring Centre', *Int J Risk and Safety in Med*, 15 (3), 235–9.
18. *League of Nations Treaty Series*, No. 8, p.187 (19XX).
19. *League of Nations Treaty Series*, No. 31 (1933).
20. Convention on Psychotropic Substances (1971); the United Nations Convention against Illicit Traffic in Narcotic Drugs and Psychotropic Substances (1988).
21. Beckley Foundation (2006), *The International Narcotics Control Board: Watchdog or Guardian of the UN Drug Control Conventions?* Beckley Foundation Drug Policy Programme, Oxford.
22. WHO (2007), *15th Model List of Essential Medicines*, World Health Organization, Geneva.
23. WHO (1996), *Classic Pain Relief*, World Health Organization, Geneva.
24. WHO (2007), *Briefing Note: Access to Controlled Medications Programme*, World Health Organization, Geneva.
25. J. Myburgh (2007), http//www.politicsweb.co.za/politicsweb/politicsweb/en/page-71619oid=8 3253.
25. M. Loudon (2005), Interview with Dr. David Graham, Natural Newscom Email Alerts, 30 August (Accessed June 2008).

27. Associated Press (2007), 'China executes former drug safety chief', *Int Hereld Tribune*, 9 July.
28. Medicines Act (1968) as amended by the Medicines Act (1971) Section 118. See I.H. Harrison (1986), *The Law on Medicines. Vols I–III. I: A Comprehensive Guide*, MTP Press, Lancaster and Boston.
29. WOG (1958), *Wet op de Geneesmiddelvoorziening* (Netherlands Law on Medicines, 1958), Art. 29 (1).
30. Government of Canada (1985), *Access to Information Act*, Ottawa.
31. J. Lexchin and B. Mintzes (2004), 'Transparency in drug regulation: mirage or oasis?' *CMAJ*, 171 (11), doi:10.1503/cmaj.1041446.
32. K. Abbasi (2004), 'Compulsory registration of clinical trials', *BMJ*, 329, 637–8. For USA see A.B. Kimball and M.A. Weinstock, 'Mandatory registration of clinical trials: a major step forward for evidence-based medicine', *J Amer Acad Dermatol*, 52 (5), 890–2.
33. Lexchin and Mintzes, 'Transparency in drug relation' (2004).
34. Ibid.
35. F.E. Silverstein, G. Faich, J.L. Goldstein et al. (2000), 'Gastrointestinal toxicity with celecoxib vs nonsteroidal anti-inflammatory drugs for osteoarthritis and rheumatoid arthritis. The CLASS study: a randomized controlled trial. Celecoxib long-term arthritis safety study', *JAMA*, 284 (10), 1247–55.
36. Writing Group of the Women's Health Initiative (2002), 'Risks and benefits of estrogen plus progestin in healthy postmenopausal women', *JAMA*, 288, 942–5.
37. K. McPherson and E. Hemminki (2004), 'Synthesising licensing data to assess drug safety', *BMJ*, 328, 518–20.
38. C. Correa (2002), *Protection of Data Submitted for the Registration of Pharmaceuticals*, South Centre, Geneva.
39. *R. v. Licensing Authority ex p Smith Kline (HL)* [1990] 1 A.C. 64.
40. C. Garratt (2005), 'Data presented to the MSF Working Group on Intellectual Property Rights', Paris, 4–5 April 2005 (unpublished).
41. B. Jøldal (1986), 'The evaluation and control of drugs in Norway', *Int. J Technol Assessment in Health Care*, 2 (4), 663–7.
42. M.N.G. Dukes and I. Lunde (1981), 'The regulatory control of non-steroidal anti-inflammatory agents', *Eur J Clin Pharmacol*, 19, 3–10.
43. M. Enstad (2004), 'Comparison of drug approval Norway – the Netherlands, 1985–1994', Thesis, University of Utrecht.
44. J. Thompson, P. Baird and J. Downie (2001), *The Olivieri Report*, James Lorimer Ltd, Toronto; Anon. (2003), 'European Court rules against blood doctor, Nancy Olivieri, in her challenge of the marketing authorization of ferriprox', http://findarticles.com/p/articles/mi_m4PRNPR Newswire18 December.
45. C. Dyer (2002), 'Woman damaged by aspirin loses court claim', *BMJ*, 324, 444.
46. KICADIS (1979), *SMON Patients vs the State and Others*, Decision of the Tokyo District Court, 3 August 1978, Kicadis Organizing Committee, Tokyo, pp. 438–9.
47. See, for example, X. Xiao-Yao, D.V. McCalley and J. McEvoy (2001), 'Analysis of estrogens in river water and effluents using solid-phase extraction and gas chromatography', J. Chromatog, 923 (1–2), 195–204; 'Prescription drugs found in drinking water across U.S.', Associated Press, 10 March 2008, http://www.cnn.com; Dear Cornelly, 'Drugs all are in the water. Does it matter?' *NY Times*, 3 April 2007.
48. M.N.G. Dukes (1985), *The Effects of Drug Regulation: A Survey Based on the European Studies of Drug Regulation.* For the World Health Organization's Regional Office for Europe, MTP Press, Lancaster and Boston.

5. Medicines for the developing world

INTRODUCTION

When seeking to define an appropriate public policy on medicines for the developing world, it is helpful to bear in mind from the outset a number of fundamental facts. They are well known, but they are not always considered together. First, medicines and vaccines are throughout the world the most widely used tool for the prevention and relief of illness and the restoration of health. Indeed, where sophisticated facilities for medical care are largely lacking, they are commonly the only tool which can reasonably provide and maintain broad access. Second, a very large proportion of the world's population – generally the poorest and least privileged – still have little or no access to medicines.[1] Despite some valiant efforts to relieve that situation, it remains catastrophic. More than 10 million children die every year, almost all in developing countries, many of them from conditions that, given access to the medicines and vaccines that currently exist, are preventable or curable.[2] In some respects the problem is becoming more severe as populations grow and the HIV/AIDS pandemic continues to spread.[3] Third, while developing countries have an obvious and uncontested duty to tackle these problems within their own borders, the international community has progressively assumed the task of providing the relief, support and guidance. Without this the challenge is unlikely to be adequately met. It would be reasonable to say that much of the industrialized world now acknowledges, at least in theory, that it has a duty in this respect.

Both nationally and internationally there is a need to define appropriate policies in this field more completely than in the past. This must include policies on R&D, and policies with respect to those global commercial activities that, for better or for worse, can have such a marked effect on drug access in all parts of the world. At the practical level there are, fortunately, a number of excellent guides to the manner in which a developing country can manage the drug field. In particular, the manual *Managing Drug Supply*, developed by the US foundation Management Sciences for Health (and now jointly sponsored with the World Health Organization (WHO)) is a first-rate resource.[4]

THE ROOTS OF THE PROBLEM

An excellent analysis of the drug access problem was that undertaken by a working group within a Task Force for the United Nations Millennium Project. The published report is entitled *Prescriptions for Healthy Development: Increasing Access to Medicines* in 2005.[5] In noting that 'the lack of life-saving and health-supporting medicines for an estimated 2 billion poor people stands as a direct contradiction to the fundamental principle of health as a human right' the Task Force aligned itself with a general proposition laid down in the Universal Declaration of Human Rights[6] and with those who earlier pointed to the fact that the right to health brings with it the right to enjoy access to treatment[7] and, in particular, to medicines.[8]

This firm view that access to medicines is a human right has since been developed further, notably by Hogerzeil et al.[9] Poverty, as the UN Task Force stressed, is the principal obstacle to access, but there is a vicious circle. Lack of access leads to a greater incidence of ill-health, which itself leads to poverty. Other causal factors encountered at the national or even local level include an inadequate commitment to making health a priority issue and a lack of human resources. In the words of the report, 'every developing country should have an overall national medicines policy and strategy founded on the essential medicines concept'. The international community, in the view of the Task Force, had not provided adequate financing, nor had it consistently fulfilled its existing promises to assist developing countries in this sector. There was insufficient coordination of available international aid. There was also a major problem relating to the development of affordable new medicines. The current incentive structure inadequately promotes R&D on medicines and vaccines to address the priority health problems of developing countries. There is an unmet need for new medicines to treat conditions such as Chagas disease, African trypanosomiasis, leishmaniasis and dengue fever. There is a need also for newer treatments for diseases that have become resistant to existing remedies, and to replace existing medicines that are poorly suited for use in the conditions often pertaining in developing countries. In addition, the Task Force criticized the pricing policies of major firms when selling to developing countries. It expressed misgivings regarding the TRIPS Agreement discussed in Chapter 2. That agreement seemed to impede access to affordable new medicines and vaccines by uniformly extending protection to patent holders – regardless of local conditions – thereby limiting the flow of low-cost generic copies.

It would seem that on many of these issues the Task Force attained

---

BOX 5.1   PHARMACEUTICAL MARKET DEVELOPMENT AND CHALLENGES IN AFRICA

Contributed by Wilbert Bannenberg MD MPH, Health Research for Action (HERA), The Netherlands

Some of the serious problems around drug supply and use in Africa are evident from readily available statistics. Africa is poor and in some respects it is getting relatively poorer. In 1980 its exports comprised 6 percent of the world market; by 2002 the figure was a mere 2 percent. Sub-Saharan Africa has more than 10 percent of the world's population but accounts for only 1.1–1.3 percent of the global drug market. The sums expended by the USA, EU and Japan on subsidizing the production of food are considerably greater than Africa's entire Gross National Product. And to look at that figure in a rather different way: while a cow in Europe is subsidized to the tune of $2 a day (and in Japan no less than $4 a day) 50 percent of Africans have to live on a daily income of less than $1. One aspect of this is that more than 50 percent of the population of sub-Saharan Africa has no access to a basic essential medicines package. Governments spend only 14–20 percent of their health budgets on public sector drugs, distribution is inefficient, local production weak, and prices in the private sector formidably high, branded items costing up to 80 ~~percent~~ *times* of the International Reference Prices.

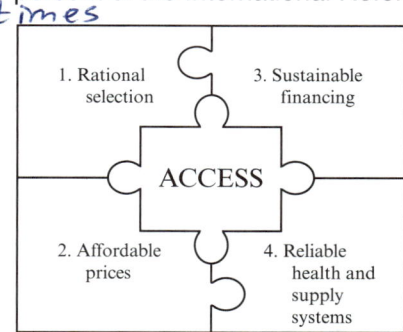

Figure 5.1   WHO access framework

While the UN's Millennium Development Goals in this field are ambitious, envisaging universal access, it has to be noted that various regional and international targets set in the past – for the treatment of malaria, HIV/AIDS and tuberculosis – have simply not been met.

The WHO 'access framework' still provides the key to ensuring access, but it needs to be followed. Similarly, the 'essential medicines' concept remains valid, but insufficiently implemented; it is still true that $2 per person yearly is sufficient to provide that basic package, but the world's governments still fail to provide that sum – a mere $1.4 billion yearly for the whole of sub-Saharan Africa; as for the world's commercial drug market, thriving at $700 billion yearly, it has priorities other than serving poor Africans. 'Pharmacy-philanthropy' by the multinational corporations is at its best (for example, the supply of ivermectin by Merck Sharp and Dohme) a useful initiative and should be further developed to tackle certain situations, but the WHO Guidelines on drug donations need to be more consistently respected than hitherto.

Clearly, action is called for on multiple fronts:

- National governments need to improve standards of drug regulation and inspection and to tackle the serious influence of counterfeiting (10–30 percent). Events in South Africa show that public pressure can be of value in inducing governments to follow a public-friendly line, for example, in favoring parallel importation and licensing.
- The patents issue calls for a new public-friendly approach; many antiretroviral drugs are widely patented in Africa, and patents are too readily granted. TRIPS allows some flexibilities, but these are underused (and undermined by 'Free' Trade Agreements); and while TRIPS holds out a promise of technology transfer, the further development of local production is unattractive with the special provisions favoring LDCs due to expire in 2016.
- There is a pressing global need for R&D to tackle hitherto untreated diseases and those for which existing drugs are encountering problems of resistance.

unanimity. On certain matters, however, the three members who represented multinational drug companies found themselves in disagreement with the majority of Task Force members whose background was in public health. No acceptable compromise proved possible, and ultimately the industrial minority produced its own dissenting report as an annex to the main document. It is instructive to observe where more or less fundamental differences of view had emerged. These related largely to issues of prices and patents. To cite the minority report: 'We do not believe that the main problem in barring medicines to the poor is patent protection, nor do we accept that individual company pricing practices are fundamental to explaining why one third of the world's poor lack access to basic, low-cost essential medicines.' The minority went on to stress the current activities of the multinational pharmaceutical industry in the developing world, including the establishment of research and manufacturing facilities, its success in various forms of public-private partnership (PPP) and its grave doubts as to whether public investment in innovation could be productive.

Bearing in mind the findings of the UN report and experience on other fronts, particularly that reflected in the work of the WHO's expert groups, it is possible to define some of the items that should characterize the national drug policy of a developing country today. In other respects, policies will closely parallel those followed in developed countries and considered in Chapters 2 and 3.

THE EMERGENCE OF ESSENTIAL DRUGS POLICIES

It is clear that national policies on medicines in developing countries cannot entirely assume the same form as those in the industrialized world. The fundamental aims are no different – one must in either situation seek to ensure that safe and effective drugs of good quality are accessible and affordable to the entire population and that they are rationally used. But the priorities are not the same. In industrialized Western countries – at least until recently – public and private budgets were enough to provide access for the entire population (if allocated responsibly), and nearly as many problems arose from over-prescribing and excess consumption of medicines as from lack of access. In a developing country much the same situation may prevail in affluent suburbs of a capital city, but elsewhere the challenges are overwhelmingly those presented by deprivation and lack of resources.

The 'essential drugs' concept as a basis for national policies in the developing world first came prominently to the fore as the central element in a new programme of the WHO under the leadership of Dr. Ernst Lauridsen of Denmark. From the time of the first World Health Assembly held in 1948, the WHO had possessed a clear mandate to work in the area of pharmaceutical products. But, during its early years it had primarily concerned itself with the harmonization of drug quality standards throughout the world. In the 1970s, however, international organizations as a whole began to turn their attention to some neglected aspects of the development process in the world's poorer countries, and especially to the social aspects of such development. As a result, as Mahmood Mamdani has expressed it:

attention turned to equity and to redistributive policies as a means of redressing the worst inequalities between groups. The international agencies translated some of this debate into policy. In 1974 the International Labour Office promoted the basic needs approach and, at the same time, the Director-General of WHO, Mahler, introduced a broad change of policy towards improving basic health services and coverage, especially in neglected rural and peri-urban populations.[10]

The 'essential drugs' concept was one of the major fruits of the new policy. Essential drugs were defined as 'those considered to be of utmost importance and hence basic, indispensable and necessary for the health needs of the population. They should be available at all times, in the proper dosage forms, to all segments of society.'[11]

In retrospect the concept was regarded in much of the world with some astonishment, especially when two years later the WHO produced the first 'Model List of Essential Drugs', comprising a mere 230 items. It is true that Sri Lanka, Papua New Guinea and Mozambique had produced limited national lists of essential drugs much earlier,[12] but in much of the remainder of the world the idea had taken root that good health required the availability of very large numbers of medicines. In Switzerland some 36,000 brand names had been noted.[13] In 1957 Dr. Lauridsen himself had encountered no less than 80,000 brand names in Egypt.[14] In Western Germany in the 1970s as many as 120,000 different products were believed to be on sale, though these included many of purely local significance.[15] There was also frank opposition, notably from the international pharmaceutical industry, which perceived in the 'essential drugs' concept the seeds of a threat to reduce the range of drugs throughout the world to such levels. This, it was asserted, would 'result in substandard rather than improved medical care and might well reduce health standards already attained'.[16]

Despite the misunderstandings and criticisms, the notion of 'essential drugs', comprising a basic minimum range of items to be available to all, took hold almost universally. Today it clearly must comprise the most fundamental item of drug policy in a developing country. In the course of time it has been refined. Quite apart from a basic national list, there is as a rule a need to distinguish those drugs on the list that should be available everywhere on free sale (over-the-counter or prescribed and self-administered), as opposed to those only suitable for use by trained personnel, in various categories of hospital, by midwives or by designated specialists.

THE PUBLIC AND PRIVATE SECTOR

At the risk of over-generalization, it would be fair to say that during the colonial era the administrations involved did not concern themselves greatly with matters of drug supply. Basic medical services were maintained, at least in the major centers of population, but needs for drugs were largely met through a private sector comprising agents and importers dealing with Western, and particularly European, manufacturers. There was also a network of mission hospitals and clinics maintained by the various churches, sometimes extending rather further into the periphery than the colonial medical services. That network made the necessary arrangements to import medicines for its own use. This general structure initially persisted into the era of independence, but with the latter soon came the realization that both rural populations and the urban poor had been seriously under-served both as regards medicinal treatment and health care in general. These populations remained largely dependent on traditional healers having quite variable standards.

The slow process of post-colonial health service reform involved, among other initiatives, the establishment of drug purchasing and distribution services, generally known as 'Central Medical Stores'. Except in a few instances where political considerations dictated that the new services should have a monopoly of drug supply, the purely private sector continued to exist, as did the mission health services.

Again generalizing, it is reasonable to say that this three-fold structure has essentially persisted to the present day. Public services seek to serve the entire population, but have commonly been constrained by lack of financing. The mission services often contrive to provide a somewhat better level of supply than the public sector can maintain, but usually require payment from patients. The private sector remains active, still serving primarily the more affluent sector of the population through pharmacies in the main cities, and providing a broader range of drugs with prices generally at international levels.

This three-fold structure seems likely to persist for a long period. It will not change until or unless economies improve to a point where a competitive private sector is able and willing to ensure an adequate supply of drugs at affordable prices, resulting in more modest need for public support, and rendering charitable mechanisms unnecessary. For the present, laws and policies in most developing countries need to provide for and facilitate the operation of all three mechanisms and encourage their creative interaction. Public sector supply institutions must, in view of their duty to the health services, be permitted and willing to remedy stockouts where necessary by purchases from the mission or private sectors, even where this involves additional expense. There must also be due provision for collaboration with donors and with bodies such as the Global Fund. The latter type of international body is likely to be dependent on public supply institutions to provide warehousing space and means of distribution. In this situation an essential item of policy must concern coordination of the various mechanisms. Unnecessary duplication must be avoided (as considered in the following section).

Public Drug Procurement and Distribution

Despite the existence of other national and international procurement channels, the public sector in a developing country is for much of its turnover likely to be dependent on its own purchasing operations. In 2008 a study carried out for the European Commission examined the present state of public drug procurement in a sample of six countries in sub-Saharan Africa.[17] Generally the process was functioning well, but a series of current problems, apparently common to many developing countries, came to the fore and were found to demand attention from policy makers. Some of the most prominent related to:

- *Failure to recruit or retain expert procurement staff.* There is commonly a shortage of trained procurement personnel. National agencies encounter great difficulty in attracting and retaining expert staff. This is commonly a financial problem. National procurement agencies, or the institutions to which they report, are often bound by salary rules applicable to government staff as a whole. They often compete for procurement staff with a private sector that is not bound by such restrictions. Experienced staff members are often lost to that sector. Also procurement staff members in the public service often find they have little chance of promotion within their institutions. Higher positions as a rule are concerned with general management, and where the opportunity arises they are likely to apply for more senior posts in other branches of the government service.
- *Lack of specialized training in procurement techniques.* One encounters, for example, tenders in which the products to be tendered for are insufficiently or incorrectly specified. Too little use is made of 'frame ordering'[18] for the fast-moving items, which often represent 70–80 percent of business.
- *Failure of associated processes in drug supply.* Viewed broadly, procurement begins with reliable estimates of need and is completed only after the goods are received and are delivered to a point in the public service where they will be reliably stored – and thereafter transmitted onward to ensure that needs are met. Too often need estimates prove to be unreliable, either nationally or with respect to certain areas of the country; at worst, they are no more than an extrapolation of earlier supply figures. The procurement process will

also be rendered ineffective if the place the drugs are delivered is inefficient at ensuring their ultimate supply through the public system to the patient. There may be leakage or theft either at the central storage point, during transport or in the periphery, reflecting either lack of efficient control or corruption.

- *Problems with quality assurance and control.* Most developing countries import the bulk of their drugs. They commonly lack the funding and facilities to inspect their foreign sources of supply. National laboratories are rarely sufficiently well equipped to check and assure the quality of all supplies as they arrive or pass through the distribution chain. Laboratory problems may reflect lack of funding or staffing, but can also result from lack of maintenance facilities for equipment. Difficulties such as these can sometimes be best solved by regional collaboration, though this can entail its own practical problems, for example, as regards postal systems and customs requirements when samples cross borders.
- *Inappropriate form and presentation of products.* Many drugs can be procured most economically in bulk, for example, in large plastic bags or bottles containing a thousand or more tablets. It may, however, not be in the best interests of public health to procure them in this form, in the absence of repackaging facilities at the final point of delivery to the patient. They may reach the latter wrapped up in scraps of newspaper, with no identification, no instructions for use and no protection from damage or moisture. The small additional cost of strip packaging in some well-chosen material, appropriate to tropical conditions and printed with some simple instructions, may well be justified.
- *Conflicts with national legislation or bureaucracy.* National drug regulatory authorities, however laudable their aims, sometimes obstruct the supply of drugs from low-cost sources by requiring specific registration of each, even when drugs are demonstrably identical to existing items and of sound quality. National procurement regulations, devised for product procurement in general, may be poorly attuned to the special conditions pertaining to drug supply. The issue of what constitutes appropriate regulation for developing countries is considered later in this chapter.
- *Insufficient donor coordination.* Here the fault sometimes lies with the national authorities, sometimes with the donors. One may encounter as many as 30 ventures alongside one another which, without a degree of joint effort, can result in duplication and waste (for example, in 'vertical supply' programs providing drugs for the treatment of malaria or tuberculosis that are operated by bilateral donors

from various countries). Other problems can arise due to a lack of understanding on the donor's part of the potential of national institutions. Some donors appear to insist on the adoption of their own agendas and modes of operation rather than those agreed upon with national or other (bilateral or international) organizations. Certain forms of donor input create operational problems, for example, the supply of bed-nets requires large storage spaces and much transport capacity for which the donor may not have made provision. The provision of massive free supplies of medicines may deprive a national store of an income that it has hitherto derived from selling them to institutions or to the public.

The storage and distribution of public sector supplies within a country can give rise to numerous problems in areas ranging from technical failure to staff corruption. Where there is a well-functioning business sector it may be possible to contract out both warehousing and transport to private firms, provided these can supply the necessary facilities in terms of security and quality (for example, with maintenance of a cold-chain of supply for products demanding uninterrupted refrigeration). In other instances, or where involvement of the private sector is considered politically unacceptable, a very considerable effort may be needed in order to maintain the standards that public health demands and to avoid wastage of scarce resources.

It would seem clear that many of the problems of procurement and distribution, insofar as they arise at the national level, can be overcome by the adoption of an appropriate national drug policy, properly adapted to the country's stage of development. But others will be resolved only as financial constraints are overcome and educational problems are alleviated. All of these are matters in which appropriate support from the international community is likely to facilitate progress.

A basic concern only now slowly coming to the fore relates to the question whether the substantial public/private funding that is now being allocated to global ventures in drug supply to developing countries is being optimally used. Hilbrand Haak (See Box 5.5), with experience in this type of activity, points to some of the difficulties that arise. They are not due to any lack of idealism or finance. It is fair to say that since bodies such as the Global Fund and the US President's Emergency Program for AIDS Relief (PEPFAR) started their operations, funding for health product procurement for certain parts of the world is no longer a problem. The essential conundrum appears to be that, while donors are anxious to see their funds move and developing countries appreciate buying goods when these are financed, insufficient attention is paid on either side to the need for correct drug management. This is despite the fact that the principles underlying proper procurement have long been recognized and that all parties for-mally subscribe to them. As one commentator puts it:

> My colleagues and I, acting as procurement experts for an international fund, have all too often seen essential drugs or antiretrovirals accumulating irregu-larly in national stores because the principal recipients have not undertaken a proper quantification of needs; storage conditions are sometimes appalling, proper distribution schedules may be lacking and staggered delivery as a means of attuning supply to consumption seems to be an alien concept. . . . Despite the fact that one brings these matters to the attention of senior fund managers, the notion of rational drug management simply does not seem to capture the atten-tion of those who are taking the decisions. They have been appointed to spend the donors' money and that is their only real concern. . .[19]

In international aid programs it can prove difficult to assimilate and benefit from well-informed and well-intentioned criticism of this nature. Those who provide the funding may not be anxious to hear that it could in part be squandered. Those who manage it have a vested interest in the reputation of the venture. Those who receive the funding will not wish to risk its being withdrawn. One might hope that the WHO, which has at least an advisory role in various of these programs, will find it possible to play a more active role in the future to ensure that they are carried through in a manner that provides optimal benefit.

DRUG INFORMATION AND EDUCATION

Whatever the extent to which the medicinal products available in a country are adequate in terms of their range, efficacy, safety or quality, their ability to serve public health largely depends on the manner in which they are used. Inappropriate use can endanger health or leave disease unchecked, or it can introduce new problems. In either case it results in economic waste. Public policy measures are then called for. In developed countries these measures have largely been based on the assumption that the rational use of drugs can essentially be entrusted to the pharmacist and physician, and to a fair extent the common sense of the user. Even in such countries that assumption is not in all respects justified (see Chapter 6). It would be perilous if this belief is allowed to dictate policy in those parts of the world where professional medical staff are in short supply and commonly over-burdened, and where public education is still constrained by the limited availability of resources. For every 100,000 population, Australia has some 250 physicians and 70 pharmacists. For an equivalent population sample, Senegal has only five physicians and one half-time pharmacist.[20]

In actual fact, the contrast is somewhat less acute since in most developing countries the limited numbers of fully qualified professionals in the health services are complemented by large numbers of staff assistants qualified to a lower level, for example, as medical assistants or prescribing nurses. Retail supply of medicines is to a large extent handled by drugstores, the managers of which may hold diplomas, for example as dispensers, while some are qualified in nursing (though many others are untrained).

Bearing in mind that the diagnosis of illness and the prescribing of medicines will to a large extent be in the hands of staff without a full medical qualification, the challenge to the makers of health policy is to provide a modicum of guidance and information such as will enable the staff concerned to serve the population as effectively and safely as possible. Where medicines are concerned, the adoption of an 'Essential Medicines List' simplifies the task, as does the fact that much of the prescriber's time will be taken up with the recognition and treatment of a relatively small range of illnesses. Many countries have developed well-conceived guides to prescribing, diagnosis and referral that have been progressively refined in the light of experience. *Malawi's Standard Treatment Guidelines*, dating from 1993 but still meeting most needs, provide an excellent example.[21] A pocket-sized volume of less than 200 pages, it succeeds in providing simple rules for diagnosing and treating more than a hundred of the conditions most likely to be encountered in the clinic, and advice on determining the situations in which a patient should be referred to a hospital. For a number of specialized and particularly problematic conditions, notably HIV infection and AIDS, countries have developed separate handbooks, largely on the basis of international guidelines.[22]

A similar approach is needed for the public that has need of basic advice in determining its attitude to medicines, and more insight as to how they should be used. A large proportion of the population, even where it is illiterate, has access to the media, particularly in the form of radio, and there are good examples of public information campaigns implemented in this way, as well as through illustrated posters displayed at clinics and drug outlets.

A final word concerns the permissibility of drug advertising, either to the professions or the public. As a rule, it has been relatively subdued, particular in view of the small market size. But agents and importers have on occasion sought to exert influence in favor of branded products, and there has been some success in seeding the notion that expensive remedies are superior to generic equivalents provided by the public health services. The success of commercial advertising in such matters is often reliant upon the weakness of public education and the absence of contradiction. There is every reason for the authorities in a developing country to demand that the advertising of a medicine adheres strictly to the claims permitted in the course of regulatory approval, and to restrict public advertising to those few items licensed for free sale and self-medication.

PRICING, REIMBURSEMENT AND SUBSIDIES

The overall issue of drug patents and pricing was discussed in Chapter 2. At this point, however, one must consider the approaches to drug pricing which are most meaningful in a developing country. Assuming that public drug procurement has been well managed so as to secure items at reasonable cost, and that there is a private sector capable of providing medicines at world prices to the minority which has the means to pay for them, the question remains as to how medicines are to be made available to the large proportion of the population that has very limited resources and is unable to pay the full costs of health care even where this is provided as efficiently and economically as possible.

Many of the countries that gained their independence in the second half of the twentieth century adopted as one of their basic ideals the notion of free health care, including the free supply of medicines. During the years that followed, it generally became apparent that, with limited and often diminishing budgets, this ideal could not be fully maintained. By 1995, a study showed that of 37 sub-Saharan African countries in which public health services had originally been free of charge, 33 had introduced health financing strategies based largely on private financing in the form of fee schemes or co-payment.[23]

This trend, which to many seemed so contrary to the ideal of free care (or at least free essential medicines) for all, came acutely to the fore when in 1987 UNICEF launched what was termed the 'Bamako Initiative'. Apparently without consulting the WHO in advance, UNICEF proposed that essential medicines for use in primary level maternal and child health clinics should henceforth be provided on condition that charges be imposed for drugs or services, the income thereby created being used to develop the health services further.[24] It soon became clear that African countries welcomed any solution that promised to relieve their funding crisis where medicines were concerned. But it became equally obvious that the Bamako Initiative had not been properly thought through. In particular, no agreement existed on how UNICEF or other agencies could contrive to supply medicines either free of charge or at sufficiently low prices to enable countries to resell them to low-income patients at a profit. All the same, in the two decades since the Initiative was launched the principle of co-payment in some form for drugs prescribed in the public sector has become widely accepted for the simple reason that it is the only course open to govern-ments that lack the funding to provide them free of charge to all.

Not only UNICEF, but also bilateral and multilateral donors have come to accept that the medicines they provide to the public sector, whether free of charge or at very low cost, will in many instances be sup-plied only against payment to many of the patients who receive them. The generally modest profit serves to sustain the health services or provide staff with a sufficient income. There are, however, a number of explicit or implicit understandings in this connection. One is clearly that the charges levied will be appropriate and reasonably modest, with exemptions for those who can make no contribution at all. There must be no profiteering and there must be no leakage of supplies to the private sector or to the black market. It would be naive to pretend that these understandings are always honored. Even where a genuine effort is made to respect them, the public interest is perhaps best served by overlooking the occasional trans-gression. It is notable that the system appears to function best at its most informal, where responsibility for levying payments and for both holding and using funds is delegated to the district or even the village level. It is at this level that local knowledge will determine which individuals can afford to pay a fee and which cannot. This arrangement that has worked success-fully in rural Kenya and elsewhere in Africa also makes it possible to avoid the bureaucracy and the corruption which are all too likely to characterize a centralized system handling finance. One final lesson that emerges from experience to date is that ability to pay and willingness to do so do not always run in parallel. However tight an individual's or a family's finan-cial situation may be, there is often both a willingness and even a desire to make at least some contribution to the cost of medicines and health care. That may reflect a sense of moral obligation, but it may also be linked to the belief that medicine that has been paid for is in some way more to be trusted than that handed down as a form of charity.

In a sense what is being discussed here is – hopefully – a transitional situation, however long the transition to full economic development may take. In the long run, any country may hope to attain the point where the economy can support the provision of free health care to those who need it. Others may hope to benefit from private health insurance coverage. Attempts have been made to introduce insurance systems in countries at a relatively early stage of development, but the concept of insurance is not well accepted everywhere.

A final word must be devoted to the issue of government priorities in this and other areas. Developing countries have sometimes been criticized for according health issues too low a priority as compared with com-mitments in other fields, including economic and military investment.

In the final analysis, such matters can only be decided by governments themselves. But it is relevant to emphasize that health is a major economic issue, with the wealth and growth of a country being strongly influenced by the state of health of its population. Issues of health, including the influence of adequate medicinal treatment on the containment of disease, are not sufficiently often analysed in economic terms. An important initiative in this direction was that taken by the World Bank in 1993 with its report *Investing in Health.*[25] Malaria is one of the conditions, curable with drug treatment, the economic impact of which has been widely studied. To quote only a single study, by Gallup and Sachs:

> Countries that have eliminated malaria in the past half century have all been either subtropical or islands. These countries' economic growth in the 5 years after eliminating malaria has usually been substantially higher than growth in the neighbouring countries. Cross-country regressions for the 1965–1990 period confirm the relationship between malaria and economic growth. Taking into account initial poverty, economic policy, tropical location, and life expectancy, among other factors, countries with intensive malaria grew 1.3% less per person per year, and a 10% reduction in malaria was associated with 0.3% higher growth.[26]

Figures such as these – and there are many more that point in the same direction – would seem to justify the view that if governments can be said to have any duty at all to the nations and peoples they govern, then on economic and strategic grounds alone a part of that duty must lie in a sufficient effort to eliminate the burden imposed by widespread yet essentially curable disease.

INAPPROPRIATE DONATIONS

Workers providing assistance in developing countries have all too often encountered instances in which these have been the passive recipients of unwanted and inappropriate aid.[27] Some charitable organizations in the industrialized world have sought to provide assistance in the belief that a developing country will be able to make good use of what others have discarded. In one instance a consultant to Mongolia found a large storeroom filled with unusable remedies that a social club in Western Europe had collected by the simple expedient of visiting many thousands of city homes and taking unwanted items from domestic medicine cabinets. Needless to say, many of the items collected proved to be life-expired, damaged or unsuited to Mongolian conditions, while all were labeled in a language with which users were unlikely to be familiar.[28] Similar problems have been noted in European countries suffering the aftermath of revolution or civil war. Indro Mattei, a Swiss pharmacist and disaster expert who co-directed an audit of the problem in Albania at a time of economic collapse, estimated that 50 percent of the donated drugs flowing into the country through non-medical voluntary organizations were 'inappropriate or useless and will have to be destroyed', and findings from Kosovo and Bosnia were similar.[29] On other occasions Western countries have without consultation provided drug supplies to the developing world as a much publicized gesture of political goodwill, only for the drugs in question to have created problems as to how they could be disposed of in an economical yet environmentally friendly manner. At worst, a number of commercial firms have disposed of surplus but outdated supplies by donating them to the developing world, thereby benefiting from tax relief provisions applicable to charitable activities.

In 1996 the WHO, having examined the various abuses of the donation system, whether involving commercial or other donors, drew up a set of guidelines[30] for its member states that are now widely respected. In some recipient countries these have been adopted into law, though failure to meet these standards is still reported. A basic principle of the WHO guidelines was that donations of medicines and medical supplies would henceforth be accepted and importation permitted only if there had been adequate prior consultation with the health authorities. A license would be granted only if the product met an existing need, was formulated in accordance with scientific principles and held recognized national licenses, and would have a sufficient period of shelf-life remaining to allow for import and distribution. A number of national regulations have added a requirement regarding appropriate labeling or accompanying leaflets. There seems no doubt that any government, institution or company proposing or undertaking donations in kind should be obliged to respect the rules in force nationally or, should these be lacking, the principles laid down by the WHO.

TRADITIONAL MEDICINES

Policies with respect to traditional medicines, largely comprising herbal remedies, are considered in Chapter 8. In developed countries they now constitute only a marginal phenomenon on the health scene, and the remedies derived from the herbal tradition are today as a rule standardized, produced and packaged under brand names. In much of the developing world, by contrast, traditional healing, with its own group of professionals, has remained a major provider of health care to populations, often being both accessible and affordable where Western medicine is not. The remedies in use and their mode of preparation, generally from herbs, vary considerably from one country to another, and even from one locality to another, because of localized traditions and the particular range of local flora. Because of this variation it is not possible to apply the usual policy standards regarding the critical assessment of quality, safety and efficacy. Policy makers, notably in Africa, have therefore concentrated on the need to create mutually supportive links between traditional and Western practice, ensuring that patients are cross-referred from one to the other where this appears to be in their best interests. The Traditional Medicines Program of the World Health Organization[31] has in this connection played a valuable advisory role.

APPROPRIATE RESEARCH AND DEVELOPMENT

As briefly noted above, the medicines needed for certain of the illnesses most prevalent in developing countries do not exist for lack of therapeutic innovation. The problem was classically delineated by Doctors without Borders in a monumental report published in 2001,[32] and others have made similar analyses. Byström and Einarsson estimated in 2001 that, between 1975 and 1997, only 13 of 1233 new chemical entities found to have useful pharmacological properties were for the treatment of diseases predominantly prevalent in poor countries.[33] The Task Force's report of 2005 for the UN Millennium Project took up the issue, seeking to identify the causes of the problem and propose possible solutions. The dilemma arises from the fact that it would, in the general view, be unreasonable to expect an industry dependent on profits from sales to devote substantial R&D efforts to products for countries with a weak economy, but also from the fact that, as noted in Chapter 2, governments of developed countries have been reluctant to interfere with the form or direction of industrial research.

As of 2008 a number of serious attempts have been made to alleviate the problem, but it continues to exist. As a senior member of the staff of Doctors without Borders put it, writing in June 2008:

> Every day, medical staff members of Médécins sans Frontières (MSF) witness first hand the failures of a market-driven pharmaceutical system, which caters to those who can pay large sums for their drugs, but leaves those who can't out in the dark. Tuberculosis is the poster child for these failures, where the newest drugs available were developed in the 1960s, and the most-commonly-used method to diagnose this curable disease – which continues to kill 1.7 million people each year – was developed nearly 130 years ago. Changing the rules of

the game will mean separating the cost of research and development from the price of products.[34]

The notion of dissociating the costs of R&D from the price of the end-product is developed in Chapter 2, with reference to proposals developed by Jamie Love and others.

Since the turn of the century there have been a number of promising developments. Much more remains to be achieved. Both governments and industry point to the creation of a number of international PPPs dealing specifically with this field of treatment for neglected diseases (Box 5.2). Industry points to a number of ventures involving the recruitment of developing world scientists in international pharmaceutical research projects. In addition, a number of research institutes in developing countries have embarked on efforts to contribute to therapeutic advance, either alone or in collaboration with others. It is evident that such efforts merit the support of governments.

BOX 5.2　SOME PUBLIC-PRIVATE PARTNERSHIPS

Global Alliance for Vaccines and Immunization (GAVI)

GAVI was launched in 2000 to improve access to established and underused vaccines and to accelerate the development of new ones. To date, GAVI has raised a total of $2.3 billion; of this, $1.5 billion was donated by the Bill and Melinda Gates Foundation. GAVI partners include governments (the United Kingdom has pledged $63 million), WHO, UNICEF, World Bank, foundations, vaccine manufacturers and research institutes. So far, $532 million has been spent in 70 developing countries, most of which has been targeted at supplying vaccines. Current research is focusing on bringing vaccines for pneumonia and viral diarrhea to market.

Medicines for Malaria Venture (MMV)

Launched in 1999, MMV funds research to discover, develop and deliver affordable new anti-malarial drugs. It has raised $107 million in total; 60 percent of this was donated by the Bill and Melinda Gates Foundation. The Department for International

---

Development (DFID) donated $10 million and the Wellcome Trust gave $3 million. In collaboration with around 40 public and private research laboratories around the world, MMV is managing 21 different anti-malarial projects. MMV estimates that it will take an additional $300 million by 2010 to take five promising products through clinical trials.

Global Alliance for TB Drug Development (TB Alliance)

The TB Alliance was created to accelerate and ensure the development of new, faster acting and affordable tuberculosis (TB) drugs. In its first five years of operation, the Alliance has been pledged ~$40 million, mostly from the Bill and Melinda Gates and Rockefeller Foundations. It has three main strands of research: developing derivatives of existing TB drugs; researching antibiotics that have not been used against TB before; and exploring entirely new drugs. One of the main priorities is to shorten treatment times and simplify regimens. It currently has ten drug development agreements. For each drug in development, an additional $60–70 million is required to proceed through Phase 3 trials.

Drugs for Neglected Diseases Initiative (DNDi)

DNDi aims to develop affordable new drugs to treat neglected diseases, by translating basic research about parasites into the development of new treatments. The charity Médécins sans Frontières teamed up with five research institutions to launch DNDi in 2003. Each partner provides financial support or research expertise on a not-for-profit basis. DNDi works closely with the Special Programme for Research and Training in Tropical Diseases (TDR). It currently has 18 projects at various stages of development to deliver better interventions for leishmaniasis, Chaga's disease, sleeping sickness and malaria. DNDi estimates that it will require ~$315 million over 10–12 years to develop six to eight drugs for neglected diseases.

Source: Adapted from Anon. (2005), 'Fighting diseases of developing countries', *Postnote No. 241, June*, Parliamentary Office of Science and Technology, London.

TRANSFERS OF TECHNOLOGY[35]

Typology of Technology and its Mechanisms of Transfer

Technology plays a key role in many aspects of prevention and treatment of disease. Public health administration systems (including hospitals and treatment centers), physicians, pharmacists, producers and users of medical devices and equipment, developers, producers and distributors of pharmaceuticals and vaccines, and patients who use them, all are dependent upon information and technology. It remains, however, a fact of global society that the capacity within nations to develop and employ technical solutions varies substantially. While the distribution of such capacity among countries is changing as a consequence of integration of the global economy, gaps in capacity remain large as between developed and developing countries, both in terms of R&D and implementation of technological solutions in the field of public health.

Technology is located across a spectrum of 'upstream' and 'downstream' points influencing the ultimate objective of preventing and treating disease. The individuals who develop and employ solutions must receive primary and upper-level education to absorb the basic foundations of science and technology. Physicians, pharmacists, nurses and other health care providers must receive technical training. Foundational or basic scientific research is conducted at universities, research institutes, teaching hospitals and private sector laboratories. The fruits of basic research must be translated into industrial technologies that can be deployed safely and effectively on a large scale. The operation of supply chains is dependent on advanced transportation and information technologies.

Transfer of technology – that is, the conveyance from one party to another of information, know-how and performance skills, technical materials and equipment – takes place in a variety of settings and ways. Educators and educational resources (books, Internet access and so on) transfer technology to students. Scientific journals, patents (and patent databases) and other technical information resources transfer technology among the scientific community. Enterprise investors transfer technology in the form of materials, equipment and training among institutions and employees. Public and private patent and know-how licensors transfer technical information, implementing skills and, in some circumstances, materials and equipment. All of these activities may take place in a variety of configurations, whether public or private, institutional or individual, through partnerships or joint ventures, and within or across national borders.

There are a number of fields of public health where improvements in the rate and quality of technology transfer are urgently needed. Throughout the world there are shortages of well-trained physicians and nurses. Research institutions throughout the developing world require access to technical data, equipment and financial resources to improve their capacity to participate in the development of better means to prevent and treat major diseases. There is, as considered above, an evident and compelling need to increase the supply and distribution of safe and effective low-cost medicines (including vaccines) throughout the developing world (and indeed to parts of the developed world as well).

The 'Global strategy and plan of action on public health, innovation and intellectual property'[36] developed by the Intergovernmental Working Group (IGWG) has addressed a number of areas where the problems of transfer of technology should be addressed. These areas can be broadly divided into those that are primarily related to 'upstream' aspects of potential technology transfer, such as in the fields of education, R&D and access to information resources, and those that are related to 'downstream' aspects of technology transfer where integration of technologies into delivery of health products and services takes place. We first focus on certain downstream aspects of technology transfer, specifically in the context of improvements to pharmaceutical production and distribution in developing countries. This is an area where public welfare gains from technology transfer could be realized with some immediacy. We then address upstream aspects of technology transfer mainly related to improvements in pharmaceutical R&D capacity.

Transfer of Technology for the Improved Production and Distribution of Pharmaceutical Products

The debate concerning local production

A number of the items included in the IGWG plan of action relate to the mechanisms by which pharmaceuticals are placed on the market in developing countries, particularly through local production, and related regulatory mechanisms.[37] Whether pursuing an increase in pharmaceutical production capacity in developing countries is an appropriate use of scarce resources has been the subject of debate. Some research has suggested that increasing local production of pharmaceuticals by developing countries may not reflect a wise use of scarce resources because only a relative handful of developing countries possess comparative advantage in this field.[38] Investing in a proliferation of smaller scale less efficient production facilities might result in an increase in local pharmaceutical prices, and might diminish quality.[39] More empirical research has been suggested regarding the effects of local production in developing countries before increasing the scale of investment toward that goal.[40]

Local production in resource-poor settings
Cognizant of the economic theory encouraging specialization, and recognizing resource limitations confronting their countries, developing country members of the WHO (including LDC members) remain strongly interested in increasing local production capacity, including with respect to establishing production and distribution facilities on a regional basis.[41] A pilot program has been initiated by UNCTAD, with financial support from the German and UK governments, to establish or improve local production capacity, principally in LDCs.[42] This pilot project, and others that may follow, should help to provide empirical evidence regarding the practical outcomes of transferring technology for the production of pharmaceutical products in comparatively resource-poor settings.

Local production as a present and future contribution[43]
It is critical to recognize that local production of pharmaceutical products in developing countries forms a significant part of existing world pharmaceutical supply. There exists an 'installed base' of pharmaceutical producers operating at different stages of the production process and with varying technological capability. Improving the technological capacity of these producers would play an important role in improving global medicine supply. Policy and regulatory efforts directed towards consolidating and strengthening local manufacturers, including upgrading facilities to meet improved Good Manufacturing Practice (GMP) standards, improving supply-chain monitoring systems, and integrating regulatory structures at the national and regional level, could strengthen developing country economies, improve innovation capacity and provide consumers with low-cost high-quality medicines.

Assuring the quality of finished products
Assuring quality control over the formulation of finished pharmaceutical products and ensuring their proper distribution requires the implementation of various technologies, and demands materials, equipment and training. The quality of pharmaceutical production depends upon the design and construction of facilities, the selection of equipment, control over quality and purity of inputs, environmental controls, training and supervision of personnel involved in the manufacturing process, training of personnel involved in quality control, purchase and implementation of supply-chain management systems (including computer software and barcode tracking equipment), and third-party verification of quality.

The extent to which developing country pharmaceutical suppliers can and do implement 'international best practices' in pharmaceutical production depends upon a variety of factors. These may include whether production is undertaken solely for the domestic market and/or for export, the extent of regulatory supervision in the domestic and/or export market, the size of the relevant markets, the demand characteristics of consumers, and the financing (and terms) available to the local producer.

Each of the foregoing aspects of pharmaceutical production requires a commitment of financial resources, and each requires the implementation of technical solutions. Although most developing country pharmaceutical producers recognize that upgrading facilities to meet international GMP standards would improve the quality of finished products, these producers often lack the financial incentive for upgrading their facilities to a sufficient extent (or at all). Such upgrades would increase their production costs, and erode whatever pricing advantages they may currently enjoy compared with foreign competitors. Such upgrades may not be financially justifiable in terms of potential increased returns from sales in the local market.

The extent to which implementation of particular standards of GMP control is necessary or appropriate depends upon the specific medicine under consideration. This discussion is not intended to suggest that all medicines and producers should be treated the same. Cost-benefit analysis is required in each situation.

Assuring API quality as a component of production

At the stage of pharmaceutical product input, developing countries around the world are dependent upon supplies of raw materials and active pharmaceutical ingredients (APIs) from a relatively small number of developed and developing country sources. API suppliers to developed countries are typically required to meet GMP standards established by the importing countries and to have their facilities inspected and approved by representatives of those countries, such as the European Union's EMEA and the US FDA. As a consequence, a part of the API supply industry (that is, that which supplies developed countries) typically meets high quality standards as a result of developed country regulatory surveillance.

On the other hand, purchasers of APIs from suppliers not inspected and approved by developed country authorities experience and report problems with the quality of imported materials. This is because the capacity of regulatory surveillance authorities in some developing countries where APIs are produced is less than that of developed country counterparts. These countries will nevertheless be obliged to rely largely on such self-regulation (and/or the efforts of the developed country regulators, which however may limit their efforts to certain export facilities).

Developing country importers of APIs thus face considerable difficulties. Quality assessment performed following the receipt of goods does not always address the same issues as GMP inspection of manufacturing plants. Because of transportation time and expense, rejecting and reordering goods create supply-chain problems. One way for developing country producers to address problems of imported APIs is to perform their own inspection of foreign suppliers, but this also presents cost and technical difficulties.

The WHO operates programs directed toward the training of developing country regulators in the performance of GMP inspections.[44] It operates programs directed toward the improvement of product quality regulatory standards, including with respect to the production of APIs.[45] The WHO presently operates a pre-qualification program that addresses the quality of pharmaceutical products used to treat HIV/AIDS, malaria and tuberculosis.[46] This program thus provides a potential model for addressing gaps in the inspection of API production facilities, but its present objectives are substantially more limited in view of the fact that it has been created purely to serve the three disease areas in question.

Regulatory barriers to trade
Another substantial obstacle to improving economies of scale among developing country pharmaceutical producers arises from differences in the practice of regulatory authorities, even (if not especially) at the regional level. Intraregional trade data for pharmaceutical products for Latin America, for example, indicate relatively low levels of cross-border penetration of locally produced generic pharmaceutical products. Local manufacturers in these markets attribute that low level of cross-border trade principally to variations in regulatory requirements, as well as to administrative barriers (such as the slow processing of applications). There are certainly cases where differences in local environmental conditions require the adoption of different standards by national regulatory authorities. For example, for tropical countries where heat and humidity are significantly higher than in more temperate countries, differences in stability requirements may be justified. However, a generally low level of intraregional trade among local producers suggests that other factors may be at work, such as a form of domestic market protection.

It seems apparent that improvements in regional production capacity based on improved efficiencies and economies of scale are dependent upon harmonization and/or consolidation of regulatory approval processes. This is not an easy matter because foreign enterprises will be able to take advantage of regional improvements just as local enterprises. On the other hand, well-financed efficient multinational producers have the resources to invest in overcoming regulatory obstacles, so that improving the situation for less well-capitalized regional producers would appear to benefit those regional enterprises to a larger extent.

Mechanisms for Preserving and Improving Local Capacity

If and as market liberalization increases as a consequence of multilateral or bilateral/regional trade rules, efficient integrated generic medicines producers from countries such as India, China, Israel and Canada will inevitably tend to displace less efficient local manufacturers, even as regards supply to the lower price segments of the market. Realistically, consolidation among local producers in developing (and developed) countries is likely to take place, continuing an existing trend. The question for many developing countries is whether they can and should develop an industrial and public health policy that will preserve and improve local production capacity in the face of increasing global competition.

In order to remain competitive, local producers in developing countries will need to increase the efficiency of their production. A significant contribution to efficiency gains can be accomplished by penetrating export markets. If a developing country producer has the ambition to penetrate developed country markets, it will need to upgrade its facilities and controls to meet US FDA, EU EMEA and other developed country GMP standards. Although this is not a foregone conclusion, compliance with FDA and/or EMEA standards should also facilitate registration with other developing country registration/approval authorities. (Developing country producers seeking to supply under procurement programs administered by the Global Fund – and other important international procurement programs – must comply with WHO GMP standards. This requirement doubtless has had a positive impact on quality control within such programs.)

Regarding APIs, notwithstanding the present efforts of the WHO, including the pre-qualification program (which is of limited scope), there is a need for substantially increasing the funding and training of developing country regulatory authorities so as to improve the oversight of API production in a way that assures the quality of domestically consumed and exported APIs. This funding and training would constitute a form of technology transfer in a very practical sense. Some form of expanded WHO inspection program might be used to address a wider range of APIs and producers than is addressed under the existing pre-qualification program, recognizing that equivalent inspection regimes are not required for all types of products or circumstances. Funding should in any case be directed to strengthening regional regulatory authorities and the harmonization of regional API standards.

As regards regulatory barriers to pharmaceuticals trade, it is important to provide financial support for meetings on the drawing up of proposals by regional regulators seeking to set agreed standards to facilitate cross-border trade between countries so as to permit local manufacturers to better penetrate regional markets.

Brazil is an example of a developing country that has recognized the importance of encouraging consolidation and movement toward global best practices in GMP compliance as a means to improve the competitiveness of its local pharmaceutical producers. It is providing development bank funding intended to encourage the consolidation of its generic pharmaceutical producers into larger scale enterprises; it is providing development bank financing to encourage upgrading and construction of new facilities to meet the highest level of local and international GMP standards; it is encouraging local production of APIs; and it has developed a highly regarded medicines surveillance authority (ANVISA). At the present time, ANVISA is preparing to commence inspections of foreign APIs producers that export to Brazil.

While it is not clear whether Brazil (or any country) can effectively use industrial policy to transform its local pharmaceutical production sector into a competitive global supplier, the government of Brazil has acknowledged that affirmative steps are needed to make this a concrete possibility. Brazil, as other developing countries, faces substantial obstacles in developing its domestic industry as a consequence of patents held by foreign enterprises. The country is taking steps to invigorate its innovative capacity so as, in the longer term, to introduce new products based on Brazilian technology. However, these long-term projects are not a complete answer to existing obstacles.

The Role of the Developed Countries in Facilitating Technology Transfer

Transfers of developed country technology are feasible with respect to virtually all aspects of improving pharmaceutical production capacity in developing countries. Such technology may include assistance with the design and construction of upgraded facilities, assistance with the purchase of capital equipment, assistance with the training of personnel at all levels of production, assistance with the purchase and installation of computer software for supply-chain management and other aspects of production, assistance with training and purchasing equipment for quality control programs, and financial assistance with the integration of regional regulatory control authorities. In addition, financial support and technical advice can be offered for programs to stimulate the consolidation of the production sector into more efficient operating units.

Although it is true that some important aspects of pharmaceutical production technology are closely guarded by their private developers, the various types of technology, including equipment and training, needed to improve generally the capacity of developing country pharmaceutical producers are largely available on the open market, as are independent technical consultants. If developed country governments are serious about assisting developing countries to improve their economic development and capacity to address public health problems, financial contributions toward programs meeting any or all the foregoing objectives would be valuable.

The key point is relatively straightforward. Most of the impediments to improving local production of pharmaceuticals in developing countries can be addressed by increasing the financial resources made available to developing countries to reduce these impediments. Most of the difficulties do not involve shortages of 'intellectual capital', although some do. Shortages of intellectual capital can be addressed in the open market of technical experts employed around the world. Many experts in pharmaceutical production technology are not currently employed by the major pharmaceutical companies. A large-scale program, potentially overseen by the WHO, to improve manufacturing capacity in developing countries is feasible if there is a will to undertake it.

The Potential Positive Impact of Production on R&D

Local producers of pharmaceuticals in developing countries clearly invest in the improvement of production processes, and in improving formulations of products already on the market, across a spectrum of technology depending on the financial resources and capacity of specific enterprises. However, with certain exceptions, local producers of pharmaceuticals in developing countries do not invest material amounts in R&D on 'new drugs'.[47] There are a number of reasons for this, the principal one being that it is expensive and risky to aim at the creation of a new drug, and most developing country producers cannot afford the investment capital needed to do so. The exceptions are in developing countries such as India, where a very few generic producers have attained a sufficient scale in the international market that revenues are adequate to permit longer term investments in 'new drug' R&D. One of the promises of improving pharmaceutical production capacity among local producers in developing countries, particularly if economies of scale on a regional basis can be achieved, is to provide the foundation for increased focus on R&D among companies that currently do not engage in that activity.

The Role of Intellectual Property

Industry structure and its financial consequences
Patents and other forms of marketing exclusivity play a very significant role in the efforts by developing countries to enhance the scale of local

production of medicines. Of the more than \$650 billion annually spent on medicines throughout the world, about \$550 billion are, as noted earlier in this volume, spent on originator patented drugs, with the remainder spent on off-patent generic products. Since virtually all of the patents on pharmaceuticals on the world market are held by enterprises based in developed countries, an overwhelming proportion of the income from the sale of pharmaceuticals around the world accrues to these companies. Even within the developed world, the distribution of income is skewed toward a few countries.

The large part of world pharmaceutical income distributed to these companies is attributed to the role they play in R&D. There is discussion within the context of the IGWG process regarding possible alternative mechanisms for funding and making available the results of pharmaceutical R&D. But however that discussion may proceed, at present developing country local manufacturers of finished pharmaceutical products are almost wholly concentrated in the production of generic off-patent products.[48]

The typical market share analysis of a developing country shows a breakdown of pharmaceutical industry income in line with the general global pattern. In dollar volume, the preponderance of sales and income accrue to multinational originator companies. Local generic producers share the internal market with branded generics of multinational originators, and with products from multinational generic producers. A change in the balance of sales and income in developing countries could be accomplished by increasing the extent of licensing of originator patented products from developed country-based enterprises to locally based enterprises. At present, evidence suggests that such licensing rarely takes place, whether on a voluntary or on a non-voluntary basis.

One issue is whether mechanisms can be developed to encourage voluntary licensing of patented products from multinational originators to local producers in developing countries. Conceptually, an approximately 'neutral' royalty rate could be determined at which a multinational originator would earn an equivalent 'net' income from licensing of its patented product for a relevant territory as it would earn from producing and making sales in the developing countries concerned.[49] Assuming that a neutral royalty rate could be established for developing countries in different situations, what types of incentives might be used to persuade multinational originators to grant voluntary licenses and thereby limit their total share of the global market?[50]

If developed country governments are inclined to promote transfers of pharmaceutical technology, tax incentives could be used to encourage licensing to developing country enterprises. In light of the large tax payments made by multinational pharmaceutical companies in the developed countries, a reduction in the overall tax burden may be an attractive incentive. Tax incentives would be a cost for the developed countries, but it might be a politically saleable cost in light of public concerns over access to medicines in developing countries.

Other forms of voluntary arrangement, including the formation of patent pools, have been proposed by contributors to the IGWG discussion. One of the key objectives of the patent pool proposal is to reduce the transaction costs associated with voluntary licensing. We do not attempt to undertake a separate analysis of each of those proposals. The general point is that increasing local supply of pharmaceutical products in developing countries requires some form of arrangement for making available patented technologies, and for political reasons voluntary arrangements may be preferable to involuntary arrangements.

There are a substantial number of political and administrative obstacles that will need to be overcome in establishing mechanisms to encourage the voluntary licensing of patented pharmaceutical technologies from the private sector. In particular there is a group dynamic problem: originator enterprises may be wary of being 'first movers' under such a system because of concerns about the behavior of their competitors. One advantage of working within the WHO is that collective approaches can be encouraged.

From the standpoint of developing countries and their producers, the utility of voluntary licensing will depend upon the technical capacity of licensees. Technology transfer objectives will be furthered by inclusion in licensing arrangements of non-patented 'know-how', assistance with registration dossiers, and other matters involved in pharmaceutical production and distribution. The negotiation and drafting of licensing agreements in the pharmaceutical sector is a specialized skill. Assistance through institutions such as the WHO might include training with respect to sector-specific negotiating and drafting skills.

A complementary approach to this issue relates to the possibility of making greater use of publicly funded technologies. As noted in earlier chapters, some important recent developments in pharmaceuticals and vaccines have originated in publicly funded research projects.[51] It would seem that there are real possibilities to encourage the use of publicly funded technologies (including research at publicly funded universities) to produce drugs and vaccines in developing countries. One of the major obstacles at present is that most of the technologies developed under public R&D programs are licensed to the private sector prior to translation into commercially marketable (or end-use) products. It is not normally practicable to bring early stage R&D to developing country producers for use in the manufacture of end-use products because developing country producers typically are not investors in translational R&D. Before these publicly funded technologies become truly useful in the developing country context it is usually necessary to move on to further stages in the development process.

One potential mechanism for improving the capacity for local production in developing countries is to work on improving capacity for later stage pharmaceutical development by funding research laboratories and clinical trials in developing countries. Another mechanism would be to condition the licensing of publicly funded technologies to originator companies on the making available of end-use (for example, finished product) technologies to developing country enterprises under financially reasonable terms. Each of these proposals is within the reasonable capability of those developed country governments which sponsor publicly funded R&D.

The WHO could play an important role in encouraging this type of activity, notably by expressing its support for such arrangements before legislative bodies in the developed countries.

The Role of Non-voluntary Licensing

Extensive negotiations have been conducted at the multilateral level over the past 30 years to establish an international framework that recognizes a role for non-voluntary (or compulsory) licensing of patents. The results of these negotiations are embodied in Article 31 of the WTO TRIPS Agreement, the Doha Declaration on the TRIPS Agreement and Public Health, and in the 30 August 2003 Waiver Decision and Protocol for Amendment with respect to Article 31*bis* of the TRIPS Agreement.[52] Neither the TRIPS Agreement, nor the Doha Declaration, nor the Waiver Decision (or Amendment) imposes a restriction or limitation on the disease burdens which may be addressed by non-voluntary licensing. The conditions established for the grant of licenses relate to procedures and remuneration. The WHO has taken steps to advise developing country governments of the availability of non-voluntary licensing mechanisms under the TRIPS Agreement and Waiver Decision.

The use of non-voluntary licenses in favor of local manufacturers of pharmaceutical products is an option open to developing countries to reduce rent payment outflows, and thereby to lower the prices to public health systems and patients for newer medicines.[53] Remuneration rates to originator companies in keeping with WTO rules may take into account the circumstances of the use of the technology.

The Role of the WHO

There are important public health reasons to encourage improvements in pharmaceutical production capacity in developing countries, including provision of greater assurance of quality and safety of medicines, and to provide for greater supervision over supply chains. The benefits from such improvements are not limited to generic products, on the one hand, or to patented products, on the other. Almost all current local production in developing countries involves generic products. Nevertheless, increasing the supply of newer on-patent products at lower prices is critically important to improving public health in developing countries, and voluntary or non-voluntary licensing of patented technologies is one important mechanism for accomplishing this.

The WHO has an important role to play in the promotion of licensing of patented pharmaceutical products by providing support to developing countries in the implementation of TRIPS flexibilities, including attention to constructing regional networks for the implementation of voluntary or non-voluntary licenses. It can do so in cooperation with other multilateral institutions, including UNCTAD, UNDP, WIPO, the World Bank and the WTO, and taking into account the interests of multilateral procurement processes.[54]

The WHO might also play an expanded role as repository and disseminator of technical information for the production and distribution of pharmaceuticals, employing both non-proprietary and proprietary know-how. Other types of useful technical information (and training) might, for example, include production process technologies. Underlying the concept of expanded WHO involvement in the transfer of production technologies (as broadly understood) is the notion of enhancing the efficiency of technology dissemination by creating a centralized repository of relevant knowledge.

Transfer of Technology for the Development of New Products

Most of the discussion up to this point has related to pharmaceutical products that are already developed, or at least at the stage of translation from basic research into commercial-scale products. Improving access to pharmaceutical products must, however, also involve transfer of R&D capability relevant to entirely new medicines commencing with basic laboratory and field research.

Public-private partnerships (PPPs)

The research gap on neglected diseases, such as leishmaniasis, is well recognized. The current major approach to addressing neglected diseases is through public-private partnerships (PPPs) such as the Drugs for Neglected Diseases initiative (DNDi). A substantial amount of planning and analysis went into the creation of DNDi, as it has gone into the creation of similar initiatives, and so far some encouraging results have emerged from the PPPs. These initiatives continue to rely on the goodwill of private sector enterprises in making available research materials and tools (recognizing that the results may also be profitable for the private sector), and on public and private charitable contributions. The main need with respect to the PPPs is for more public and private funding. Additional support is also needed to facilitate testing and registration of new PPP products, as well as in design and approval of production facilities that will supply the treatments. The WHO may be able to increase its support for the 'downstream' aspects of introduction of new PPP products.

Additional resources for developing country researchers

Research facilities in developing countries in general are much less well funded than their counterparts in the developed countries. Computer equipment and software is often out of date. Newer analysis and testing equipment is frequently unavailable. A straightforward form of transfer of technology from developed to developing countries would involve the financing or direct contribution of equipment and supplies needed by developing country research facilities.

Research on new pharmaceutical products employs libraries of potential disease targets that are used to screen compounds and biological materials. The libraries of targets used in screening are generally held by private sector enterprises based in the developed countries. They may also be held by laboratories of universities and public or private research institutes. Improving the capacity of developing country researchers to find new pharmaceutical products depends upon access to libraries of compounds and biological materials.

The international community has accumulated a considerable amount of experience in collecting and providing public access to biological materials in the context of the Food and Agriculture Organization (FAO). The idea of creating publicly accessible resource banks that would even take into account the protection of intellectual property derived from research on such materials is not new. While the FAO primarily relies on access to materials provided by public institutions, the model suggests the possibility of libraries that would take advantage of the resources of the private sector while taking into account the contributions of that sector. The WHO might well consider a study of the FAO model for sharing of food-related resources as might be applied to the context of pharmaceutical R&D.

Transnational R&D collaborations regarding biological resources

A considerable amount of attention is being paid to the relationship between patents and biological resources in the context of properly implementing the Convention on Biological Diversity (CBD). The preponderance of biodiverse resources are located within developing countries. The preponderance of financial and technical resources for R&D on the use of biodiverse resources in pharmaceutical products is located in the developed countries.

There is clearly a need to improve the climate for collaboration between developed and developing countries for the exploration and potential use of biological materials as preventives and treatments for disease. Steps to improve this climate would include initiatives by enterprises based in the developed countries to enter into collaborative R&D efforts with researchers and institutions in the developing countries on terms that adequately recognize the contributions from both sides, and that also have the objective of strengthening the R&D capacity of research institutions in developing countries.

One of the main objections of the commercial biotechnology industry with regard to recognition of the rights and obligations established by the CBD is that a lack of clarity regarding rules may lead to insecurity of intellectual property rights, including patents that may result from research on biological materials. While claims to patent rights are never entirely secure, it would seem that concerns of biotechnology originators would be substantially reduced in an environment in which agreements were entered into that defined the respective rights and obligations of bio-prospectors and the host countries. The WHO, in collaboration with representatives of developing country governments, industry and NGOs might consider working toward the development of 'standard form' bio-prospecting agreements that could be entered into and deposited (confidentially) at the WHO. The objective would be to reduce the transaction costs associated with CBD compliance in the interests of furthering R&D on biological resource-based products.

APPROPRIATE POLICIES FOR THE DEVELOPING WORLD

As long ago as 1975, the World Health Assembly requested the WHO to provide guidance to member states on the development of national drug policies. With that guidance, many countries have developed drug policies in some form, but it is not possible to estimate in any simple manner how many have constructed and implemented policies that are suited to their needs. More than half the member states have adopted essential drugs lists and many have updated them. Many have formally adopted national drug policies in the form of legislation or formal declarations of intent. Except in a few cases where specific studies have been carried out it is, however, impossible to determine how thoroughly these measures have been carried into effect. Insight into consultancy reports seems to show that in many instances implementation has been only partial, but in such instances the steps taken have been specifically aimed at correcting the most serious shortcomings, whether these relate to defective distribution, misleading promotion or the circulation of counterfeits.

There will never be complete agreement on what constitutes an appropriate level of regulation in any individual country. While ideal regulatory standards for countries in general can be defined (see Chapter 4), one will always encounter in an individual country those who advance arguments in favor of a special standard because of prevailing circumstances. In a developing country one may be able to advance either reasons why local industry should be allowed a greater degree of latitude in order to develop under difficult conditions, or conversely grounds for dealing more stringently with situations favoring the spread of pharmaceutical counterfeiting. The WHO, from the perspective of public health, has done much to advise individual countries in these matters as well as enunciating the underlying principles[55] while the World Bank has seemed to aim for a balance between the various interests (Box 5.3).

As noted earlier in this chapter, policy makers in developing countries have sometimes tended to accord too low a priority to health issues. If one accepts that governments have a duty to their populations in this respect this situation will need to be corrected, even though general constraints on resources may mean that, with that correction, full access to medicines and health care is still likely to be long delayed.

Many developing countries, particularly those classified as 'least developed', remain at an early level of industrial development. They are unlikely in the near- to medium-term to catch up with those few countries in the world that have not only taken the lead in the development and manufacture of pharmaceuticals, but are now accentuating and consolidating it. In pharmaceuticals those few comprised, for many decades, the United States, Japan and several countries in Europe. Since 1970 they have been joined by India and China (Boxes 5.3 and 5.4) with their large populations, technological abilities and wealth of natural resources. Others, such as Korea, Singapore and Israel, have developed important, though more limited, roles, while countries such as Brazil are investing heavily to join the major suppliers. Only a few other countries seem likely to join this group for the foreseeable future, especially given the fact that

BOX 5.3   REGULATORY CHALLENGES IN ASIAN PHARMACEUTICAL DISTRIBUTION

Contributed by Andreas Seiter and Yolanda Tayler, the World Bank, Washington, DC

At the present time the two leading economies in Asia, China and India, are continuing to grow rapidly. This is particularly due to their low cost of production and their ability to serve a large market, both domestic and international. In some respects it may also reflect the fact that they have a relatively loose regulatory environment. In both these countries the regulatory infrastructure is lagging significantly behind world developments. Regulators are underfunded, face difficulties in identifying qualified personnel, and are impeded by political interference, particularly where the regulatory structure is decentralized. Although there has been progress in improving the situation (for example, the passage of the so-called Schedule M in India that approaches but does not attain WHO standards of manufacturing practice), enforcement of standards remains weak. There are, for example, significant gaps in ensuring that products reaching the market are GMP compliant, and the recent enlargement of China's inspectorate team is still inadequate. In India the imposition of GMP is in fact still widely opposed, as is the maintenance of adequate drug licensing procedures. Where R&D in pharmaceuticals is concerned, both countries have PPPs, mainly focusing on commercial opportunities, though some ventures may have a public health component. India seems interested in providing some support to R&D, as evidenced by its recent decision to reduce or eliminate an existing tax on clinical trials. China is seeking to support industry in developing R&D by creating a strong government-financed system of research and innovation. There is, however, a long way to go; it has been found that Chinese pharmaceutical firms spend only 0.5–5.0 percent of their revenue on R&D.

Various questions now arise as to future policies in these two countries, for example, whether they should take steps to protect local ownership of their domestic producers. In principle, open markets appear to be preferable, but there is some distrust of market forces. If local producers are sufficiently strong to compete on international markets, one might also ask whether there is any justification for subsidizing them internally. Decisions will also need to be taken regarding the enforcement of competition law, since the impression that competition is sometimes unfair could prove to be a barrier to investment.

Of the other Asian countries with potential in this field, Singapore is of particular interest. Though it has no significant domestic market, it has proved to be astute in other fields in attracting foreign investment. It could well prove to be a suitable s te for a 'high tech' park for global players, and in principle one could imagine China and/or India establishing R&D hubs there.

Several low-income countries in Asia, such as Bangladesh, could in due course have potential as manufacturing platforms for other developing countries. Much will, however, depend on the interpretation put upon the TRIPS agreement in the coming years, and upon the ability of these countries to create the credible regulatory oversight that up to the present has often been lacking. In Bangladesh there are some good companies that would benefit from the introduction of a stronger regulatory system, but the latter initiative is viewed as a threat by the many weaker firms operating to lower standards.

Finally, in this region, the impact of FTAs (such as those concluded by the United States with Korea and Thailand) will need to be examined as regards the price and availability of drugs. Since 95 percent of essential drugs are already out of patent there may be no major impact, but it could mean that novel and innovative drugs will in future be less exposed to low-cost generic competition.

the pharmaceutical industry itself is now in a phase of rapid consolidation through mergers and acquisitions, creating a very small group of powerful entities based in highly developed areas.

It would seem advisable for many of the world's poorer countries to direct their ambitions to what seems reasonably attainable and to their best advantage. The environment could well favor the study and development of natural remedies based on traditional knowledge, or the creation of the small-scale centers of excellence of the type which today bear such extraordinary promise in biotechnological innovation. There is also a place for the creation of specialized manufacturing centres where active components from other parts of the world are processed into forms that are well attuned to the conditions prevailing in developing markets. This might maximize the public benefit of their necessarily constrained investments.

BOX 5.4   EVOLUTION AND CHALLENGES OF THE ASIAN PHARMACEUTICAL MARKET

Contributed by Dilip G. Shah, Secretary General, Indian Pharmaceutical Alliance

According to figures published by the WHO in 2007, the proportion of the GDP expended on health attained 14.6 percent in the United States, 10.9 percent in Germany and 7.6 percent in Great Britain. In Asia's two largest markets the figures are today not far behind those of Britain: 6.1 percent in India and 5.8 percent in China. The involvement of state health care in the provision of services is, however, very different: 83.4 percent in Britain, as against only 33.7 percent in China and a mere 21.3 percent in India. Where pharmaceuticals are concerned, the entirety of Asia, Africa and Australasia, with 73 percent of the world's population accounts for only 7.7 percent of the market, while North America with 5 percent of the world's people has 47.8 percent of the market.

Within Asia some countries have experienced a very considerable growth in their pharmaceutical industries, and in this connection special attention must be paid to India and China. Within India the domestic industry's share of the home market has risen from a mere 15 percent in 1970 to 80 percent in 2004. National policy measures that significantly affected the development of the local industry included the Patents Act of 1970 which at the time abolished product patents, while policy changes in 1978 and 1986 related to the mandatory production of APIs within the country, the mandatory use of these indigenous ingredients and the introduction of stringent price controls. Developments have also been influenced by the presence of multinational corporations and the availability of enterprising technocrats in large numbers. Exports have increased rapidly, attaining 166,346 million rupees in 2004–05, and Indian industry has become a major player in the supply of affordable medicines for global markets; sales to Europe, North America, East Asia and Africa are particularly prominent. Future developments will clearly be strongly influenced by the passage of a series of new statutes between 1999 and 2005 putting into effect most of the requirements set by TRIPS, but also redefining innovation: Section 3(d) of the current law rules that a new form of a known substance (including a salt, ester, polymorph and suchlike, and even one of its metabolites) shall not be regarded as an innovation; nor, according to Section 3(d) shall a substance obtained by a mere admixture, resulting only in the aggregation of the properties of the components, be regarded as an innovation. Other current provisions allow third parties to oppose the granting of a patent, and make provision for export under compulsory license to countries which have themselves issued such licenses.

The US industry association PhRMA has, not surprisingly, vigorously attacked Indian policies, estimating that in 2005 foreign firms suffered damages to the extent of $2.5 billion because of insufficient patent protection and a further $1 billion because of inadequate data protection, a total of $ 3.5 billion. On similar grounds PhRMA has estimated that in China, which by 2010 will be the world's seventh largest pharmaceutical market (with generics accounting for 70 percent of turnover), foreign firms controlled only 24 percent of the market and were in 2005 damaged to the extent of $3.1 billion. PhRMA has demanded that the US Trade Representative for India insist on a series of changes in the law to put an end to these fetters on foreign firms.

BOX 5.5　HEALTH PRODUCT MANAGEMENT IN DEVELOPING COUNTRIES: DEMANDING EXCELLENCE

Contributed by Hilbrand Haak MD, MPH, Consultants for Health and Development, the Netherlands

Health systems in developing countries have often suffered from an overall lack of essential health products. Since the systems that were needed to manage supply chains for these products were often weak as well, national and international agencies focused on strengthening the selection, quantification, cost-effective procurement, and storage and distribution of these items. Some also tried to improve the 'rational' use of health products. Up to the mid 1980s, management of health products was largely an unexplored area, and

and inefficiency and waste were widespread. All that began to change when modern management principles were applied to 'drug management'. The first edition of the well-known volume *Managing Drug Supply* was published in 1982, followed by a fully revised edition 15 years later. Courses based on the principles set out in *Managing Drug Supply* were held throughout the world and even found their way into university curricula. A basic principle in this new approach was that, given the scarcity of funding for health product procurement, the benefits of budgets should be maximized. Costs should be kept as low as possible and losses should be minimal.

Whereas some systems successfully applied certain or all of the principles of *Managing Drug Supply*, others continued to be plagued by inefficiency and waste. Unwise selection, poorly quantified needs, inefficient procurement, inappropriate (and potentially wasteful) storage conditions, and ill-defined distribution schedules and systems are still all too commonly encountered as features of health systems in developing countries. International and bilateral donors and development agencies have spent resources on the development of improved drug management systems, but apparently with limited success. Public drug management systems proved relatively resistant to developmental efforts, and one can speculate about the underlying reasons. Agencies apparently learned to live with such deficiencies. On the one hand, they realized that it could be difficult to change such practices, while, on the other hand, there was a proper respect for national autonomy; this, it was felt, was an area in which external agencies could perhaps be accorded only a modest role.

At the turn of the century a number of new and powerful financing mechanisms came into operation, notably the Global Fund to Fight AIDS, TB and Malaria (the 'Global Fund'), the US President's Emergency Program for AIDS Relief (PEPFAR), GAVI and others. With these new mechanisms, unusually large financial resources quite suddenly became available. Countries were now able to procure goods in quantities that had been unheard of in earlier times. The new financing agencies focused on 'performance' and wished to show that delivery of effective care was feasible and could be achieved, and they desired to demonstrate to their own financiers and taxpayers that funds had been well spent.

Understandably, some grant recipients, confronted for the first time as it were with a horn of plenty, hastened to propose the rapid procurement of considerable quantities of goods, whatever the system into which these were to be fed. Some were procured in national markets at high cost, since this often meant that they were available without delay; sometimes unrealistic quantities were procured; sometimes they had to be delivered to storage facilities which still left much to be desired. This eagerness to use the available funds at once was understandable, since in the past their failure to use funds in one disbursement period had resulted in reduced funding in the next. Somehow, with goods in plenty, the principles of correct management of health products now appeared less important, and a 'why worry?' attitude seemed to prevail. Some countries and systems clearly still lacked the skills to deliver excellence in health product management, while others had become accustomed to procuring high-cost brand name products and expected to continue doing so with the new international funds, particularly since these were so plentiful. Some failed to understand the fragile nature of certain health products and proposed to procure them just as in past decades, delivering them into conditions where they would be only too likely to decay and expire before they served their intended purpose. Establishing excellence in health product management seemed of lesser importance. It was as if spending funds was now the correct thing to do, and certainly the most spectacular, rather than spending time and energy on effective improvement of health product management.

The need to 'perform' has in some cases been seen to lead to poor selection of products (for example, ordering of non-essential consumables or equipment) and poor quantification of product needs leading to over- or under-ordering; poorly functioning storage conditions have led to waste (for example, where non-heat stable ARV products for use in HIV/AIDS programs have been stored at room temperature); flaws in procurement procedures have led to unnecessarily high prices for goods; and dysfunctional systems have resulted in inefficient distribution. These are mere examples, but it is alarming to see that they represent real shortcomings in the present situation and in the way money is used. They are also alarming because the principles of correct health product management have been well known and accepted for more than 20 years, yet it apparently remains difficult to apply them in practice.

t is fair to say that the new financing mechanisms have sought to adhere to correct managerial principles where health product procurement and supply management are concerned. However, there has at the same time been a timetable for disbursement to which one is supposed to adhere; not surprisingly, desk officers have often chosen the course that seems to demand priority, with disbursement winning the day while drug management has somehow receded into the shadows. At times it even seems that both funder and recipient have worked in harness to play out this scenario, with 'good performance' being sought and assessed very largely in terms of the volume of goods supplied rather than the quality and effects of the overall operation.

Those charged with the evaluation of programs have sometimes made a case for employing 'rapid solutions' for weaknesses n the practice of procurement and supply management. Tasks handled by weak systems could, for example, be temporarily contracted out to capable institutions, or UN agencies could take on the joint role of principle recipient and implementing agency. Technical assistance was in a number of cases proposed to strengthen or restructure defined components of the procurement and supply management system, for example, storage facilities, procurement departments or laboratory facilities. These technical assistance experts have duly been set to work, but they tended to follow the same developmental approach as was adopted in the 1980s and 1990s, when lack of resources was the common denominator and systems had to be built up in the absence of funds for the procurement of health products. Typically such technical assistance teams have recommended a sequence of actions involving 'project identification' missions, subsequent stakeholders' conferences', and 'consensus building' efforts, ultimately followed by the development of 'Masterplans' and the development and imposition of a series of 'capacity building' exercises. Outcomes have not always been measured in terms of improved availability of health services to populations. Often these efforts have lasted longer than the grant cycles in which they were initiated, and the direct benefits to the grant implementation process can in some cases be questioned. And all the time the clock is ticking, demanding that pre-set indicators and goals be met within the limited time allocated for the use of a grant. Whereas the most urgent needs were in some cases met, technical assistance, which one might expect to offer solutions when systems are insufficient, has often failed to find ways to provide rapid improvement in defective operations.

As the new financing mechanisms have generated ever more resources and countries have pressed ahead to develop further grant proposals, some undesirable processes have become apparent. One is the unavoidable pressure to spend the resources allocated, to the extent that relatively less attention is paid to determining whether the demands being made cn the funds are truly appropriate. The other is the plodding trad tional approach adopted to technical assistance, aiming for gradual long-term development when what is now needed is a series of rapid improvements in the system, to ensure the planned outcomes in patient care are achieved within the lifetime of the grants.

A question still insufficiently answered is why some health care and supply systems continue to function as poorly as they do. Experts who have been working in development for many years know that poor performance seems to be perpetual in some systems. State-of-the-art medical stores have been financed and constructed by the international community in various countries, and it is not uncommon to find that key staff in Ministries of Health have obtained Masters and PhD degrees from reputable institutions in industrialized countries. Staff training is sometimes so frequent that it becomes a hindrance to regular care delivery and supply management. With all these inputs one can wonder why poor systems and standards continue to be so common. Could it be that the international community has become used to under-performance in developing countries and that its continuation is raising too few eyebrows? Could it be that the international community is expecting too little excellence in grant implementation from recipient countries?

In today's world, private sector investments are on the rise in many developing countries. These investments are less likely to be provided or continued without demanding excellence, and the 'credit worthiness' of recipients is carefully evaluated. Those with the best 'credit worthiness' ratings tend to receive more investments; those who do poorly receive less investment. The new financing mechanisms operate to some extent as investors, although returns are not monitored in monetary terms, but in terms of improved health outcomes or health systems improvements. If the 'health returns' are good, the new financing mechanisms can be expected to find more parties prepared to invest into their operations (for example, for the Global Fund where the investors are national governments and private sector parties).

Bringing about improvement in public sector functions is notoriously difficult, especially in developing countries. All the same, one is tempted to think that in the current environment, and unless disbursement pressure comes into play, most financing agencies are likely to make a merely verbal protest, and to continue giving on a 'no objection' basis. This cycle is likely to continue, unless the international development community is able to define new methods that reward excellence and penalize poor management practices. Defining these methods and rewards may be one of the most important challenges for the years immediately ahead. In the developmental approach there is too little demand for excellence in grant implementation, and too much opportunity for poor practices to persist. Stockouts of vital health products (for example, antiretroviral drugs, condoms, anti-malaria medicines) are unacceptable and will ultimately result in emergency purchases of such products from national suppliers at significantly increased prices. This will offer opportunities for national industries, but may not be what the donors contemplated.

Today one quite frequently encounters the realization in developing countries that these large-scale international development funds will not be available forever. It could be that the recipients are rather more aware of the ticking of the clock than the givers. So long as those funds are at hand they must be used wisely and competently. If that means that some part of the funding should be used to bring about rapid improvement in health product management, so be it. The resources are there – indeed they are there in abundance. It is intolerable to find that they are not used to the best advantage. It should not be so, and it does not need to be so. Time will indeed one day run out, and it is vital that we do not lose the opportunity we now have to use every available dollar and euro to the best advantage to bring about lasting improvement in public health in the developing world, especially in the poorest countries.

NOTES

1. United Nations Millennium Project (2005), *Prescriptions for Healthy Development: Increasing Access to Medicines*, Earthscan, London.
2. R.E. Black (2003), 'Where and why are 10 million children dying every year?', *Lancet*, 361, 2220–34.
3. DFID (2008), *Increasing Access to Medicines in the Developing World*, UK Department for International Development, London.
4. MSH (1997), *Managing Drug Supply: The Selection, Procurement, Distribution and Use of Pharmaceuticals*, 2nd edn, WHO Action Programme on Essential Drugs, Geneva, and Management Sciences for Health, Kumarian Press, West Hartford, CT.
5. United Nations Millennium Project (2005), *Prescriptions for Healthy Development*.
6. United Nations (1948), *Universal Declaration of Human Rights*, Art. 25 (1) UN Resolution 217A (III), United Nations, New York.
7. J. Mukherjee (2004), 'Basing treatment in rights rather than ability to pay', *Lancet*, 363, 10971–2.
8. H.V. Hogerzeil (undated), *Evidence Presented to the UN Task Force on Access to Drugs*, 2003.
9. H.V. Hogerzeil, M. Samson, J.V. Casanovas and L. Rahmani-Ocora (2006), 'Is access to essential medicines as part of the fulfilment of the right to health enforceable through the courts?' *Lancet*, 9532, 305–11.
10. M. Mamdani (1992), 'Early initiatives in essential drugs policy', in N. Kanji et al., eds), *Drug Policy in Developing Countries*, Zed Books, London, p. 13.
11. WHO (1975), 'Prophylactic and therapeutic substances', Document A22/11, World Health Organization, Geneva.
12. Mamdani (1992), 'Early initiatives in essential drugs policy', p.14.
13. M. Muller (1982), *The Health of Nations; A North-South Investigation*, Faber and Faber, London.
14. E. Lauridsen (1984), 'The World Health Organization Action Programme on essential drugs', *Danish Med Bull*, 31, 1.
15. M.N.G. Dukes (1985), *The Effects of Drug Regulation*, World Health Organization (Regional Office for Europe), Copenhagen, p.12.
16. M. Peretz (1977), Statement to *Scrip* as cited by I. Prudencio (1988): *El concepto del medicamento esencial*, Mario Negri Institute, Milan.
17. M.N.G. Dukes, J. Hygino and G. Weeda (eds) (2008), *Procurement Policies and Practices for Drugs in Sub-Saharan Africa; A Study Performed for the European Commission and Recommendations of a Workshop Held Jointly with the World Health Organization*, EC, Brussels (Final Draft, June).
18. A frame order is a general agreement between purchaser and seller that particular goods will be available for purchase within a certain period on agreed terms. Within this period specific orders for exact quantities are then placed as and when they are required. This procedure avoids the need for repeated negotiation of prices and conditions.
19. Anon. (2008), Commentary to the authors by an experienced procurement consultant.
20. Figures calculated from *World Health Statistics 2008*, World Health Organization, Geneva.
21. Ministry of Health Malawi (1993), *Malawi Standard Treatment Guidelines*, 2nd edn, Ministry of Health, Lilongwe.
22. UNAIDS (1999), *Developing HIV/AIDS Treatment Guidelines*, UNAIDS, New York.
23. L. Gilson and A. Mills (1995), 'Health sector reforms in Sub-Saharan Africa: lessons of the last 10 years', *Health Policy*, 32, 215–43.
24. G. Walt and J.W. Harnmeijer (1992), 'Formulating an essential drugs policy', in N. Kanji, J.W. Harnmeijer and A. Hardon (eds), *Drugs Policy in Developing Countries*, Zed Books, London.

25. World Bank (1993), *The World Development Report 1993: Investing in Health*, World Bank, Washington, DC.
26. J.L. Gallup and J.D. Sachs (2001), 'The economic burden of malaria', *Am J Trop Med Hyg*, 64 (1–2 Suppl.), 85–96.
27. D. Rienstra (1999), *Report on a European Expert Seminar on Appropriate Drug Donations*, Wemos, Amsterdam.
28. M.N.G. Dukes (1996), 'Report to Danida on a mission to Mongolia' (unpublished).
29. J. Ciment (1999), 'Study finds that most donations to developing countries are appropriate', *BMJ*, 319, 942.
30. WHO (1996), *Drug Action Programme: Guideline for Drug Donations*, Document DAP 96/2, World Health Organization, Geneva.
31. WHO (2003), 'Traditional medicines', Fact Sheet No. 134 (revised), World Health Organization, Geneva.
32. MSF (2001), *Fatal Imbalance – The Crisis in Research and Development for Drugs for Neglected Diseases*, Médécins sans Frontières (Doctors without Borders), Geneva.
33. M. Byström and P. Einarsson (2001), *TRIPS: Consequences for Developing Countries: Implications for Swedish Development Cooperation*, SIDA, Stockholm.
34. E. 't Hoen (2008), 'Drugs for developing countries: trial in Singapore', *Int Herald Tribune*, 3 June.
35. This section is based on an unpublished background paper on 'Transfer of Technology' prepared by Frederick Abbott in November 2007 for use by the WHO Secretariat in connection with discussions in the Intergovernmental Working Group on a Draft Global Strategy and Plan of Action on Public Health, Innovation and Intellectual Property.
36. Sixty-first World Health Assembley, WHA61.21, 24 May 2008, Annex ('Global strategy and plan of action on public health, innovation and intellectual property'). Element 4 of the draft global strategy and plan of action is expressly addressed to 'Transfer of technology', but elements and paragraphs throughout the plan encompass transfer of technology.
37. A/PHI/IGWG/2/2. Element 4, for example, includes: '(4.1) promoting transfer of technology and the production of health products in developing countries

    (a) explore possible new mechanisms and make better use of existing mechanisms to facilitate transfer of technology and technical support to build and improve innovative capacity for health-related research and development, particularly in developing countries
    (b) promote transfer of technology and production of health products in developing countries through investment and capacity building
    (c) promote transfer of technology and production of health products in developing countries through identification of best practices, and investment and capacity building provided by developed and developing countries where appropriate.

    (4.2) supporting improved collaboration and coordination of technology transfer for health products, bearing in mind different levels of development

    (a) encourage North–South and South–South cooperation for technology transfers, and collaboration between institutions in developing countries and the pharmaceutical industry' Element 3 includes: '(3.2) framing, developing and supporting effective policies that promote the development of capacities for health innovation *(a) establish and strengthen regulatory capacity in developing countries*'. Element 6 includes: '37 Support for and strengthening of health systems is vital for the success of the strategy, as are the stimulation of competition and the adoption of appropriate pricing and taxation policies for health products. Mechanisms to regulate the safety, quality and efficacy of medicines and other health products, coupled with adherence to good manufacturing practices and effective supply chain management, are critical components of a well-functioning health system.' The cited elements and paragraphs are by no means exhaustive of the draft action items that are relevant to production and distribution of pharmaceuticals.

38. See Warren Kaplan and Richard Lang, 'Local production of pharmaceuticals: industrial policy and access to medicines, an overview of key concepts, issues and opportunities for future research', HNP Discussion Paper, World Bank, January 2005.

39. Ibid., pp. 1–3, 11–12, 32–5. Basic trade and economic theory teaches that in a world of reasonably open markets, countries should and will concentrate production in areas of comparative advantage and that, as resources are allocated by each to their most productive uses, global economic welfare will improve. If the economy of a particular country is best adapted to production of agricultural products, its citizens collectively will be better off producing agricultural products while importing medicines from countries better adapted to producing pharmaceuticals. If the international trading system functions as expected, the production of medicines might ultimately be concentrated in efficient large-scale factories (with lower average costs) located in a relatively few countries that export to the global consumer.

40. Ibid., for example, p. 35.

41. See, for example, Report of the WHO Regional Director, *Local Production of Essential Medicines, Including Antiretrovirals: Issues, Challenges and Perspectives in the African Region*, AFR/RC55/10, 17 June 2005, adopted by the Regional Committee, 55th Meeting of the WHO Regional Committee for Africa, 22–26, August 2005, AFR/RC55/20.

42. See UNCTAD's Work in the Area of Technology Transfer and Intellectual Property Rights, *Report to the WTO TRIPS Council 2007* and Frank Schmiedchen, German Ministry of Economic Cooperation and Development, 'Local production of pharmaceuticals', PowerPoint presentation, Addis Ababa, 22 March 2007.

43. Background for this discussion on mechanisms to improve local production and distribution of pharmaceuticals was developed in the course of implementing a project on transfer of technology in the pharmaceutical sector in Latin America, funded by the US Agency for International Development, which involved extensive interviewing of industry participants, researchers, government regulators and policy makers, and further involved tours of a number of pharmaceutical production facilities. References to sources of information are included in a study based on this project that is not yet public.

44. See, for example, 'WHO basic training modules on GMP', http://www.healthtech.who. int/pq/trainingresources/pq-pres/gmptrainingGMPBasicTraining.htm, last accessed 19 March 2009.

45. The WHO is presently undertaking a substantial amount of work in the revision of GMP standards for the production of APIs. See, for example, 42nd Expert Committee on Specification for Pharmaceutical Preparations, Proposal for revision, 'WHO Good Manufacturing Practices (GMP) for active pharmaceutical ingredients (APIs)', Working Document QAS/07.239, September 2007.

46. Pre-qualification Program, 'Priority essential medicines, a United Nations programme managed by WHO', available at http://www.who.int/prequal/default.htm, last accessed 19 March 2009.

47. 'New drugs' is used here to refer to new chemical entities or biologicals that are different from pharmaceutical products previously approved by relevant regulatory authorities.

48. In the API sector some multinational originators contract for the manufacture of supplies from developing countries such as China and India.

49. That 'net' income figure would naturally exclude expenses related to sales and marketing in the developing country(s) territory (since those expenses would not be incurred), it might include only a fraction of the administrative and marketing costs associated with general overhead, sales and marketing outside those developing countries, and it might reflect only such portion of R&D costs that might reasonably be allocated to the geographic territory covered by the license. In order to maintain the approximately net-neutral character of the royalty arrangement, sales by developing country producers would need to be restricted to developing country markets, perhaps on a regional basis (in order to allow production at efficient scale).

50. Voluntary licensing requires production at sufficient scale to justify investment by licensees. In many cases licensing terms that permit distribution on a regional or similar scale would be required.
51. For example, a recently introduced vaccine for cervical cancer marketed by GlaxoSmithKline is based on research conducted for the US NIH.
52. Texts of these instruments are available at http://www.wto.org, last accessed 19 March 2009.
53. In 2007, the governments of Brazil and Thailand have taken advantage of the flexibility provided by the TRIPS Agreement to issue non-voluntary licenses with respect to important treatments for HIV/AIDS and coronary disease, two of the leading causes of morbidity and mortality in developing countries. In each case the initial grant of a license was undertaken to permit importation of generic versions of otherwise patented drugs. In each case the government indicated its longer term intention to manufacture the drugs.
54. The procurement rules of the Global Fund authorize countries to request funding for legal support in making use of TRIPS Agreement flexibilities.
55. WHO (2001), *How to Develop and Implement a National Drug Policy*, 2nd edn, World Health Organization, Geneva; WHO (2000), *WHO Medicines Strategy. Framework for Action in Essential Drugs and Medicines Policy 2002–2003*, World Health Organization, Geneva.

6. The use of medicines: education, information and persuasion

POLICIES ON THE USE OF MEDICINES

In Chapter 4 the purpose of public policy in the field of medicines was defined; it was to ensure that effective and safe medicines of good quality were accessible and affordable to the entire population and that they were rationally used. The latter part of that definition carries public policy beyond technical involvement with medicinal products themselves and into the area of behavior. In Chapter 9 we confront the topic of over-medication, a practice that can be detrimental to public health, but also wasteful in direct economic terms. Ensuring rational use is, however, more than a question of discouraging such incorrect use. It should also involve a positive effort to identify and promote those uses of medicines that will provide the greatest benefit coupled with the least risk. That will mean dealing with the public, and also with the health professionals concerned and those who influence all these parties. Establishing and maintaining public policy involves much more than creating or enforcing rules. Successful policy must also be based on the promotion and maintenance of wide understanding and support for the thinking that underlies that policy.

Education, information and persuasion are complementary processes to this end, but they are often confused – sometimes deliberately so. In particular, some questionable practices in commercial advertising and promotion may be claimed by their proponents to represent useful forms of information and even of education. One must make a distinction between these elements. In essence, one might say, *education* is intended to transmit a sound way of thinking, *information* is a process of transmitting facts, and *persuasion* represents an attempt to transmit a conviction.

EDUCATION

In most of the world's countries government has played a major role in enabling and financing the development of professional education, but has been reticent (often commendably so) to interfere with the style and content of teaching. In these latter matters universities and colleges have traditionally enjoyed much independence, seeking the necessary advice and support from their own advisory councils or from organizations representing the professions rather than from government. This has sometimes led to a relatively conservative approach and some slowness in adapting to social change. That has certainly been the case in both medicine and pharmacy where teaching about medicines is concerned.

The Physician

Basic education

Until quite late in the twentieth century, a medical student in most centers in Europe and North America acquired his or her knowledge of medicines and their uses in a curiously impractical manner that in essence had not changed for a hundred years or more. Basic teaching in pharmacology, built around animal models, was taught in the lecture theatre and laboratory during the early pre-clinical years before the student had been confronted with patients.[1] Later, during the years of clinical teaching, the educational emphasis was on diagnosis; a basic understanding of medicines was assumed, and teaching as to their use was sometimes little more than an appendix to a lecture, with some remarks on dosage. Such teaching may have been adequate when the range of medicines available was still no greater than was the case until the time of the Second World War, when the patient was still seen by many as the mere passive recipient of treatment who could generally be relied upon to react to it in a predestined manner, and in an era when the risks of adverse reactions and interactions were still hardly recognized. These things began to change with the pharmacological revolution that grew up in mid-century with the arrival of penicillin and the antihistamines.

Medical curricula were here and there experimentally reformed to confront the student with real patients from an early phase of teaching, and the concept of 'rational use of drugs' came to the fore. The ancient dictum that a good physician will treat the patient and not the disease was given new validity. Lewis J. Sherman in the USA pointed out in 1959 that 'patients are not treated in a vacuum and that they respond to a variety of subtle forces around them in addition to the specific therapeutic agent under investigation'.[2] But at the same time, with the growth of the new National Health Services and government-sponsored insurance systems, it became obvious that a distinct policy was needed if the community were to benefit properly from the new era.[3] The new medicines somehow had to be financed to a large extent from the public purse, often at rapidly increasing cost, meaning that there would be a need to prescribe parsimoniously. Above all, the realization dawned in some quarters that the physician who had been trained in the traditional manner was not well equipped to deal with the growing complexities of drug therapy, or to face the onslaught of aggressive pharmaceutical selling.

The need to develop what was now being called 'clinical pharmacology' came to the fore, and in 1969 the WHO convened a study group to demarcate the scope of this relatively new discipline.[4] Progress was nevertheless irregular. In Britain a small group of pioneers brought about change relatively soon; by 1989 as many as 21 teachers of clinical pharmacology at British universities were available to argue before a Royal Commission on the National Health Service that the new science had a series of interlinked tasks to perform for the benefit of the public, and they defined them in the light of their own experience:

1. Acute care of patients with general medical problems.
2. Provision of specialist advice on drug therapy, and drug-associated problems: this would include patients with adverse drug reactions, patients with inadequate responses to therapy, and patients requiring careful pharmacological control for prolonged periods of time (for example, patients on long-term treatment with anticonvulsants, anticoagulants, hypotensive drugs or anti-Parkinsonian agents).
3. Care of patients suffering from poisoning with drugs or other chemicals (whether accidental or deliberate).
4. The establishment and supervision of drug prescribing systems and prescribing policies within district hospitals, and amongst general practitioners.
5. Monitoring of drug costs with the hospital and the local general practitioner community.
6. Responsibility for postgraduate education in clinical pharmacology and therapeutics of medical staff in the district and particularly of general practitioners. This should also include monitoring of the activities of pharmaceutical firms' representatives.[5]

In retrospect one might disagree with some of the priorities presented in 1989, but this broad definition of what a specialty of this type could contribute to health care remains essentially valid. In that same year Ingenito et al.[6] in the United States were similarly urging greater progress in basic and applied training in clinical pharmacology. Under the influence of such authoritative appeals, views on medical education began to change. But they did not change very fast, and many observers have remained frankly critical of the lack of adequate reform.[7] Nearly 20 years later in 2008,

Richir et al., who had over the years implemented ambitious teaching programs in the Netherlands on the subject of clinical pharmacology for medical and pharmacy students, noted the serious lack of similar developments elsewhere.[8] Governments for their part have over the years often examined various segments of the problem – heavy drug expenditure, occurrence of side effects, costly drug promotion and suchlike – without as a rule obtaining a broad understanding of what has been wrong or developing a comprehensive approach to bring about improvement in prescribing practices.

The clinical pharmacologist and the clinical pharmacist

The increasing realization that the various tasks to be performed in the name of 'clinical pharmacology' were all essential to public health did not everywhere mean that this was widely viewed as a discipline having a need for its own specialized practitioners. Desmond Laurence in London, who produced the first edition of his textbook *Clinical Pharmacology* in 1960, was one of the first to be appointed to a full-time Chair of Clinical Pharmacology and Therapeutics. Pioneers in a number of other countries seeded the discipline there, but its further development as a distinct branch of the medical profession was irregular. One reason, undoubtedly, was the resistance offered by existing medical specialists. Internists in particular appear to have regarded the clinical pharmacologist as poaching on their preserves, but many other physicians seemed reluctant to accept what they saw as the prospect of a clinical pharmacologist constantly looking over their shoulder or checking their prescribing. Such a situation was not unprecedented in medicine. In much of the world radiology was long refused specialist status, the argument being that any physician worth his or her salt should be capable of reading an X-ray without specialized assistance.

In the case of clinical pharmacology, however, a second complicating factor was involved. Within the profession of pharmacy, where the loss of its traditional role in formulating and compounding medicines was felt so acutely, the concept arose of the 'bedside pharmacist' or 'clinical pharmacist' – a specialized pharmacist who could assist the physician in the choice and use of medicines and in monitoring the outcome of treatment.[9] The clinical pharmacist was unavoidably a competitor of the medically trained clinical pharmacologist. Whether either of the two specialists developed in a particular academic or hospital environment was very much dependent on the presence of a pioneer who could attract support, but who could also succeed in providing useful service and was not merely regarded as an intruder. What is striking is that professional clinical pharmacology and professional clinical pharmacy rarely developed harmoniously together. In a given academic center one or the other was likely to win the day, eclipsing the other. In the United States clinical pharmacy has become particularly prominent.

The problems in the growth of clinical pharmacology as a profession were compounded by cost factors in an era of rising prices. As the WHO put it in 2005:

> As a new discipline clinical pharmacology has had to fight for recognition, both in medical schools but also in the wider world of health care delivery. . . [T]he demand for a new lecturer in molecular biology in a medical school, a new cardiologist in a teaching hospital or a further administrator in a health service commonly takes precedence over creating a position for a clinical pharmacologist.[10]

The pharmacist

Pharmacy enjoys a curious history. A learned profession that for many centuries centered on the compounding of medicines for the individual patient lost this task almost entirely within a few decades as mass-produced products from the pharmaceutical industry took over. The dispensing pharmacist still had a formal duty to check the clarity and apparent correctness of a prescription, to take the right product from the shelf and to answer any questions that a customer might raise, but the essence of the old dispensary dating from the days of the apothecary's laboratory had vanished. While many pharmacists, following their lengthy scientific training, settled down to a (profitable) role as retail sellers of packaged drugs, others in the profession looked for new directions that pharmacy might usefully take. Technical and investigational work within the new industry offered employment to relatively few, and the scientific civil service with its regulators and inspectorates even fewer. The monitoring of adverse effects and interactions seemed to offer an appealing challenge, but it soon became largely the province of medical prescribers.

Two directions soon evolved: the clinical pharmacist, considered above, might develop a role in supporting the physician or sharing his or her work in patient care, especially in a hospital environment. The '*community (retail) pharmacist*', for his or her part, could aspire to become a trusted counselor and provider of information to the patient on all matters involving the use of medicines. This latter role is still developing, but it bears promise.[11] The heavily burdened general medical practitioner may find too little time to discuss extensively with the patient the correct way in which a medicine should be used, the adverse effects that may occur and whatever precautions need to be respected in taking it. If the community pharmacist can assume rather more of that role it will be to the benefit of many a patient. An individual may be more hesitant to seek advice when standing before a sales counter than when seated in the privacy of the doctor's office, but in some countries pharmacies have begun to provide dispensing cubicles, and even consulting rooms where privacy is assured. What remains to be achieved is the development of a sufficient degree of public trust in the retail pharmacist as a professional, commensurate with that which his or her predecessors enjoyed in the age of compounding.

The public

The much-cited Alma Ata declaration of 1978, essentially a world health charter, stated that 'people have the right and duty to participate individually and collectively in the planning and implementation of their health care'.[12] Since then, the WHO has consistently stressed the fact that public information and education on drug use are key elements in national drug policy,[13] and independent foundations have propagated the same view.[14] Yet, as the US-based foundation Management Sciences for Health noted 20 years later in a review of the topic: 'despite the progress in some countries, drug use education for the public is seldom allocated the necessary human and financial resources. It is frequently treated as a marginal activity or one to be tackled only when the other elements of drug policy are in place.'[15]

Quite apart from a lack of understanding of some of the positive aspects of medicines, one commonly encounters frank and even dangerous misunderstandings, such as the notion that two drugs are better than one, that two doses are more effective than one, and that traditional medicines are always safe and can be used alongside prescribed drugs without problems. Conversely, one encounters patients who are so hesitant to take any medicines that they leave their prescriptions unfilled.

In a far-sighted paper published as long ago as 1978, Anne Somers of Rutgers Medical School defined the need to set priorities in educating the public about health.[16] As examples of what could be achieved she pointed to the results of the Stanford Heart Disease Prevention Program and the anti-smoking effort sponsored by the American Heart Association and the American Cancer Society. Given the successes achieved by limited public health education programs in a number of specific fields, she found it deplorable that health education was 'so neglected in national health policy and in the allocation of national health resources'. In her view, the US Congress tended to respond to particular interests rather than the national interest, adding: 'There is no effective constituency for health education or health promotion.' Thirty years later, and viewed across the world, that is still very largely the case despite valiant efforts by the WHO and others,[17] often with specific emphasis on rational use of drugs by the public.[18] Nationally sponsored public education programs, where they exist at all, tend to concentrate on fields in which crises have already erupted, as in the case of traffic accidents and heavy smoking. By setting priorities in lifestyle teaching, and backing these with other measures, as Somers argued, society could well achieve much more in terms of healthy living, longer life and reduced financial expenditure. Given what is already known regarding such matters as over-medication and inappropriate use of medicines and their adverse influence on health, a great deal could be achieved by well-directed efforts to rally public interest and support for an effort to use drugs more effectively and more safely.

The course of public policy

Although less has been achieved than might have been hoped for when Anne Somers wrote her paper in 1978, there are at least signs that educational policy in health matters is now being more broadly conceived, with many voluntary initiatives and a measure of official involvement in various aspects of training both of professionals and the public at large. The WHO has produced valuable material on what can be achieved through sound professional education in rational drug use, on the one hand, and properly directed health promotion, on the other.

In June 2008 Britain's Secretary of State for Health announced the creation of Medical Education England (MEE),[19] one of the recommendations of a review of the National Health Service. MEE would be an 'independent advisory arms length non-departmental body' working to improve both basic and postgraduate medical training.[20] Details have yet to be developed, and there is already concern that this body will have no financial means to influence the educational process. But, provided that one of its objectives is to ensure well-directed physician training with respect to drugs, both at the undergraduate and postgraduate levels, it could represent an important step forward. On the other hand, the voluminous 2005 report of Britain's House of Commons Select Committee on Health, in dealing with pharmaceuticals, provided little help on such training matters. While noting extensively the extent to which the pharmaceutical industry now financed postgraduate medical education, it was almost entirely silent on the possibility of providing an adequate counterweight in the form of objective teaching.[21]

In the United States, the American Board of Clinical Pharmacology today oversees the accreditation of training programs in clinical and applied pharmacology and conducts examinations, ensuring a continuity of standards in these specialties.[22] Unfortunately, most medical schools still lack a formal course in clinical pharmacology, and physicians, pharmacists and other scientists in training may not have access to formal teaching of this subject. The clinical center of the NIH does, however, provide some training on the subject to assist candidates to prepare for the

Board's examinations.[23] This is encouraging, but a broader education for physicians in rational prescribing is still largely lacking.

As to the rest of the world, however, much as one may regret the wasteful competition between clinical pharmacology and clinical pharmacy in a range of developed countries, it has at least ensured that in one way or another the proper use of medicines is becoming a recognized and respected field of study and specialization. Sporadic but encouraging efforts have also been made in numerous situations to improve professional insights into the principles of good prescribing. In much of the developing world simple prescribers' handbooks,[24] backed by follow-up training courses, provide valuable teaching and support to physicians, as well as to medical assistants, nurses and dispensers who in that environment are still frequently expected to play the doctor's role.

There are similarly good though sporadic examples of official efforts to instruct the public on these matters. In France, for example, simple books have been published and distributed to schools, teaching children to understand both the role and the risk of medicines. Illustrated posters on the safe use of drugs today enliven the walls of many a rural clinic from Tanzania to East Timor.[25] In Canada one sees that, in the teaching of public health, increasing attention is being paid to the issue of what is called 'health dissemination to the public' so that lay concepts of healthy living – including rational use of drugs – become less dependent on notions spread by the mass media.[26] In the United States, the National Council on Patient Information and Education actively develops posters, leaflets, radio spots, information folders and activity sheets.

The results of such efforts are not always measurable, but where there has been due enquiry, one finds that they are effective. The tools to bring about improvement are largely there, but they have been used in a piecemeal manner. What is still lacking is a consistent overall effort on the part of major governments to ensure that medicines achieve their full potential to the benefit of all.

INFORMATION

Data Sheets

The creation of drug regulatory systems for the approval of new products and the official assessment of older ones (see Chapter 4) brought with it a procedure for evaluation of a 'data sheet'. Whatever the title accorded to it in various legal systems, this was essentially a product's passport. It meant that the product had not merely been approved for sale after examination of all the evidence, but had been accepted subject to some specific understandings regarding its properties (both desirable and undesirable), the indications for which it was to be used and the manner of use. The approved data sheet was, from that moment, the golden standard by which all promotion, documents and statements would be assessed. The packaging text and package insert might be less extensive, but they would be required to conform to the text of the data sheet. Advertisements might be couched in more appealing terms, but they would essentially have to deliver the same message. Only if new evidence were to emerge and be approved by the authorities would any change to the data sheet be approved.

The data sheet has not always been respected, and as a technical document it is not always easy to read. Yet it remains an essential and eminently sensible instrument of policy and regulation. The fact that the data sheets for many drugs are today made available to the health professions in the form of printed or electronic compendia[27] means that they are usually available on the physician's desk or screen to be consulted in case of need.

Professional Journals

It has been estimated that there are some 7,000 medical journals in the world, some emanating from professional associations, but the vast majority issued by independent publishers. They are the channel through which the bulk of research papers appear, as well as comprehensive reviews of particular topics and authoritative editorials. In principle, therefore, one might expect the medical journals to provide the physician from week to week with an ongoing flow of information and comment on medicines on which he or she might base prescribing practice.

To some extent this is the case, but one has to bear a number of provisos in mind. First, the number of truly authoritative and impartial journals providing the entire medical profession in the country of their publication with peer-reviewed studies and broad reviews is very small. France has its *Press Medicale,* Britain both The *Lancet* and the *British Medical Journal,* and there are similar situations in much of Western Europe. Canada, Australia and the United States. There is, however, nothing comparable in most countries of Asia, Latin America or the developing world. Second, current studies of drugs are scattered over many hundreds of medical journals, many difficult to access and some of dubious repute carrying sponsored papers that have not been objectively scrutinized. The practicing physician without access to a national peer review journal is therefore hardly capable, alongside his or her daily work, of maintaining contact with more than a small fraction of what is happening in the world of medicines. Finally, it is regrettable that even some journals of established repute have become so dependent on income from the pharmaceutical sector that this has jeopardized their editorial independence and balance. Very largely this is a question of their dependence upon drug advertising.[28] To quote some of the evidence adduced by Lexchin and Light:

> Companies may refuse to advertise in journals that publish articles that are critical of the drugs industry. In 1992, the *Annals of Internal Medicine* published an article that critically examined the scientific accuracy of advertisements for drugs in 10 leading medical journals. Reviewers (doctors and pharmacists) judged that 34% should have been revised before publication, and 28% should not have been published. After publication of this article, the decrease in drug advertisements in the *Annals* was greater than in four leading general medical journals. The journal lost an estimated $1–1.5 million in advertising revenue by publishing the study. The editor said, 'The episode revealed the true colours of the pharmaceutical industry, which was willing to flex its considerable muscles when it felt its interests were threatened.' The potential effects of articles on advertising revenue may consciously or subconsciously affect editors' decisions about publication or may influence which authors are asked to contribute.[29]

It has also been authoritatively argued that too great a part of the content of major journals consists of reports on drug studies that have been selectively designed and edited to produce the results desired by the sponsor. Acceptance for publication of a sponsored study can produce very substantial income in the form of paid reprints.[30] Many journals are also willing to publish paid supplements covering industry-sponsored symposia. The scientific content of these supplements is commonly of a lower standard than that of the main journal.[31] Conversely, an industrial sponsor is generally in a position to ensure that a study resulting in negative or problematical findings does not reach the journals. All these factors can result in an imbalance in journal content where medicines are concerned.

Public Information

Public education and public information are a continuum. The conclusions regarding education earlier in this chapter are also relevant here. However, irrespective of the means by which information on medicines has traditionally been directed to the public, any examination of the scene as it is now developing must center on the Internet. Providing as it does both information and persuasion, not always clearly distinguished from one another, the Internet – with its ready accessibility to the bulk of the public and its input from multiple sources – has become the dominant influence in many fields. Where medicines are concerned, it is particularly likely to be consulted by the individual who has a very personal concern in an issue of treatment, and is looking for sound information and advice. It can prove difficult (or impossible) to assess the reliability of the various sources offering such help, or to choose between the conflicting viewpoints offered:

> In a survey conducted with the assistance of graduate students in 2008, an Internet search was conducted to seek advice on the treatment of arteriosclerosis (a number of synonyms were also used), limiting the query to English language material from a recent period. A total of 68 items were identified as being likely to be found in a layman's search of the subject. Of these, 6 were firmly identified by name as emanating from academic or other expert sources which could be regarded as having special experience in the field. Three more originated with official information sources. A further 17 were classified as originating from sources which by claim or implication possessed a measure of expertise but could not be recognized by the group as authoritative; the information provided was in general subjective and poorly founded, and some of the data were mutually contradictory. Four further sources, as adjudged by their content, clearly emanated from the pharmaceutical trade or industry without acknowledging this fact; one of these referred in extremely positive terms to a 'promising' therapeutic development that (in the light of current literature) could only be considered speculative. Seven were provided by sources, commercial or otherwise, based in traditional medicine. Two websites were described as designed to provide drug information to practicing physicians, but were naturally accessible to any viewer. The remaining 29 items were in the nature of personal 'blogs', generally expressing personal opinions or experiences or making apparently unfounded assertions.[32]

No two Internet searches on such a topic are likely to provide quite the same result.

Public Policy on Drug Information

In developing a sound public policy on drug information, it is necessary for both professionals and the public to have access to at least one source of information, accessible both in print and electronically, that is universally acknowledged as being independent and as objective as is possible. Prof. Joe Collier, recalling after many years his initiation in 1969 as a writer for the *Drugs and Therapeutics Bulletin*, has sought to explain what this can mean:

> I was to scrutinise all the relevant published data, read and note all of the comments made by article reviewers, and use all this information to prepare the article for publication, ensuring clarity, reliability, and impartiality. The published article must reflect the scientific knowledge available and distinguish what was known about the product from what was derived from conjecture, bias, or the uncritical position of the establishment. Moreover, there would be no place for my own (preconceived) biases. Readers were to

be given information they could trust and be confident that the advice given had no hidden agenda no ulterior motive. Four decades on, and I am still discovering the full implications of these ideals . . . What has emerged over the years is that my views have needed to be much more than independent. To be of real value, they have needed to be delivered in a way that the message was clear, pertinent, honest, and unambiguous. Advice that can be misinterpreted or leaves room for misunderstanding is often unusable and may be dangerous.[33]

As regards the Internet, public policy faces a dilemma. The material flows freely across borders, so that even where national provisions on the acceptability of content are in force they are unlikely to be of much significance. There is firm resolve in most countries to avoid political censorship of the Internet, yet on some fronts (for example, where the medium becomes a means for disseminating instructions for making bombs), it is widely considered that measures are needed to avoid its misuse. For such purposes, various countries and states have imposed duties, backed by sanctions, on Internet service providers.

The field of drug information does not lend itself to such an approach. The viewer may be misled by inadmissible commercial promotion, but is at least as likely to be confused by the proliferation of conflicting views, some advanced by experts and others merely reflecting bias or incompetence. The most promising approach for public policy is likely to be the provision of recognition and support to the development and maintenance of well-recognized and impartial sources – in this case, websites of impeccable and declared origin which reflect an authoritative consensus. Insofar as commercial promotion is concerned, the same corrective mechanisms will be available as in the case of other media, with official measures complementing the operation of voluntary codes of advertising practice maintained both by the pharmaceutical industry[34] and by Internet service providers themselves.[35] Without endorsing a particular information provider, a few major Internet websites are emerging as candidates as authoritative and unbiased sources for information concerning medicinal treatment.

In developing policies, one also must distinguish between complementary and alternative medicine offerings that may represent traditional treatments used effectively for many years, on the one hand, and medical 'quackery' that also has been around in one form or another since the beginning of time, on the other. Assisting Internet users to distinguish the baby from the bath water represents a challenge. As noted above, more attention is needed from the policy community in regard to developing standards and/or certifications that Internet users can rely upon when they visit medicines-related websites. Internet users may still be able to find quackery, but at least they may do so knowingly. Those seeking more authoritative information should be able to identify trustworthy sources with confidence.

As for many other fields as well, the Internet presents both opportunity and challenge. The medium has almost unlimited potential for providing useful information instantaneously and at very low cost, which is inherently beneficial. At the same time, there is tremendous opportunity for transmitting and receiving 'bad' or incomplete information. At all events, the Internet is not going away. Its ever-increasing role as an information source regarding medicines must be accounted for in the development of policy.

PERSUASION

Commercial Promotion to the Professions

As a matter of business economics, it is generally accepted that commercial advertising has been an important instrument in the development of a thriving economy. It creates interest in new and improved products leading to their more rapid acceptance, thereby providing a stimulus to further R&D. At times that has been the case in pharmaceuticals, just as in other fields. When Banting and Best discovered the possibility of treating diabetes with insulin in 1921, the medical profession was largely taught how to use it by traveling representatives of the companies that in their laboratories had turned it into a dependable and standardized product.[36] In the mid 1920s the average traveling representative was an academic who had been trained to play a specialized teaching role. In later years there was, however, a distinct change of emphasis. With the growth of massive corporate competition in the pharmaceutical field, aggressive selling by commercially trained representatives became the order of the day. Today, as every pharmaceutical company well knows, a drug stands and falls with the manner in which it is promoted, especially to prescribers. A product that is more effective, safer or more convenient in use than others will certainly have a somewhat greater potential for success in the field, but unless it is promoted astutely it may well lose out to a somewhat inferior competitor. There is, therefore, a turning point at which the effects of advertising count for more, in terms of financial return, than the actual merits of the product.

To take only a single example, sufficiently old for the facts to be viewed accurately in retrospect: In May 1981 a prominent three-page color advertisement appeared in medical journals in Britain, dominated by a picture of a sky clearing from mist to bright blue and the heading 'Why is there a wind of change in the treatment of arthritis?'[37] The drug was Opren® (benoxaprofen), claimed to have 'more fundamental' effects on the arthritic process as well as being better tolerated and more potent than existing compounds. Though rejected in some other countries where these claims were not regarded as proven, Opren® was marketed in the United Kingdom and rapidly achieved a substantial sale because of the promises made for it. It was withdrawn in 1982 because of severe adverse effects including sometimes fatal hepatic complications in the elderly. The company was subsequently criticized on various grounds including its intensive marketing campaign.[38]

It seems clear in the light of this and similar cases that heavy promotion – especially in the early phases of introduction of a medicine, and before there is an opportunity to recognize whatever benefits or drawbacks it may possess in practice as compared with existing products – may lead to much unnecessary injury. It is at the very least likely to bring about a substantial shift in prescribing patterns, whether medically justified or not, and to lay a considerable added burden on the public purse.

A more general problem with the emphatic advertising of new medicines to health professionals is the facile assumption that they will, because of their training and experience, be capable of distinguishing wheat from chaff and will, therefore, have little need of protection from misleading advertising claims. Given the complexity of modern pharmacology, this is hardly the case. A physician seeking to ascertain the credibility of the statements and suggestions advanced in advertising would need complete access to the (often unpublished) reports and references on which they are based, and sufficient insight into the methodology employed to form a view on the conclusions advanced. Even for a clinical pharmacologist this would be a daunting task. For a general physician it is an impossible one.

The most directly relevant standards set by the community for a drug advertisement are, as noted earlier in this chapter, those of the data sheet approved at the time of licensing. Advertising must according to the law be *compatible* with this approved text. This standard is helpful, but not simple to apply in practice, since there is no requirement that the promotional text be *identical* to that of the data sheet, though many national laws require that any printed advertisement be accompanied by a full copy of the data sheet text. The latter is, however, likely to be printed on a separate page, all too often compressed into inhospitable 8-point type, and does not make easy reading. It is clearly the main promotional text – usually attractively presented and illustrated and framed in simple and seductive terms – that is intended to influence the reader and does so. It is likely to involve a sufficient measure of poetic license and advertising hyperbole to suggest that the product concerned is considerably more virtuous and novel than is actually the case.[39]

At least as helpful as the individual data sheet in practice in assessing the acceptability of a text advertisement (and much more helpful in ensuring that such texts conform) is the existence of a voluntary code of advertising practice adopted by the national organization of pharmaceutical manufacturers. Many such codes exist and some are highly detailed.[40] As noted above in connection with the advertising of products for self-medication, a code of this type can be effective because a manufacturer monitors the advertising practice of its competitors and is likely to seize upon any contravention of agreed standards as representing unfair competition. In some instances, the association requires prior approval of an advertisement by a committee of advisors, and in most systems there is provision for the examination of complaints and the imposition of sanctions of varying degree. The Australian monitoring system, maintained by the industry association, issues detailed quarterly reports on complaints that have been investigated under its auspices, and it is instructive to consider its mode of operation in some detail, as typified by the case summarized in Box 6.1. In the right circumstances, an industrial system to maintain acceptable advertising standards may be more effective than a national authority, since official mechanisms tend to move slowly and constitutional rules on freedom of speech may inhibit advance censorship of materials.

Third, there are the existing legal and regulatory standards for drug promotion, such as those established in 1992 by the European Community[41] and subsequently incorporated into municipal law in the member states. The extent to which these are enforced by national authorities varies, but it is again striking that the voluntary codes of the manufacturers' associations concerned seek to follow the Community guidelines and provide their own mechanisms to ensure adherence.

While these three mechanisms do a great deal to keep text and visual advertising within reasonable limits, serious problems arise in ensuring that other forms of promotion are in conformity. The metamorphosis of the industry representative in the course of a few decades from a traveling purveyor of documented information into a high-pressure salesperson (often termed a 'detailer' or even 'drug consultant') has been sketched above. It is not uncommon today in the United States for the detailer to be a young woman with background that may include a position on the cheerleading squad for the university football team. The detailer, visiting all the physicians in his or her area of work to promote a particular manufacturer's products, is regarded by many in the industry as the most potent promotional weapon of all. The detailer may build up a relationship of trust with his or her medical clients, and exercise a considerable persuasive

BOX 6.1   MONITORING OF ADVERTISING
THROUGH A VOLUNTARY CODE:
AN AUSTRALIAN CASE

In 2006 Pfizer Australia brought a complaint against the AstraZeneca company relating to its promotion for the lipid-lowering drug Crestor® (rosuvastatin calcium). It was alleged that certain promotional items overstated the benefits of Crestor and created a false and misleading impression of its safety profile, ease of use and appropriate starting doses. The Medicines Australia Monitoring Committee decided unanimously that the claim that Crestor was the most effective statin at lowering LDL-Cholesterol was in breach of the relevant sections of the Advertising Code as it did not adequately reflect the body of evidence and made a comparison with other statins that could not be substantiated. The Committee noted that the front page of the promotional item emphasized a starting dose of 10 mg while the full text that followed listed both 5 mg and 10 mg starting doses. The officially approved data sheet recommended either a 5 mg or 10 mg starting dose. Some members of the Committee proffered the view that it was not in the best interests of the industry or quality use of medicines to promote the highest starting dose for a medicine and not make balanced reference to both the 5 mg and 10 mg starting doses. By a majority the Committee found a breach of the Code as prescribers could be misled, believing that 10 mg was the most appropriate starting dose. Members of the Committee were of the view that although the promotional item referred to 'once daily, any time of the day and with or without food' the term 'simple to initiate' was understating all of the officially recognized contraindications and precautions for the initiation and continuation of therapy with Crestor. The Committee noted that doses above 20 mg daily required specialist supervision. By a majority the Committee found a further breach of the Code because doctors could be misled by the statement that treatment with Crestor was simple. The Committee considered the claim that Crestor had a favorable risk-benefit profile which appeared at a trade display in 2006. Although acknowledging that a medicine must have an acceptable risk/benefit profile in order to be registered for use in Australia, members were of the view that the juxtaposition of the statement with the graphs was an implied comparison between Crestor and other statins (suggesting that Crestor's risk/benefit profile was superior to that of the other statins) that could not be substantiated. The Committee was also of the view that this statement was a hanging comparative. Members commented that the graphs adjacent to the claim were difficult to interpret – there were no error bars or numbers of patients treated to assist in interpretation and evaluation of the claim. Members were also of the view that the referenced source was not easily accessible or critically reviewable by prescribers and the graphs appeared to be selective presentation of evidence. Some members commented that they had concerns over the use of data from several older studies for other statins in the composite graph and it was not clear that the information presented came from several sources.

Having found a number of breaches of the Code, the Committee determined that AstraZeneca should cease distribution and use of the materials found in breach of the Code and that a corrective letter should be sent to all general practitioners in Australia who had been detailed with, or mailed, the promotional material, all doctors enrolled in the Crestor Early Access Program and to all attendees at the 2006 conference at which the trade display appeared. The Committee also determined that a fine of $75,000 should be imposed. An appeal was lodged by AstraZeneca on four counts against the findings of the Code of Conduct Committee. The Appeal Committee upheld the appeal on two of the four counts. It maintained the view that the materials found in breach should be withdrawn and that the requirement for a corrective letter should remain. The Committee agreed that the fine should be reduced to $40,000 in consideration that the appeal had been partly upheld.[a]

In the event, this sanction was apparently insufficient to ensure complete correction of the faults that had been found. In 2008 the system reported on a further complaint raised by Pfizer, alleging that at a post graduate weekend event in November 2007 a trade display banner carrying claims for Crestor previously found to be in breach of the Code was prominently displayed to the 120 health care professionals in attendance. Pfizer considered this to be a significant repeat breach. AstraZeneca denied any deliberate attempt to intentionally mislead health care professionals. An internal investigation concluded that a breakdown in the company's withdrawal procedure for promotional material had resulted in the inadvertent use of the materials previously found in breach of the Code. In a unanimous decision the Committee found that a repeat breach had occurred. A sanction of A$80,000 was imposed. The Committee did not impose a corrective letter itself in consideration of the fact that AstraZeneca had volunteered that it would send a corrective letter to all doctors in attendance at the educational meeting.[b]

Notes:
a. MA (2007), *Medicines Australia Code of Conduct Report: Finalised Complaints July–December 2006*, Medicines Australia, Deakin, ACT, Australia, pp. 48–56.
b. MA (2008), *Code of Conduct Quarterly Report, January–March 2008*, Medicines Australia, Deakin, ACT, Australia, p. 16.

influence on their prescribing. From the point of view of the community, it has proved extraordinarily difficult to ensure that the message conveyed by the detailer is in conformity with the approved claims. Both official regulations and voluntary codes insist that traveling representatives adhere to prescribed standards, but neither mechanism can entirely ensure that this happens. Unapproved indications may be discussed, problems glossed over and reprints of biased material provided. Gifts, lunches and excursions may be offered. There is no doubt that a proportion of practitioners do appreciate this effort-free manner of acquiring information on new developments. It is also clear that some firms and representatives make a genuine effort to portray the facts fairly. From society's point of view, however, the fact that an important channel of drug promotion evades any form of impartial assessment or supervision undermines to a considerable extent the application of a healthy medicines policy at a crucial juncture in its application.

To some extent there has been an attempt, particularly through the operation of industry codes, to impose limits on one other form of promotion having a questionable character. This relates to the provision of gifts, travels and other favors to health professionals, notably prescribers. This type of activity is commonly concentrated on those health professionals who are viewed by industry as opinion leaders capable of exerting influence on their colleagues. A trip to attend an industry-sponsored symposium in Hawaii may represent a tempting benefit to an individual physician, nurturing his relationship with the commercial sponsor of the event, yet the cost involved may be only a percentage point of the advertising budget for a new product with ambitious sales projections that the symposium is intended to serve. There has been increasingly strong criticism of such practices, and in July 2008 drug companies in the United States announced plans for the almost complete cessation of gifts to doctors, ahead of much more radical proposals on the matter which were being considered by the federal authorities.[42] By contrast it would appear that recent voluntary guidelines put forward by drug companies in Europe fall short of any obligation for the industry to ban gifts to health professionals or disclose its funding of medical organizations, educational events and financial arrangements with doctors. A recent survey conducted by Consumers International concluded that none of the major pharmaceutical companies that have made commitments in the United States had clear plans to take similar action in EU markets.[43] This could be an area in which only firm official action will be capable of bringing about significant improvement on a broad front, and it could be that developments are beginning to move in that direction. Measures in preparation by the General Medical Council in Britain are reported to include a procedure under which physicians receiving significant gifts from the pharmaceutical industry may be deprived of their right to practice.[44]

Public policy perspectives
In those Western countries – where the persuasive role of the manufacturer and seller has in many fields played a significant role in economic growth – there has been a marked reluctance to impose any generalized form of authoritative control on advertising and promotion. In some legal systems, as noted above, the national constitution prohibits any advance censorship of advertising materials. The old legal principle 'let the buyer beware' (*caveat emptor*) remains a valid rallying cry addressed to the good sense of the public, but it hardly enables the user to protect himself or herself in an area of technologically advanced products, promoted in a manner that may be both subtle and seductive. Where medicines are concerned, the rule that promotion must be in accordance with the data sheet approved by the authorities at the time of registration provides a valuable standard by which to judge promotion and to apply correctives where necessary. Some more general standards – such as the rule applied in many countries that drugs must not be the subject of promotional sampling – are clearly of value. Beyond that, the community has benefited most markedly from the voluntary advertising codes maintained by industry itself, with one firm essentially policing another. It seems likely that these principles will underlie most public policy with regard to drug promotion in the years to come. However, a caveat is called for. Astute commerce has sometimes outrun ethics by a considerable margin. Just as subliminal advertising in any field was proscribed in much of the world 50 or more years ago, one

must be alert to new promotional developments that call for specific measures before they are capable of upsetting the delicate balance that has been achieved to date.

As noted earlier in this chapter, there is above all a pressing need for the public sector to ensure an effective counterweight to the massive and highly persuasive promotional pressure exerted by the industry and trade. There is no absolute need to put a stop to the latter, for it represents a widely accepted practice and can in some respects play a useful role. The important thing is to correct the serious and indefensible imbalance that exists at present between impartial and highly partial sources of information and advice. For the future, several mechanisms could well provide some degree of correction to this situation.

The first, already touched on, could be the more widespread creation or development of impartial sources of drug information and assessment. In many countries these exist already in the form of modest 'drug bulletins' sponsored variously by independent foundations, health insurance agencies or consumer associations and commonly enjoying some measure of official support or subsidy. Irrespective of whether these are officially sponsored or simply enjoy some form of authoritative recognition or support,[45] they enjoy a great deal of trust and exert a considerable influence. Britain's *Drugs and Therapeutics Bulletin* provides a well-known example observing strict criteria of impartiality,[46] as does America's *Medical Letter*.[47] Both have international influence, with the latter (published in English and French) reaching 200,000 subscribers, many outside the United States and Canada. More than a hundred such bulletins across the world currently work together through the International Society of Drug Bulletins,[48] exchanging information and experience to ensure an optimal dissemination of reliable and unbiased assessments of drug therapy. There is no need for such initiatives to be limited to printed bulletins. Increasingly their material is being made available in other forms, particularly through the Internet.

A second type of initiative that has been developed only sporadically, but has shown great promise, is the appointment of traveling information consultants, visiting physicians in the same manner as do the detailers of the drug companies – but providing impartial information. This approach, pioneered by Avorn at the Massachusetts Institute of Technology in the 1980s, proved as effective as its commercial counterpart in influencing prescribing, but in this case providing objective advice. The effects were measurable in terms of greater economy in prescribing, and therefore attractive to a health insurance or reimbursement authority seeking to counter excessive expenditure.[49] The initiative has been followed up successfully in a number of countries and states. For example, in France the principal health insurance agency (L'Assurance Maladie) now conducts localized academic detailing programs which have achieved considerable success in correcting the prescribing of antibiotics and lipid-lowering drugs.[50] In Australia the government pays for a nationwide program of physician detailing that covers 60 percent of the country's primary care doctors.[51] In the United States similar academic detailing programs are now in operation in Pennsylvania[52] and Oregon.[53]

A third approach, apparently developed most effectively in the Netherlands but not unknown elsewhere, is to assist the practicing physician in handling commercial pressures. One initiative, developed at the University of Groningen, involves inviting detailers from various firms to make presentations to an audience of medical and pharmacy students, and encouraging the latter to respond critically. Teachers would be present in the background and would, after such a commercial presentation, help the students to recognize the sales techniques to which they had been exposed, and to consider whether their response had been adequate. A complementary initiative that has had some success in the same country involves arrangements by which detailers from industry no longer visit the individual physician, but come by appointment to make sales presentations on pre-arranged topics to local groups of physicians and pharmacists. Experience has shown that in this situation the detailers come better prepared to provide well-founded information and to enter into serious discussion.

We do not propose to suppress drug promotion. However, steps can and should be taken to ensure that the audience for such promotion becomes more critical, more aware of the fact that it is often being seduced rather than informed, and better capable of looking elsewhere for truly authoritative advice. Drug promotion will not go away. But faced with a counterbalancing influence it may well become more responsible and more useful. It may be stimulated to develop in a manner that better serves the interests of the community as well as those of the seller.

Direct to Consumer (DTC) Advertising of Prescription Medicines

In most of the industrialized world, the clear regulatory distinction between those drugs that can be sold only on medical prescription and the group available on free sale for self-medication (in the United States referred to as 'over-the-counter' or OTC – see Chapter 4) is carried through into the area of promotion. Commercial advertising for prescription drugs is limited to the professional audience. Only two Western countries – the United States and New Zealand – as of 2009 have permitted the public advertising of prescription items. The view more widely held is that since these medicines can be issued only at the physician's discretion, it is at least unnecessary and at worst undesirable that the public be exposed to commercial promotion for products on which they cannot be expected to form a critical or rational view. DTC advertising of prescription items was emphatically rejected by the European Parliament in October 2002.[54] At the time of this writing, the debate on this topic has been reopened in Canada with an industry-based body challenging the country's prohibition of DTC promotion on grounds that such a prohibition is inappropriate and unconstitutional.[55]

Between the First and the Second World War, many countries enacted measures to prohibit the public advertising of remedies for major illnesses and epidemic diseases. In Britain advertisements for the drug treatment of venereal disease were prohibited in 1917 and for cancer remedies in 1939, while a broadly based Pharmacy and Medicines Act of 1941 prohibited the advertising of any medicine to the public for the treatment of a further range of serious conditions. These specific edicts were, however, no more than symbolic of what was becoming broadly accepted practice in industrialized countries. Drugs intended for use under medical supervision were no longer advertised directly to the public. This principle was for some decades fully accepted by the industry, for example, in its advertising codes: 'Medicines which cannot legally be sold or supplied to the public otherwise than in accordance with a prescription . . . must not be advertised to the general public.'[56] The same principle was incorporated into the WHO's guidelines on *Ethical Criteria for Medicinal Drug Promotion* of 1988.[57]

In the course of time, however, a number of firms aggressively seeking expansion began to view this limitation as frustrating and sought a way to bypass it. Newspaper campaigns designed to alert the public to particular symptoms and disorders, and the need for treatment without any mention of a specific drug, became popular in the United States well before 1990, and soon began to appear elsewhere. The industry also began to reach the public in new ways, particularly by feeding ready-edited texts to medical journalists and issuing 'press releases' on what were claimed to be significant innovations. By 1993, explicit promotion for prescription drugs was being directed prominently to the US public, encumbered only by an FDA requirement that any advertisement must include extensive lists of precautions and adverse effects. That restriction was relaxed in 1997, after which this type of advertising became a dominant feature of the US scene in both print and electronic media.

From the point of view of many major pharmaceutical firms, public promotion of prescription drugs in those few industrialized countries where it is permitted has become a highly attractive practice resulting in a greatly increased turnover. When it is challenged, the industry presents a series of arguments to support the practice, arguing that:

- Prescribers react constructively to the consumer pressure engendered by such advertising by ensuring that they have available the relevant information on a DTC-promoted drug and its indications, and are thus able to take well-informed prescribing decisions.
- The doctor-patient relationship will be improved as a result of increased contact and discussion regarding patient health care.
- Earlier knowledge of treatment possibilities will ease anxiety about disease risk, particularly since those with limited education and severe illness may receive simple accessible information about potential therapy.
- Medicines will be used to treat illness earlier, resulting in better patient outcomes.
- In some cases where professional advice would not otherwise be sought, preliminary awareness and diagnosis by patients will improve therapy by enhancing patient understanding and increasing the likelihood that they will consult professionals. A prohibition on DTC advertising would 'keep patients in the dark'.
- Innovation for new medicines will be brought forward as physicians are encouraged to replace older drugs by newer and better ones.

However, as DTC advertising has become increasingly emphatic, so have the challenges to it.[58] The industry arguments are dismissed as unproven, while critics advance evidence that DTC:

- leads to inappropriate use of medicines where doctors succumb to patient pressure to prescribe a particular medicine;
- undermines the doctor-patient relationship where patients aggressively demand a particular product and may leave the practice or threaten to do so if it is not prescribed;
- results in confused or misinformed consumers because they have too little information about a medical condition, and the information available to them is unbalanced;
- generates consumer anxiety through exaggerated promotion of the risk of disease, which may adversely impact on vulnerable populations, such as the uneducated or those with severe or chronic illness; creates 'disease mongering', where everyday sensations and minor discomforts are cited as evidence that an illness is present and demands treatment;

- leads to wide use of medicines in the community before a population risk profile has been developed;
- promotes a view of medicines as 'life solutions', to the detriment of better alternatives, such as diet and exercise, resulting in increased medicalization of society, with an associated increase in the risk of medical misadventure;
- escalates costs to subsidize medicines and patient visits to doctors, particularly where consumers are 'doctor shopping' in an attempt to find a doctor prepared to prescribe a particular medicine.

The legal situation

As noted above, the situation as of 2009 is that DTC is very prominent in the United States and New Zealand, is explicitly prohibited in the EU and in most other industrialized countries, but is tolerated to some extent in parts of the developing world. From the legal point of view, it has been argued for industry that the First Amendment to the US Constitution[59] prohibits banning this type of promotion.[60] Current FDA rules go no further than to require that such advertising provide a fair balance of information and is couched in consumer-friendly language.[61] Similarly, in New Zealand, it has been argued that Section 14 of the New Zealand Bill of Rights Act of 1990 protects freedom of speech (including commercial speech) in a manner rendering prohibition impossible.[62] The Medicines Act of 1981 and the Medicines Regulations of 1984[63] merely prohibit 'unbalanced' or 'inappropriate' DTC advertising. The situation has been complicated by the agreement of December 2003 between Australia and New Zealand to establish a joint Therapeutic Products Authority and to harmonize their legislation on medicines. However, a draft advertising code drawn up in this connection recognizes that while DTC advertising is permitted in New Zealand, it is not permitted in Australia. In the European Union, the 'Codified Directive' of 2001 states categorically that 'Member States shall prohibit the advertising to the general public of medicinal products which are available on medicinal prescription only.'[64] Despite the firm opposition to DTC advertising expressed in the European Parliament in 2002, industry pressure continues on the European Commission to secure a more liberal regime. The Commission was persuaded that advertising of prescription drugs for certain selected conditions (HIV/AIDS, asthma, diabetes) for a trial period of five years could be acceptable, but it remains doubtful whether the Parliament will be amenable to any such compromise.

Professional and social views

Professional associations, individual health professionals and consumer bodies have been engaged in vigorous debate on the future of DTC advertising, particularly in Europe, Canada (in view of current litigation) and Australia (because of the harmonization of drug law with New Zealand). Views have diverged, as indicated above, but some have made a firm effort to distil lessons from practice to date in the countries where DTC advertising has been permitted. In New Zealand, in 2003, a group of health professionals delivered an extensively documented report to the Ministry of Health supporting the case for a ban on consumer advertising for prescription drugs.[65] The group noted 'significant and growing dissatisfaction' with the existing situation. There was

> clear evidence that DTCA stimulates demand for the advertised brand drugs, many of which offer little benefit and less clear safety profiles over existing products . . . this has deleterious effects on resource allocation within an already stretched health system, unduly influences the prescribing process, and leads to further medicalization of health.

Neither self-regulation nor official control on direct to consumer (DTC) advertising practice had proved effective, and the only sound policy option was, in the authors' view, to prohibit it entirely. It is notable that the report received overwhelming support from professional bodies and consumer associations.

In such a field it is all too easy to use data selectively in order to support a particular point of view, and hard facts regarding the influence of DTC advertising are often lacking. A few authors or groups do appear to have provided well-documented analyses.

Basara in 1996 conducted an interrupted time series analysis and found that use of the migraine drug sumatriptan increased after commencement of a DTC advertising campaign and decreased after the campaign finished.[66] Mansfield has commented on this work that

> Most DTCA is for new drugs. Many new drugs are inferior to older treatments, and over two-thirds are no better but are often more expensive . . . in the likely case that the results of this study can be generalized to most DTC campaigns it is likely that DTCA is sometimes beneficial but more often harmful.[67]

Mintzes et al. in 2002–03[68] performed a comparative cross-sectional study in different countries and concluded that 'more advertising leads to more requests for advertized medicines, and more prescriptions. If DTCA opens a conversation between patients and physicians, that conversation is highly likely to end with a prescription, often despite physician ambivalence about treatment choice.'

't Jong et al. in 2004 carried out a further time series analysis, studying the impact of an industry-promoted disease awareness campaign in the Netherlands that did not actually mention the name of the drug being promoted.[69] Like Basara, these authors found that the use of the advertiser's drug increased after commencement of a campaign (about toe nail fungus infections) and decreased after the campaign finished. They concluded that overall the campaign they studied was harmful:

> The effects on work load in primary care of the lay media marketing medicinal products for cosmetic indications which cannot be treated with over the counter drugs should not be underestimated. Several synchronous campaigns like this would cause a serious adverse impact on general practitioners' workloads and costs. This may affect patients who need care for more serious problems.

DTC advertising – public policy for the future
With marked differences between the various views that are being expressed so strongly, a lack of consistency across the globe as regards policy and law on this matter and a vigorous debate in progress, it is not simple to foresee the early emergence of a consistent global policy on DTC advertising of prescription medicines. In the field of medicines as a whole it is an unfortunate fact that well-defined policies have emerged only after serious accidents dictated the need for them. It is not inconceivable that, in the field of DTC advertising as well, policies will emerge only in the wake of events. Two trends could emerge. One could reflect economic constraints: as health systems and health insurers have become increasingly concerned at the level of health expenditure and, in particular, the sums needed to meet the costs of drug prescribing. That has already led to a series of measures relating to pricing, reimbursement levels and the provision of impartial information to physicians. Bearing in mind the evidence that DTC advertising strongly increases the use of newly introduced products (with which there is still little field experience but which tend to be disproportionately expensive), this could very well lead to insistence by these bodies on limits to public advertising for new drugs. A second trend towards a more restrictive regime could reflect safety concerns, given the high incidence of adverse effects that may result when massive sales of a new product under the influence of DTC advertising precede the emergence of safety information in practice. The events relating to Vioxx® (rofecoxib) are a case in point. By the time the drug was withdrawn in 2004 because of the occurrence of severe and sometimes fatal cardiac complications, it had as a result of DTC advertising acquired a much larger proportion of the market for anti-inflammatory drugs than might have been expected for a new drug with no marked advantages. Dr. David Graham of the FDA estimated that an estimated 88,000–140,000 excess cases of serious coronary

heart disease probably occurred in the United States over the market life of rofecoxib.[70] It is figures such as these, now emerging for a series of drugs that entered the market precipitously with the backing of DTC advertising, that may influence the coming shape of public policy.

NOTES

1. D.A. Flockhart, S. Usdin Yasuda, J.C. Pezzullo and B.C. Knollmann (2002), 'Teaching rational prescribing: a new clinical pharmacology curriculum for medical schools', *Naunyn Schmiedebergs Arch Pharmacol.*, July, 366 (1), 33–43.
2. J. Sherman (1959), 'The significant variables (in) psychotherapeutic research', *Amer. J. Psychiatr.*, 116, 208–14.
3. MPM (1975), 'Report of the Working Party on the Continuing Education of Doctors in Medical Therapeutics', Medico-pharmaceutical Forum, London.
4. World Health Organization (WHO) Study Group (1970), 'Clinical pharmacology scope, organization, training', *World Health Organ Tech Rep Ser*, 446, 5–21.
5. RCNHS (1978), 'Evidence to the Royal Commission on the National Health Service. 2. From the Committee of Professors of Clinical Pharmacology and Therapeutics, Association of Professors of Internal Medicine', *Br J Clin Pharmacol.*, 5 (6).
6. A.J. Ingenito, C.M. Lathers and H.J. Burford (1989), 'Instruction in clinical pharmacology: changes in the wind', *J Clin Pharmacol.*, 29, 7–17.
7. W.H. Han and S.R. Maxwell (2006), 'Are medical students adequately trained to prescribe at the point of graduation? Views of first year foundation doctors', *Scott Med J*, 51 (4), 27–32.
8. M.C. Richir, J. Tichelaar, E.C.T. Geijteman and T.P.G.M. de Vries (2008), 'Teaching clinical pharmacology and therapeutics with an emphasis on the therapeutic reasoning of undergraduate medical students', *Eur J Clin Pharmacol.*, February, 64 (2), 217–24.
9. J.M. Burke, W.A. Miller, A.P. Spencer et al. (2008), 'Clinical pharmacist competences', *Pharmacotherapy*, 28 (6), 806–15.
10. WHO (2005), 'Unfinished business: clinical pharmacology and world health (personal perspectives)', *WHO Drug Inform.*, June, 7 ff.
11. W.R. Doucette, D.H. Kreling, J.C. Schommer et al. (2006), 'Evaluation of community pharmacy service mix: evidence from the 2004 National Pharmacist Workforce Study', *J. Amer. Pharmacists Ass.*, 46 (3), 348–55.
12. WHO/EURO (1978), *The Declaration of Alma Ata: Conclusions of the International Conference on Primary Health Care*, Alma Ata, 6–12 September.
13. WHO/DAP (1994), *Public Education in Rational Drug Use: Report of an Informal Consultation*, Document WHO/DAP/94.1, World Health Organization (Drug Action Programme), Geneva; WHO/DAP (1996), *Rational Drug Use: Consumer Education and Information*, Document WHO/DAP/MAC.8/96.6, World Health Organization (Drug Action Programme), Geneva.
14. IMBRF (1993), 'Improving patient information and education on medicines', International Medical Benefit/Risk Foundation, Geneva.
15. MSH (1997), 'Encouraging appropriate drug use by the public and patients', in *Managing Drug Supply*, 2nd edn, Management Sciences for Health, Boston, MA, pp.497–8.
16. A.R. Somers (1978), 'Priorities in educating the public about health', *Bull NY Acad Med*, 54 (1), 37–41.
17. WHO (2005), *Promoting Health: The Bangkok Health Promotion Charter, as Accepted at the 6th Global Conference on Health Promotion*, Bangkok, August 2005, World Health Organization, Geneva.
18. UWC (1998), 'Promoting rational medicines use in the community', Programme of

a training course organized with the WHO, university and institutional sponsorship, August 2008, University of the Western Cape, Bellville, South Africa.

19. Hansard (2008), 'Alan Johnson: oral answers to Questions in the House of Commons: children, schools and families (NHS Next Stage Review)', *Hansard's Parliamentary Reports (House of Commons)*, 30 June Col. 596.

20. J. Stephenson (2008), 'Medical Education England', BMJ Careers (online), 6 August.

21. House of Commons (2005), *House of Commons: Select Committee on Health*, Fourth Report, HMSO London, April.

22. ABCP (2007), 'The American Board of Clinical Pharmacology' (website, accessed July 2008).

23. NIH (2008), 'Principles of clinical pharmacology', Course Prospectus, National Institutes of Health, Bethesda, MD.

24. Ministry of Health Kenya (2002), *Clinical Guidelines for Diagnosis and Treatment of Common Conditions in Kenya*, Government of Kenya, Ministry of Health, Nairobi, Ministry of Health Malawi (1993), *Malawi Standard Treatment Guidelines*, 2nd edn, Ministry of Health, Lilongwe, Malawi.

25. Management Sciences for Health (1997), pp. 496–512.

26. L. Hoffman-Goetz and S. Dwiggins (1998), 'Teaching public health practitioners about health communication: the MPH curriculum experience', *J Community Health*, 23 (2), 127–35.

27. Good examples include the *Physicians Desk Reference* in the United States, the *Data Sheet Compendium* in the UK and the *Laegemiddelkataloget* in Denmark. In some countries commercial volumes such as the *Dictionnaire Vidal* (France, Russia and elsewhere) have essentially the same content.

28. A. Hussain and R. Smith (2001), 'Declaring financial competing interests: survey of five general medical journals', *BMJ*, 323, 263–4.

29. J. Lexchin and D.W. Light (2006), 'Commercial influence and the content of medical journals', *BMJ*, 332, 1444–7.

30. R. Smith (2005), 'Medical journals are an extension of the marketing arm of pharmaceutical companies', *PLoS Med*, 2 (5), e138.

31. R. Smith (2003), 'Medical journals and pharmaceutical companies: uneasy bedfellows', *BMJ*, 326, 1202–5; M. Cho and L. Bero (1996), 'The quality of drug studies published in symposium proceedings', *Ann Intern Med*, 124, 485–9.

32. M.N.G. Dukes (2008), 'Internettinformasjon: studentenøvelse' (unpublished).

33. J. Collier (2006), 'The price of independence', *BMJ*, 332, 1447–9.

34. CGR (2002), *Guidelines for Advertising and Information Relation to Prescription-only Medicines on the Internet*, Stichting Code Geneesmiddelenreclame (Drug advertising Code Foundation), Gouda, the Netherlands.

35. EFA (2006), *Internet Censorship Laws in Australia*, Electronic Frontiers Australia, North Adelaide, SA, Australia.

36. M. Tausk (1978), *Organon: De geschiedenis van een bijzondere Nederlandse onderneming*, Dekker & Van de Vegt, Nijmegen.

37. Dista Products (1981), Advertisement No. OPR 34/JAN 81, as published in *Update*, 15 May.

38. J.K. Aronson (ed.) (2006), *Meyler's Side Effects of Drugs*, 15th edn, Elsevier, Amsterdam, Boston and Heidelberg, pp. 420–1.

39. Where an advertisement is considered to be inconsistent with the standard set by the data sheet, the authorities will in most countries be able to demand that it cease to appear. At one time the United States FDA was in addition able to require publication of an equally prominent correction. This is no longer the case, but it can require that a manufacturer send a corrective letter to health service providers. See, for example, the corrective letter sent by Janssen Pharmaceutica on 21 July 2004 concerning misstatements on the safety of Risperdal^R (risperidone).

40. PhRMA (2008), *PhRMA Code on Interactions with Healthcare Professionals*, Pharmaceutical Research and Manufacturers of America, Washington, DC; CGR

(2008), *Gedragscode Geneesmiddelenreclame* (Medicine Advertising Code, the Netherlands), Stichting Code Geneemiddelenreclame, Gouda; MA (2007), *Code of Conduct*, 15th edn, Medicines Australia, Deakin, ACT, Australia.

41. EC (1992), *Directive 92/28 of March 31st 1992 on the Advertising of Medicinal Products for Human Use*, European Community, Brussels.
42. PhRMA (2008), *Code on Interactions with Healthcare Professionals* (revised July 2008), Pharmaceutical Research and Manufacturers Association, Washington, DC.
43. CI (2008), *EU Now Trailing US on Irresponsible Drug Promotion*, Consumers International, London.
44. M. Day (2006), 'Doctors who take drug "freebies" risk being struck off', *Daily Telegraph* (London), 8 July.
45. In mid 2006 it was announced that the authorities in Britain proposed as an 'economy measure' to withdraw the subsidy which had made it possible to send the *Drugs and Therapeutic Bulletin* to all health professionals as an objective aid to sound and economical prescribing. At the time, the annual cost of providing the *Bulletin* was less than one-thousandth of the promotional budget of the pharmaceutical industry. Fortunately, a solution was found and the *Bulletin* continued.
46. Collier (2006), 'The price of independence'.
47. 'The Medical Letter – A non-profit organization', http//:www.medicalletter.org.
48. ISDB Information Booklet (2007), 'International Society of Drug Bulletins', http://66.71.191.169/isdbweb/pag/index.php.
49. J. Avorn and S. Soumerai (1983), 'Improving drug-therapy decisions through educational outreach: a randomized controlled trial of academically based "detailing"', *N Engl J Med.*, 308, 1457–63; J. Avorn (2007), 'Every clinician deserves an un-sales rep', Medscape General Medicines (website), posted 19 January.
50. Websites reporting on academic detailing in France and defining the methods employed include http://www.puppem.com and http://puppem.com/APO.aspx.
51. Avorn (2007), 'Every clinician deserves an un-sales rep'.
52. Ibid.
53. http://www.oregon.gov/DAS/OHPPR/ORRX/HRC/evidence_based_reports. shtml#Prescription_Drugs.
54. HAI (2002), 'European Parliament soundly rejects move towards direct-to-consumer advertising', Press Release, Health Action International, Amsterdam, 24 October.
55. Information provided by the Ministry of Justice, Toronto, Ontario, February 2008.
56. ABPI (1984), *Code of Practice for the Pharmaceutical Industry*, 6th edn, Art. 22.2, Association of the British Pharmaceutical Industry, London.
57. WHO (1988), *Ethical Criteria for Medicinal Drug Promotion*, World Health Organization, Geneva.
58. CA (2001), *Policy Report. Promotion of Prescription Drugs: Public Health or Private Profit?* Consumers' Association, London.
59. 'Congress shall make no law respecting an establishment of religion, or prohibiting the free exercise thereof, or abridging the freedom of speech, or of the press; or the right of the people peaceably to assemble, and to petition the government for a redress of grievances.'
60. C. Meek (2001), 'Direct-consumer Advertising of Prescription Medicines. A review of international policy and evidence: a report for the Royal Pharmaceutical Society of Great Britain', http://www.rpsgb.org.uk/pdfs/dtcarep.pdf.
61. J. Hoek, P. Gendall and J. Calfee (2004), 'Direct-to-consumer advertising of prescription medicines in the United States and New Zealand: an analysis of regulatory approaches and consumer responses', *Int J Advertising*, 23 (2), 197–227.
62. Ibid.
63. New Zealand Legislation website, http://www.legislation.govt.nz.
64. Council Directive 92/28/EEC, 31 March 1992.
65. L. Toop, D. Richards, T. Dowell, M. Tilyard, T. Fraser and B. Arroll (2003), *Direct to Consumer Advertising of Prescription Drugs in New Zealand: For Health or for Profit?*

Report to the Minister of Health, New Zealand Departments of General Practice, Christchurch, Dunedin, Wellington and Auckland Schools of Medicine.

66. L.R. Basara (1996), 'The impact of a direct-to-consumer prescription medication advertising campaign on new prescription volume', *Drug Inf J*, 30, 715–29.

67. P.R. Mansfield (20XX), *Submission from Healthy Skepticism to the New Zealand Ministry of Health Consultation on DTCA*, p. 2.

68. B. Mintzes, M.L. Barer, R.L. Kravitz et al. (2003), 'How does direct-to-consumer advertising (DTCA) affect prescribing? A survey in primary care environments with and without legal DTCA', *CMAJ*, 169 (5), 405–12.

69. G.W. 't Jong, B.H. Stricker and M.C. Sturkenboom (2004), 'Marketing in the lay media and prescriptions of terbinafine in primary care: Dutch cohort study', *BMJ*, 17 April, 328 (7445), 931.

70. D.J. Graham, G. Campen, R. Hui et al. (2005), 'Risk of acute myocardial infarction and sudden cardiac death in patients treated with cyclooxygenase 2 selective and non-selective non-steroidal anti-inflammatory drugs: nested case-control study', *Lancet*, 365, 9456, 22 January (early online publication); Anon. (2005), 'Vioxx caused 88,000 to 140,000 cases of serious heart disease', Press Release, DrugInjuryLaw.com.

7. Regulation and the role of the courts

The role which governments have increasingly assumed of protecting the public interest in the field of medicines in no way obviates the role of the public in defending its own interests by exerting pressure through representative organizations or the media, or more importantly by taking legal action in the civil courts where necessary. Such action may be taken against various parties such as physicians, pharmacists, hospitals or public health authorities. The discussion that follows is primarily concerned with legal action brought against the pharmaceutical trade or industry, on grounds that may range from the publication of misleading advertisements to the sale of dangerous products. In some matters there is also a role for administrative sanctions and for the institution of criminal proceedings by the regulatory agency itself.

From the point of view of public policy, civil litigation in this field may at its best be seen as complementing the protective role of the state. As Australian John Braithwaite concluded, surveying the scene in depth as long ago as 1984:

> In most countries, but especially the United States, product liability law rather than criminal law has provided most of the deterrence against corporate crime in the pharmaceutical industry. Compensation, not deterrence, is the recognized function of product liability law. Yet the conclusion from my interviews was that pharmaceutical executives report fear of product-liability suits as a reason for obeying the Food, Drug and Cosmetic Act of immensely greater importance than fear of criminal prosecution or any other regulatory action.[1]

The state may choose to facilitate civil liability proceedings, notably by providing financial support for litigants who appear to have sound cases ('legal aid'). However, in some situations, it may discourage or even exclude its use, notably proscribing litigation against a firm in connection with a drug that has received the full approval of the regulatory authority (see below).

The extent of the awards (or the settlements reached in lieu of judicial awards) has in some major cases reached a level where it is bound to affect company finances significantly, and hence provide a useful deterrent.

193

However it must be borne in mind that some of the products concerned had already delivered massive profits, and in these cases the companies may well have regarded the costs of litigation as little more than one of the expenses occurred in attaining commercial success. The $80,000 fine imposed on the Richardson-Merrell group back in the 1960s in connection with MER-29®, and even the estimated $200 million involved in its subsequent settlements in civil cases, must be set against the fact that the firm had anticipated annual sales of the drug amounting to $4.25 billion.[2] This type of discrepancy between deterrent and commercial temptation has continued to occur.

In June 2005 the Eli Lilly Company announced a $700 million settlement of approximately 8000 cases that were filed against it on the grounds that the atypical anti-psychotic drug Zyprexa® (olanzapine) caused patients to develop diabetes and diabetes-related injuries. The lawsuits claimed that the firm had failed to adequately warn patients and their doctors about the drug's known association with these adverse events.[3] The drug's annual sales, however, remained high, at $4.4 billion in the year 2006.[4]

In November 2007 Merck & Co. agreed to pay $4.85 billion to settle 27,000 cases brought by patients who had severe adverse (cardiac) effects after taking its product Vioxx® (rovecoxib). An essential element in this situation was the existence of evidence that the firm had been in the possession of clinical evidence of this adverse effect prior to its marketing, but had not made this available to the FDA. The product was withdrawn from the market in 2004 in the midst of widespread concern about its safety. The drug was found to have more than doubled the risks of heart attacks and strokes among patients who used it to ease arthritis pain. As noted in Chapter 6, one scientist estimated that it had caused a vast number of heart attacks and fatalities in the United States.[5] Though the settlement is for a substantial sum, business commentators have suggested that cases still to be filed by other lawyers could lead to a further major increase in the damages to be paid.[6] The drug's sales had averaged $2.5 billion per year prior to the litigation.

Grounds for Action

Since the criteria for acceptability of a medicine have been well defined in national law, litigation has a much firmer starting point than in some other fields, though the approach adopted will vary with the legal system involved. A plaintiff who has been injured in some way by a drug may claim that it was defectively designed or manufactured or that there was a failure to warn consumers of the dangers associated with the product. In some cases one may bring a claim for negligence or for negligent misrepresentation – as well as a fraud-based claim such as fraudulent misrepresentation. There are also warranty claims, both expressed and implied, as well as statutory causes of action relating to unfair and deceptive trade practices. In the countries of the European Union, the Product Liability Directive of 1985 will be applicable and in some cases the General Product Safety Directive of 1992.

Whether or where the strict liability principle will apply, thereby freeing the injured party of the need to prove either the existence of a duty or failure to exercise due care, is much disputed. Where the doctrine is adopted in its purest form, it will be no defense for a manufacturer to show that it acted according to the 'state of the art'. Liability will be established if damage and proximate cause alone are demonstrated, unless the firm can establish one of the defenses provided for in the relevant product liability law. Adoption of strict liability where pharmaceutical manufacturers are concerned is primarily a matter of convenience for the community, but in fact it involves accepting a legal fiction: namely, that the manufacturer is in some sense guilty of any serious adverse effect despite the fact that in the pharmaceutical field such adverse effects are in practice often unavoidable and, in some contexts, unpredictable.

Misleading Advertising

While drug regulatory agencies have, as noted in Chapter 6, increasingly exercised a measure of control over drug advertising, some promotional practices remain open to challenge. A classic case involving advertising that offered a guarantee of efficacy is that of the Carbolic Smoke Ball, heard in London in 1893.

A British manufacturer introduced the Carbolic Smoke Ball, which emitted aromatic vapors to prevent or relieve upper respiratory congestion. In an advertisement (Figure 7.1) he offered £100 to any individual who, after exposure to the vapors, contracted 'INFLUENZA, Colds, or any Diseases caused by taking Cold . . .'[7] A Mrs. Carlill suffered this experience and claimed the sum to which she considered herself entitled, bringing an action for breach of warranty when the manufacturer refused to pay. The producer argued that there was no contractual relationship between him and the claimant. The Court of Appeal, however, found for the appellant on the ground that an offer had been circulated to the general public, which ripened into a contractual relationship when a particular section of the general public had met the conditions attaching to the offer.[8]

Guarantees as specific as this have become unusual, but civil courts have frequently found it necessary to examine advertising claims in order

CARBOLIC SMOKE BALL

WILL POSITIVELY CURE

COUGHS Cured in 1 week	**CATARRH** Cured in 1 to 3 months.	**HOARSENESS** Cured in 12 hours.	**THROAT DEAFNESS** Cured in 1 to 3 months.	**INFLUENZA** Cured in 24 hours.	**CROUP** Relieved in 5 minutes.
COLD IN THE HEAD Cured in 12 hours.	**ASTHMA** Relieved in 10 minutes	**LOSS OF VOICE** Fully restored.	**SNORING** Cured in 1 week.	**HAY FEVER** Cured in every case.	**WHOOPING COUGH** Relieved the first application.
COLD ON THE CHEST Cured in 12 hours.	**BRONCHITIS** Cured in every case.	**SORE THROAT** Cured in 12 hours.	**SORE EYES** Cured in 2 weeks.	**HEADACHE** Cured in 10 minutes.	**NEURALGIA** Cured in 10 minutes.

As all the Diseases mentioned above proceed from one cause, they can be Cured by this Remedy.

£100 REWARD

WILL BE PAID BY THE

CARBOLIC SMOKE BALL CO.

to any Person who contracts the Increasing Epidemic.

INFLUENZA,

Colds, or any Diseases caused by taking Cold, after having used the **CARBOLIC SMOKE BALL** according to the printed directions supplied with each Ball.

£1000 IS DEPOSITED

with the ALLIANCE BANK, Regent Street, showing our sincerity in the matter.

During the last epidemic of **INFLUENZA** many thousand **CARBOLIC SMOKE BALLS** were sold as preventives against this disease, and in no ascertained case was the disease contracted by those using the **CARBOLIC SMOKE BALL.**

THE CARBOLIC SMOKE BALL,

TESTIMONIALS.

The DUKE OF PORTLAND writes: "I am much obliged for the Carbolic Smoke Ball which you have sent me, and which I find most efficacious."

SIR FREDERICK MILNER, Bart., M.P., writes from Nun, March 7, 1890: "Lady Milner and my children have derived much benefit from the Carbolic Smoke Ball."

Lady MOSTYN writes from Carshalton, Cary Crescent, Torquay, Jan. 10, 1890: "Lady Mostyn believes the Carbolic Smoke Ball to be a certain check and a cure for a cold, and will have great pleasure in recommending it to her friends. Lady Mostyn hopes the Carbolic Smoke Ball will have all the success its merits deserve."

Lady ERSKINE writes from Spratton Hall, Northampton, Jan. 1, 1890: "Lady Erskine is pleased to say that the Carbolic Smoke Ball has given every satisfaction; she considers it a very good invention."

Mrs. GLADSTONE writes: "She finds the Carbolic Smoke Ball has done her a great deal of good."

Madame ADELINA PATTI has found the Carbolic Smoke Ball very beneficial, and the only thing that would enable her to rest well at night when having a severe cold."

AS PRESCRIBED BY

SIR MORELL MACKENZIE, M.D.,

HAS BEEN SUPPLIED TO

H.I.M. THE GERMAN EMPRESS.

H.R.H. The Duke of Edinburgh, K.G.
H.R.H. The Duke of Connaught, K.G.
The Duke of Fife, K.T.
The Marquis of Salisbury, K.G.
The Duke of Argyll, K.T.
The Duke of Westminster, K.G.
The Duke of Richmond and Gordon, K.G.
The Duke of Manchester.
The Duke of Newcastle.
The Duke of Norfolk.
The Duke of Rutland, K.G.
The Duke of Wellington.
The Marquis of Ripon, K.G.
The Earl of Derby, K.G.
Earl Spencer, K.G.
The Lord Chancellor.
The Lord Chief Justice.
Lord Tennyson.

TESTIMONIALS.

The BISHOP OF LONDON writes: "The Carbolic Smoke Ball has benefited me greatly."

The MARCHIONESS DE SAIN writes from Padworth House, Reading, Jan. 13, 1890: "The Marchioness de Sain has daily used the Smoke Ball since the commencement of the epidemic of Influenza, and has not taken the Influenza, although surrounded by those suffering from it."

Dr. J. RUSSELL HARRIS, M.D., writes from 6, Adam Street, Adelphi, Sept. 24, 1891: "Many obstinate cases of post-nasal catarrh, which have resisted other treatment, have yielded to your Carbolic Smoke Ball."

A. GIBBONS, Esq., Editor of the *Lady's Pictorial*, writes from 172, Strand, W.C., Feb. 14, 1890: "During a recent sharp attack of the prevailing epidemic I had none of the unpleasant and dangerous catarrh and bronchial symptoms. I attribute this entirely to the use of the Carbolic Smoke Ball."

The Rev. Dr. CHICHESTER A. W. READE, LL.D., D.C.L., writes from Bunstead Downs, Surrey, May 1890: "My duties in a large public institution have brought me daily, during the recent epidemic of influenza, in close contact with the disease. I have been perfectly free from any symptom by having the Smoke Ball always handy. It has also wonderfully improved my voice for speaking and singing."

The Originals of these Testimonials may be seen at our Consulting Rooms, with hundreds of others.

One **CARBOLIC SMOKE BALL** will last a family several months, making it the cheapest remedy in the world at the price—10s., post free.

The **CARBOLIC SMOKE BALL** can be refilled, when empty, at a cost of 5s., post free. Address:

CARBOLIC SMOKE BALL CO., 27, PRINCES ST., HANOVER SQ., LONDON, W.

Source: The *Illustrated London News*, 1892.

Figure 7.1   Carbolic Smoke Ball Advertisement

to assess a plaintiff's case and have on occasion pointed to the grossly misleading character of some promotion in which scientific facts are cited but are presented in a distorted manner that in effect amounts to a promise of success.

In a California case (reviewed below) involving an ephedrine-based slimming aid that had caused injury, the Court noted a typical claim to the effect that users of the product had a 3860 percent greater fat loss than non-users. This was based on a small company-financed study finding that users lost 1.93 percent of their body fat, while non-users lost 0.05 percent. The effect was thus, in any practical sense, entirely insignificant.[9]

The basic legal rule regarding advertising to health professionals is that it must be technically in line with the material approved by the regulatory agency at the time of drug approval, or as subsequently modified with the agency's permission (see Chapter 6). Both agencies and courts will tolerate a certain degree of promotional hyperbole, but in its entirety the material must not be misleading. Since agencies rarely have sufficient resources to monitor all advertising, the role of civil litigation is again of value in detecting misleading promotion and, in effect, providing a deterrent to further malpractice.

Drug Injury

The most prominent and usual type of claim brought against a pharmaceutical manufacturer relates to drug injury.

Perhaps one of the most influential cases of this type, which appears to have done much to accelerate the further development of drug regulatory policy, was that brought by numerous civil litigants against the Merrell Company in the United States from 1961 onwards because of injury attributable to the cholesterol-lowering drug triparanol (MER-29®). There was also a criminal case brought by the FDA itself (reviewed later in the present chapter) in which the defendants entered a *nolo contendere* (no contest) plea, since a guilty plea would have impaired its standing in any subsequent civil litigation. Nevertheless, some 500 civil cases followed and the settlements reached with plaintiffs were estimated to have totaled about $200 million.[10]

When private proceedings are brought against the producer of an approved product, a relevant consideration is whether the firm in question had a clear conscience regarding its scientific performance and the presentation of its data to the regulatory authorities. This issue has repeatedly been crucial, and companies have frequently preferred to settle cases rather than see information relating to their misdeeds enter the public domain through a trial.

In 1988 Ms. Ilo Grundberg of Utah, who had been prescribed triazolam (Halcion®) as a sleeping aid, noted on several occasions that while she was taking the drug she experienced changes in her behavior, including the occurrence of paranoia and delusions. She nevertheless resumed the treatment. In the course of it she shot and killed her mother to whom she had always been devoted. A criminal court acquitted her of murder since she was deemed to have acted under the influence of a toxic substance. She then brought a civil action against the Upjohn Company for $21 million in damages (notably the loss of her mother). Data collected in support of her case showed that the product license had been suspended in the Netherlands in 1979 because of reports of similar reactions,[11] and that Upjohn had been in the possession of data from human Phase I studies conducted on prisoners in the United States which demonstrated this type of psychosis-triggering effect. It had not made this information available to regulatory agencies. An Upjohn spokesman in Britain admitted incomplete submission of data but attributed this to a 'transcription error'.[12] Shortly before the trial in 1991, the company settled with Ms. Grundberg for what was reported to be a very substantial sum.[13] It is known that similar settlements were also reached in other cases of a similar type relating to Halcion®.[14]

It may be noted that since the Grundberg case was heard, issues of federal pre-emption of state tort cases have arisen. These are considered later in this chapter.

Where a foreign manufacturer of a drug or component materials is likely to be inaccessible to litigation, the legal situation when drug injury occurs can be confusing. Certain firms based in Switzerland appear to have been notoriously unwilling to allow access to their internal data. In some instances involving foreign suppliers, it may be possible to bring an action against a national firm importing or further processing the product.

In 2007–08 certain supplies of the injectable anticoagulant ('blood thinner') heparin, in use in many countries, were found to be causing severe allergic and other reactions, eighty one cases proving fatal in the United States alone.[15] A starting material was an extract of pig's intestines supplied from China. The adverse effects were attributed by some experts to a particular contaminant,[16] but this was contested. The drug was recalled in the United States, Australia, Japan and in several European countries where material from the same source had been in use.[17] Claims for damages have been lodged in various countries, those in the United States being brought against the importer and processor, Baxter International Inc. of New Jersey. It appears clear that Baxter recognized a duty to inspect the primary supplier's plant in China and claimed to have done so. The FDA would normally inspect such a supplier of starting materials as well, and initially stated that it had done so, but according to press reports the agency later modified this statement since it admitted that its records confused two different Chinese manufacturing plants.

Cases Relating to Inefficacy

Chapter 4, discussing the principles underlying drug regulation, makes the point that efficacy is a relative concept. No drug can be expected to be effective in every case in which it is used. In some problematic conditions drug therapy can at best be expected to provide relief or cure only in a minority of patients.

The oral contraceptives provide a partial exception to this rule, since from the start there was a general understanding that their efficacy in preventing pregnancy approached or attained 100 percent. Very occasional cases alleging contraceptive failure were brought against some manufacturers, though apparently without success. It appears from several cases on both sides of the Atlantic that the courts, for example, in Michigan, were prepared to accept by implication the existence of virtually absolute efficacy for these products.

In *Troppi v. Scarf* (1971)[18] a tranquillizer was mistakenly dispensed instead of a contraceptive, and pregnancy followed. The Court considered that the dispensing error was responsible for the pregnancy. The dispenser was held liable for child support until the child reached the age of majority.

With such exceptions, tort cases in which a plaintiff seeks damages for lack of efficacy are almost unknown, except where the seller has been so reckless as to offer a guarantee, as in the Carbolic Smoke Ball case noted above. Anita Bernstein has, however, recently advanced arguments to support the view that courts should deem ineffectiveness an actionable injury.[19] As she puts it:

> Courts already extend this recognition when they hear claims for deceptive practices based on inaccuracy in pharmaceutical labeling. Yet deception does not cover all the harm that ineffective drugs cause. An ineffective drug is also a source of bodily injury. One manageable way to acknowledge this physical harm would be to permit a plaintiff who suffered from a drug's lack of safety to recover – if and only if she can prove that the drug did not live up to the claims on its label – for its ineffectiveness as well.

The Restatement of Torts 2d points to the relevance of efficacy. It states that if the benefits of a prescription drug 'outweigh its known risks, and if the manufacturer has provided suitable warnings and directions for use, the defendant's product will be deemed reasonably safe, and the plaintiff will not recover'.[20] However, any argument that lack of efficacy (that is, failure to attain the desired cure or measure of alleviation) or lack of effectiveness (that is, failure to attain the claimed effect on bodily function) should be actionable goes considerably further than this. Were the law to be amended to render such claims admissible, the great difficulty of proving the individual case would remain, and the industry could in any case easily react by introducing modest but uniform changes to the labeling of all drugs, making due reference to the uncertainties inherent in therapy.

Cases Related to Quality Defects

Patients are extremely unlikely to bring tort claims relating primarily to quality defects even if these are visible or tangible, for example, tablets infested with mould or eye drops containing visible particles. Such obviously defective products are simply likely to be discarded or returned for replacement. A tort claim is only likely to emerge if the product is used and has serious ill-effects. It will be these effects, rather than any physical defect of the product (of which the user is unlikely to be aware unless it is grossly visible), that will form the basis of the action. The current cases involving heparin of Chinese origin, noted earlier, are typical in that the severe adverse effects became apparent at a time when the nature of the alleged quality defect underlying the problems was still unclear.

Standards of Public Expectation

It is pointed out in Chapter 4 that standards of efficacy, safety and quality are not absolute. The standards applicable at any moment will depend on what is attainable and what actually has been attained. If in 1930 an antibiotic had been developed that could cure 15 percent of cases of pneumococcal pneumonia, a condition that at the time was commonly fatal and almost entirely untreatable, it would have been a major advance. If such a drug were to have been launched after the introduction of penicillin, which was capable of curing most such cases, it would have been regarded as having no practical value. Public notions as to what can reasonably be expected of a medicine are not always realistic or well informed, but they tend to follow this same principle, and courts have shown themselves willing to accept it as a starting point in issues concerning efficacy or safety.

From about 1960 onwards a number of firms had marketed a 'first generation' of oral contraceptives, followed some years later by a somewhat modified 'second generation'. Because the second generation contraceptives were highly effective, they were welcomed particularly since the original products of this type (that is, the first generation) proved capable, in a percentage of users, of causing thromboembolic complications (that is, blood clots which were sometimes fatal). In products of the second generation this risk was considerably reduced because the content of active material had been successfully lowered. After some years the patents on the APIs used in these products were, however, due to expire. Three firms took the initiative prior to 1990 to market products comprising a so-called 'third generation' of oral contraceptives based on new active ingredients. These met regulatory criteria for efficacy and safety, but within a number of years evidence appeared that the incidence of thromboembolism had again risen. No evidence was produced that the third generation offered any particular benefit, such as might have outweighed an added risk.

Legal proceedings were brought against the three firms on behalf of a number of British women who had suffered thromboembolism, in some instances fatal, while taking the new products. It was argued before the court that women as a whole had now come to regard the second generation oral contraceptives as comprising the accepted standard and that subsequent products falling below this standard should be regarded as 'defective'. While the deliberations of the court appeared to accept this, it had been agreed with the parties in advance that, in view of the uncertainties of clinical statistics, the existence of a sufficiently increased risk to render the third generation products 'defective' in the eyes of the law could only be regarded as proven if it were shown that the thromboembolic risk had at least doubled. The final judgment was that, according to the best evidence available, the risk had probably been increased, but by a lesser amount (apparently some 70 percent) and the action therefore failed.[21]

The Regulatory Defense and Pre-emption

As noted above, the regulatory status of a product may be relevant if its efficacy or safety come into dispute in civil court proceedings. The industry has on many occasions advanced the view that if efficacy, safety or quality has been subject to approval by the national drug licensing authority, they cannot be challenged in the civil courts. In the United States, this view was sometimes accepted, to a certain extent several decades ago. In a case heard in Oregon in 1966, a court held that:

> a drug, properly tested, labeled with appropriate warnings and approved by the Food and Drug Administration, and marketed properly under federal regulation, is, as a matter of law, a reasonably safe product. Accordingly, a person claiming to have suffered adverse effects from using such a drug, unless he can

prove an impurity or an inadequacy in labeling, may not recover against the seller for breach of warranty. . .[22]

Outside the United States, the argument for preemption has hardly been accepted. In a typical series of judgments handed down in The Netherlands on claims brought by patients claiming to have been injured by the sleeping remedy Halcion® (triazolam), courts tended to the view that regulatory approval would not exclude a company's liability for tort. The Arnhem District Court considered that

> The control exercised by the government authorities relates to the minimum standards which a pharmaceutical must attain, and not the totality of prudence which is the duty of the party proposing to market the drug. The fact that the Committee for the Evaluation of Medicines had advanced no objections to the text of the introductory folder and the package insert does not therefore mean that the Upjohn Company cannot have failed in its duty of care.[23]

In dealing finally with the same issue, the Supreme Court of the Netherlands explicitly stated that registration of a drug by the authorities does not abolish the liability of the manufacturer at civil law.[24]

In Britain one can discern an intermediate view, with at least one court characterizing the Licensing Authority's approval of a medicine as a preliminary finding of fact that it will be 'reluctant to criticize'.[25] One can have some understanding of this intermediate view, since a regulatory agency is generally better equipped to form a valid view on the merits and safety of a drug, at least at the moment of assessment, than is a court of justice. The fact remains, however, that agencies prove in some cases to have been misled (for example, where applicants' files are incomplete, as in the cases of triazolam and rovicoxib); and also, as in the case of benoxaprofen in Britain, even the best scientific data available does not always lead to definitive conclusions. For these and other reasons, regulatory bodies are not infallible.

The situation as it has developed in the United States since the Oregon case of 1966 is summarized in Box 7.1, the most significant change being that in the attitude of the FDA[26] which came to favor the pre-emption principle; it has been suggested that this change was a consequence of political and industrial pressure exerted on the agency.[27] While as of March 2009 the principle has been rejected by the US Supreme Court, it should be noted that the issue may at any time be reopened and that the state of Michigan has followed its own course in this matter.

Michigan adopted a law that, since 2006, eliminated causes of action for defective warning or design when the product complained of is an FDA-approved drug.[28] It has been suggested that this statute came into being

BOX 7.1   PROPOSED PRE-EMPTION OF TORT CLAIMS IN THE USA

With Acknowledgments to Daniel W. Sigelman, Attorney at Law

Since 2002, the FDA has progressively adopted the view that the Federal Food, Drug and Cosmetic Act by implication pre-empts many failure-to-warn claims in state courts regarding drugs approved by the Agency. In 2002 it filed *amicus* briefs asking courts to dismiss such cases. In January 2006 the FDA formalized this position in the preamble to a rule revising requirements for drug labeling. In a reversal of its long-term neutrality regarding such litigation, the agency now maintains that state-law failure-to-warn cases threaten its ability to protect the public health. A determination in a tort case that an FDA-approved label fails to warn adequately of risks may force manufacturers to add warnings that are not approved by the FDA, thus rendering the product 'misbranded'. As noted in Chapter 1, the issue was raised before the US Supreme Court in 2008/9 in the case of Wyeth v. Levine. In March 2009 the court rejected the principle of pre-emption of state tort causes of action for mislabelling. See http:www.supremecourtus.gov/opinions.html. One must wonder however whether this is the end of the discussion; the interests at stake are such that the controversy is likely to continue.

Critics of the FDA view[a] point out that:

1. The moment the FDA approves a new drug is the one moment the agency is in the best position to be the exclusive arbiter of a drug's safety and effectiveness. Once the drug enters the marketplace, risks that are relatively rare, that manifest themselves only after an extended period of time, or that affect vulnerable subpopulations begin to emerge. The FDA's tools for gathering post-approval information are relatively crude and ineffective. Even since its resources were supplemented by new legislation (the FDA Amendments Act) in January 2007[b] they amount only to a tiny fraction of those available to industry, which are mobilized when tort litigation comes into play. Only a small fraction of adverse reactions are reported to the FDA. For that reason the tort system, which provides new evidence

from the field and which by reason of the discovery process has access to all internal industry materials, has historically provided important information about these newly emerging risks, to physicians, patients and the FDA.

2. Even with respect to its initial assessment of a drug the agency is relatively weak. Studies by the Government Accountability Office and the Institute of Medicine have been critical of the agency's ability to keep unsafe drugs off the market and to respond effectively to unforeseen hazards with newly approved drugs.[c]

3. Any attempt to eliminate the role of tort law in protection of the public where medicines are concerned starts from the implied assumption that the FDA is infallible. A long series of errors on the agency's part shows that it is not, even in instances where the manufacturer has provided it with all the relevant data in its possession.

4. A judgment for the plaintiff against a pharmaceutical company does not mean that the labeling must be changed and new warnings added, hence undermining the FDA's authority. It merely awards damages against the firm. If the firm in the light of this changes the labeling, it has the right and indeed the duty under existing legislation to do so promptly in situations where there is reasonable evidence of risk, simply being obliged to inform the FDA of the change and submit a Supplemental New Drug Application that the FDA then reviews after-the-fact.[d]

5. While litigation does not necessarily have a rapid effect, it is clear from experience that neither does an FDA decision to call for a warning. Although the 2006 FDA Amendments Act enables the FDA to impose a warning, it requires the agency to negotiate first with the company, and this can be a lengthy procedure. Time and again, failure-to-warn litigation has preceded and clearly influenced FDA decisions to modify labeling and, at times, to withdraw drugs from the market.

6. Although the FDA asserts that its current view on pre-emption is in line with its earlier long-term policies, it is in fact a reversal of policy.

Notes:

a. FDA (2006), *Requirements on Content and Format of Labeling for Human Prescription Drug and Biological Products*, 71 Fed. Reg. 3922, 3933–6 (24

January 2006). To be codified at 21 CFR. pts 201, 314 (601); E. Pringle (2006), 'Bush uses FDA to shield big pharma from lawsuits', *Top Scoops*, 15 May.
b. Food and Drug Administration Amendments Act of 2007, Pub. L. No. 110-85 State 823 (2007).
c. Risk and Responsibility: *The Roles of the FDA and Pharmaceutical Companies in Ensuring Safety of Approved Drugs, Like Vioxx. Hearing before the H. Comm. On Government Reform.* 109th Cong. 23, 55 (2005) (testimony of Steven Galson, Acting Director, Center for Drug Evaluation and Research, FDA); A. Bacin, A. Stratton and S.P. Burke (eds) (2006), *The Future of Drug Safety – Promoting and Protecting the Health of the Public.* Institute of Medicine of the National Academy of Sciences, Washington, DC. pp. 153–4.
d. 21 CFR §201.57c(6)(i)(2006) and §201.80.

Source: This account has drawn on D.A. Kessler and D.C. Vladeck (2008), 'A critical examination of the FDA's efforts to preempt failure-to-warn claims', 96, *Geo LJ*, 461 ff.

under the influence of the pharmaceutical industry lobby.[29] Michigan law does not permit federal pre-emption if the manufacturer obtained FDA approval by omitting or fraudulently misrepresenting information. The statute survived a challenge based on an earlier interpretation of state constitutional law by the US Supreme Court dating back to 2003.[30] As far as issues of fraud on the FDA were concerned, the Supreme Court held in 2001, in *Buckman v. Plaintiff's Legal Comm.*,[31] that 'stand-alone' state law claims for fraud on the FDA conflicted with the FDA's authority to police such fraud.

In the meantime, in 2000, 27 residents of Michigan sued the Warner Lambert Company under the Michigan statute claiming personal injury arising from the use of the firm's product Rezulin® (troglitazone) for diabetes. The serious adverse effects complained of were well documented in the literature and were not at issue (leading in 2000 to withdrawal of the drug by the FDA), nor did the issue of fraud on the FDA arise. Warner Lambert argued in its defense that the Michigan statute was pre-empted since 'permitting state courts to second-guess the FDA's product-approval and fraud-detection process interferes with the agency's essential functions and promotes regulatory uncertainty'. The Michigan plaintiffs responded that federal pre-emption did not apply to traditional state tort claims for wrongful death or injury.

The case was tried in Federal District Court in New York, which ruled that the fraud provision in Michigan law was pre-empted by federal law and dismissed the action. However, in 2007 the US Court of Appeals for the Second Circuit overturned that decision, allowing the case to proceed. Warner Lambert applied to the Supreme Court for a writ of *certiorari*, and the Supreme Court accepted to hear the case. In a somewhat unusual turn of events, the Supreme Court affirmed the decision of the Court of Appeals in a per curiam 4-4 decision based on the recusal of Justice Roberts (who owned shares of Pfizer, the parent of Warner Lambert) (*Warner Lambert v. Kent* 552 US (2008).

Yet this did not put an end to the pre-emption question. Instead, the facts shifted to Vermont where a plaintiff had sued Wyeth in state court for failing to adequately label against using a certain type of injection procedure (IV Push) with its anti-nausea drug (Phenergan). The FDA had approved a label that described certain risks associated with the type of injection used, but did not preclude it. A jury in Vermont awarded $6 million to the plaintiff whose arm was amputated as a consequence of gangrene resulting from an improperly administered IV Push injection, and the Supreme Court of Vermont affirmed the judgment (*Levine v. Wyeth*, 2006 VT 107 (2006)). The US Supreme Court granted *certiorari* and heard oral arguments in the case. In March 2009, as noted in Box 7.1, it rejected the pre-emption principle.

In our view, it is regrettable that, prior to this decision, some courts in the US had already accepted the FDA's view on pre-emption as representing good law. In our view, broad acceptance of pre-emption in the pharmaceutical area would run seriously counter to the public interest since on numerous occasions the ability of litigation to serve the public interest has been demonstrated. By mobilizing legal and judicial resources, and making use of the right to subpoena relevant data from any source including industry files, the process has repeatedly brought significant facts to light. Often enough it has gone on to lay blame where blame is due, and sometimes it has pushed both industry and the drug regulatory authorities belatedly into action; though even at this stage the process may be thwarted by the aggressive manifestation of commercial self-interest. Three prominent (and in part related) examples, all from the United States, are cited (essentially as summarized by Kessler and Vladeck in 2008).[32]

Litigation uncovered the fact that Pfizer, the maker of the anti-inflammatory drug Celebrex® (celecoxib), had in 1999 conducted an unpublished clinical study to determine whether the drug could be used to treat Alzheimer's disease. In the course of this study a statistically significant increase was found in the incidence of heart attacks. Pfizer, however, delayed submitting the study to the FDA until 2001, after the FDA had convened an advisory committee meeting to consider whether drugs of the Celebrex class should carry warnings for heart attack and stroke. The advisory committee recommended that a warning be added to the labeling for Vioxx®, Celebrex's main competitor. Unaware of the Pfizer study linking Celebrex® to increased heart attacks and strokes, the committee did not make a similar recommendation for Celebrex®.

Litigation also brought to light the fact that Merck, the maker of Vioxx® (rofecoxib), had been acutely concerned about the heart attack risk associated with its drug before the FDA understood the risk and before Merck alerted the FDA to the risk. During tort cases brought against Merck, the plaintiff's lawyers uncovered internal company memos and e-mails that were not provided to the FDA. One memo warned that a study of Vioxx® should be limited to patients taking aspirin, otherwise there would be a 'substantial chance that significantly higher rates' of cardiovascular disease would show up in the Vioxx® group. A senior company doctor recommended that potential subjects with high risk of cardiovascular problems be kept out of the study so that cardiovascular problems 'would not be evident'.

Litigation also revealed evidence that manufacturers of a certain class of antidepressant medication – the selective serotonin reuptake inhibitors (SSRIs) – had withheld adverse event data. Here the New York State Attorney brought a civil action against GlaxoSmithKline, alleging that the company had fraudulently withheld clinical studies showing that its SSRI drug, Paxil® (paroxetine), increased the risk of suicide in children and young adults without effectively treating their depression. The complaint further alleged that the company's internal memos urged company officials to 'manage the dissemination of data in order to minimize any potential negative commercial impact' while, at the same time, encouraging sales representatives to tell doctors that 'Paxil demonstrates remarkable efficacy and safety in the treatment of adolescent depression.' Three months later, GlaxoSmithKline settled the case by, among other things, agreeing to make its data public.[33] Shortly thereafter, the FDA required warnings on SSRIs to highlight the association between use of SSRIs and an increased suicide risk in children and adolescents.[34] In Britain, where the drug was known as Seroxat®, similar evidence was presented that unfavorable data from clinical trials had been withheld by GlaxoSmithKline from the Medicine and Health Products Regulatory Agency. Prosecution of the firm was considered but not pursued because of some lack of clarity in the relevant law.[35] However, as a direct consequence, the government undertook to make release of data from clinical trials compulsory by law, and to seek a modification of European law to the same effect.[36]

One particularly useful role played by litigation has involved those drugs which entered the market prior to the establishment of current regulation. In principle, they are permitted to remain on the market under what in the United States is termed the 'grandfather clause' provision, and in the United Kingdom the issuance of 'licenses of right', until the agency reassesses them according to current standards. The reality is, however, that few regulatory agencies have succeeded in performing a complete assessment of these older drugs, either because of lack of capacity or because the experimental or clinical evidence available is outdated and does not permit full evaluation. When these products prove to be the cause of injurious effects, litigation may be the most suitable means of ensuring that some degree of justice is done. The case of clioquinol was outlined above. An unusually complex and serious problem involved diethyl-stilbestrol (DES) which, although available worldwide for half a century, was most intensively used in the Netherlands.

DES was developed in the United Kingdom prior to 1940 as an effective low-cost estrogenic (female) hormone. For altruistic reasons the inventor left it unpatented. It was therefore manufactured by many firms. Two US physicians propagated its use in pregnancy as a means of preventing habitual or threatened abortion, and some physicians concluded that it would be wise to administer it to all pregnant women, although its efficacy was unproven. Only some 30 years after its introduction did evidence come strongly to light that female children from these pregnancies tended to develop vaginal changes when reaching adolescence or adulthood, and that these could become malignant. There was also a high incidence of fertility disturbances among these women. Some analogous changes were found in the males. The treated mothers too were prone to develop adverse effects, and there was, in some, emergent evidence of an adverse effect on the third generation. Several thousand claims were brought to court, mostly directed against manufacturers, but some against the FDA. Problems of proof were significant because of the lapse of time between the claimed treatment and the emergence of adverse effects. In the Netherlands, after judicial proceedings, a compromise was reached under which the firms that had manufactured or sold DES contributed to a compensation fund for victims. It is not an ideal solution and the details of the settlement have been rightly criticized[37] but it perhaps comes closer to justice than other approaches.

To summarize, litigation in this field, especially where patients have been exposed to risks of which they had not been warned, can to an important degree complement the role of regulation, calling all parties to order and setting straight both incomplete and distorted records, quite apart from its ability to ensure that compensation for injury is paid. Three of the major cases cited here all relate primarily to events in the United States and to situations in which pharmaceutical companies had behaved in a manner less than conducive to the public interest. However, this should not obscure the fact that litigation on such matters can also do good (and has done good) in other legal systems and in situations where faults have been due to honest error, and not solely to improper practice. Critics of litigation in this field argued for a long period that it would discourage and destroy innovation,[38] the same argument that was raised against government regulation of medicines. There is very little reason to believe that this has happened except perhaps as regards vaccines, where special measures were called for (see Chapter 8). However, litigation has probably been one of the factors catalyzing the concentration of the industry into larger and stronger units. A litigation process can be cumbersome, costly and slow, but it would be highly regrettable if at any time society were to abandon a major protective and remedial mechanism that has served the interests of various populations so well.

Unregulated and Deregulated Products

Products that have the character of medicines, but that for one reason or another do not fall within the scope of medicines regulation, are likely to be covered to some extent by the general regulation of consumer products or 'wares'. This regulation will be narrower in its scope and will not normally relate to efficacy. An unusual situation was created in the United States in 1995 when a large number of products, which up to that time had been regulated as 'drugs' by the FDA, were removed from the agency's field of operation as part of a series of deregulatory measures.[39] Although the class of products involved was primarily characterized by the legislature as 'Dietary Supplements', it involved some that had pharmacological activity. The case of ephedra or ephedrine, which had come into popular use as an aid to weight reduction, gained notoriety after its deregulation, when serious adverse effects including fatalities were reported. The death of Steve Bechler, a well-known baseball player, was prominently reported and numerous users or their families brought civil actions against firms selling the products.

One class action was brought in a California case against Cytodyne Technologies, the makers of the ephedra-based product Xenadrine®. The plaintiffs pointed in particular to the advertising claims, which were characterized as false and misleading. The court gave judgment for the plaintiffs and ordered the firm to return $12.5 million in profits on sales of the product in California over a five-year period, the sum to be deposited in a pool for distribution among the users. The FDA subsequently prohibited the sale of products of this type.[40]

Legal Aid

Funding of litigation
In a number of countries, including the United Kingdom, considerable sums in public money are available to plaintiffs to pursue tort cases,

including those involving pharmaceuticals and vaccines. The point of departure is the view that, in principle, an unlawfully injured party should be in a position to pursue a case for damages, irrespective of his or her financial means. The availability of funding is, however, dependent upon budgetary limitations and on the chances of success in any particular case. The body administering the funds in the UK (the Legal Services Commission) may at any time during a case reassess the prospects and amend its decision.

In the period 1993–95 a very large series of cases was in preparation on behalf of clients who had suffered from the dependence-producing properties of the benzodiazepine tranquillizers, the allegation being that the manufacturers were aware of the risk well before it became public knowledge and users were alerted to it. After extensive studies the prospects of success appeared to be poor. Funding was withdrawn after some £30 million had been contributed by the Commission. After the failure in 2002 of the case against the manufacturers of the third-generation oral contraceptives (summarized above), it was estimated that the costs had reached some £5 million. In 2003 the Commission withdrew legal aid for proposed litigation against three manufacturers of the measles, mumps and rubella (MMR) vaccine after an independent paper concluded that the proof of a causal association between the vaccine and one of the most commonly alleged adverse effects (autism) was weak. The legal costs up to the moment of withdrawal were some £5–10 million.[41] In 2004 the Commission restored aid to a minority of the families whose claims related to complications other than autism, which appeared to be better founded.[42]

It seems clear that, from the point of view of public policy, legal aid should be made available wherever possible to enable plaintiffs having a reasonable case to obtain justice, whatever the limitations of their finances. It is, however, equally clear that the legal process can be extremely costly, that assessment of the prospects involves in effect a prior judgment on the merits of a case, and that public funding can only be granted where the circumstances justify it.

Over-regulation

In Chapter 8 the view is noted that opiates and other controlled drugs are sometimes the subject of excessively restrictive public policies, rendering them inaccessible in situations of real medical need. It is unusual to experience a tort case dealing with over-regulation in national or state law, but in July 2008 a claim was lodged by the Pain Relief Network against Washington State, alleging that patients in need of relief for extreme pain were being deprived of the necessary treatment as a result of over-restrictive policies applied by a number of state officials.[43] The group noted that it had targeted Washington because the state had been a leader both in pain treatment and in restricting doctors' prescriptions of pain relief medication, and that its policies were being followed widely across the United States. Its guidelines, which apply only to treatment of chronic pain, recommend that the total daily dose of opioids should not exceed 120 mg of morphine or its equivalent if both pain and physical function are not improving. In the group's view such guidelines do not take into account the needs of individuals, and they make doctors afraid to give larger doses when necessary.

Criminal Law

Drug regulatory agencies are generally endowed with powers to prosecute offenders, and a great many cases have, over the years, been brought by the U.S. FDA for alleged offences of greater or lesser seriousness. For example, in 1959 the Wallace and Tiernan company marketed the tranquillizer Dornwal® (amphenidone) despite the strenuous objections of the company's own medical director. Other members of its staff had warned that the drug could cause serious effects on blood formation (hemopoiesis). The company was subsequently notified of nine cases of bone marrow disease and three fatalities. The firm was found guilty on criminal charges.[44]

At the federal level, the False Claims Act was originally passed in the Civil War era to discourage fraudulent military contracts, but can be applied to bring criminal charges of false promotion in any field where public expenditure is involved. It was first invoked in the pharmaceutical industry against Genentech, which settled a 1999 lawsuit for $50 million. Since then, federal prosecutors have used the law against major drug companies in 15 cases, all of which have been settled. Lawyers who represent drug companies have noted that while the legal premise of such lawsuits – that improper marketing can defraud the government – may not stand up in court, companies choose to settle rather than risk losing government reimbursement for their products.[45]

It is evident that where a regulatory system is in existence, the sale and advertising of unapproved products will be unlawful and will render the seller liable to prosecution.

In April 2008 Britain's Medicines and Healthcare Products Regulatory Agency (MHRA) prosecuted a general practitioner, Dr. Dinesh Maini, for advertising (and possessing with intent to sell) the unlicensed drug Lipostabil® for cosmetic purposes. In 2005 Dr. Maini had advertised the drug under the name 'Fat Jab' in a Nottingham newspaper. After having been warned by the MHRA, he continued to advertise the drug on a website. Inspectors subsequently seized stocks of the drug from his surgery. He was found guilty on all charges and ordered to pay a substantial sum in costs and fines.[46] It may be noted that Lipostabil® was legally on sale in Germany but for another indication.

Exceptionally, individuals within pharmaceutical firms may be charged with offences for which they can be held personally responsible. This course has often been followed in the United States. An English case is cited here. In a case brought by the Department of Health and Social Security, Roussel Laboratories was accused of issuing an advertisement for their drug Surgam® (tiaprofenic acid) which 'was misleading in that the claims for gastric protection and selective prostaglandin inhibition were not justified or substantiated by clinical or other appropriate trials or studies', and of claiming in the absence of adequate evidence that 'Surgam® was safer and had fewer or less incidence of side effects than indomethacin in the treatment of arthritis'. The medical director of the company, Dr. Christopher Good, was accused of consenting and conniving in the matter underlying these claims. With respect to four of the five advertisements in question, Roussel Laboratories and Dr. Good were found guilty, and substantial fines and costs were imposed. The sentence was upheld on appeal.[47]

One of the most significant criminal cases of the last half-century in this field involved the prosecution in the United States of the William S. Merrell Company, as well as members of its staff, in connection with the extensive injury caused by the cholesterol-lowering drug MER-29® (triparanol).

MER-29 was introduced in the United States and a number of other countries in 1960. Frequent adverse effects were soon reported from the field, including baldness, skin damage, changes in the reproductive organs and blood, and serious damage to vision (including cataract). The drug was withdrawn in April 1961. Criminal investigations revealed malpractice within the firm including replacement in the toxicity studies of monkeys that had shown undesirable effects, deletion and distortion of records relating to adverse effects in three animal species, and manipulation of clinical studies to avoid unfavorable outcomes. Prosecution on a variety of criminal fraud counts involved the Merrell Company itself, its parent corporation Richardson-Merrell and also three Merrell employees, including two members of the medical staff and a vice-president. Fines were imposed on the companies, and the three individual defendants were each sentenced to six months probation.[48]

In Canada, in 2004, criminal charges were brought both against institutions and individuals in a case where a blood product tainted with the

HIV and hepatitis viruses had entered the blood transfusion system and infected several thousand patients. The product had been supplied by the Armour Pharmaceutical Company in the United States, and supplied under the authority of the Canadian health authorities to the Canadian Red Cross. Prosecutions were brought against the Armour Company, and also against its former vice-president, a former director of the Canadian Red Cross, and two Canadian health officials, on grounds of criminal negligence causing bodily harm and commission of a common nuisance. All the accused were acquitted. The Ontario Superior Court agreed that the events under consideration constituted a 'disaster'. But in its view the evidence showed neither wanton disregard for public safety nor a departure from the standards of a reasonable person. The former Director of the Red Cross continued to face separate criminal charges related to allegations that the Red Cross had not taken adequate measures to screen blood donors. The Red Cross had earlier pleaded guilty to a violation of the Food and Drug Regulation Act and apologized to the infected patients, and the federal government paid compensation to the victims.[49]

Concluding Observation

It is evident to the authors that private civil litigation in the field of medicines plays a significant and useful role in promoting not only a measure of justice for injured individuals, but also in promoting the common welfare by bringing to light facts that may otherwise remain hidden. In a number of important cases action by private lawyers on behalf of their clients has caused the withdrawal from the market of pharmaceutical products that should not have been there in the first place, and which products were causing substantial harm. Government regulators do not always have the resources, and in some cases may lack the inclination, to actively police this very large and very public market.

NOTES

1. J. Braithwaite (1984), *Corporate Crime in the Pharmaceutical Industry*, Routledge and Kegan Paul, London, p. 346.
2. P. Knightley, H. Evans, E. Potter and M. Wallace (1979), *Suffer the Children*, Viking Press, New York, p. 65.
3. S.M. Goldberg (2005), 'Pharmaceutical litigation: Zyprexa, $700 million settlement', Press release, Steven M. Goldberg Co., Solon, OH.
4. V.B. Kennedy (2007), 'Lilly CEO: 22007 Zyprexa sales seen flat', *Market Watch*, 14 March.
5. B. Patsner (2008), 'The Vioxx settlement: salvation or sellout?' www.law.uh.edu/

healthlaw/perspectives, C. Johnson (2007), 'Merck agrees to blanket settlement on Vioxx', *Washington Post*, 10 November.

6. D. Fisher (2007), 'Will the Vioxx settlement work?' *Forbes*, 13 November.
7. Advertisement (1892), 'Carbolic Smoke Ball will positively cure . . .', *Illustrated London News*, 21 Jan, 119.
8. *Carlill v. Carbolic Smoke Ball Co.* (1893), 1 QB, 256.
9. F. Fessenden (2003), 'Judge orders ephedra maker to pay back $12.5 million', *New York Times,* 31 May.
10. Braithwaite (1984), *Corporate Crime in the Pharmaceutical Industry*, p. 346.
11. M.N.G. Dukes (1990), 'The van der Kroef syndrome', in *Side Effects of Drugs Essays*, Elsevier, Amsterdam, New York and Oxford, pp. 29–38.
12. L. Hunt (1991), 'Side effects of sleep aid omitted in report to FDA', *Washington Post,* 28 August.
13. D. Hooper (2000), 'The Halcion nightmare', in *Reputations Under Fire*, Little, Brown and Company, London, pp. 187–206.
14. J. Abraham and J. Sheppard (1999), *The Therapeutic Nightmare: The Battle over the World's Most Controversial Sleeping Pill*, Earthscan, London.
15. FDA Press release, February 2008, http://www.fda.gov/oc/po/firmrecalls/baxter02_08.html.
16. http://attorneypages.com/hot/unknown-heparin-contaminant-baffles-fda.htm (accessed 27 June 2008).
17. http://attorneypages.com/hot/heparin-recall-italy-france-denmark-australia.htm.
18. *Troppi v. Scarf* (1971), 31 Mich. App. 240, 187 NW 2d 511.
19. A. Bernstein (2007), 'Enhancing drug effectiveness and efficacy through personal injury litigation', Emory University School of Law, Public Law and Legal Theory Research Paper Series. Paper No. 7-13.
20. *Restatement (Second) of Torts* § 402A comment *k (*1965).
21. Queen's Bench Division, High Court (London), XYZ and others (Claimants) versus (1) Schering Health Care Limited, (2) Organon Laboratories Limited and (3) John Wyeth and Brother Limited. Judgement by the Hon. Mr Justice Mackay. London, 29 July 2002. Case No. 0002638. Neutral Citation No. (2002) EWHC 1420 (QB).
22. *Lewis v. Baker* (1966), 2d 400, 404 (Or. 1966) (en banc).
23. Rechtbank Arnhem (Court of Arnhem), 28 June 1984. Reported in *Tijdschr v. Consumentenr.*, 1985, pp. 82–9 and *Tijdschr v. Gezondheidsr.*, 1985, pp. 109–14.
24. Reported in *Ned. Jur. Bl.,* 9 February 1990, afl. 6, 225–9.
25. *Smith, Kline and French Laboratories Ltd v. Licensing Authority* [1989] 1 All ER 578.
26. Kessler and Vladeck (2008), 'A critical examination of the FDA's efforts to preempt failure to-warn claims'.
27. Pringle (2006), 'Bush uses FDA to shield big pharma from lawsuits'.
28. Mich. Stat. Ann. § 600.2946 (5) (2006).
29. A. Cohen (2007), 'They say we have too many lawsuits? Tell it to Jack Cline', *NY Times*, 14 January, Week in Rev., p. 11
30. *Taylor v. SmithklineBeecham Corp.*, 658 NW 2d 127 (Mich. 2003).
31. *Buckman v. Plaintiffs' Legal Comm.*, 531 US 341 (2001).
32. Kessler and Vladeck (2008), 'Critical examination of the FDA's efforts to preempt failure-to-warn-claims'.
33. Press Release (2004), 'Settlement sets new standard for release of drug information', Office of the NY State Attorney General, 26 August.
34. S. Vedantam (2004), 'Depression drugs to carry a warning: FDA Order Notice of risks to youths', *Washington Post,* 16 October, p. A1.
35. J. Goldstein (2008), 'UK to tighten rules as GSK avoids prosecution', *Wall St J*, 6 March.
36. Anon. (2008), 'GSK escapes prosecution over drug trial data', *New Scientist*, 14 March.
37. E.F.M. 't Hoen and M.N.G. Dukes (2007), 'Compensation for diethylstilbestrol injury',

Lancet, 369 (9557), 173–4; F.E. Van Leeuwen, E.J.M. Van Erp, T.J.M. Helmerhorst and P.A.M. Heintz (2007), 'Compensation for diethylstilbestrol injury', *Lancet*, 369 (9569), 1258.

38. L. Lasagna (1991), 'The chilling effect of product liability on new drug development', in P.W. Huber and R.E. Litan (eds), *The Liability Maze: The Impact of Liability Law on Safety and Innovation*, pp. 334–48.

39. US Congress (1994), 'The Dietary Supplement Health and Education Act', *Public Law*, 103–417, 103rd Congress.

40. Fessenden (2003), 'Judge orders ephedra maker to pay back $12.5 million'.

41. C. Dyer (2003), 'Commission withdraws legal aid for parents suing over MMR vaccine', *BMJ*, 327, 640.

42. J. Dowad (2004), 'MMR parents win legal victory', *Observer,* 26 December.

43. *Complaint for Declaratory and Injunctive Relief, Damages; a class action lawsuit by Laura Cooper (lead attorney)* et al., filed: 24 June 2008.

44. J. Braithwaite (1984), *Corporate Crime in the Pharmaceutical Industry*, Routledge and Kegan Paul, London, Boston and Henley, p. 56; A. Johnson (1976), *Research Conducted by the Drug Industry: A Conflict of Interest*, Public Citizen, Washington, DC.

45. Anon. (2006), 'WRF Attorney quoted on False Claims act prosecution in pharmaceutical industry', *Baltimore Sun*, 7 May.

46. Anon. (2008), 'Doctor prosecuted for advertising and selling an unlicensed medicine – "Fat Jab", UK', *Medical News Today*, 28 April.

47. Central Criminal Court (1986), *Queen v. Roussel Laboratories and Christopher Saxty Good*. Judgment by J. Capstick, 19 December.

48. Braithwaite (1984), *Corporate Crime in the Pharmaceutical Industry*, pp. 60–5.

49. Reuters Business and Finance (2007), 'Doctors acquitted in Canada tainted-blood trial', 2 October, www.cbc.ca/canada/story/2007/10/01/taintedblood-verdict.html.

8. Specialized policy areas: vaccines, biologicals and blood products; alternative and traditional medicines; self-medication; counterfeit medicines

VACCINES, BIOLOGICALS AND BLOOD PRODUCTS

Vaccines and certain 'biologicals' (for example, immune sera and toxoids as well as blood products) merit somewhat separate consideration from drugs. Although in many respects the situation with regard to overall public policy, responsibility for quality and liability for possible injury is the same, a number of differences can arise. Those differences can reflect particular social and religious concepts, but also the nature of these products and the circumstances that dictate their use.

VACCINATION AND THE CONCEPT OF PREVENTATIVE TREATMENT

Since Edward Jenner in England and John Redman Coxe in America pioneered vaccination against smallpox at the beginning of the nineteenth century,[1] the prevention of major epidemic diseases in this way has come to comprise a major component of public health policy. From the outset, however, it was realized that the process of mass vaccination had to be managed with the greatest care, especially since it involved exposing healthy individuals to a degree of risk. It is striking that in this field considerations of efficacy, safety and quality came to play a major role in policy a century before they became established with regard to medicines in general. Issues of legislation, information and access, too, were decided early, since it was clear that if mass prevention was to be successful the law must impose duties, public support must be recruited and free access unhindered by financial barriers must be assured. In the course of only a few decades, coordination of policy across the world became a further necessity as international travel burgeoned, with the real danger that unchecked epidemics might spread rapidly and disastrously from one continent to another.

The principal characteristic of vaccination, as opposed to most types of drug treatment, is as already noted that it is generally administered for preventative purposes to entirely healthy individuals. While a person planning to visit an area where a disease is endemic or prevalent may undergo vaccination in his or her own interests, a high proportion of all vaccinations are administered population-wide under national programs. Except in those cases where it is medically contraindicated, such administration is often required by specific legislation (or emphatically recommended by the authorities), as a means of protecting the community against epidemic disease. In this situation the interests of the community as a whole may override the interest of a particular individual. To quote a decision of the US Supreme Court dating back to 1905 and bearing on smallpox vaccination at the time when an epidemic was threatening:

> In every well-ordered society charged with the duty of conserving the safety of its members, the rights of the individual in respect of his liberty may at times under the pressure of great dangers be subjected to such restraints, to be enforced by general regulations, as the safety of the general public may demand.[2]

Vaccination also has a number of other distinguishing characteristics, notably:

- Whereas a medicinal drug is designed to counter the agent causing disease and/or to suppress its ill-effects, a vaccine is derived from the causative agent itself. It is artificially attenuated so that the chance of its inducing the disease in the recipient is very slight, but it retains sufficient potency to stimulate the user's immune system to build up his or her defenses so that the user can repel or destroy the same virulent causative agent if it is subsequently encountered. One must add however that, even in the modern era, there have been very occasional instances where insufficiently attenuated vaccines were introduced and proved pathogenic, as in the case of the oral poliomyelitis vaccine (OPV) formerly used in the United States.[3]
- Although vaccines are primarily used as part of a public health program, and not for self-medication, the products are sometimes administered (notably in the course of mass vaccination campaigns) without the intervention of a physician. Semi-skilled staff may administer them, while oral vaccines may be taken by the individual without assistance or supervision.

● In most countries the procedures for registration of these products differ from those applicable to pharmaceuticals. There may be special legislation on 'sera and vaccines' or on 'biologicals', with a separate regulatory agency, as well as separate bodies studying adverse reactions.

● Where the vaccine is administered superficially, the potentially infectious material used can cause injury to a third party. The historic example is that of a smallpox vaccination subject transmitting infection to an infant with eczema, resulting in *eczema vaccinatum*. A corresponding risk exists with poliomyelitis vaccination.

● The positive benefit/risk ratio, which provides the justification for public vaccination programs, is not necessarily constant. The potential benefit of a vaccine may be largely or completely lost if a new viral strain appears against which it is ineffective.

● Vaccines can, however, also be toxic because of impurities, sometimes comprising materials that in the current state of knowledge cannot be removed. This can bring them within the doctrine of 'unavoidably unsafe products', which may mean that the manufacturer cannot be held strictly liable though it will still be under a normal obligation to warn of the known risks.[4]

The situation with sera, used to confer immediate protection against imminent or current infection by administering antibodies of animal origin (for example, from infected horses) is somewhat different. The principle problem encountered here is that the serum contains foreign (animal) protein that can give rise to hypersensitivity reactions, including fatal anaphylactic shock.

With both vaccines and sera, errors may occasionally occur in the field, involving improper or inadequate sterilization, use of incorrect doses or routes of administration or accidental substitution of drugs for diluents or vaccines.[5]

Manufacturing and Quality Control of Vaccines

The principles applicable to the licensing of vaccine manufacturing plants and the maintenance of effective inspection and quality control are not greatly different than those which hold good for drugs generally. One significant difference is the fact that in a number of countries the manufacturing of certain vaccines has been undertaken by state-owned or non-profit institutes rather than by commercial firms.

In France the Institut Pasteur was established as a non-profit foundation, and it was in this capacity that it initially became the country's first major producer of vaccines and sera. In later years, despite receiving a measure of state support, it became increasingly dependent on commerce, and it is now heavily supported by the profits from a commercial vaccine production facility in its own group.

In Denmark the State Serum Institute originated at the end of the nineteenth century within a university department of pathology and bacteriology. Inspired by the work of Roux at the Institut Pasteur in Paris on the preparation and use of an anti-diphtheria serum, the director obtained state support for the creation of a research and manufacturing unit in this field, the original plan being to supply the serum free of charge to the medical profession. In the century since its foundation the Institute has been in the forefront of vaccine development and production, working particularly in the fields of tuberculosis and poliomyelitis. Though it receives financial support for its research both from the state and from private foundations, the Institute is a highly successful and profitable state-owned producer of sera and vaccines.

In the European Community, by virtue of Directive 89/381/EEC, stable industrially prepared blood products intended for a large number of patients, namely albumin, coagulation factors and immunoglobulins, now fall under the Community's pharmaceuticals legislation. These products are, therefore, subject to the same rules on manufacturing and marketing as pharmaceuticals.[6] The same Directive gives binding force to the measures recommended by the Council of Europe and the WHO on the selection and control of blood donors, and supplements them with quality procedures specific to blood derivatives.

Conscientious and Religious Objections to Vaccination

In most countries some form of provision is made for an individual's right to refuse vaccination of himself or herself or of a child, for example, for religious reasons. This would seem entirely reasonable, but some provision needs to be made for a situation in which the refusal appears to be based on a serious misconception or on unreasonable pressure from a third party and where the danger of epidemic infection is real and imminent. The individual patient is more likely to accept an approach from his or her trusted physician on these matters than from the authorities, and health professionals may need guidance on how to deal with such situations wisely and in the patient's best interests.

In the United States, more than 25 immunization procedures are currently recommended prior to entry to a kindergarten. Certain states require particular immunizations to be carried out as a prerequisite to school attendance. Approximately 73 percent of children in the United States are in fact immunized. However, a sizable minority of parents have concerns about immunization, and a proportion refuse some or all vaccines.[7] In 1999 a national telephone survey indicated that almost one-quarter of parents felt uncertain about the increasing number of childhood vaccines, and there has in recent decades been some active lobbying against compulsory vaccination.[8] As once-common childhood diseases become rare, disease awareness decreases, and parents' perspectives about vaccine risks and benefits change. Some religious groupings (Islam, Christian Science) oppose all forms of vaccination.[9] Parents with alternative orientations were found to have more concerns and were relatively more likely to have misconceptions about vaccines. Both accurate and inaccurate information on immunization is available to parents from many sources, including the Internet,[10] creating understandable confusion. As of 2004, Fredrickson et al. noted that 48 states in the United States allowed religious exemptions, and 18 allowed philosophical exemptions.[11]

Cases of poliomyelitis have occurred in the Netherlands in strict Calvinist communities which reject vaccination since disease is considered an Act of God that must not be obstructed. In 1992–93 110 cases occurring in a close-knit church community in the village of Elspeet were attributed to this situation.[12] Vaccination in the Netherlands is strongly recommended but not obligatory.

Thus, in many countries there is understanding of the desire of members of the public to refuse vaccination of themselves or their children, either because they consider it risky or for other reasons. One must, however, bear in mind that mass vaccination is carried out, not primarily for the sake of the individual vaccinee, but to protect the public as a whole. One can make the case that according a right of refusal may contribute to what has been called a 'tragedy of the commons'.[13]

Liability of the State for Injury Resulting From Mass Vaccination Programs

As noted above, large-scale programs of vaccination against disease have either been made obligatory by governments or strongly recommended. The question arises as to the state's responsibility when injury results.

The matter is not merely theoretical. In the more distant past there were periodically serious outbreaks of vaccine-induced injury, generally attributable to quality defects and most notably to the survival of potent infectious material in 'killed' or 'attenuated' vaccines.[14] With improved scientific understanding and manufacturing standards, that type of injury has become much less common, as surveys and statistics show,[15] but injury does continue to occur.[16] The 'Cutter incident' in the United

States in 1955 involved the accidental release onto the market of a batch of poliomyelitis vaccine containing live poliovirus, with disastrous consequences for the recipients.[17] It has been calculated that, in that year, 260 individuals throughout the world developed poliomyelitis as a result of immunization with 'killed' vaccine.[18] Most other forms of vaccine have on occasion killed or injured persons to whom they were given. The same applies to sera. For example, serum sickness may follow the use of anti-tetanus serum.[19]

It may be noted that written consent to vaccination in the framework of such public programs is not generally considered to be necessary, though in some countries practitioners and local authorities have introduced consent forms in the hope of avoiding legal liability for possible complications. Verbal consent is commonly sought but tends to be implied if the individual or the family do not raise objections, for example, on religious grounds. By contrast, it has been pointed out that a company or organization seeking to immunize all its employees in the interests of the staff as a whole must still obtain their consent, and that in this situation it is particularly necessary to ensure that no form of duress is either exerted or experienced.[20] The state is clearly in a somewhat different position.

In 1976 Childress set out a number of simple criteria to assess whether the community could be held liable for injury to an individual resulting from an officially required procedure. Although he had clinical research procedures in mind, his proposed rules seem applicable here.[21] In his view, compensation is needed at least where:

1. the injured party either accepts or is compelled to accept a position of risk *or*
2. by accepting the position the injured party is exposed to objective risks that he or she would not have encountered otherwise *or*
3. the activity that has injured the individual is (at least in part) for the benefit of society.

The issue of a government's liability for the adverse consequences of its vaccination program was squarely presented in public discussion of cases of alleged brain damage due to whooping cough (pertussis) vaccination in the United Kingdom and a number of other countries. The fact that pertussis vaccine carries a degree of risk is universally recognized, but to date it has not been possible to separate the protection-inducing factor of the vaccine entirely from the possible toxic factors,[22] and the degree of risk may vary with the product and by geography. A thorough review in the United States by the Institute of Medicine in 1993 assessed the risk of an acute neurological reaction at less than one per 10.5 million vaccinations.

However, concern in such matters may be dictated by the severity of the reaction rather than by its frequency.

Apart from the fact that, as already noted, the risks may genuinely be greater in one country than in another, several factors have caused views on government liability to differ. In those developed countries where it is difficult or impossible to bring a tort action against the state, it has been argued that, unless government makes some special provisions for compensation in this field, a child injured in a state vaccination program will be poorly off as compared with one injured by the ordinary administration of a commercial vaccine (where one can bring proceedings against the manufacturer). Conversely, it has been suggested that, if a state compensation scheme is created, the beneficiaries may enjoy an unfair advantage over individuals who were not vaccinated at all, but suffered injury as a result of incurring the disease spontaneously. Henk Leenen, writing in 1981 from the Netherlands where vaccination was recommended by the state but not made obligatory, considered that in this context one could not hold the government liable for any ill consequences that might ensue.[23] Yet others have pointed to the inadequacy of tort law in this field, since it may be very difficult to demonstrate negligence. Nor will it be possible to argue that incorrect advice was provided by the authorities to health staff on precautions or contraindications, since it is often unclear what would have been the best advice.

Against this background of uncertainty, a series of countries did proceed to institute procedures allowing for compensation where damage resulted from compulsory (and in some instances recommended) mass vaccination programs. Switzerland[24] and Japan[25] appear to have led the way in 1970, with the United Kingdom following in 1979 and the United States in 1986 (see below).

In the United Kingdom the entire issue was considered by a Royal Commission on Civil Liability and Compensation for Personal Injury. The Commission recommended that since vaccination was advised by the state the public authorities should be strictly liable in tort/delict, and that children suffering apparent vaccine damage should be entitled to a weekly benefit paid as a supplement to normal child benefits. The Vaccine Damage Payments Act of 1979 as ultimately passed[26] covered damage caused to a person by vaccination (including vaccination of the mother while pregnant) against a series of designated diseases, including whooping cough, tetanus, smallpox, tuberculosis, measles, rubella, poliomyelitis and diphtheria. Other diseases could be designated as qualifying diseases by Order in Council. The Act also covered persons disabled by close contact with a person who had been vaccinated against one of the qualifying diseases. Under the Act, claims are decided by an independent tribunal (with medical expertise) on the balance of probabilities, and a reasoned decision must be given. If a causal link can be shown and disability is at least 80 percent, a fixed sum is payable by way of compensation. This sum was initially £20,000 but has since been increased in line with inflation.

The British legislation expressly permits a civil action for damages to be raised as well. The success of the latter will naturally depend on the ability to prove negligence, clearly a difficult matter.[27]

In the United States, the National Childhood Vaccine Injury Act was passed in 1986 largely in response to concerns from parents and vaccine manufacturers arising out of litigation over the diphtheria, pertussis, tetanus (DPT) vaccine.[28] The complex situation in the United States is summarized separately in Box 8.1.

BOX 8.1   VACCINE LIABILITY ISSUES IN THE UNITED STATES

The issue of liability for vaccine injury has passed through various phases of debate in the United States. The developments have not been paralleled elsewhere, but for the sake of completeness they are summarized here.

1. Prior to 1982, litigation against vaccine manufacturers was increasing in parallel with other forms of medical litigation. Tort actions against the US government were not permitted except where the government explicitly accepted them.
2. In 1982 a TV program *DPT Vaccine Roulette,* apparently inspired by an earlier British paper,[a] claimed that many children were neurologically impaired as a result of receiving diphtheria pertussis tetanus (DPT) vaccine, one component of which was whole-cell pertussis (whooping cough) vaccine. Though the link was medically contested, many hundreds of lawsuits against DPT manufacturers followed, and all except one of these manufacturers ceased to make the product, leading to a vaccine shortage.
3. As a consequence, Congress passed the National Childhood Vaccine Injury Act in 1986, introducing no-fault compensation for a number of listed types of vaccine injury following certain types of vaccination. As later extended, the list includes DPT, MMR (measles/mumps/rubella), *Haemophilus influenzae b,* hepatitis B or varicella vaccines, all of which were recommended for routine use in children.

A simplified adjudication process was created. Awards could be made if the balance of probabilities pointed to a causal link. Within a decade more than 1100 awards had been made under the Act. As a consequence, litigation became uncommon, and four firms continued to produce one or more vaccines. The procedure is intended to pre-empt state court actions.

4.   In June 2007 claims were brought on behalf of the parents of 4900 autistic children claiming that their children's condition was due to MMR Vaccine.[b] The Act allows for claims for unlisted conditions (such as autism) to be considered if evidence is adduced. The medical evidence for a link is today much disputed,[c] and as of April 2009 the litigation continues.

5.   Meanwhile routine smallpox vaccination, abandoned in 1972, except for military personnel, has been reintroduced on a limited scale under the Homeland Security Act (in force 2003) because of possible use of the virus as a biological weapon. Vaccination is offered to volunteer 'smallpox response teams' and a stockpile of vaccine and of vaccinia immune globulin has been created to cover the entire population. Under Section 304 of the Act no claim for any resultant injury can be brought against volunteers administering the vaccine or against manufacturers, but a remedy will lie against the US government.[d]

Notes:
a.   G.T. Stewart (1977), 'Vaccination against whooping-cough: efficacy versus risks', *Lancet*, 234, 1.
b.   B. Patsner (2008), 'Childhood vaccines and autism; special courts and torts', *Health Law Perspectives*, February, http://www.law.uh.edu/healthlaw/perspectives/homepage.asp.
c.   Institute of Medicine (2004), *Immunization Safety Review: Vaccines and Autism*, National Academies Press, Washington, DC.
d.   A. Baciu, A.P. Anason, K. Stratton et al. (2005), 'The smallpox vaccination programme', in *Public Health in an Age of Terrorism*, National Academies Press, Washington, DC.

Source: Based on G. Evans (1998), 'Vaccine liability and safety revisited', *Arch Pediatr Adolesc Med*, 152, 7–10.

Victims of vaccination in Germany in a sense enjoyed protection at a very early date since a general law dating back to 1961,[29] modified to some extent in 1971,[30] exploited a principle inherent in the laws of German states that for many years provided for the state to compensate injury suffered by individuals as a consequence of any type of official act. This principle had already been employed prior to 1961 to provide compensation in cases of injury by compulsory smallpox vaccination, and even by the 'recommended' vaccination against tuberculosis. The new law likewise covered both obligatory and recommended forms of vaccination. To be eligible for compensation the vaccinee must have suffered an injury exceeding the normal consequences of vaccination. Indirect damages and injury to third parties by transmission of the virus are covered, as is aggravation of a pre-existing illness. During the first eight years of operation of the system, some 200 claims were allowed. But, after the abandonment of smallpox vaccination, the number of claims fell very drastically.

BLOOD AND BLOOD PRODUCTS

In many respects, the problems relating to blood and blood derivatives intended for transfusion are closely analogous to those considered with respect to drugs. Blood or one of its derivatives, supplied for administration to patients, can reasonably be considered a 'defective product' in the sense of the EEC Product Liability Directive if it does not provide 'the safety which a person is entitled to expect,'[31] and there is copious evidence that injury can result from errors associated with its collection, processing or administration. Public policy requires that blood and its derivatives be readily available without quality defects or barriers of price, and there is in many places a preference for non-commercial supply channels. As with vaccines, religious and ethical objections are sometimes raised to the use of blood, and reasonable allowance has to be made for them. There has been much ethical debate and litigation, both in the United States and elsewhere, involving the possible right of a physician or hospital to override a patient's religious objections to receiving a transfusion.[32] The outcomes have varied, but both medical authorities and courts have been notably hesitant to allow parents to refuse the administration of blood to their children.

For a great many years the most common injury that was reported in this area resulted from the administration to patients of incompatible or life-expired blood, a fault generally due to errors made by hospital staff. Allergy was also a recurrent complication. In recent years these problems have been dwarfed by those resulting from the supply and use of infected blood, especially material carrying the HIV virus (and thus potentially capable of transmitting AIDS).

In so far as the responsibility and liability of the supplier is concerned, there is no medical reason to treat cases of injury involving unsafe blood differently from those involving unsafe drugs. As with drugs, there is an obvious obligation to maintain acceptable standards of quality, which in the case of blood or its derivatives is largely a matter of ensuring that it comes from a healthy source, is rigorously checked, properly processed and is stored under proper conditions. The logistics of blood supply tend, however, to be different from those of drug supply. Outside the United States, whole blood destined for transfusion and labile products derived from it (for example, clotting factors or packed erythrocytes) are not generally considered commercial products. Because of its human origin blood is often obtained, supplied and processed by government or voluntary non-profit agencies (for example, the Red Cross). This form of supply can affect the legal situation if a conflict arises. If a court believes that there has been fault on the part of the supplier, it will not (in the absence of a sales contract) be able to call upon any form of commercial law to provide a remedy. It may, however, be able to rely on statutory law relating to blood products that in many countries sets very specific requirements. By contrast, if a court does not believe that a remedy is called for, it may well find some means of rejecting a claim even where the blood is of commercial origin.

In an old but still commonly cited New York case heard before the Court of Appeals in 1954 (*Perlmutter v. Beth David Hospital*), a private patient was given an infusion of tainted blood and contracted hepatitis. The blood was charged separately to the patient's account. The court refused to find that the blood had been sold as a product. It said that there was a contract for the supply of services that contained no implied warranty of fitness.[33] It may be noted, however, that in a 1988 case, a New York Court did hold that HIV contaminated blood was a 'substance' for purposes of the statute of limitations,[34] thus enabling a victim who later contracted AIDS as a result of transfusion to lodge a claim. The 1954 decision seems to have been one of policy, pronounced at a time when, as the Court concluded, there was 'neither a means of detecting the presence of the jaundice-producing agent in the donor's blood nor a practical method of treating the blood so that the danger may be eliminated'. The contrast between the two cases thus also reflects the general principle, touched on in other chapters, that standards of quality unavoidably change as methods to improve and control them improve. Though the duty to another party will not change, a court will only hold a producer to standards that are reasonably attainable given the state of the art. The old Perlmutter case may also illustrate the fact that courts do their best to avoid placing an unreasonable burden upon physicians or hospitals supplying blood to save lives. The blood in that case was of commercial origin. But it is undoubtedly true that courts will also seek to be as lenient as possible towards non-commercial suppliers of blood products acting in the public interest, such as the Red Cross.

Risk of HIV Contamination

The end of the 1970s and the mid 1980s saw society confronted with very large numbers of patients worldwide who were infected with HIV through exposure to contaminated blood products, principally Factor VII and Factor IX administered in concentrate form to those suffering from hemophilia-type clotting disorders. In some countries the problem was largely a consequence of fractionation of commercially procured blood donations, obtained by the main US commercial enterprises in this field, which were contaminated with viruses at the time they were purchased. The history of this epidemic has been extensively described elsewhere[35] and need not be recounted here, but its extent is grave. Of 2000 registered hemophilics in Japan, some 400 had by 1996 died of HIV infection.[36] In France, between 1992 and 1994, a special fund established by the government to pay damages to transfusion patients infected with HIV granted compensation to 4000 patients. In 820 cases the amount of the settlement could not be agreed between the parties, and was settled by a court.[37]

It should be pointed out that the HIV molecule was not identified until about 1984, and thus no direct screening was possible, donor selection and surrogate testing for hepatitis B virus being the only possible protection.

Countries have found very different means of dealing with the problems of HIV-infected blood. New legislation has been introduced and older legislation adapted to ensure that the blood transfusion service maintains adequate standards of quality at all stages. In several countries litigation brought against health authorities or the blood transfusion service has either been successful in court or has been settled. The situation in a number of countries is summarized briefly below.

European Union

Insofar as courts have been willing to regard items in this field as 'products' and the institutions processing them as fully analogous to commercial drug producers, they can fall under the European Union's provisions dealing with product liability and consumer protection. However, even prior to these European rules, various countries had sought and found solutions to the liability problem. Germany had provided compensation under its drug regulations and developed a system for reporting adverse effects,[38] In Denmark, independent of EU rules, a state compensation fund was established in 1995 to compensate persons infected with HIV from Factor VIII transfusions. The move followed the rejection in the High Court of a case brought against the Health authorities and the Danish manufacturer. It was demonstrated that the authorities had twice delayed switching from the Danish supplier to a foreign source of more expensive

Factor VIII that had been heat-treated to eliminate the virus. The Court considered the delay 'irresponsible but not culpable'.[39]

United States

In the United States, state statutes usually indicate that the suppliers of blood products are not to be held strictly liable. Sometimes, in order to avoid strict liability, these statutes will provide that the supply of blood is a service and not the sale of a product (see Perlmutter case cited above).[40] The blood supplier may, however, be liable in negligence if infected blood has not been screened out. Rigorous screening is of the greatest importance since blood from multiple donors is mixed during processing and infection from a single donor may thus injure many recipients.

In a 1992 case, a non-profit blood bank, UBS, was sued by the Quintana family for failing to screen their blood donors properly for potential infection with HIV. As a result, Mrs Quintana, who had undergone emergency surgery and received several pints of blood collected and processed by UBS, contracted infection with the virus. The Court held that there was a presumption in favor of defendant UBS if it adhered to the industry standard of care. However, the plaintiff is permitted to rebut that presumption by presenting expert testimony to indicate that the standard of care adopted by the school of practice to which the defendant adheres is unreasonably defective by not incorporating readily available practices and procedures which are substantially more protective against the harm that plaintiff experienced.[41]

Class actions, admitted in the United States for drugs, have not been admitted for cases involving blood. In the Rhone-Poulenc Rorer case of 1995[42] the Seventh Circuit Court of Appeals decertified a class action relating to infected blood that had been certified by the District Court 'on particular issues only' relating to the general question of negligence. The Court of Appeals pointed out that most federal courts do not permit the use of a class action in mass tort claims in any field,[43] unless the weight of numbers makes the use of a class action irresistible.

In 1987 in the case of *John Doe v. Cutter Biological & Others*,[44] the judge similarly decided against a class action in a case involving blood, in terms that still provide useful guidance as to the criteria that are likely to be applied.

> Personal injury cases generally are not appropriate for class action treatment because such actions do not have the predominant communality of issues necessary for class treatment. This case is no exception. Any plaintiff in this litigation will have to establish (*inter alia*) what coagulation factor materials he took and when; what warnings his physician received or did not receive, and when; what information was available to the plaintiff, and when; the state of medical and scientific knowledge at those times pertinent to his claims that

the anti-haemophilic factor concentrate he took was factually the cause of his injury; that the producer of that concentrate was negligent in one or more of the ways alleged; and that such negligence was the proximate cause of the particular plaintiff's injury. Proof of each defendant's breach of duty and whether that breach proximately caused the injury claimed by a particular plaintiff would have to be tried separately for each plaintiff. These issues will have to be decided individually on a case-by-case basis. There is no common nucleus of operative facts which could be resolved in a general trial applicable to all plaintiffs, and there are no common issues which predominate over individual issues.

In August 1996 an Order was made in the US District Court for the Northern District of Illinois Eastern Division for the certification of a settlement class and preliminary approval of a settlement agreement in favor of all US persons with hemophilia who were HIV positive and had been exposed to Factor VIII concentrate manufactured by any of the four main defendants. The settlement amount was $100,000 net of counsel's fees and costs. This relatively modest sum was no doubt attributable to the perceived difficulties of proof, especially in relation to the identity of the proper defendant.

In an unusual case also involving HIV infection from transfused blood, the United States was held liable for the fault of a naval surgeon; the latter had performed a tonsillectomy in such a manner as to demand not only a direct transfusion but also a follow-up transfusion at another hospital where the available blood was apparently from a contaminated source.[45]

By 1997, a number of producers of blood derivatives in the United States had agreed on pacts both with the federal government and with 20 of the states, laying the basis for a multi-million dollar lawsuit settlement over Factor VIII and IX products that had transmitted AIDS or the HIV virus to hemophiliacs.[46]

Japan
As of 1 July 1995, a new Product Liability Law came into effect that covers injury attributable to blood products; a parliamentary amendment however excludes liability for 'complications of blood transfusion such as those caused by contamination by viruses the complete removal of which by existing technology is impossible'.[47]

United Kingdom
In cases of HIV infection in the United Kingdom, the government and courts faced a series of problems prior to the enactment of the Consumer Protection Act. As in some other countries, it sometimes proved impossible to determine the source of a contested product. Massive litigation

brought against the Department of Health related variously to its failure
to provide a safe regime for donor selection, processing of blood and
treatment of patients. After defending a series of cases, the government
ultimately recognized its responsibility in these matters and established the
Macfarlane Trust, a charitable fund of £10 million for the relief of hardship
among HIV positive hemophilia sufferers. In addition it provided a direct
donation of £20.000 per person as well as settling outstanding cases with
an overall payment of £42 million to be shared among all those affected
whether or not they had joined in the legal proceedings. A major step was
the establishment of a National Blood Authority to assume overall responsibility for the National Blood Service. The Authority was incorporated in
late 2005 into a new body known as NHS Blood and Transplant.

Hepatitis C Infection

The relative success of the HIV hemophilia litigation in the UK, and the
technical investigations carried out in the course of it, paved the way
for the investigation of similar claims in relation to the hepatitis C virus
(HCV) acquired both from whole blood transfusions and concentrates
and other blood products.

The most significant case regarding HCV contamination is that decided
in England in 2001 under the strict liability provisions of the 1987
Consumer Protection Act that from 1988 onwards adopted the rules laid
down in the EC Product Liability Directive.[48] The case is proving influential in other EU member states[49] because it considers the manner in which
knowledge evolves with respect to blood products – a topic of study and
concern at many centers throughout the world – and, in that connection, the relevance in this field of the disputed 'development risk defense'
allowed by the Directive.[50]

The case involved claims by 114 persons infected with HCV following blood transfusions given to them in the course of medical treatment
between specified dates in 1988 and 1991. Type C serum hepatitis was
only identified in 1988, and a screening test to eliminate the risk of contamination was introduced in the UK in 1991. Both parties agreed that
blood was a 'product' within the meaning of the law and that the National
Blood Authority et al. were the producers. Mr. Justice Burton's judgment
strongly supported the spirit of the EC Directive in its desire to facilitate compensation irrespective of issues of negligence. He distinguished
a 'standard' product (that is, one that is and performs as the producer
intends) from a 'non-standard' product that is in some way deficient or
inferior. The product supplied to the plaintiffs was non-standard because
of the presence of HCV. The defendants pleaded the development risks

defense, but the Court pointed out that the risk was known by 1988. Mr. Justice Burton added: 'The existence of the defect is in my judgment clearly generic. Once the existence of the defect is known, then there is the risk of that defect materializing in any particular product.' From that moment, the producer would supply the product at its own risk. The fact that the defendants were not capable before 1991 of discovering the defect in their own particular product was not considered sufficient ground to accept the development risk defense (discussed earlier). The claim against the defendants was allowed.

In this case, no warning regarding the risk of hepatitis C had been supplied with the product. It is possible that, had such a warning been given, the Court might have found for the producers.

It is also notable in this case that the parties agreed that the National Blood Authority et al., could be regarded as producers of the blood. This deviates to some extent from the provisions of the European Directive which relates to bodies that are 'in business' (Art. 7(c) of the Directive), and in another court this view might be challenged. But it is one supported by legal commentators,[51] and where blood products are concerned it seems eminently reasonable.

Liability of Donors

A question that does not yet appear to have been tested in court is the possible liability of an individual blood donor who proves to be a source of contaminated blood. Learned authors have stressed the fact that the donor bears an important part of the responsibility for the safety of transfusion practice. As early as 1977, the League of Red Cross Societies defined it as the duty of the donor towards the recipient to provide safe blood.[52] This duty involves taking note of the information given to them on 'safe donor behaviour', and informing the transfusion service accordingly on any aspect of his health or behavior which could be in conflict with this standard.[53] A donor who gave blood after knowingly exposing himself to the risk of AIDS infection would certainly transgress this norm. Several legal systems specifically impose criminal liability on a blood donor who knowingly makes a false statement regarding his state of health prior to giving blood.[54]

Issues of Consent

It is sound and normal practice for a conscious patient to be informed in an appropriate manner by a physician, when a transfusion is planned, as to the possible benefits and risks of the procedure. Often there will be no formal request for consent, but this will be taken as implied if the patient does not object. As with drugs, the extent of the information provided will depend upon the individual and the circumstances. As Christopher Newdick (1994) has pointed out, an enquiring patient 'ought to be told much more than one who says: "I'm in your hands, doctor. You know best." '[55]

As in the case of vaccines, consent in written form by the patient or guardian is not customary for a transfusion, though it may be part of a broader process (for example, hospital admission for surgery) for which consent has already been obtained. Jean Pierre Soulier (1994) has suggested that in certain situations, for example, the use of new types of blood product with which there is still little experience, written consent should be obtained.[56] In Japan written patient consent to transfusion is now becoming more common since the exclusion of many transfusion complications from the new Product Liability Law, as noted above.[57]

Criminal Liability

In various countries criminal charges relating to tainted blood have been brought against individuals and institutions. In France, as early as 1985, two physicians were convicted of distributing non-heat-treated antihemophilic concentrates in the course of 1985, knowing that they could be contaminated by HIV, and without warning the Haemophilia Association of the risks that its members were running. Two health authorities received suspended sentences on similar charges. It may be noted that the specific conviction of the two physicians was criticized, particularly since a much wider group of professionals and advisors appears to have shared responsibility for the error.[58]

In Canada, where by late 1985 2,000 people were reported to be infected with HIV and up to 60,000 with HCV, the Supreme Court of Canada found the Canadian Red Cross negligent in that it had failed to screen blood donors effectively for HIV infection.[59] A series of criminal charges followed and are considered in Chapter 7.

Overall Policy with Respect to Blood Products

Differences in social and political tradition unavoidably lead to dissimilar approaches where blood products are concerned. Irrespective, however, of whether the actual activities in this field are handled by state institutions, non-commercial bodies or business firms, there is a very broad agreement that the community needs to be involved in rule making, inspection and ensuring the quality of service at all steps from donor selection to bedside transfusion. These are products which are directly used to save lives, but they can equally directly threaten survival. The long history of problems with various forms of virus contamination has forced recognition of the community's role, and there is reason to insist that such a role be strictly maintained in order to face threats in the future. Where, in spite of every precaution, injury does occur, there will still be a place for compensation schemes and a supportive role for litigation – backed very occasionally by the sanctions of the criminal law.

ALTERNATIVE AND TRADITIONAL MEDICINES

While the great bulk of medicinal therapy today is based on the principles of scientific medicine and pharmacology, and considerations of policy take this as their starting point, there has been an increasing degree of public interest in the possible merits of treatments developed outside Western scientific tradition. Extraordinary difficulties have attended attempts to develop policies in this matter that will best serve the public interest. The medical scientist is unwilling to accept conclusions and teachings that are not based on his or her own rigorous approach to proof. From traditional medicines practitioners, one may encounter unassailable convictions that cannot easily be questioned. The points of departure for public policy must, on the one hand, be a willingness to accept alternative preferences and points of view but, on the other hand, maintain the overarching principle of safeguarding the individual from undue risk.

For practical purposes it is helpful to make a distinction here between the situation of alternative therapies of relatively recent origin and that surrounding longstanding traditional forms of medicinal treatment.

Alternative Medicines: Homeopathy

Although a series of alternative approaches to medicinal therapy have been developed within Western countries, the following discussion will center on the practice of homeopathy, which is the most extensively practiced of these teachings and has been the subject of much policy debate. The method originated with the German Christian F.S. Hahnemann (1755–1843) who published his system in 1810.[60] A series of observations had led him to the conclusion that, whereas certain chemical substances could produce undesirable effects on the body mimicking those of disease, the use of these same chemicals in extreme dilution could counter these same effects. The greater the dilution, the more potent the effect. He proceeded to develop a series of remedies based on this principle. His successors extended its application, resulting in the availability of the wide range of homeopathic medicines that are manufactured and sold today.

It has not proved possible to find a place for the homeopathic approach in orthodox medical teaching. Critics have pointed to what are regarded as elementary errors in Hahnemann's original observations. Impartial studies of the administration of homeopathic medicines have failed to detect any significant beneficial effect. It is indeed argued that some of the more extreme dilutions are such that not a single molecule of the active substance is likely to be present in the normally recommended dose. Benefits attributed to these remedies are considered to be based on observations of individual cases, in which the 'placebo' effect of suggestion and the natural defenses of the body have resulted in relief – no role being attributable to the remedy. Adherents to the homeopathic method respond by arguing inter alia that homeopathic treatment is individualized, and that one therefore cannot expect positive results to be obtained in a normal comparative clinical study in which a standard dose is employed in a series of patients.

In this situation one cannot anticipate a wide consensus regarding the claimed efficacy of the Hahnemann method. In view of the extensive following that it enjoys, however, many regulatory agencies have shaped their policies to allow for individual choice, taking into consideration the fact that, in view of the extreme dilutions employed, the possibility of any adverse effect hardly arises.

Special provision has, therefore, been made for the licensing of homeopathic remedies provided that manufacturing conditions are fully satisfactory and that the labeling of any product sold under this regime is appropriate. This must include an explicit statement that the product is accepted as representing the homeopathic tradition only, and that it has not been evaluated for efficacy by the agency concerned.

A comparable approach would appear to be acceptable for other alternative forms of treatment involving the use of medicinal remedies, provided that manufacturing quality is assured and sufficient reason is present to exclude any significant risk.

Traditional Medicines

The situation of traditional medicines differs vary considerably from that of alternative therapies of relatively recent origin. Many countries in all parts of the world have a tradition of folk medicine, largely though not exclusively based on the use of herbs, and sometimes dating back for many thousands of years. In a large part of the world traditional medicines coexist with Western evidence-based medicine, often complementing it and providing poorly resourced populations with trusted care at relatively low cost. It will no doubt continue to do so for a long time to come. Quite apart from this, a proportion of the most valuable drugs available to Western medicine were discovered as a result of traditional medical practices. The identification of digitalis as the active component of the foxglove leaf by William Withering and its adoption into cardiac medicine in the late eighteenth century was particularly prominent, but it is only one in a long series of such developments. Opium from the poppy (as a source of morphine for the relief of severe pain) provides a more ancient example, while the adoption of senna as a laxative and the various forms of atropine to treat numerous symptoms and disorders involving the autonomic nervous system are equally significant. This type of assimilation of traditional knowledge into Western medicine continues. The vinca alkaloids for the treatment of malignant disease were only recognized in the mid twentieth century, and artemesin was adopted from Chinese practice for the treatment of drug-resistant malaria only after 1980. Undoubtedly, given the vast number of herbs used medicinally across the world, and their regional variations, developments of this type will continue, though hopefully in an increasingly systematic manner.

From the point of view of public policy in Western countries, products claiming to be based on a foreign medicinal tradition present something of a dilemma. In the public interest, it is desirable to ensure that principles of efficacy, quality, safety and truth applicable to Western medicines are respected. However, except where particular remedies have been fully assimilated into scientific medicine, the data that one needs to ensure that traditional medicines attain these standards are largely lacking. There has rarely been a systematic study of their desired and undesired effects in human subjects. The manner of proper preparation is rarely documented in full, if at all. The situation is further complicated in many countries by the fact that these products have usually been commercialized, and there is no certainty that the packaged commercial product represents the original tradition in a genuine and trustworthy manner. In some cases it clearly does not. In The Netherlands, a commercial product claimed to be based on Korean ginseng, which is reputed to have tonic properties, was found on analytical examination to consist of turnips floating in French wine.[61]

As in the area of alternative therapies, however, these medicines have progressively attained a considerable following outside the countries where the original tradition grew up. There is public demand that they be available. Where a manufacturer or importer is in a position to provide documented evidence of their properties, they can be treated as ordinary medicines, but as a rule such materials are not available.

In principle, it would be desirable to adopt an approach analogous to that developed for homeopathic medicines outlined above, that is, such products may be licensed for sale, provided it is made clear that they represent a particular tradition and have not been authoritatively tested for efficacy. This, however, leaves open the issue of safety – not a negligible matter in view of the fact that the plant world is the source of some of the most potent poisons known. Unless rigid manufacturing specifications can be set and maintained, serious accidents can occur.

The deregulation in the United States of products based on ephedra, considered in Chapter 7, provides an example of the quality problem. After a number of serious and even fatal cardiovascular complications among users of these products was reported, it was found that there had in some manufacturing plants been an 18-fold variation in the content of ephedrine and that other ephedrine-like substances were sometimes present. All this would point to the fact that serious over-dosage with these substances, which are known to raise blood pressure, could occur.[62]

The degree of risk presented by commercialized traditional medicines is not known. Most of the products in question are used in the framework of self-medication. Adverse effects therefore fail to enter the professional based adverse reaction reporting systems. Edzard Ernst in the United Kingdom has, however, for many years maintained a sympathetic but close watch on worldwide reports of adverse events due to complementary therapies as a whole. It is evident from his collected material that they can and do induce a wide range of serious and sometimes fatal unwanted effects.[63] This problem clearly merits ongoing attention from the public health perspective. Insofar as these traditional remedies are being manufactured and marketed worldwide – in an environment far removed from that in which they have traditionally been prepared and used on the basis of inherited knowledge – there would seem to be an increasingly powerful argument for subjecting them to a critical regulatory regime, at least in order to attenuate whatever risks may be associated with their use.

SELF-MEDICATION

The Nature of Self-Medication

Any attempt to define an appropriate public policy applicable to self-medication is complicated by the fact that the view of society generally – and of the professions – as to the self-diagnosis and self-treatment of illness has changed several times over the past century, and continues to change. Attitudes toward self-medication are determined only in part by what is technically desirable or wise. They also reflect social views, including attitudes toward the empowerment of the layperson, and the proper

BOX 8.2   HERBAL MEDICINE: THE NEGLECTED SUPPLIER OF GLOBAL HEALTH

Ryan Abbott, MD/JD Candidate, MTOM LAC

Introduction

Herbal medicine has been used to treat disease for thousands of years as part of virtually all cultures and medical systems, and nearly one-third of pharmaceutical drugs were originally derived from plants.[a] Herbal medicine is both self-administered and utilized by practitioners of traditional medical systems, such as traditional Chinese medicine (TCM) and Ayurveda. Worldwide, the use of herbal medicine is considerable, and represents a global market of $60 billion.[b] In industrialized nations, the resurgence of herbal medicine can be related to the larger renaissance of Complementary and Alternative Medicine (CAM). In developing nations herbal medicine is used as a matter of necessity, because it is efficacious and because it is embedded in indigenous cultural and medical systems; in these countries the use of herbal and traditional medicine may surpass the use of pharmaceutical and allopathic medicine, while in the poorest areas of the world, herbal medicine is sometimes the only affordable and accessible source of treatment. For example, in Ghana and Kenya a single course of pharmaceutical treatment for malaria costs $1.60 compared with $0.10 for herbal treatment.[c] Considering that the annual per capita out-of-pocket health expenditure for these nations is about six dollars, pharmaceutical medicine is simply beyond the means of much of the population. In addition to being more affordable, herbal medicine is more accessible. Of the 57 nations with a critical shortage of physicians, nurses and midwives, 36 are in sub-Saharan Africa. In these countries, such as Uganda, the ratio of traditional practitioners to allopathic practitioners may be as high as 40:1. Because allopathic practitioners are further concentrated in cities, access to pharmaceuticals is even more limited in rural populations.

Benefits of Herbal Medicine

Where pharmaceutical treatments are unavailable, inaccessible or ineffective, herbal medicine may represent a viable alternative.

As a complementary treatment, herbal medicine may be able to decrease reliance on more expensive and invasive interventions.

While the breakthroughs of pharmaceutical medicine in the past century have led to stunning successes in the treatment of many infectious and acute conditions, such as tuberculosis and smallpox, they have not had similar results with many chronic diseases. With improved life expectancies, cancer and stroke have become the leading causes of death, and chronic pain and infirmity are on the rise. Pharmaceutical medicine has fallen short in adequately addressing the maintenance of health and improving quality of life, as well as the treatment of chronic, stress-related illnesses.[d]

Pharmaceutical research has also tended to focus on the most profitable conditions rather than those representing the most significant burden to global health. While the treatment of erectile dysfunction has proven highly lucrative, one-sixth of the world's population suffers from one or more neglected tropical diseases, associated with a high degree of morbidity and mortality. Diseases neglected by Pharma for lack of financial desirability already have established herbal treatments. Herbal medicine could also help those patients who experience only partial relief of their symptoms from medication or who may be unable to tolerate pharmaceutical intervention. For diseases that lack effective pharmacological treatment, patients are increasingly turning to herbal medicine for treatment.[e]

In the management of conditions for which efficacious pharmaceutical treatments exist, herbal medicine remains significantly less expensive. Herbal medicine is widely and inexpensively available to practitioners of alternative medicine and the public, and its use is supported by an extensive traditional knowledge base. Whereas the development of new pharmaceuticals requires significant monetary investment, the herbal armamentarium is already extensively developed and does not qualify for patent protection. Herbal medicine may prove to be cost-effective both directly and indirectly by reducing reliance on more expensive medications, and by limiting the side effects and complications associated with pharmaceutical medicines.

The significant adverse effects attributable to pharmaceuticals far surpass those attributable to herbal medicine. Even when appropriately prescribed, virtually all pharmaceutical-based interventions include some risk to the patient of side effects or complications, particularly over a long-term course of use. The more powerful the drug, the more likely it is to have harmful side effects. To the extent that pharmaceutical treatment could be supplemented or replaced with herbal medicine it would be expected to reduce the incidence of harmful side effects and minimize iatrogenic effects. Preliminary evidence supporting the cost-effectiveness of herbal medicine is promising, but additional research is needed.[f]

Barriers to Integration

Despite the widespread use of herbal medicine, the allopathic medical community has largely failed to address the issues surrounding its manufacture, therapeutics and application. Herbal medicine is poorly regulated worldwide, even with regards to good manufacturing practices. Some research has found that commercially available herbal medicines may be adulterated or contain high levels of heavy metals or undeclared pharmaceuticals.[g] Perhaps most importantly, there is a critical paucity of research evaluating the use of herbal and traditional medicines, particularly with regards to efficacy, safety, drug-herb interactions and cost-effectiveness. Part of the reason that herbal medicine has received so little attention may be that most conventional health care providers know very little about herbal medicine.[h] The research designs and systems created to evaluate pharmaceuticals would require modification to address the unique challenges posed by herbal medicine. Herbal medicine also shows little financial promise to the pharmaceutical industry. Because existing and novel herbal remedies cannot apply for patent protection, they infringe upon the market for pharmaceuticals while at the same time failing to produce monopolistic profit. Perhaps partially for these reasons, many stakeholders in the current health care system oppose the use and research of herbal medicine. Even the relatively modest amount of funding devoted to researching herbal medicine is a vehemently debated political issue.

To improve the health of the global population while remaining within the restraints of the global economy, it is vital that policy makers, health professionals and the public make well-informed decisions regarding the development and use of herbal medicine.

Although herbal medicine has always played a major role in global health care, it continues to exist at the periphery of allopathic medicine. Integrating the use of herbal medicine with pharmaceutical medicine where appropriate may produce a health care system that retains the advantages of the existing system while addressing its limitations. Integrating herbal medicine could prove safer, more accessible, more affordable and more effective in dealing with the health care challenges of the twenty-first century.

Notes:
a. World Health Organization (2002), *WHO Traditional Medicine Strategy 2002– 2005*, Geneva, Switzerland.
b. UNCTAD (2000), Systems and National Experiences for Protecting Traditional Knowledge, Innovations and Practices, Background Note by the UNCTAD Secretariat. Geneva, United Nations.
c. C.K. Ahorlu (1997), 'Malaria-related beliefs and behaviour in southern Ghana: implications for treatment, prevention and control'. *Trop Med and Int Health,* **2** (5), 488–99.
d. G.F. Anderson, V. Petrosian and P.S. Hussey (2002), *Multinational Comparisons of Health Systems Data*, The Commonwealth Fund, New York.
e. J.A. Astin (1998), 'Why patients use alternative medicine: results of a national study', *JAMA*, 279 (19),1548–53.
f. P.M. Herman, B.M. Craig and O. Caspi (2005), 'Is complementary and alternative medicine (CAM) cost-effective? A systematic review', *BMC Complement Altern Med*, 2 (5), 11; A.R. White and E. Ernst (2000), 'Economic analysis of complementary medicine: a systematic review', *Complementary Therapies in Medicine*, 8, 111–18.
g. Institute of Medicine (2005), *Complementary and Alternative Medicine in the United States*, National Academies Press, Washington, DC.
h. C. Zollman and A. Vickers (1999), 'What is complementary medicine?', *BMJ*, 319, 693–6.

role of the health professions. In addition, they are necessarily influenced by the availability of professional services. In a country where certain conditions are epidemic and access to the physician is limited, one may accept a broader role for self-medication than elsewhere.

The term self-medication refers primarily to the use of those over-the-counter (OTC) medicines which have been formulated and manufactured explicitly for purchase and use by the lay patient, without the need to consult a physician. These medicines will be sold in pharmacies (or in some countries much more widely) and, as a rule, they can be advertised directly to the public.

There are, however, several gray areas that need to be born in mind in policy making. One involves the use of a small group of prescription medicines which are highly unlikely to be abused, yet which will be required so frequently over a long period by the chronically ill that it would seem unduly burdensome to demand frequent prescriptions. Pharmacies may be authorized to issue these without prescription at their discretion to known clients. The injection of insulin is the example usually cited. There is also the situation in some parts of the world where, irrespective of laws and edicts, many pharmacists or drug retailers sell a wide range of drugs (for example, antibiotics) without prescription that could better be used under medical supervision. As a rule this practice is, in fact, illegal in the countries concerned. It clearly involves risk either to the individual user (for example, because contraindications are not respected) or to the community (for example, when widespread use of antibiotics results in the development of bacterial resistance). Countering this practice is likely to be in the public interest, but it will involve a long-term process of public education and, in many cases, improved access to medical care.

At the beginning of the twentieth century self-medication in developed countries was widespread, but regarded as discreditable. The field was dominated by the sale and intensive promotion of largely overpriced medicines of dubious value and secret composition for which undocumented claims were advanced. Medical writers and professional organizations in various countries condemned the practice. Dr. F. Zernick in Germany, around the turn of the century, published analyses and assessments of many such remedies in the *Deutsche Medizinische Wochenschrift*. The Bruinsma brothers in the Netherlands had taken a similar initiative a generation earlier.[64] In 1909 and 1912 the British Medical Association published a series of analyses and critical reviews of products offered for self-medication in the UK, showing that most were both overpriced and useless.[65] It is, therefore, hardly surprising that, as health services became more widely accessible in developed countries, the view began to develop in some quarters that self-medication with its suspect history no longer had any place in society. It soon became clear, however, that the new health services were struggling to cope with the volume of work they were expected to undertake. There was not always good reason to trouble the doctor for a minor symptom. There was a reasonable place for a number of simple but genuine remedies that could be used by the lay public to relieve everyday symptoms without the need for medical diagnosis or supervision. By 1970, positive policies based on that view were gaining adherence and a vigorous and entirely reformed self-medication industry was responding with well-formulated products. These were approved by regulatory agencies and generally advertised in a responsible manner. A 1975 document drawn up by the Council of Europe declared that a logical self-medication policy could be based on a joint consideration of eligible diagnoses, symptoms and medicines.[66] Where a condition could be readily self-diagnosed (for example, the common cold, headache, constipation) and could normally be relieved by simple, familiar products presenting no substantial degree of risk, the latter could be made freely available for short-term use in the home. Products such as mild analgesics and laxatives, nasal decongestants and antacids were clearly acceptable. This view was later adopted in studies by the WHO.[67] In the developed world standards such as these are now generally part of the legal framework of regulation.

By 1990, there was a move towards an even broader scope for self-diagnosis and self-treatment of illness. Liberal OTC availability standards were sometimes challenged by medical practitioners arguing that some medicines might, in lay hands, give a degree of symptomatic relief masking serious conditions. The underlying condition would, therefore, remain undiagnosed and untreated. But strict application of this principle would be inconvenient, and unnecessary provided that adequate warnings were provided to the user that such medicines were intended only for short-term use. More products were released for self-medication. These include antiperistaltics for the relief of 'tourist diarrhea', a number of compounds more effective than the antacids for gastric distress, and creams containing low concentrations of corticosteroids to relieve skin irritation.

On some specific issues there have been controversies and occasional changes of view, dictated either by experience or by changing social concepts. At least one anti-inflammatory drug, released in some countries for home use to relieve pain, was returned to prescription control because of the incidence of side effects.[68] Free availability of post-coital contraceptives (the 'morning after pill') was initially refused, but subsequently approved in many countries subject to continuing criticism, particularly from religious organizations.[69] From a different religious standpoint, the general availability of medicines containing alcohol has been proscribed.[70] On certain other matters, criticism of a more liberal regime has been expressed primarily from the medical point of view. The release of a blood-lipid lowering agent for free sale in the United Kingdom in 2004 was condemned because of what some view as the already considerable over-use of such products, the ultimate medical value of which has been questioned.[71]

It is not clear how far and how fast the trend toward greater liberalization of self-medication will or should proceed. Bearing in mind that not only varying medical attitudes, but also social, educational, moral and religious views, enter the debate, it is unlikely that broad international consensus will be attained, except on some general principles. The list of products considered proper to release for home use will continue to differ from one country to another. It is also possible that the current trend toward greater liberalization will be followed by something of a backlash. There is already concern regarding overmedication in industrialized society (see Chapter 9).

With the controversial advertising of prescription medicines to the public in certain countries, the user has gained a measure of control over his physician's prescribing, thus effectively extending the range of self-medication. Should clear evidence emerge that the public is now insufficiently protected from itself, these matters will certainly merit policy review.

Designation of Products for Use in Self-medication

The broad principles laid down by the Council of Europe in 1975 according to which a product can be considered eligible for use in self-medication are now widely accepted, even if their exact interpretation differs. In Europe designation of a drug as being eligible for use in self-medication is undertaken by the regulatory authorities according to principles laid down by the European Union Directive 92/26/EEC of 1992. Entirely new chemical entities will not be so released. Their status can, however, be reassessed later when a request to this effect is made by the holder of the market authorization, and once sufficient field experience with them has been gained to pass definitive judgment on the drugs' value, risks and manner of use. Designation of a drug for 'over-the-counter' use can, according to the European Union's rules, also be withdrawn after five years in the light of experience. But, it is likely that if any problem were to arise an agency would not hesitate to withdraw the designation at an earlier date

The US FDA has established an Office of Non-prescription Drugs, backed by an Advisory Committee and its Center for Drug Evaluation and Research. It has established and continues to draw up monographs to cover each class of OTC drugs currently available. Most such drugs or their equivalents have been on the market for many years. The FDA has been reluctant to release newer products for free sale. It is notable that in December 2007 the FDA, departing from the precedent set by the British authorities, rejected for the third time an industry application to release a cholesterol-lowering statin for use in self-medication on the grounds that 'too many of the wrong people would use the drug if it no longer required a prescription'.[72]

Labeling and Promotion

If self-medication is to be sufficiently safe, product information and instructions for use that are provided to the public must be appropriate and reliable. Health professions, regulatory authorities and to some extent the specialized industry working in the field have developed standards for teaching the public to self-medicate in a responsible manner. The 'Code of Advertising Practices' of the Consumer Healthcare Products Association in the United States urges member companies to promote the responsible use of these remedies and provides a series of detailed rules,[73] as do the corresponding codes from manufacturers' associations in Britain,[74] Australia[75] and elsewhere. Like other codes maintained by drug manufacturers, these tend to be effective since the members of the associations in effect police one another to ensure adherence, departure from a code being regarded as a form of unfair competition.

Although, as with prescription drugs, the distinction between information and promotion is sometimes artificial, it is generally reasonable to make this distinction where medicines for self-medication are concerned. The package insert and the labeling are intended to provide the basic information needed by the user. Existing codes and standards make it clear that this information must be complete and must not be promotional in character. In addition, it should warn against excessive use of the product and point out the possibilities of its causing harmful effects, which should be specified. Where advertising is conducted in the media it must be recognizable as such and not be camouflaged as editorial matter. In addition:

1   Public advertising for medicines should be informative and clear, and not give the impression that the product is capable of doing more than it actually can.
2   It should not advocate the habitual taking of medicine, and there should be advice to consult a doctor if a problem persists.
3   It should be precise about the therapeutic merit of the preparation and not speak simply of a general enhancement of well-being.
4   It must avoid creating an imagined need.

The question whether safety information should be included in an advertisement to the general public is not entirely settled. Some countries have required such information to be included. Others have not, and the European Community's Directive 92/28/EC is ambiguous on the matter. The industry has pointed to research indicating that inclusion of safety information in public advertising is ineffective. A commonly accepted practice is now for a public advertisement to refer the reader or viewer explicitly to the official data sheet or packaging text for information on safety and other matters. It seems likely that the lack of clarity at Community level will persist until it is resolved either by the Community itself or judicially in cases of injury attributed to lack of safety information.

Certainly, the fact needs to be stressed in all information provided with OTC drugs that self-medication must only be used briefly and the physician consulted if the symptoms are not promptly relieved, since this is a basic principle in responsible self-treatment. Should a manufacturer find itself facing charges that it has failed to provide adequate warnings, it will be important for it to be able to demonstrate that its warnings were not only present, but were obvious and clearly formulated. As with prescription medicines, the risk of over-information must be avoided. In 1994 the US FDA announced measures to simplify and shorten packaging texts for OTC drugs in order to reduce confusion. It was pointed out that the current label for aspirin contained more than 500 words including some, relative to risk prevention, which certain consumers would not understand.[76]

Once again, however, the difference in standards internationally must be stressed. What is today regarded as unacceptable practice in the United States or Western Europe remains common practice in some other parts of the world. A court dealing with an individual case will be unlikely to acknowledge standards of behavior that have not been recognized in the community in which it is administering justice.

Liability for Injury Due to Self-medication Products

There is no doubt that a manufacturer can be held liable for failure to warn a user of the risks of a self-medication product, perhaps even where these dangers might be considered well known to the public.

In a US case brought against the manufacturer of the paracetamol-based analgesic Tylenol® (paracetamol) in 1994, the plaintiff claimed that as a result of his drinking wine daily his liver had been sensitized to the hepatotoxic effects of the drug. After taking the drug for several days for influenza, he experienced acute liver toxicity demanding hospitalization. It was alleged that the defendant knew of the danger of using Tylenol® if alcohol were regularly taken, but had not warned users of the risk. Instead, the advertising had implied that the drug was 'doctor recommended' and entirely safe. A federal court awarded some $8 million in damages.[77] It is notable that, in this case, the fact that the instructions folder had been approved by the FDA did not constitute a valid defense.

COUNTERFEIT MEDICINES

The counterfeiting of medicines is, as of 2009, a global problem of vast dimensions. While the sale of such products is undoubtedly most widespread in the developing world, they are to be found in all markets. Because of the fact that they are disseminated internationally, the problem can only be solved by coordinated international effort.

At the outset, distinction needs to be made between those copies of recognized drugs which, while illegal and in breach of trademark and patent laws, essentially possess the properties of the original, and those products that are false and misleading in that they merely have a superficial resemblance to the genuine product and are of no medicinal value. Both types of product are of concern to the bona fide industry and trade, which makes efforts to track them down to their source and bring prosecutions. But the latter type represents a major danger to public health and will be the central topic of this review. A so-called penicillin ampoule that contains only powdered sugar or starch may cost the life of a child with pneumonia. A batch of falsified artemesin, sold for the cure of resistant malaria, may decimate the population of an African village. In either instance the fraudulent product is likely to have been made under far from ideal conditions, meaning that it may be polluted with toxic impurities or pathogenic microorganisms.

Exact definitions in this field are of crucial importance, especially since the creditable activities of the research-based industry to eliminate counterfeits have sometimes been regarded as closely linked to its more controversial efforts to counter the trade in genuine generic drugs. In May 2008 the WHO-based International Medical Products Anti-Counterfeiting Taskforce (IMPACT) introduced into the World Health Assembly a resolution to update the WHO's definition of a counterfeit medicine. It found itself vigorously opposed by India, which regarded the change as one that would impede the country's export of generic products in good standing.[78]

The major originator pharmaceutical companies are pressing very strongly for aggressive enforcement measures to address the problem of counterfeiting. Regrettably, these same companies have for several decades pressed equally strongly to prevent producers of generic pharmaceutical products from entering 'their' markets, even when the generic producers were acting within their legal rights. It is not surprising that demands coming from the originator industry for governments to take strong action to suppress counterfeiting are often greeted with skepticism by developing countries, by public health advocacy groups and by generic industry groups. The problem is exacerbated when originator demands take the form of proposed legislation that would indiscriminately target legitimate generic producers and bad-faith counterfeiters. This is not merely an unfortunate legacy of the abuse of power. It is an ongoing problem. Unless the originator industry and the legitimate generic industry are able to ratchet down the level of hostility in the interest of protecting the public, cooperation on solving the problem of dangerous counterfeits will remain difficult to achieve.

The Extent and Sources of Counterfeiting

No global survey exists of the extent of counterfeiting or the sources of counterfeit products, but individual country studies give a sufficiently clear picture of the seriousness of the situation and the need for action.

A country-wide survey in Cambodia in 1999 showed that 60 percent of 133 drug vendors sampled sold, as the anti-malarial mefloquine, tablets that contained the ineffective but much cheaper sulphadoxine/pyrimeth-amine combination (obtained from stocks that had been earmarked for destruction), or fakes that contained no active substance at all.[79]

Newton et al. found that in five countries of mainland South-East Asia 38 percent of tablets claiming to contain the anti-malarial artusenate were fake and of no value.[80] Reviewing six such studies in 2007, Moloney noted estimated regional rates of counterfeiting ranging from 38 percent to 53 percent.[81]

In developing countries counterfeit medicines sometimes enter the public and private health systems on a massive scale through machina-tions in international commerce, for example, where counterfeits are supplied from abroad although a genuine product has been ordered and paid for in advance. In developed countries counterfeits can also infiltrate established supply systems to some extent. A relatively new area of abuse is the sale of drugs through Internet pharmacies, which commonly offer to undercut the retail trade but may supply worthless products.

Large-scale counterfeiting is most likely to be found in countries with a considerable capacity for pharmaceutical manufacturing coupled with an insufficiently effective system of control and inspection. Many such prod-ucts have been traced back to South-East Asia, a considerable number originating in China, India and Pakistan. The control system in China was for a time seriously corrupt, while the regulatory system in India, split between federal and state authorities, is known to inspect only a small fraction of the manufacturing facilities in the country. Products from Asia have been found to move through the Central Asian Republics to the Middle East and onwards into Africa, and they are found on sale in all these areas.

The Detection of Counterfeiting

With the sophisticated methods of pharmaceutical analysis available at the present day, such as the so-called DART method (direct analysis in real time),[82] a counterfeited product can be distinguished from the origi-nal relatively easily. The difficulty is that, in many parts of the world, the most advanced methods are either unavailable or are in use only in central national laboratories. These laboratories are already heavily occupied with routine quality control and are unlikely to have sufficient capacity to undertake large-scale detection of fraudulent products. Most countries also maintain a network of less sophisticated laboratories handling local analyses. but these are more simply equipped and may be unable to detect increasingly sophisticated counterfeits.

The experience of the Republic of Laos is typical. Over a period of some 20 years the nature of counterfeit products entering the country appears to have changed as a reaction to efforts to combat the trade. At first the counterfeits were relatively crude imitations of recognized products. The printing and packaging were primitive, and with a little teaching the deceit could be detected both by a sales agent and a lay user. When the public became more alert to the practice, the presentation of the counterfeits improved, though the content was as useless as ever. At this stage some original manufacturers began to rely on the addition of a hologram to the packaging materials. Fraudulent manufacturers, however, produced a sufficiently close copy of the hologram to deceive consumers, and in due course they appear to have acquired sophisticated holographic equipment enabling them to copy original holograms precisely. In the meantime, there was a similar development towards greater sophistication as a means of reducing the likelihood that fraud would be detected. In the early 1990s, because of the appearance of false copies of the anti-malaria drug artusenate in which the active substance was completely absent, the Laotian authorities equipped their regional laboratories with simple equipment capable of determining whether artusenate was present in a given product. Shortly afterwards, the counterfeit producers began to include miniscule amounts of artusenate in their materials, quite insufficient to have any medicinal effect but adequate to provide deceptively positive readings on the available equipment.[83]

Principles of Policy and Law

A paper by Paul Newton et al. published in the *British Medical Journal* appeared under the title 'Murder by fake drugs'. The authors drew attention not only to the morbidity and mortality resulting from the trade in effective counterfeits, but also to the fact that certain of these products actually contained harmful ingredients.[84] While the term 'murder' was used here in a rhetorical rather than a legal sense, there is no doubt that this trade leads directly to loss of life. It is evident that counterfeit drugs breach both national law and agreed international standards. In addition, their production and dissemination represent criminal activities, even though, in view of the international nature of the trade, there might be

considerable difficulties in proving individual causation if charges of homicide were to be brought. The judicial concepts of 'reckless homicide' or
'depraved heart murder' which feature in various systems of law might be
helpful in this regard.[85] They appear to be applicable to cases of marketing
of a product known to be defective, but also to any form of reckless behavior which might reasonably be considered to endanger life, even though it
is not directed against a known and specific individual.

It is possible to document individual cases where this was necessary in
order to bring charges. In another paper from the Newton group, this time
referring to 'manslaughter', one individual case was reported in detail as
an example that was considered typical of many more. In February 2005
a 23 year-old man presented with fever to a rural hospital in Burma and
was diagnosed as suffering from uncomplicated falciparum malaria. He
was treated with an adequate dose of oral artusenate, labeled as having
been made by Guilin Pharmaceutical in Guangxi, People's Republic of
China. Since artusenate derivatives were introduced in the area, not one of
600 patients with parasitemia studied prospectively had died. In this case,
however, the patient became unconscious on the third day with aggravated
parasitemia and died despite intensive treatment. The artesunate used to
treat the man was found to be counterfeit. It carried a falsified hologram,
and the main ingredient was paracetamol (acetaminophen), with a small
amount of artusenate added.[86]

Ultimately one might hope to see an international criminal court being
endowed with the authority to handle cases relating to this trade, but this
does not presently appear a realistic prospect. International procedures
to bring criminal proceedings are sometimes feasible where gross political
crimes are concerned, but there is still no real hope of international corporate crime being dealt with in an analogous matter.

An extensive report on counterfeit drugs drawn up by the WHO in
1999,[87] with guidelines for tackling the problem, provided an encyclopae-
dic overview of what might be done at various levels and by all parties.
A major conference on the subject was convened in Rome in 2006,[88] and
the WHO subsequently established a Task Force (International Medical
Products Anti-Counterfeiting Taskforce (IMPACT)). Despite these (and
other) manifestations of concern, there is still little sign of a truly coordinated global effort commensurate with the extent of the problem. When
the International Conference of Drug Regulatory Authorities in 2004
examined a WHO proposal to tackle the matter through international law,
it literally concluded 'that further discussions are needed before a global
treaty is introduced to tackle the growing trade in counterfeit drugs',[89]
a response that is sadly typical of the hesitant approach to the issue to
date. It is clear that action is needed at every point, from the source to the

final destination of the counterfeit product. The counterfeit movement is fuelled primarily by a dishonest urge for enrichment, but it is catalyzed at every level by ignorance, indifference or both. A policy intended to defeat the problem is only likely to be successful if the matter is comprehensively addressed. At this point, one can do no more than present some examples of significant efforts in particular fields.

Elimination at Source

In September 2007 Dr. Zhong-Yuan Yang reported to the International Scientific Committee of the US Pharmacopoeia on an initiative developed in China where pharmaceutical inspectors have been equipped with 40 mobile laboratories capable of taking samples from pharmaceutical production units for immediate examination. The equipment will render possible the detection on site of counterfeit products, enabling measures to be taken without delay.[90]

Elimination From the Trade and Internet

In developed countries drug control agencies and inspectorates have been active in detecting infiltration of the pharmaceutical supply chain by counterfeits.

An investigation undertaken in 2002 by the MHRA resulted in the seizure of counterfeit drugs to the value of 2.2 million euros, intended for illegal sale to the public. The effort followed a series of such seizures at UK airports by customs officials. The medicines, sourced by a group that had specialized in the counterfeiting business, were filtered for sale through licensed wholesalers to pharmacies in the UK, and through Internet sites based both in the UK and abroad. In September 2007 the individuals responsible within Britain were prosecuted and sentenced.[91]

The risk of counterfeit drugs being supplied when an order is placed with an unknown Internet site appears to be substantial. In New Zealand the Medicines and Medical Devices Safety Authority has warned prescribers and the public of the risks involved in purchasing drugs through offshore Internet sites because of the considerable likelihood that they will be counterfeits.[92] The Authority maintains a list of authorized pharmacies that can validly accept orders on the Internet. Similarly in the United States, the National Association of Boards of Pharmacy maintains a public register of authorized Internet sources for drug purchases, and the FDA has explicitly warned against Internet purchases from others, listing by name a large number of sites that have been shown to supply counterfeits.[93]

From the standpoint of those interested in the protection of public health, the idea – and the reality – that well-organized groups are deliberately introducing dangerous products into the medicine supply chain is difficult to grasp. It illustrates the very worst aspects of human nature. Perhaps it is a certain level of incredulity among the policy community that accounts for the tepid response. And, most regrettably, a history of 'crying wolf' by the originator industry in the face of legitimate generic competition has not helped matters. Counterfeiting is however a reality and one of the most serious problems that the medicine supply chain must address. The perpetrators are dangerous people, and serious law enforcement mechanisms are needed to confront them, with force if necessary. An appeal to conscience does not appear a viable approach.

NOTES

1. E. Jenner (1798), *An Inquiry into the Effects of the Variolae Vaccinae*, S. Low, London; J.R. Coxe (1802), *Practical Observations on Vaccination: On Inoculation for the Cow Pock*, J. Humphreys, Philadelphia, PA.
2   *Jacobson v. Massachusetts*, 197, US 11 (1905).
3. L.N. Alexander, J.F. Seward, T.A. Santibanez et al. (2004), 'Vaccine policy changes and epidemiology of poliomyelitis in the United States', *JAMA*, 292, 1696–701.
4   *Toner v. Lederle Laboratories*, 732 P. 2d 297 (Idaho 1987); *Graham v. Wyeth Laboratories*, 666 F.Supp. 1483 (D-Kan. 1987).
5. S. Dittmann (1990), 'Adverse events following immunization', in *Proceedings, 1st World Congress on 'Safety in Medical Practice'*; Elsinore, Denmark, 28–31 May 1990; S. Dittmann (1991), 'Surveillance programs in immunization', in M.N.G. Dukes and J.K. Aronson (eds), *Side Effects of Drugs Annual, 15*, Elsevier Science Publishers, Amsterdam, London and New York, pp. 340–1.
6. P. Brunko (1994), 'Les exigences communautaires relatives aux médicaments dérivés du sang et du plasma humains', *Ann Pharmaceut Franc*, 52, 89–98.
7. S.P. Candrillo (2004), 'Vanishing vaccinations: why are so many Americans opting out of vaccinating their children?' *Univ Mich J Law Reform*, 37, 353–439.
8. K.M. Severyn (1996), '*Jacobson v. Massachusetts*: impact on informed consent and vaccine policy', *J Pharmacy Law*, 55, 260–1.
9. A. Lyren and E. Leonard (2006), 'Vaccine refusal: issues for the primary care physician', *Clin Pediatr*, 45, 399–404.
10. R.M. Wolfe, L.K. Sharp and M.S. Lipsky (2002), 'Content and design attributes of antivaccination websites', *JAMA*, 287, 3245–8.
11. D.D. Fredrickson, T.C. Davis, C.L. Arnold et al. (2005), 'Childhood immunization refusal – provider and parent perceptions', *Clin Res Meth*, 36 (6), 431–9.
12. P.M. Oostvogel, J.K. van Wijngaarden, H.G.A.M. van der Avoort et al. (1994), 'Poliomyelitis outbreak in an unvaccinated community in the Netherlands, 1992–93', *Lancet*, 344, 665–70.
13. G. Hardin (1968), 'The tragedy of the commons', *Science*, 162, 1243.
14. G.S. Wilson (1967), *The Hazards of Immunization*, Athlone Press, London; W.C. Cockburn (1977), 'Hazards of immunization', in *Bull WHO*, Suppl. 2, 13–1.
15. WHO/EUR0 (1986), *Immunization Policies in Europe*, Report on a WHO Meeting, Karlovy Vary, Czechoslovakia, 1984. World Health Organization, Regional Office for

Europe, Copenhagen; S. Dittmann (1996), 'Immunological preparations', in M.N.G. Dukes (ed.), *Meyler's Side Effects of Drugs,* 13th edn, Elsevier Science Publishers. Amsterdam, Lausanne, New York and Oxford, pp. 918–61; See, for example, national figures for the Netherlands quoted in Anon. (1993), *Adverse Reactions to Vaccinations,* Report of a Committee of the Health Council of the Netherlands, No. 14e, Gezondheidsraad, The Hague.

16. K.R. Stratton, C.J. Howe and R.B. Johnson (eds) (1994), *Adverse Events Associated with Childhood Vaccines,* National Academy of Sciences, Washington, DC; S. Dittmann (1995), 'Risiken von Schutzimpfungen, internationale Erfahrungen bei der Erfassung von Impfschaden', in G. Maass (ed.), *Impfreaktionen-Impfschaden,* Kilian, Marburg.

17. Dittmann (1996), 'Immunological preparations', p. 918.

18 WHO (1977), 'Proceedings of the International Conference on the Role of the Individual and the Community in the Research, Development and Use of Biologicals', *Bull WHO,* Suppl. 2, 13 ff.

19. E. Rudzki (1985), 'Arzneimittel in Polen: eine Literaturübersicht über die Symptome von Nebenwirkungen' (Drugs in Poland: a literature survey on symptoms of adverse reactions), *Dermatosen,* 33, 136.

20. L.E. Rozovsky and F.A. Rozovsky (1990), *Consent of Employees to Vaccination,* Lefar Health Associates.

21. J.F. Childress (1976), 'Compensating injured research subjects: I. The moral argument', *Hastings Centre Report,* 6 (6), 21–7.

22. Anon. (1993), *Adverse Reactions to Vaccinations,* p. 8.

23. H.J.J. Leenen (1981), *Gezondheidszorg en Recht* (Health care and law), Samsom Uitgeverij, Alphen aan den Rijn and Brussels, p. 228 (In Dutch).

24. Fenille Federale (1970), No. 52, 31 December, Section 23 (3).

25. Japanese Public Health Report (1970), 'Law on compensation for vaccine injury', *Jap Publ Hlth Rep,* 672, 28 September.

26. Vaccine Damage Payments Act, 1979, C.17.

27. A.L. Diamond and D.R. Laurence (1986), 'Product liability in respect of drugs', in P.F. D'Arcy and J.P. Griffin (eds), *Iatrogenic Diseases,* 3rd edn, Oxford University Press, Oxford, New York and Toronto.

28. Pub. L. No. 99-660, 100 Stat. 3755 (codified as amended at 42 USC $300aa-1 to -34 (West 1991 and Supp. 1992).

29. *Bundesgesetzblatt* (1961), p. 1012.

30. *Bundesgesetzblatt* (1971), p. 1401.

31. C. Newdick (1994), 'Product liability for defective blood', *Haematologia,* 26, 49–53.

32. S. Finfer, S. Howell, J. Miller et al. (1994), 'Managing patients who refuse blood transfusion: an ethical dilemma', *BMJ,* 308, 1423–6.

33. *Perlmutter v. Beth David Hospital* (1954), 308 NY 100; 123 NE 2nd 792-798 CA.

34. *Prego v. City of New York,* 534 NYS 2d 95 (Supp.1988).

35. For example, C. Koch (2000), 'Blood, blood components, plasma and plasma products', in M.N.G. Dukes and J.K. Aronson (eds), *Meyler's Side Effects of Drugs,* 14th edn, Elsevier Science Publishers, Amsterdam, New York and Lausanne, pp. 1111–39.

36. H. Beppu (1996), 'The case of contaminated blood products in Japan', *Int J Risk Safety Med,* 9 (3), 157–60.

37. J.B. Meijer van Putter (1994), 'Schadevergoeding aan hemofiliepatiënten' (Injury to haemophilic patients), *Ned. Tijdschr. Geneesk.,* 138, 2415.

38. H. Radtke, K. Bachmann, G. Pindur et al. (1995), 'Der gesetzlich vorgeschriebene Stufenplan bei Beanständungen oder Nebenwirkungen von Blutkomponenten' The legally required guidelines for reporting risks or side-effects caused by blood components, *Infusionsther. Transfusionsmed.,* 22 (3), 186–95.

39. M. Dolley (1995), 'Danish court clears drug firm of blood contamination', *BMJ,* 310, 552.

40. *Torts and Compensation,* 2nd ed., Am. West Casebook Series, p. 9702.

41. *United Blood Services, Div. of Blood Systems Inc. v. Quintana,* 827 P 2d 509 (1992).

42. *Rhone-Poulenc Rorer Inc.* 5l F 3d 1293, 16th March 1995.
43. Rule 23 of Federal procedure, setting out three situations in which class actions can be brought.
44. *John Doe v. Cutter Biological & Others*, US District Court for the District of Hawaii, 8 December 1987.
45. D. Brahams (1991), 'Negligence, extra blood transfusions, and risk of AIDS', *Lancet*, 337, 545. For original report see *Doe v. United States of America*, US District Court, District of Rhode Island [1990] 2 Med L R, pp. 131–2.
46. Anon. (1997), 'Medical firms reach pacts clearing way for AIDS settlements', *Wall St J*, 1 May, B8.
47. M. Yawata (1994), 'Transfusion and Japan's product liability law', *Lancet*, 344, 120.
48. Council Directive 85/374/EEC of 25th July 1985 on the approximation of the laws, regulations and administrative provisions of the Member States concerning liability for defective products.
49. R. Best (2002), 'A comparison of civil liability for defective products in the United Kingdom and Germany', *German Law J*, 4, April, 1–5.
50. S. Williamson (2003), 'Compensation for infected blood products. A and others v National Blood Authority and Another', *Electr. J. Compar. Law*, 7.5, December.
51. Newdick (1994), 'Product liability for defective blood', p. 52.
52. Z.S. Hantchef (1977), 'The development of blood transfusion and its legislative and economic impact (editorial)', *Transfusion-Noter*, 11 and 12, League of Red Cross Societies, Geneva.
53. A.B.M. Los and C.T. Smit Sibinga (1989), 'De persoonlijke verantwoordelijkheid van de bloeddonor voor de veiligheid van de bloedtransfusiepraktijk' (The personal responsibility of the blood donor for the safety of transfusion practice), *Ned Tijdschr Geneesk*, 133, 1157–8.
54. Australia (Northern Territory) (As in force at 7 April 1999) Consolidated Acts: Notifiable Diseases Act, Sect. 26(E): Liability of blood donor.
55. Newdick (1994), 'Product liability for defective blood', p. 52.
56. J.P. Soulier (1994), 'Responsibility in transfusion practice: reflections after the French trials', *Haematologia*, 26, p. 57.
57. Yawata (1994), 'Transfusion and Japan's product liability law', p. 120.
58. J.P. Soulier (1994), 'Responsibility in transfusion practice; reflections after the French trials', *Haematologia*, 26, 55–7. See also A. Dorozynski (1995), 'Garetta case causes clash with French public opinion', *BMJ*, 310, 552.
59. BBC (2001), 'Aids scandals around the word', BBC News, 9 August.
60. C.F.S. Hahnemann (1810), *Organon der rationellen Heilkunde*, Arnold, Dresden.
61. M.N.G. Dukes (1980), Personal communication.
62. M.N.G. Dukes (2005), *The Law and Ethics of the Pharmaceutical Industry*. Elsevier, Amsterdam, Boston and Heidelberg, p. 321.
63. E. Ernst (2000), 'Risks associated with complementary therapies', in M.N.G. Duke and J.K. Aronson (eds), *Meyler's Side Effects of Drugs*, 14th edn, Elsevier, Amsterdam, New York and Lausanne. See also updated monographs on individual drugs in E. Ernst (2005), *Meyler's Side Effects of Drugs*, 15th edn.
64. G.W. Bruinsma and J. Bruinsma (1878), *De kwakzalverij met Geneesmiddelen*, Leeuwarden.
65. BMA (1909), *Secret Remedies,* British Medical Association, London; BMA (1912), *More Secret Remedies,* British Medical Association, London.
66. COE (1975), *Abuse of Medicaments: Report by a Working Party 1972–1973*, Council of Europe, Strasbourg.
67. WHO/EURO (1986), *Guidelines for the Assessment of Medicinal Products for Use in Self-Medication,* World Health Organization, Regional Office for Europe, Copenhagen; DAP (1995), *Report of the Expert Committee on National Drug Policies*, Action Programme on Essential Drugs, World Health Organization, Geneva.

68. Anon. (1994), 'Ketoprofen switched to Rx in Italy', *Scrip,* 21.
69. M. Kramlich (2003), 'Taking life at the corner drugstore', United States Conference of Catholic Bishops (pro-life website), http://www.usccb.org/prolife/publicat/lifeissues/121903.shtml.
70. IOMS (1995), *The Judicially Prohibited and Impure Substances in Food and Drugs,* Report on a Seminar convened by the Islamitic Organization for Medical Sciences.
71. S. Chowdhury (2005), 'Simvastatin over the counter: a prescribing controversy', *Nurse Prescribing,* 3 (3), 29 May.
72. Associated Press (2007), 'Cholesterol drugs won't be sold over the counter', 13 December.
73. CHPA (Update 2008), *Code of Advertising Practices for Nonprescription Medicine,* Consumer Health Products Association, Washington, DC.
74. PAGB (Update 2008), *Medicines Advertising Codes,* Proprietary Association of Great Britain, London.
75. ASMI (2008), *ASMI Code of Practice,* Revised edn, Australian Self Medication Industry, North Sydney, NSW.
76. 'FDA simplifies OTC labels', *Marketletter,* 19 September 1994.
77. *Benedi v. McNeil Consumer Products Inc.* (1994), case as cited by J.W. Moch and A. Borja in J.W. Moch, A. Borja and J. O'Donnell (eds) (1995), *Pharmacy Law,* Lawyers and Judges Publishing Co., Tucson AZ, pp. 42–3.
78. B.A. Liang (2008), *Counterfeit Drugs – Defining the Problem,* Partnership for Safe Medicines, Vienna, VA.
79. J. Rozendaal (2000), 'Fake antimalarials circulating in Cambodia', *Bull Mekong Malaria Forum,* 7, 62–8.
80. P.N. Newton, S. Oriux, M. Green et al. (2001), 'Fake artusenate in southeast Asia', *Lancet,* 357, 1948–50.
81. J. Moloney (2007), Literature review for the research Thesis: 'Analysis of factors contributing to community vulnerability to substandard antimalarials', Department of General Practice and Community Medicine, University of Oslo.
82. F.M. Fernandez, R.B. Cody, M.D. Green et al. (2006), 'Characterization of solid counterfeit drug samples by desorption electrospray ionization and direct-analysis-in-real-time coupled to time-of-flght mass spectrometry', *ChemMedChem,* 1, 702–5.
83. S. Sengaloundeth (2007), Personal communication to Dr M.N.G. Dukes, Vientiane, Laos, August 2007.
84. P.N. Newton, N.J. White, J.A. Rozendaal and M.D. Green (2002), 'Murder by fake drugs', *BMJ,* 324, 800–1.
85. K.M. Collins (2002), 'Negligent homicide/manslaughter (involuntary)', *International Encyclopedia of Justice Studies,* Monticello, AR; L.P. Strobel (1980), *Reckless Homicide? Ford's Pinto Trial.* South Bend, IN; M. Somarajah (1975), 'Reckless murder in Commonwealth law', *Int Comp Law Q,* 24 (4).
86. P.N. Newton, R. McGready, F. Fernandez et al. (2006), 'Manslaughter by fake artusenate in Asia – will Africa be next?', *PloS Med,* 3 (6), 1–4.
87. WHO (1999), *Counterfeit Drugs: Guidelines for the Development of Measures to Combat Counterfeit Drugs,* Document WHO/EDM/QSM/99.1, World Health Organization, Geneva.
88. 'Combating counterfeit drugs: building effective international collaboration' Rome Conference, 16–18 February 2006.
89. M.L. Gibson (2004), 'Drug regulators study global treaty to tackle counterfeit drugs', *BMJ,* 328, 486.
90. USP (2007), Statement by Prof. Zhong-Yuan Yang, Member, Advisor to the Guangzhou Municipal Institute for Drug Control, China, at the meeting of the US Pharmacopoea International Scientific Committee, Tampa, FLA, September.
91. A. Lewcock (2007), 'Massive counterfeit drug ring cracked', In-Pharma Technologist com, 18 September (accessed June 2008).
92. NZMMDSA (2005), 'Counterfeit medicines – don't fake concern', Statement by

the New Zealand Medicines and Medical Devices Regulatory Authority, *Prescriber Update*, 26 (1), 15-16.

93. FDA (2008), *Buying Medicines and Medical Products Online*, Food and Drugs Administration, Rockville, MD.

9. The rich, the poor and the neglected

Problems in ensuring access to medicines are in no sense limited to the developing world. In high-income countries there are generally sufficient budgetary resources to supply entire populations with needed treatments, but because of inequalities in wealth distribution and as a consequence of government policy failures, significant access gaps remain. On the reverse side of the coin, high-income countries face a largely unaddressed problem of over-consumption of medicines, the causes of which include poor prescribing practices and commercial promotion of treatment. And in the meantime a considerable number of illnesses, many of which in principle might be eligible for some form of medicinal therapy, remain neglected by researchers.

In several of these matters one is in effect dealing with a state's duty to minorities. Such a duty is well recognized in international law, where the minority is characterized in terms of ethnicity or religion and the state's duty towards it is primarily a question of respecting its rights and practices.[1] By analogy, however, one might well consider that a state has an obligation to afford a disadvantaged minority a degree of special treatment, enabling it so far as possible to overcome its impediments, whether the latter arise from poverty, age or the burden of a rare disease. This is hardly an extrapolation from existing law, rather an interpretation of it. It has often enough been argued that the state has a duty to eliminate poverty and, so long as it has not been eliminated, to provide relief from its most severe consequences. Similarly, there is a widely agreed public duty to care for the elderly to the extent that they cannot care adequately for themselves. This concept of the duties of the state or community would seem to be most firmly embedded in national law in the social democracies of Northern Europe, but in every country it has its prominent advocates. How far such duties, when agreed in theory, will be carried in practice in a particular country is a question of political interpretation, but the view that they exist hardly seems to be open to challenge.

OVER-CONSUMPTION: THE RICH, THE AFFLUENT AND THE MERELY OVER-EAGER

In 1986 a critical French journal devoted to prescribing issues drew attention to the over-use of medicines with a cartoon that has become a classic (Figure 9.1). An elderly man emerges from a city pharmacy pushing a supermarket trolley loaded with medicines. The example may represent gentle exaggeration, but the message it conveys is valid and well documented from the field. Marcia Angell has cited a report on the case of a US woman who was found to be taking 18 prescription drugs at a cost of nearly $16,000 per year. She comments that what this patient probably

Note: Illustration by Claude Serre (1938–98) published in the journal *Revue Pressure* (Paris) in 1988.

Figure 9.1 Over-prescribing: a cartoon from France

needed was less medication and more medical attention.[2] While a large part of the world's population is deprived of ready access to the medicines it needs (see Chapter 5), another group is consuming them to excess, sometimes grossly so. Over-consumption represents waste, but the practice itself introduces new health risks. As such it should be a valid concern for policy makers.

In 2008 a publication by the British Medical Association[3] provided a number of situations in which prescribing within the National Health Service must be considered to be excessive: 'profligate prescribing may be considered to exist where the prescriber(s) consistently prescribes excessive amounts of high cost products or inappropriate, high quantities of medicines that are significantly at variance with comparable clinical scenarios and where the prescriber(s) is/are unable to provide a reasonable explanation'.

The causes of over-medication vary, and if public policy is to counter it, these causes need to be understood. Where prescribed medicines are concerned, Dr Angell and others stress the proven influence of extraordinarily heavy advertising directed to the physician and secondarily to the pharmacist. The physician may also have been pressured by his patient to prescribe, and feel unable to resist the pressure. This seems much more likely to occur where the pharmaceutical industry is permitted, as is the case in the United States and New Zealand, to advertise prescription medicines directly to the public, but the patient may also have become habituated or addicted to a product and therefore insist on continuing it even though there is no medical justification for its further use. There are also individuals who appear to regard the generous consumption of medicines as one of the privileges to be enjoyed where there are no financial obstacles. In other instances over-consumption of a prescribed medicine is a result of confusion on the patient's part.[4] The British Medical Association paper cited above found that excessively expensive prescribing could sometimes have a financial explanation:

> prescriptions where the drug is initiated or switched, e.g. within a therapeutic class/indication, with the effect that reimbursement is based on a product that provides a larger purchase margin for the prescriber(s) and the product(s) selected cost the NHS more, unless there is good clinical evidence to support the switch . . .

In many instances, however, it seems clear that the explanation for excessive prescribing simply lies with the fact that a physician has not learned the principles of rational drug use and that his or her use of medicines is nothing less than a bad habit or, more precisely, a series of bad habits. Even where a medicine has been well chosen and well prescribed, the patient may independently raise the dose in the hope of attaining a more rapid or complete effect. A parallel phenomenon is the practice of excessive self-medication, often alongside the use of prescribed medicines, a topic that was considered in Chapter 8.

The consequences of over-medication for the individual patient vary from one person to the next and are often difficult to foresee. Instances in which 18 drugs are being taken at the same time may be exceptional, but cases in which five, six or more products are being taken are readily documented, the indication for one sometimes duplicating the indication for others. Since each of these will have its own adverse effects and may interact with any of the others, it will be impossible to predict the total effect in any given user. The International Centre for the Study of Psychiatry and Psychology has frequently drawn attention to the use of multiple psychoactive drugs in mental states where there may be a confusing overlapping of diagnoses and treatments, while some of the conditions in fact require no medication at all.[5] Some, such as Attention Deficit Hyperactivity Disorder, have been dismissed in certain quarters as mere products of 'disease mongering' (see Chapter 6). Without considering the merits of such a challenge, the fact that it is possible indicates how uncertain the basis of some prescribing practices and even some popular medical notions may be.

The consequences for society as a whole of excessive medication are well documented both in terms of health and of finance. The case of the over-use of antibiotics is particularly striking and was been massively documented by Geoffrey Cannon, who in 1995 was able to look back on four decades of their use and observed a progressively worsening situation.[6] By 1990, with the antibiotic market in the United Kingdom reaching approximately £300 million yearly, roughly half this sum appeared to be wasted as a consequence of unnecessary prescribing.[7] That adverse effect paled, however, into insignificance when compared with the immense and growing problem of antibiotic resistance across the world, itself largely a consequence of ill-advised use of these medicines both in industrialized countries and the developing world, and extending to their use in animal husbandry and fish farming as well as in human medicine. In that same year a study in Boston of the extent to which children harboured an *E.coli* bacterium that had become resistant to antibiotics noted its presence in 21 of 39 individuals, while in China 96 percent of individuals were found to carry a resistant strain of the organism and in Venezuela 98 percent.[8] Over several decades, physicians faced with resistance to one antibiotic have been able to turn to another of more recent date, but the supply of new and superior antibiotics is weakening, while multi-antibiotic resistance has become more common and constitutes an increasing threat to the world community as a whole.

The reasons for an authoritative approach in policy to the problem of over-consumption are therefore two-fold. First, it represents a form of waste, often at the expense of the public health services or more generally as a burden on society as a whole. Second, it represents a risk to the health both of the treated individual and of the community. This latter menace can also, if one finds this more persuasive to political policy makers, be expressed in financial terms (see Chapter 2).

The principal policy approaches to over-consumption involve both regulation (see Chapter 4) and education (considered primarily in Chapter 6). Teaching health professionals the concept of rational use of medicines is not excessively difficult. According to a simple definition of the challenge by the WHO, rational use of medicines is attained when patients receive adequate medication for their clinical needs, at doses corresponding to individual requirements, and at the lowest possible cost for the patient and society.[9] As far as the public health services are concerned, there may also be a possibility of raising financial barriers to over-consumption, as discussed in the paper from the British Medical Association's publication cited above. In the UK it had long been realized that the provision of entirely free medicines would lead some users to take them to excess. At the time of its creation in 1948, the British National Health Service provided prescribed medicines entirely without charge but, because usage appeared excessive, prescription charges were soon introduced and raised progressively during subsequent decades.[10] Provided such charges are not increased to the point where they lead to drug deprivation and are imposed with provision for exceptions, the approach is defensible.

THE POOR: STRUGGLING IN THE MIDST OF PLENTY

In industrialized countries lacking universal health coverage, problems of access are particularly likely to affect the elderly with their generally lower incomes and relatively greater need of drugs. The United States is commonly cited as experiencing this problem to a marked degree, though it is not unique. According to the authors of a 50-state study of non-adherence to prescribed medicine published in 2007, 40 percent of seniors responding to the survey reported not adhering to their 'doctor's orders' regarding their medication regimens, commonly leaving prescriptions unfilled for financial reasons.[11]

Some seniors in the United States have taken to crossing the border into

Canada,[12] where national price controls mean that prescription products are generally available at less than 50 percent of the United States price:

> In the United States, unaffordable drugs prices limit the accessibility of necessary treatments. For the elderly especially, prescription meds can become a major expense. . . . By 2010, annual prescription drug spending per elderly American is projected to increase to $2,810 – a hard price to pay just to stay healthy . . . . High costs force patients to look elsewhere for cheaper meds. Other countries, such as Canada, have created an alternative market for the same medicine at a much lower price. In fact, our neighbors to the north offer the same prescription pills for less than one-third the cost. Many consumers have already turned to Canada to take advantage of these savings. According to one study, 7% of American buyers get their medication from Canada.[13]

The United States is not the only country in which this problem has arisen. Even in countries with a comprehensive system of public health care, a limit may have been imposed on the total sum that can be allocated yearly for the supply of medicines to a particular individual. An elderly patient having need of more extensive medicinal treatment may encounter difficulties in financing it, though there are as a rule special provisions to meet cases of real need.

THE NEGLECTED: SUFFERERS FROM RARE DISEASES

When considering those conditions for which no adequate treatment exists, it is helpful to understand the nomenclature generally in use. In 2005 the European Organization for Rare Diseases (EURORDIS) provided some helpful definitions:[14]

- *Rare diseases* are characterized by their low prevalence (less than 1/2000) and their heterogeneity. They affect both children and adults anywhere in the world.
- *Neglected diseases* are common, communicable diseases that mainly affect patients living in developing countries. They are considered primarily in Chapter 5.
- *Orphan diseases* comprise both rare diseases and neglected diseases. They are 'orphans' of research focus and market interest, as well as of public health policies.
- *Orphan drugs* are medicinal products intended or suited for the diagnosis, prevention or treatment of rare diseases, but receiving little attention because of the poor prospects of a financial return.

The problems resulting from failure to develop or supply drugs for neglected diseases occurring in developing countries were considered in Chapter 5. In principle, that particular issue should be capable of solution because the number of individuals affected is so great. The situation is different as regards rare and unusual illnesses occurring in the world as a whole. Where the number of patients affected by a condition amounts at most to a few hundred in a million it is understandable that commercial innovation is likely to pass them by and that a government will for the sake of its duties to the majority find it impossible to accord a high and truly adequate priority to the special needs of the few. Some would define the problem more broadly: in the United States an orphan or rare disease is generally considered as one having a prevalence of fewer than 200,000 affected individuals in that country,[15] and the Office of Rare Diseases of the NIH lists nearly 7,000 conditions which are considered to fall within this definition. In France, where a similar definition is maintained,[16] it has been calculated that there are 15000 people suffering from sickle cell anemia, 8,000 people suffering from amyotrophic lateral sclerosis, 5,000–6,000 people with cystic fibrosis, 5,000 diagnosed with Duchenne muscular dystrophy and 400–500 patients with leukodystrophy. In France there are also a handful of cases of progeria (premature aging), of which less than 100 cases are known to exist in the world.

The arguments in favor of according a higher priority to the world's rare diseases are straightforward. Sixty-five percent of such diseases are serious and debilitating. They tend to appear early in life (frequently in early childhood), many being marked by chronic pain or suffering, and motor, sensory or intellectual deficiencies are present in half of all cases. This leads to an incapacity that commonly reduces autonomy, rendering the individual heavily dependent on community support. Finally, in more than half of all cases life is considerably shortened. Any survey of the field shows not only that it includes a very large number of conditions for which there is currently no reasonably adequate means of providing relief or cure, but in addition that the prospects of developing entirely adequate treatments commonly appear to be remote. The burden that this lays on the individual sufferer, but also on society as a whole, is clear.

France is one of very few countries that has sought to develop a clear public policy regarding rare diseases. Its *National Rare Diseases Plan 2004 – 2008* was essentially based on sections of a law of 9 August 2004[17] that related to the handicapped generally. The Plan adopted ten strategic approaches intended, in the words of the legislator, 'to ensure equity in the access to diagnosis, to treatment and to provision of care' for people suffering from a rare disease. The policy would set out to:

- Increase knowledge of the epidemiology of rare diseases.
- Recognize the specificity of rare diseases.
- Develop information for patients, health professionals and the general public concerning rare diseases.
- Train professionals to better identify rare diseases.
- Organize screening and access to diagnostic tests.
- Improve access to treatment and the quality of health care provision for patients.
- Continue efforts in favor of orphan drugs.
- Respond to the specific needs of accompaniment of people suffering from rare diseases and develop support for patients' associations.
- Promote research and innovation on rare diseases, notably for treatments.
- Develop national and European partnerships in the domain of rare diseases.

Any or all of these approaches could be helpful, but when considering the duties of the state in this matter, one has to consider how far these duties can realistically be expected to go. Several of the items on France's list relate to ensuring sufficient access by the patients concerned to facilities that currently exist, and it is an inventory to which one can wholeheartedly subscribe. Only two or three items relate to the creation of new means of treatment, and it is obvious that here the state, with all the uncertainty that surrounds the creation of new medicines or other therapies, can make no promises, especially since it is not a major participant in the R&D process. Essentially its role here will be to encourage and where possible support promising initiatives taken by others. On some fronts it may be appropriate for it to finance already promising trends; EURORDIS has, for example, argued that 'the public funding of rare disease clinical trials should be promoted through national or European measures'.[18]

One approach with which policy makers could well be associated concerns the detection and exploitation of what might well be termed missed opportunities. The best examples of this approach relate to the search for drugs of value in neglected diseases rather than rare diseases, but they need to be considered here.

The Drugs for Neglected Diseases Initiative (DNDi), already touched on in Chapter 5, is one such initiative at the international level. Though the emphasis in its work to date has necessarily been on some widespread diseases of the developing world, its philosophy can be applied to any neglected disorder. Not having resources comparable to those of the major commercial R&D bodies, DNDi chose to examine the very large numbers of substances which have been created in the past in the framework of medicines research, but then for one reason or another were set aside. In many instances these substances have been abandoned because they were insufficiently promising in attaining the research goal that they had been intended to reach, but many are pharmacologically or biologically active and could prove suitable to serve another purpose.

DNDi was established in 2003, largely following preliminary work by the humanitarian organization, Médécins sans Frontières (MSH), and is currently joined by seven other organizations. There are now five national participants – the Oswaldo Cruz Foundation from Brazil, the Indian Council for Medical Research, the Kenya Medical Research Institute, the Ministry of Health of Malaysia and France's Pasteur Institute, alongside the UNDP/World Bank/WHO's Special Programme for Research and Training in Tropical Diseases (TDR). There is collaboration with many research bodies, both public and private, and financial support has been received from various sources including the Bill and Melinda Gates Foundation. Essentially, DNDi seeks to capitalize on existing, fragmented R&D capacity and to complement it with additional expertise as needed. This 'virtual' approach is meant to keep research costs within attainable limits, while creating the possibility of identifying missed opportunities in medicinal discovery. Significant successes of DNDi to date have been the development of two non-patented but highly effective drug combinations for the low-cost treatment of malaria.

A different but equally promising initiative is the establishment of the San Francisco-based Institute for OneWorld Health. OneWorld Health was founded in 2000 as a non-profit firm by the pharmacologist Victoria Hale who had experience both with the FDA and the generic industry, and was herself aware of drugs which had been abandoned for reasons that apparently had little or nothing to do with any lack of therapeutic promise. For its initial project, a drug falling into this category which appeared valuable in Kala-azar, OneWorld Health obtained substantial funding from the Bill and Melinda Gates Foundation. The Institute went on to develop a product for use in Chagas Disease, the active component having been produced within a small biotechnology firm that did not have the capacity to carry its development further.[19] More recently, the Institute has commenced collaboration with a major pharmaceutical firm in Switzerland to develop a low-cost remedy for diarrheal disorders.[20]

Again, as with DNDi, there is an obvious likelihood that this type of work will primarily benefit sufferers from the neglected diseases of the developing world, but the possibility that it will bring about progress in dealing with certain other neglected conditions is clearly present. It would seem clear that in seeking to achieve developmental aims such as those devised for public policy in France, states will do well to support non-commercial initiatives such as these.

There are in addition some various initiatives by the originator pharmaceutical industry to address specific neglected diseases. Where the fruit of these initiatives appear to bear scientific promise, but are unlikely to be commercially viable, the existence of bodies such as DNDi and OneWorld and a number of smaller initiatives with analogous ideals in narrower areas may well offer opportunities to develop them further.

Finally, it is important to examine the official measures taken with respect to rare diseases in two areas of the industrialized world, namely the United States and the European Community.

In January 1983 the US Congress passed the Orphan Drug Act. The granting of orphan drug status allowed for under the Act was designed to encourage the development of drugs where this would be prohibitively expensive or unprofitable under normal circumstances. Firms undertaking such development are rewarded with tax reductions and marketing exclusivity on that drug for an extended period (seven years post-approval). During the first 20 years after the passage of the Act, drugs developed under its provisions include products to treat glioma, multiple myeloma, cystic fibrosis, phenylketonuria and venomous snakebites. Up to June 2004, a total of 1129 different orphan drug designations had been granted by the Office of Orphan Products Development, and 249 orphan drugs had received marketing authorization. In contrast, the decade prior to 1983 had seen fewer than ten such products entering the market.

A similar status exists in the European Union, administered by the Committee on Orphan Medicinal Products of the European Medicines Agency (EMEA) under rules adopted in January 2000.[21] Market exclusivity in this case is offered for a period of ten years.

In 2007 the FDA and EMEA came to an agreement whereby the same application could be used for both agencies, thereby reducing the time and finances required of companies to apply for orphan drug status. However, the two agencies still maintain separate approval processes.[22]

One should add that, although these systems have been emulated in other parts of the world,[23] there has been criticism of the approach adopted to date,[24] particularly since the existing systems have tended to attract ventures that offer the ultimate prospect of very considerable profit. In 2003 the orphan drug with the largest worldwide turnover was reported to be erythropoietin (Epogen®), used for various forms of anemia, with sales of $2.4 billion. Governments may still, it is argued, offer little incentive to develop products for truly rare conditions.[25] It has been suggested that the system creates unjustified monopolies, and it has been proposed that profits on such drugs should be limited in view of the fact that their development has in effect been subsidised by the taxpayer. However, in a balanced review of achievements up to 2008, Haffner et al. have noted some of the benefits of orphan drug legislation accruing to sufferers from a small number of truly rare diseases.

> Pegademase was the first instance of an enzyme-replacement therapy for a metabolic disease. (34) After pegademase, five enzyme replacement therapies were developed to treat Gaucher's disease, Fabry's disease, and enzyme deficiencies of the urea cycle. (35) Pegademase also involved the first use of a polyethylene glycol delivery system to increase the half-life of a drug and decrease immunogenicity. (22) This approach has had more widespread applicability in Pegasys, a pegylated interferon subsequently approved for the treatment of hepatitis C. (36) From monoclonal antibodies such as rituximab, to conjugated monoclonal antibodies such as to situmomab, to small molecules such as imatinib mesylate, it is apparent that orphan legislation is not just supporting me-too products derived from advances in more prevalent disorders, but rather development of orphan products has been and is part of the discovery of innovative treatments.[26]

It seems clear that orphan drug provisions as they currently exist are less than perfect and are subject to some abuse. They will no doubt be revised as time passes, especially in the light of the changing pattern of drug innovation as biotechnology (see Chapter 3) comes to the fore. Amendments to the US legislation already have been introduced on several occasions,[27] and more changes will likely follow in order to attune policy as closely as possible to real need.

NOTES

1. A.S. Akermark (1997), *Justifications of Minority Protection in International Law*, Kluwer Law International, London, The Hague and Boston; J.H. Carens (2000), *Culture, Citizenship and Community: A Contextual Exploration of Justice as Evenhandedness*, Oxford University Press, Oxford; J. Pejic (1997), 'Minority rights in international law', *Human Rights Quarterly*, 19 (3), 666–85.
2. M. Angell (2004), *The Truth About the Drug Companies*, Random House, New York, pp. 171–2.
3. BMA (2008), *Caring for the NHS@60*, British Medical Association, London.
4. Y.Y. Wang, T. Liabsuetrakul, V. Chongsuvivatwong et al. (2007), 'Under- and overconsumption intermittent TB treatment among rural TB patients in south-west China', *Int J Tubercul Lung Dis*, 11 (12) 1345–51.
5. ICSPP (2006), 'Mental health and the law', Digital video disk of ICSPP Annual Conference.
6. G. Cannon (1995), *Superbug: Nature's Revenge – Why Antibiotics Can Breed Disease*, Virgin Publishing, London.
7. Ibid., p. 20.
8. Cited by Cannon (1995), *Superbug: Nature's Revenge*, pp. 205–6.

9. WHO (2002), *Promoting the Rational Use of Medicines: Core Components*, World Health Organization, Geneva.
10. S. Jacobzone (2000), 'Pharmaceutical policies in OECD countries: reconciling social and industrial goals, labour market and social policy', Occasional Papers No. 40, Organization for Economic Cooperation and Development, Paris.
11. I.B. Wilson, C. Schoen, P. Neuman et al. (2007), 'Physician-patient communication about prescription medication nonadherence: a 50-state study of America's seniors', *J Gen Intern Med*, 74.
12. Unsurprisingly, the US pharmaceutical industry has vigorously opposed the filling of prescriptions in Canada, stressing among other things the risks of buying drugs abroad. Since many of the drugs dispensed are, however. US approved products exported to Canada, this argument does not entirely ring true.
13. J. Berk (2008), 'America's drug problem', *P.H. Yale Public Health*, (5) 1, 1–4.
14. EURORDIS, (2005), 'Rare diseases: understanding this public health priority', European Organization for Rare Diseases, www.eurordis.org, November 2005.
15. ORD(NIH) (2008), 'Rare disease and related terms', Office of Rare Diseases of the NIH website. National Institutes of Health, Bethesda, MD.
16. MOH (2004), Ensuring Equity in the Access to Diagnosis, Treatment and Provision of Care: The French National Plan for Rare Diseases, 2005 – 2008, Ministry of Health and Social Welfare, Paris.
17. Law on the Equality of Rights and Opportunities, the Participation and the Citizenship of the Handicapped. Adopted on 3 February 2005, Paris.
18. EORDIS 2005, 'Rare diseases'.
19. D. Perlman (2002), 'Drug firm seeks cures over cash', *San Francisco Chronicle*, 19 August.
20. B. Tansey (2008), 'OneWorld teams with Roche for diarrhea cure', *San Francisco Chronicle*, 17 April.
21. EC (2000), Regulation (EC) No. 141/2000 of the European Parliament and of the Council on Orphan Medicinal Products.
22. D. Young (2008), 'U.S., EU will use same orphan drug application', *BioWorld News*, 28 November.
23. EP (1999), *Orphan Drugs*, European Parliament Publications, Strasbourg.
24. D. Loughnot (2005), 'Potential interactions of the Orphan Drug Act and pharmacogenomics: a flood of orphan drugs and abuses?, *Am J Law Med*, 31, 365–80; J. Love (1999), 'Brief note on the abuse of orphan drug programs in creating monopolies', 5 January 1999, http://www.cptech.org/ip/health/orphan; T. Maeder (2003), 'The orphan drug backlash', *Sci Am*, 288, 80–8.
25. Reuters (2004), 'Drugmakers ignoring cancer in children? No incentives to develop treatments for small market', *Reuters News Agency Report*, 10 May.
26. M.E. Haffner, J. Torrent and P.D. Maher (2008), 'Does orphan drug legislation really answer the needs of patients?' *Lancet*, 371, 2041–4.
27. OOPD (2008) Office of Orphan Products Development, http://www.fda.gov/orphan, Website updated 22 May 2008.

10.   Global and regional policies: the way ahead

THE WAY AHEAD

Worldwide the pharmaceutical sector is currently marked by a series of tensions, which are separate but interlinked and which periodically explode into the public consciousness when acute crises arise. Some of those tensions relate directly to the role of the pharmaceutical industry; others result from the development of public policies that have placed too great a weight on maintaining the status quo rather than working creatively to build a healthy future. This clearly underlies the inherent tension between exclusivity rules in the pharmaceutical market, as promoted in the WTO's TRIPS Agreement, and the need to provide wider access to medicines. The first major conflict in that connection erupted in South Africa in 2001 and involved a direct but unsuccessful challenge by a group of major pharmaceutical companies to the public health policies of the government.[1] Other direct conflicts have occurred in Asia, and the foundations for further conflict are still being laid in the negotiation of 'Free Trade Agreements' that, in fact, restrict the ability of developing countries to interpret the TRIPS Agreement in the interest of their own populations.

Linked to these problems is widespread discontent with the high level of drug prices, which can render products inaccessible to the poor but can also raise problems in affluent societies.

A third source of tension is the increasing realization that useful pharmaceutical innovation has become a rare commodity.

Continuing conflict sometimes seems to be an inevitable manifestation of a global system for the development and supply of pharmaceuticals that is dependent on the ability of corporations to attract capital to what is inevitably a high-risk business in a competitive global market for investment. To succeed in attracting such capital requires the promise of a high rate of return.

Simplistic solutions to such complex situations never carry one very far. In some developing countries the notion of nationalizing the industry has been raised, but promptly dismissed as entirely unrealistic where one is dealing largely with massive multinational corporations, many of which are larger entities than single countries and entirely capable of shifting their operations around the globe to benefit from opportunities in one environment, evading unwelcome laws in another. Even radical proposals to restrict an industry's pricing and profits run into problems when it emerges, as it always will, how tightly the industry is now integrated into the overall economy. Many a state pension fund is able to serve its beneficiaries largely because it has invested heavily in pharmaceutical companies delivering high and dependable returns on investment.

Looking at things from a positive point of view, one is obliged to conclude that the genius of the free market as a whole lies in its ability to harness the ambition and energy of women and men striving for wealth, fame, personal satisfaction and other (perhaps more modest) indicia of accomplishment. In the specific area of medicines the major companies succeed in managing complex R&D, production and distribution chains and providing (at least on demand) reasonable assurances of quality. There is also a beneficial (though not always peaceful) balance between the role of the innovative industry and the generic producers, with the latter stepping in to establish competitive markets and offer moderate prices after the R&D firms have had an opportunity to recoup their investigational expenses.

There is, however, also much reason to look at the situation critically, for it has some distinct flaws. The free market is prone to provide its greatest rewards for the sale and consumption of products that the public for one reason or another seem to like (or can be persuaded to like) but that do not necessarily address real public health problems. The consolidation of industry and a degree of risk-averse behavior is found to inhibit the development of breakthrough products. The concentration of power in a few major market actors can distort governmental decision making. Market exclusivity can be pressed beyond reasonable limits by the evergreening of patents and use of other devices.

Advertising may have more to do with dubious techniques of seduction than with emphatic presentation of the plain truth, and the expense involved may considerably exceed the investment in innovation. Firms promising early generic competition may be bought out or scared into a state of paralysis by aggressive litigation. Corrective measures by government may be impeded by suppression of data or political pressure to obstruct price controls.

None of these negative aspects justifies such measures as would tie down the free market excessively, let alone eliminate it, but they all call for firm correction. In that, national and regional measures must complement one another.

THE GLOBAL IDEAL

By and large, human beings are physiologically the same all over the world. They are susceptible to the same diseases, though their exposure to them varies; they respond to the same forms of treatment and they have – or deserve to have – the same rights. By this simple logic, then, all individuals across the globe should have access to a collection of the best medicines that can be devised, and it should be possible to set universal standards by which to judge the eligibility of any particular drug for use in human subjects and the manner in which a good drug can best be used. Those standards should essentially extend to a drug's quality, safety and efficacy, as well as the statements that can justifiably be made about it and the manner in which it should be made and stored.

The Arguments for a Global Policy Approach

There are certain practical considerations favoring a global approach to medicines policy. To deal at a purely national level with matters which surely could be handled globally inevitably involves duplication of effort. Some 150 of the world's countries maintain their own drug approval procedures. Not all are technically equipped to perform the task in its entirety, but many are. That means that in a great many committee rooms around the world experts are gathered together to take decisions on the same matters and on the basis of the same evidence. Where their decisions are identical, one could argue that time and money have been wasted. Where their decisions differ without good reason, the process of introducing new and perhaps necessary drugs may be complicated, delayed and rendered more expensive. As for those countries which lack – and may for many years ahead continue to lack – the technical and financial resources to handle drug regulation competently – in theory these would benefit from the institution of a global regulatory body that would work on their behalf.

We cannot pretend that all the world's citizens enjoy the benefits of uniform standards. Sometimes a country is let down by its regulatory system, sometimes by its inability to insist in practice on maintenance of the standards to which it in principle adheres. For many years after the fearful effects of thalidomide on the unborn child had been extensively documented and the drug had been withdrawn,[2] its effects continued to occur around the globe. David Lee describes another tragic instance of a lag in the corrective process (Box 10.1), when the same substance – the harmful properties of which had sparked drug regulatory reform in the United States in 1938 – was subsequently permitted to wreak havoc in a

BOX 10.1   PROTECTING THE PUBLIC
           HEALTH: ANOTHER PREVENTABLE
           DIETHYLENE GLYCOL TRAGEDY

*David Lee, MD Management Sciences for Health, Arlington,
Virginia*

In October 2006 the Ministry of Health and the Social Security
Fund of Panama issued a recall of seven medicinal products.[a]
Twenty-one persons had died of acute renal failure and with
international technical assistance, the deaths were traced to the
presence of diethylene glycol (DEG) in these over-the-counter
medicines produced by the Social Security Fund's own production laboratory. By January 2007, the official number of known
DEG-related deaths was 51,[b] and there was a likelihood that
more had yet to be recognized.

The toxicity of DEG had been known since 1937, when DEG
was used as an excipient in a sulfanilamide product and caused
105 deaths in the USA.[c] Since 1992, DEG contamination of glycerine used in pharmaceuticals led to similar outbreaks of deaths
in India,[d] Haiti,[e] Argentina,[f] Nigeria[g] and Bangladesh.[h] What went
wrong in Panama?

It is clear that the regulatory system failed to provide adequate
mechanisms to assure the quality of medicines in the market and
protect the public from substandard and dangerous medicines. It
appears that the Social Security Fund did not follow operational
principles for good pharmaceutical procurement[i] when the glycerine was purchased. First, a competitor claimed that the glycerine
supplier did not submit all the required documentation. If this is
true, that supplier should not have been allowed to participate in
the procurement. Second, order quantities were apparently not
based on reliable estimates of actual need; the DEG-contaminated
glycerine was purchased in 2003, but because of over-stocking
it was not used until 2006. Third, despite wide agreement that
prospective suppliers should be pre-qualified, and that selected
suppliers should be monitored through a process that considers product quality, service reliability, delivery time and financial
viability, these essential standards were not met. The imprisoned
owner of the company subsequently admitted to altering the expiration date on the labels of the contaminated containers (from

2003 to 2007), stating that it was 'common practice' in the trade.[j] Finally, there were concerns about the lack of transparency of the procurement process. The procurement directorate should not have purchased the glycerine at all in 2003, since at that time the Social Security Fund authorities were discussing the future of the medicines production laboratory and had ordered a stop on further procurement of raw materials.[k] The laboratory did not have the capacity to comply with international standards for GMP, and as early as 2000, the pharmacist in charge had sent various reports on the inadequate laboratory conditions to the Social Security Fund authorities, but the latter apparently did not take concrete action to improve the situation. Despite these shortcomings, the Ministry of Health continued to authorize the laboratory to produce medicines, at least until April 2006.

Only three tests (specific gravity, purity, microbiology) were actually performed on the batch of DEG-contaminated glycerine even though methods for the detection of DEG as published in the US Pharmacopoeia require gas chromatography and mass spectrometry, for which the laboratory was not equipped. However even a simple test such as that for specific gravity should have determined that the DEG-contaminated glycerine was not 100 percent as labeled, and this finding should have been enough to prevent its use, even if the impurities had not been identified.

It was not until a significant number of patients had experienced acute renal failure, half of them dying, that the relevant authorities became aware of the public health crisis. More than three months had then passed since the DEG-contaminated products were manufactured and released for distribution. Initial suspicions of an infectious cause for this unusual epidemic shifted to a toxicological causal agent.

With international technical assistance, supported by field investigation and sophisticated technological resources, the public health authorities quickly identified DEG as the toxic substance involved. A public information campaign and a massive door-to-door search in the capital city recovered over 120,000 bottles of potentially contaminated medicines. A number of arrests followed.

According to the local supplier, the glycerine had been purchased from a Spanish company that had procured it in China. It is still not known at what point on this long supply chain the DEG contamination occurred. In the 1998 DEG poisoning epidemic in Haiti the DEG-contaminated material was similarly traced to a manufacturer in China, but the latter had closed its operations, moved on to another location, and its records were no longer available.[1] The Panamanian DEG tragedy raises a series of questions concerning the complex issues surrounding policies, regulation and its enforcement, and the quality assurance of essential medicines in developing countries:

- Should the Social Security Fund be manufacturing medicines, albeit 'over-the-counter' products that are considered relatively safe? What are the costs of in-house production compared to effective and efficient procurement from local manufacturers or importers, given the conditions and need for heavy investments to achieve GMP standards? Do the purported benefits outweigh the risks?
- Should the Ministry of Health continue to allow pharmaceutical manufacturing, public or private, if there is no commitment to require and enforce compliance with internationally recognized GMP? Do the benefits outweigh the public health risks if GMP is not followed? What will be required to get local manufacturing operations to achieve GMP compliance?
- What is necessary and sufficient to ensure that there is adequate and effective national capacity to assure the quality of medicines that are marketed? How can activities and resources be prioritized to optimize effectiveness? In the increasingly complex world of pharmaceutical manufacturing and trade, active and inactive ingredients are produced in geographic sites other than those in which the finished products are compounded, packaged or repackaged.
- What should be done to enhance monitoring of product quality and medicines related problems and the system's response to minimize harm when problems do occur?
- How much is a life worth? The acquisition cost of the DEG-contaminated glycerine was US$18,500, resulting in more than 51 deaths from acute renal failure and many more cases who survived but required treatment. The government proposed an amount of US$6.5 million to indemnify victims and their families.
- How can international collaboration be enhanced to reduce the trade in substandard and counterfeit medicines, including raw materials?

The DEG tragedy in Panama was preventable. It occurred because of a systemic failure. The system did not procure from a reliable supplier, did not require or enforce GMP standards, did not adequately assess the quality of ingredients before manufacturing, and did not control the quality of the finished product. Once an infectious cause of the cases of renal failure had been excluded, external assistance was needed to examine and confirm the suspicion that a medicine-related quality problem was involved. Official handling of the crisis was not transparent. Unfortunately, this situation is characteristic of the pharmaceutical regulatory and quality control systems in many, if not all, developing countries. Until these systems are adequately strengthened, the world will continue to periodically suffer similar dramatic and preventable tragedies.

Notes:
a. M. Vega Loo (2006), 'Alteran jarabe en CSS', *La Prensa*, 12 October.
b. J. Arcia (2007), 'Otro muerto por los jarabes contaminados', *La Prensa*, 12 January.
c. This led to the passage of the US Food, Drugs and Cosmetics Act (FDCA) in 1938, which required evidence of safety as a requirement for marketing authorization.
d. J. Singh, A.K. Dutta, N.K. Dubey et al. (1998), 'Diethylene glycol poisoning in Gurgaon, India', *Bull WHO*, 79, 88–95.
e. K.L. O'Brien, J.D. Selaniko, C. Hecdivert et al. (1998), 'Epidemic of pediatric deaths from acute renal failure caused by diethylene glycol poisoning', *JAMA*, 279 (15), 1175–80.
f. R. Drut, G. Quijano, C. Jones and P. Scanferla (1994), 'Hallazgos patalógicos en la intoxicación por dietilenglicol', *Medicina (Buenos Aires)*, 54, 1–5.
g. H.O. Okuonghae, I.S. Ighogboja, J.O. Lawson and E.J. Nwana (1992), 'Diethylene glycol poisoning in Nigerian children', *Ann Trop Paediatr*, 12 (3), 235–8.
h. M. Hanif, M.R. Mobarak, A. Ronan, D. Rahman, J.J. Donovan Jr, M.L. Bennish (1995), 'Fatal renal failure caused by diethylene glycol in paracetamol elixir: the Bangladesh epidemic', *BMJ*, 311, 88–91.
i. World Health Organization, United Nations Children's Fund, United Nations Population Fund, World Bank (1999), *Operational Principles for Good Pharmaceutical Procurement*, WHO/EDM/PAR/99.5, World Health Organization, Geneva.
j. R. Rodriguez (2006), 'Dueño de Medicom habla', *La Prensa*, 16 November.
k. J. Arcia (2007), 'Ex directores en la mira', *La Prensa*, 6 January.
l. UN Commission on Human Rights (1999), 55th session, Item 10 IIIA, 20 January.

range of other countries, culminating in an epidemic of injury in Panama nearly 70 years later. Incompetence, ignorance, indifference and lack of financial resources all seem to have played a role in these tragedies.

If we pursue this line of reasoning to its ultimate conclusion, the endpoint could only be the establishment and maintenance of a global drug regulatory agency with powers of enforcement, operating perhaps under the auspices of the WHO, or some comparable body with the well-being of all as the reason for its existence.

Obstacles to Global Policy and Regulation

Yet there are obstacles and objections to truly global regulation. Some of these obstacles may prove to be genuinely insuperable. Some of the objections may represent no more than the protests of self-interested parties. It is necessary to consider a number of these elements, with reference to examples. We begin with two basic problems.

Not all evidence, whatever its apparent authority, is beyond doubt. So-called proof of the efficacy and safety of a new drug (and many older ones) can be so incomplete or ambiguous that even the most qualified experts differ as to interpretations. One can cite numerous examples to support this statement, such as the introduction in the mid 1980s of the combination of L-DOPA and an enzyme inhibitor to treat Parkinsons Disease. Some agencies were persuaded of a therapeutic breakthrough and voted for its approval. Others, who gave weight to the suspicion that the enzyme inhibitor might cause injury by inhibiting enzymes important in other bodily processes, held up regulatory approval in their institutions until practical experience elsewhere convinced them that their doubts were unfounded. But in other cases the doubters proved to be correct. In the mid 1980s benoxaprofen was approved in the United Kingdom as a major advance in the treatment of rheumatic conditions and was launched with great fanfare. In the Netherlands, where the same evidence was reviewed, the agency had misgivings regarding the safety of this new therapeutic approach. It posed serious objections, maintaining them in the face of scorn and indignation. Belgium and Luxemburg pursued the same course. Six months later, numerous elderly people in the United Kingdom were found to have died of liver complications after taking the drug, and it was hastily withdrawn worldwide. In circumstances such as these it is fortunate that there are a number of competent regulatory agencies in existence, all forming their views independently. Each will have its own perspective, and each will on occasion be mistaken, or display too great or too slight a measure of caution.

Current needs and wants are not the same in all places. Physiology may be more or less the same across the world, but current needs, priorities and demands are not. The primary aim of medicines policy as it evolved in the increasingly affluent West, particularly from the 1960s on, was to react quickly and forcefully to the entry into the market of medicines that were dangerous, ineffective or badly made. Other goals, however important in principle, were of secondary importance. In the world of 2009, by contrast, the two most evident problems demanding action are grossly inadequate access to drugs in many developing countries, and the failure of most drug research to address the pressing problems of the South, such as malaria and the massive spread of multi-drug resistant tuberculosis. The regulatory problems of half a century ago are still there, but we know how to address them. In an increasing number of countries we succeed. But we have not yet identified the best way to overcome the current therapeutic challenges.

There are subtle differences between countries relating to traditions and patterns of demand. For example, herbal and traditional medicines survive and thrive in much of the world because they are believed to have proven their worth over generations. and because they are available where Western medicines are not. Many of these traditions undoubtedly have demonstrable therapeutic virtues. Even where they do not, there may be merit – assuming in retaining deeply rooted and trusted traditions because even placebo effects are helpful.

Differences in national and local demand can have equally deeply rooted explanations, reflecting longstanding popular habits and preferences. A physician moving his or her practice from one European country to another is immediately confronted with these differences. One nation is happy with tablets and capsules, another trusts only injections, a third believes above all in suppositories. Families on one side of the North Sea call for antibiotics for the mildest infection, while on the other people are hesitant to use them. Will a Finnish physician rely on the results of a clinical study from Italy? The satirist's concept of the Northern European Medical Credibility Zone[3] is not entirely without basis in reality. One needs only to have spent a little time in an international committee debating pharmaceuticals to realize the extent of (sometimes quite good-natured) cross-border distrust between scientists in this field.

When political considerations enter into the dialogue, with a particular government apparently more concerned about the well-being of its national pharmaceutical industry than the welfare of its people or those of other nations, cross-border cooperation may seem a distant dream.

Working Towards Global Solutions

Considerations such as those above suggest that it will be anything but simple to create and maintain a rigid homogenous globally applicable system of drug policy, and that this may not be entirely desirable. This being said, in fact a great deal of international policy has emerged over a period of 60 years and it is worth considering this history.

Back in 1946 when the Constitution of the WHO was drafted, the drafters competed with one another to formulate clauses that would ensure the WHO would have no legislative or regulatory authority whatsoever.[4] Countries that had been fighting wars to preserve their freedom were averse to any agreement or institution resembling supranational control. Since then, 60 World Health Assemblies have demonstrated that member states are as reluctant as ever to formally endow the WHO with any real governing power. The debates in the Assembly preceding the adoption – in a much scaled-back form – of the WHO's *Ethical Criteria for Medicinal Drug Promotion* in 1988 were marked by heated interchanges. Some member states appeared to place much greater weight on the freedom of action of their national drug producers than on the public health interest. What the WHO has demonstrated over time is the extent of the influence that can be exerted in this field through scientific credibility and expertise alone. Perhaps the most successful of the WHO's many initiatives was its creation of the 'Essential Drugs' concept (outlined in Chapter 5). This led to wide acceptance of the idea that world health as a whole is best served by first making a basic range of well-proven drugs universally accessible rather than by placing all the emphasis on the marketing of new and more expensive drugs.

Numerous WHO publications have established principles for such ventures as the adoption of a national drug policy,[5] the containment of costs[6], the conduct of valid and safe clinical trials[7] and the role of clinical pharmacology,[8] all gaining credibility from the independent expertise involved in their compilation. In recent years the WHO has, with the support of such bodies as the European Medicines Evaluation Agency, provided opinions on the merits of particular drugs in order to assist small regulatory agencies having limited staff and expert advisors. Something similar was tried on a reduced scale in the Organization's Regional Office for Europe 30 years ago, but at that time it was met with strong resistance from both industry and national agencies as representing the thin end of the dreaded supranational wedge. In that respect we have come a long way in a generation. The WHO has also succeeded in collaboration with other agencies in establishing pre-qualification procedures for the international recognition of dependable sources of drug supply[9] for certain specified purposes. For some programs of assistance, adherence to the list of pre-qualified suppliers is now compulsory. The WHO has established and maintains a virtually worldwide system for the detection and study of new adverse drug reactions and interactions occurring in the field.[10] More recently, it has created an international register of clinical trials.[11] Despite occasional tactical blunders and heavy lobbying of WHO's staff and management by parties with self-interest in the field of medicines, cautious but determined progress in such directions seems likely to continue.[12]

Other specialized agencies operating globally, notably UNICEF, with its assurance of low-cost drug supplies to poor countries (essentially by functioning as a non-profit wholesaler) and the World Bank with its ability both to advise individual member states on policy development, to fund economic progress and sometimes to assist in expert procurement of medicines, have played roles complementary to that of the WHO. Here, too, some spectacular results have been achieved by persistent hard work, sound advice and reliable performance over a long period. Insulated some-what from the constant international political debate, institutions such as UNICEF can develop initiatives and be in a position to succeed before there is an opportunity for skeptics to question their desirability.

REGIONAL POLICIES

While reflection on the multilateral situation may lead to cautious opti-mism regarding the prospect of broad and truly global policy and practice, less caution is needed as regards developments at the regional level. Highly promising developments regarding joint regional action in this field seem to show that, between relatively homogenous groups of nations, common structures can be created and can function.

The countries of the Eastern Caribbean provide a good example.[13] The Eastern Caribbean Drug Service (ECDS) has for many years provided a pooled drug procurement service to nine Ministries of Health in the small island nations of the Caribbean. The success of the operation, which allowed ECDS to reduce unit costs for pharmaceuticals by over 50 percent during its first procurement cycle alone, reflects the importance of such joint efforts of political will and institutional alliances, and of a common approach to medicines policy as a whole. The nine countries had essen-tially the same view on the medicines that their populations required and the criteria for their entry into the market. There was also a community-wide policy on such matters as standardizing pack sizes, dosage forms and strengths, as well as generic bidding and therapeutic alternative bidding. Above all, these were countries in which medicines were (and still are) being used in very much the same way.

The regional collaboration in the medicines field that has been achieved in South-East Asia provides a larger and now more ambitious example. The Association of South East Asian Nations (ASEAN) was formed in 1967 by Indonesia, Malaysia, the Philippines, Singapore and Thailand, and has since expanded to ten countries with others currently seeking membership.[14] As part of the ASEAN's broad program of cultural and economic development, there are regular consultations between the member states on the approval of medicines for sale. ASEAN has also promoted measures to increase access to medicines in its member states, to increase the use of low-cost generic products, and to collaborate on knowledge of traditional medicines across the region.

The Southern African Development Community (SADC), embracing 15 countries, has developed ambitious plans for common and cooperative approaches to drug policy, and will be putting these into operation, with donor support, beginning in 2009.

The most far-reaching regional collaboration in the medicines field is that developed in the European Union (Box 10.2), which has not only maintained close and regular consultation between national drug regulatory agencies for two decades but has progressively introduced harmonized laws, regulations and standards and has established a central approval procedure.[15] The initial definition of general standards dates from 1965, while specific rules for toxicological and pharmacological tests were issued in 1975. An advisory committee of experts, the Committee for Proprietary Medicinal Products (CPMP), was active beginning in 1978. Starting in 1987, a 'concertation procedure', compulsory for biotechnological products and voluntary for 'highly innovative' products was introduced. This created a procedure for issuing a straightforward EU marketing authorization that came into play as soon as a firm sought marketing authorization in any member state, this state acting as Rapporteur. During the early years of operation of the new system, member states could object to the Rapporteur's decision, which decision would then be reconsidered by the CPMP. The latter could then provide a non-binding advisory opinion on the matter. This procedure was drastically strengthened and extended in 1995, when a central European Medicines Evaluation Agency (EMEA) was established in London, supported by advice from the CPMP. The Rapporteur is now appointed by the EMEA and CPMP, though the manufacturer may express a preference. Finally, beginning in 1998, the licensing competence of national authorities was limited to their own markets. They would henceforth operate independently only with respect to drugs intended for marketing in their country and nowhere else in the European Union.

This very brief summary of the complex developments in the European Union might suggest that progress was smooth and fairly rapid. In fact, despite the relative homogeneity of the Western European countries that comprised the European Union during most of this period, it was a venture with ups and downs. Some of these aspects are considered in Box 10.2 and need not be described again here, but a number of points deserve to be stressed in view of their broader significance.

A major failure concerned an attempt, in the early days of the CPMP,

BOX 10.2   DRUG REGULATION IN EUROPE:
SOME LESSONS AND QUESTIONS

Contributed by Graham Dukes, MD LLM and Ellen 't Hoen, LLM

Harmonization and centralization of drug regulatory procedures in the European Union have been introduced progressively since 1966, during which time the number of member states has grown from six to 25. Initially only broad principles were laid down, but by the late 1970s more detailed rules for drug approval were made binding on member states and monthly consultations between national agencies established. At the same time, detailed approval standards for particular classes of drugs were established. A centralized approval procedure has since then been created and its competence progressively extended. Some conclusions and impressions are presented below.

1. In countries with limited national capacity or experience, standards have been much improved. Corruption and undue influence have been largely eliminated. However in some countries that already had high regulatory standards one does observe a degree of relaxation. This reflects in part the need to compromise, in part the fact that a national agency anxious to serve as a port of entry for European applications will seek to render its procedures as attractive as possible to applicants.

    Fees have risen considerably, but only in part due to Europeanization; they also reflect acceptance of the belief that drug approval procedures, formerly largely state funded, should now be fully funded from fees.

2. The formulation of clear standards (in the form of guidelines, largely developed with the United States and Japan in the International Conference on Harmonization) has benefited all parties, reducing inconsistencies between national requirements. These standards are suitable for most industrialized countries, though they may not always be entirely appropriate for the developing world.

3. The initial expectation that joint effort would both accelerate assessment and reduce operational costs has not been fulfilled. The complexity of the procedures needed to

secure consensus, as well as the massive volume of interpretation and translation, cause expense and delay. Some larger member states have actually increased their national staffing and resources to ensure that they can play a full part in European procedures and that their national views on policy are adequately reflected in European decisions.

4. The policies and decisions of the European Union are directly applicable in the member states and the states of the European Economic Area; the latter have agreed to accept EU rulings and standards as a means of ensuring open trade with the Union. The standards applied and decisions taken for the European Union have also come to be regarded throughout the world as scientifically authoritative.

5. Though current European Union standards apply to new drug applications, a considerable time can elapse before all drugs accepted earlier at the national level in member states are reassessed according to current standards.

6. Some criticism of drug policies at the European level reflects the fact that the European Union originated as an economic community, the primary purpose of which was to ensure the free movement of goods and services between member states. This was, therefore, the starting point for the harmonization (and progressive unification) of drug policies, reflecting the needs of industry and trade. This was in contrast to the situation in most individual countries, where drug regulation was based primarily on considerations of public health.

7. Successes achieved in Europe should probably not lead to the conclusion that an even larger group of nations could and should seek to achieve unified policies in this field. Much depends on the cultural and political homogeneity of the community concerned.

8. Europe has sometimes been accused of reacting too slowly to crises, for example, the emergence of serious adverse effects with a particular medicine. However this has not always been the case.

9. The European Union has since 1987 applied fairly strict data exclusivity (DE) rules, that is, for a fixed period of time, drug regulatory authorities will not allow the registration

files of an originator to be used to register a therapeutically equivalent generic version of that medicine.

10. In the context of recent debates on the need to encourage R&D for neglected diseases the role of the central assessment body (the EMEA) in assessing products destined for use outside the EU has been expanded, for example, enabling it to provide advice to the WHO on the merits of certain drugs intended for developing countries.

11. There is today an increasing realization that populations need to be protected by an overall drug policy, extending beyond pure regulation of individual medicines to matters such as price controls, industrial and trade profits and earnings, research, guidance on prescribing, provision of objective public information and education, and sufficient provisions regarding 'marginal products' (such as herbal remedies). It is not clear that the European Union will make consistent progress in this direction since its involvement in drug issues has from the outset been defined as relating to technical regulatory issues in the narrow sense. On other matters, considerable discrepancies between member states exist, for example, a drug may be several times as expensive in one country as in another.

to establish the principle of mutual recognition, by which a medicine approved in one member state would, with certain caveats, be eligible for approval by all others. In retrospect, it is clear that this approach failed because of lack of mutual trust. In particular, one of the first applications eligible for approval in this manner was based on national registration already granted in Italy. Other member states, represented in the CPMP, expressed a serious lack of trust in the evidence on the basis of which the Italian license had been issued, and the product was subsequently discredited, as was the management at the time of the Italian agency.[16]

It is clear that much of the strength of the European procedures today is drawn from the unanimity gradually attained between a series of countries with relatively similar systems and standards. With that agreement as a basis, it is currently proving possible to extend the application of the system to newer member states, namely a number of countries in Central and Eastern Europe in some of which drug regulatory traditions and standards were previously less well developed.

A final point, evident from Box 10.2, relates to the fact that regional procedures are likely to involve a deal of debate, compromise and delay. The costs of obtaining a drug marketing license today in most European countries are a large multiple of those incurred a generation ago. That appears, however, to be the price one must pay for struggling towards a degree of uniformity in a heterogeneous world.

Finally, a word must be devoted to the work in the drug regulatory field of the International Conference on Harmonization (ICH).[17] Whatever its name, this should be regarded as an inter-regional rather than an international body, having been established in 1990 by the US FDA, the European Union and the Japanese drug regulatory agency. With the International Federation of Pharmaceutical Manufacturers Associations (IFPMA) providing the secretariat, expert groups meet regularly and develop highly specific guidelines for methods to establish the quality, safety and efficacy of medicines. Active participants are scientists from the regulatory agencies and from the originator pharmaceutical industry. The WHO is involved, but only as an observer.

The declared aim of the ICH is to establish agreed upon standards to which the agencies involved will adhere, thereby serving the public interest and avoiding unnecessary discrepancies. While the standards are obligatory only for the agencies directly involved, the hope has often been expressed that the same standards would be applied throughout the world.

There has been little in the way of opposition to the technical standards developed by the ICH that generally represent current norms for good research practice. Some have expressed the view that the strong industry influence has tended to play down certain requirements, namely as regards chronic toxicity studies. The principal criticism of ICH is in a sense diametrically opposed to this, and questions the ICH view that its regulatory standards should become universally applicable. Critics contend that they represent, in fact, advanced standards that can only be maintained by large research organizations in submissions to large and well-equipped regulatory authorities.[18] Much of the world is, however, currently dependent on medicines that have never been tested to these standards, and may not require such sophisticated investigation. Quality in particular, as pointed out in Chapter 4, is a relative concept. Simple long-established remedies with a broad efficacy/safety ratio may not have been proven to be ideal in every respect, yet they play a vital public health role. In this view, the global research-based industry may be seeking, by its propagation of ICH norms, to further strengthen its position to the exclusion of all others, notably smaller manufacturers and generic suppliers. It could indeed be that, in the long run, standards such as these will prove helpful or even essential for the introduction of highly innovative drugs, the therapeutic spectrum and toxicity of which is still in doubt, but for the foreseeable future lesser standards will continue to be regarded as adequate in some situations.

Finally, in considering this issue of drug quality, one needs to note the increasing uniformity of the world's pharmacopeas.[19] Although many countries still maintain their own national pharmacopoeias as official standards of quality, there has been a strong move towards harmonization. Most European countries now accept the European Pharmacopoeia and contribute to it rather than producing their own volumes. The British Pharmacopoeia still exists but is increasingly based on the European texts. The US Pharmacopoeia, now translated into both Russian and Spanish, is acquiring a dominant influence on quality practices in Latin America and the CIS countries that emerged from the former Soviet Union, and it is working closely with China. Japan still updates its own texts but is increasingly influenced by these other volumes. Just as there is something to be said for the existence of a number of regulatory agencies across the world, so it would seem desirable that a certain number of centers continue to produce quality standards of this type. To some extent interpretations will continue to differ and progress is likely to be enriched by a certain amount of diversity.

THE DEVELOPED AND DEVELOPING WORLDS

The acknowledgement that standards may be allowed to differ obliges us to consider how far public policy in the field of medicines has proceeded towards an attainable ideal; first considering the situation between developed and developing countries, then examining the relationship between the two. The distinction between these two groups of countries, formerly termed the 'First World' and the 'Third World', has never been sharply delineated. Today an intermediate group of large countries undergoing rapid development (for example, Brazil, Russia, India and China, or BRIC) is now receiving considerable attention. For the sake of discussion, it is helpful to compare the state of public policy in the two extreme situations.

The Developed World

The two main characteristics of the developed world in the medicines field include the accessibility of existing drugs to the population and the existence in the larger economies of originator multinational pharmaceutical firms with thriving export businesses. The extent to which public policy has actively created this situation, rather than simply facilitating its emergence, varies among developed countries. Access to medicines and medical care without financial barriers has most clearly been a long-term target of the social democracies of Northern Europe. More liberal economies have moved less far and less fast, putting faith in private initiatives and allowing a measure of laissez-faire. The development of successful pharmaceutical industries has been only partly due to deliberate public policy. Yet wealthy countries have stimulated the process of industry development because of its economic benefits, primarily by their fiscal policies, though at the same time imposing significant regulatory requirements. Negative developments in these countries have included a trend to excessive use of medicines and a commercial trend to excessive promotional pressure. The effects of these trends now call out for corrective action in the interests of public health and well-being.

The Developing World

The developing world, as considered at length in Chapter 5, is unfortunately still largely characterized by situations of shortage and deprivation. Because of low average per capita incomes, many drugs on the world market are out of reach of the bulk of a poor population, and the health situation is marked by a high incidence of conditions for which modern drugs have simply not been developed. National economies are too weak to provide correction. Little innovative research is possible. All these problems are aggravated in many cases by inexperienced government, circulation of counterfeit medicines, corruption, a shortage of trained personnel at all levels and a generally weak infrastructure.

Policies in Two Worlds: Bridging the Gap

There is a universal consensus that, in this field as in others, developing countries must, for their own sake and that of the world as a whole, develop further, and that they have need of assistance in doing so. There are, however, different opinions as to the desired end-point of this process, the priority to be accorded to it and the means by which it can best be achieved. A number of the most promising approaches are considered briefly here.

Donor aid

Industrialized countries have in the post-colonial era accepted that they must provide donor assistance to developing countries. The countries of Scandinavia have in recent years devoted as much as 1.5 percent of their own GDP to this end,[20] while other industrialized nations such as the

United States have become prominent in the field primarily because of their size and economic strength. The drug field has been a popular area of concentration because of the evident needs that exist, with programs often being initiated in situations of crisis and taking the form of massive drug donations in kind. Though in a later phase such initiatives have tended to be succeeded by efforts to improve infrastructure, the HIV/AIDS epidemic has led to renewed programs of donations in kind. Either approach or both may be appropriate provided they are attuned to adequately documented needs and are efficiently administered to avoid waste and corruption. With such provisos, donor assistance in the medicines field, whether provided bilaterally or through broad cooperative programs, is generally a useful element in the process of development. Within a recipient country there is, however, a constant need for coordination of donor efforts if wasteful duplication is to be avoided.

Promotion of appropriate research

Chapters 2 and 3 make the point that if research is to be guided into areas where the need for innovation is greatest an appropriate system of rewards must exist. The patent system is not, in its present form, a tool that encourages the type of innovation of which the developing world, with its limited ability to pay for new and better medicines, has the most need.

As discussed in Chapters 2 and 5, there are a number of potential mechanisms for promoting innovation most needed in developing countries, including prizes targeted to specific diseases and subsidies with prescribed end-points. In addition, R&D initiatives undertaken by public-private partnerships and others can engage in segmentation of patent-based distribution rights along geographic and/or purchasing entity (for example, public or private) lines, allowing for different pricing arrangements to take effect for the same product.

Market segmentation approaches already have been used by PPPs such as the Drugs for Neglected Diseases Initiative (DNDi) and the Foundation for Innovative New Diagnostics (FIND). Arrangements with private sector companies do not exclude the patenting of innovation, but they allocate geographic (and other) distribution markets between public and private collaborators based on income and other factors in the relevant markets, so as to permit individuals in developing countries to take advantage of low-priced supplies of new products.

Other approaches to making innovation more widely available include the potential buying out of patent rights with respect to defined markets, or the contribution of patents into pools that can be drawn from under different terms and conditions.[21]

The fact that these and other approaches to the reorientation of medicines innovation are at the moment the subject of vigorous debate and some experimentation is a good indicator that the way ahead is still open and that several solutions may ultimately need to be used in parallel.

Transfer of technology (see also Chapter 5)
In a field such as pharmaceutical R&D, it is clear that many countries with traditionally limited resources do have the potential to contribute to the process if they are given the opportunity. Transfer of pharmaceutical-related technology, from enterprises or institutions with technology resources to enterprises or institutions that lack such resources, is one option for increasing pharmaceutical-related R&D worldwide. The benefit will not be merely one-sided. Traditional knowledge, native skills and natural resources can enrich the overall process to universal benefit.

To the extent that governments are the owners of technology (for example, as is often the case with the National Institutes of Health in the United States), they may constructively provide such technology to foreign governments or to public or private institutions. The WTO TRIPS Agreement establishes a transfer of technology obligation for developed country members in favor of LDC members.[22] Recent free trade agreements negotiated by the United States include certain (admittedly soft) commitments with respect to technology transfer.[23]

The process of transferring technology unfortunately becomes more problematic when private enterprise is the prospective transferor. Technology is typically considered a valuable proprietary asset, and a typical commercial enterprise does not wish to build up competitors. In a sense, the private sector is always engaged in seeding technological development in the developing world, for example, by establishing and equipping local manufacturing plants that will train and employ local personnel. Such plants are, however, too often fated to remain dependent on the foreign parent company in many respects, including input of innovation and supply of active ingredients, and they are unlikely to play a major role in the development of an independent and globally competitive local industry. This is a problem that governments in Brazil, India, and even Canada, are currently attempting to address. There are potential downsides to seeking to disseminate drug production too widely. The nature of the process is such that, for the world as a whole, very considerable economies can be achieved by concentrating production in centers where massive volumes can be attained. Yet, while recognizing the importance of economies of scale, those scale economies do not dictate a particular geographic distribution of productive capacity. That capacity could well be distributed among a number of countries adhering to appropriate GMP standards.

Solving the Counterfeiting Problem

The fact that the issue of counterfeit drugs is relegated to the last place in the present discussion must in no sense be regarded as an indicator that it is of secondary importance. It exists worldwide, and as Chapter 8 makes abundantly clear, it is now substantially affecting the drug trade in much of the developing world, presenting a major risk to public health. Here, too, however, one must make some careful distinctions. The first concern of a manufacturer of a patented drug will be the fact that its product has been illegally reverse-engineered and reproduced, and that it will thereby lose revenue. From the public health point of view, the essential issue is not the fact of the illegal copying, but the possibility that public health will be placed at risk. Priority must be given to eliminating those false products that are either toxic or useless. Useless counterfeit penicillin must have cost countless lives. Now it is artemesin – life saving for many malaria patients – that is being criminally falsified on a vast scale. Addressing this problem requires substantial investment in effective supply chain management and quality control at every step, with action taken in each country involved in the manufacture, trade or retailing of such products.

PUBLIC REGULATION AND SUPPORT OF INNOVATION

As noted in Chapters 2 and 3, while most governments have not become directly involved in pharmaceutical innovation, some have taken steps to facilitate drug discovery, for example, by tax measures favoring innovation. They also have been accused of impeding or discouraging innovation through their regulatory activities (see Chapter 3).

A number of countries maintain state-funded research institutes with activities in the fields of medicine and pharmacology, often dating from a period when industrial research hardly existed. These institutes have been primarily concerned with basic scientific research. The discoveries with potential practical application have mainly been exploited by others.

A US Government Accountability Office report on pharmaceutical innovation highlights the problem of moving basic innovation from the laboratory into commercial-scale production.[24] This problem has been raised elsewhere, for example, in Brazil, where large-scale government funding is provided for basic research towards the development of new pharmaceutical inventions, but where there are limited links between the research community and the industrial pharmaceutical sector.[25] In a number of European countries, such as The Netherlands, quiet but effective links appear to be maintained between the state institutes and industry which are beneficial to both. The proven ability of industry to translate basic research into demonstrations of effectiveness in animals, and thereafter in human studies, makes it an eligible partner to undertake this task. The essential condition is that work funded by the taxpayer should not become primarily a source of enrichment for industry. The benefits must be equitably shared.

As noted in earlier chapters, controversy has arisen several times in the United States when major new drugs found their origins in work performed within the NIH, such as at the National Cancer Institute. Essential work leading to the development of the important anti-cancer drug paclitaxel was developed at the National Cancer Institute and brought to market by a US-based multinational (with further assistance from a university research center) under the name Taxol®. Critics[26] argued that neither the taxpayers nor the NIH benefited sufficiently from the income generated from the sales of this very successful product. Nor, it has been argued, did many potential users, since Taxol® was marketed at an extraordinarily high price, thus depriving many patients of access to its benefits. The industrial response to criticism in this and similar cases has been that the community reaps an adequate reward in the form of corporate taxes and the development of exports, while the institutes concerned benefit from profitable royalty agreements. While it is difficult to generalize, there is good reason to take as a starting point that the public should be the principal beneficiary of the fruits of research achieved largely at public expense, and that the burden should lie on private beneficiaries or licensees of such innovation to justify prices that appear excessive.

SOCIETY AND THE PHARMACEUTICAL INDUSTRY

Events such as those relating to Taxol®, and the sharp controversies that often surround them, require a student of public policy in this area to consider carefully the role that the pharmaceutical industry currently plays in society, and the extent to which this is desirable. Unavoidably, any debate on this subject largely turns around the practices and power of the multinational corporations that have come to dominate the field. If one compares the picture of the originator industry painted by its most vociferous critics against that offered by the industry itself (and more particularly by its sophisticated public relations arm), one is faced with a stark contrast. In the eyes of the critic, the industry has become the epitome of capitalist greed, grossly overcharging for its products, manipulating the professions and the public in its own interests, investing much more heavily and successfully in seduction than in innovation, economical with the truth and indifferent to the needs of the developing world. In the originator industry's well-manicured self-portrait, on the other hand, it is characterized as a public benefactor of the highest order, moving in the vanguard of medical progress and faithfully serving the patient, the investor and the community according to the standards of good business, professional ethics and sound science.

In theory, one might argue that a sound public policy will ultimately emerge from such a clash of diametrically opposed views, but in reality both are too simplistic to be helpful. Both rely in part on the selective use of information to prove their case. What is more, there is a serious imbalance between the two in the manner of their presentation and the impact that they exert on policy. The imbalance is in part a question of style; the critical view is commonly presented in the measured tones of academic or professional debate, while industry mobilizes all the tools of persuasion to its cause. There is also an imbalance of volume. Democracy has over the years been built around the assumption that society consists of individuals, whose votes and needs must determine the pattern of government. The fact of the matter is, however, that in the course of the centuries societies have sometimes been dominated and policies imposed upon governments less by individuals than by massive corporate entities. The East India Companies of Britain, the Netherlands and Denmark developed that role in the eighteenth century, manipulating entire parliaments and even armies to their advantage. More subtly, the multinationals that grew up two centuries later learned the art of lobbying. According to the US Center for Public Integrity, from January 2005 through June 2006 alone, the pharmaceutical industry spent some $182 million on federal lobbying,[27] and the industry was stated to have 1,274 registered lobbyists in Washington, DC, as well as lobbying teams in the individual states. The number of individuals lobbying for consumer and patient interests is a relative handful.

The structure of government can result in a further imbalance of interests. In many national administrations the departments or ministries handling trade, the economy, and industrial and commercial development play a substantially greater role in policy formulation than do the generally smaller and weaker departments handling education, culture and health. Where medicines and the pharmaceutical industry are concerned, all these departments come into play, and the health interest may all too often be overridden. That may be understandable, but it is hardly justifiable, even from the economic point of view. In 1993 the World Bank devoted its annual *World Development Report* to the issue of 'Investing in Health'.[28] The belief that the health of a country's population is a factor promoting both welfare and wealth was anything but new, but the report documented the link in an impressive manner, especially for the developing world. It is today equally well demonstrated for industrialized economies; a study conducted for the European Union in 2005[29] documented systematically the high cost falling on Europe's economies as a result of illness. It assembled a wealth of evidence to demonstrate how good health promoted earnings and labor supply, while poor health increased the likelihood of early retirement with the resultant loss of working capacity. Taken together, such evidence provides a powerful argument for governments of every hue to invest adequately in the health of their populations, not only because better health is a desirable objective in its own right, but also because it is an important determinant of economic growth and competitiveness.

Add to that the clear evidence of the importance of medicines in advancing health, and one might expect governments to devise medicine policies that are fully in the public interest. On certain fronts that has happened, notably with the introduction of procedures for the critical evaluation and approval of new drugs to ensure their quality, safety and efficacy. Yet one repeatedly finds situations emerging in which consumer voices arguing in the public interest are in direct confrontation with the views of the pharmaceutical industry, with the latter sometimes exerting the greater effect on political decisions. A single example already touched on in Chapter 6, must suffice: Britain's independent *Drugs and Therapeutics Bulletin,* was for many years distributed free of charge to health professionals thanks to an official subsidy. Its influence in encouraging critical and economical prescribing was out of all proportion to the negligible costs involved – approximately one-thousandth of the drug industry's expenditure on promotion. Not surprisingly, the *Bulletin* ran foul of certain spokespersons for the drug industry and some of its close allies.[30] Yet it remains astonishing that, at a time when British parliamentarians were debating with concern official reports on the level of drug advertising and the costs of prescribing, the country's Secretary of State for Health decided to withdraw support for the *Bulletin* as an 'economy measure'.[31] The *Bulletin* was ultimately saved, but it is a compelling illustration of the imbalance in lobbying pressures.

Undoubtedly, the pharmaceutical industry has on too many occasions brought criticism upon itself by persisting in various malpractices and the development of grand but questionable ambitions. Aldous Huxley's fictional portrayal in 1932 of a fully medicated society[32] has sometimes seemed temptingly within reach of those commercial ambitions. Tonics, vitamins and oral contraceptives have all in turn been sold profitably, though relatively innocuously, to healthy populations. Rather less innocent was the tranquillizer era. By 1979 no less than 31 million prescriptions for these drugs were issued in Britain alone,[33] and this must to a large extent be traced back to the promotional insistence that there was a universal need for them. An introductory advertisement from the 1950s under the heading, 'Whatever the diagnosis. . . LIBRIUM', was not atypical.[34]

It sometimes seems as if that mid-century boom in market expansion and profitability, backed by a wave of innovation, endowed some leaders of industry with a sense of invincibility and impregnability that persisted into an age where more modest self-assessment might be called for. Many of those who speak on behalf of the pharmaceutical industry today appear over-defensive and resistant to change, even when, as some industry leaders are now saying, the time for change has come. When Sir Richard Sykes, a prominent figure in the British pharmaceutical industry, appeared before the House of Commons Select Committee in 2005, he was very direct in his statements: 'Today the industry has got a very bad name. That is unfortunate for an industry that we should look up to and believe in, and that we should be supporting. I think there have to be some big changes.'[35]

Precisely how those changes will be brought about is still unclear, but it seems evident that public policy in this field must increasingly strike a balance between the desirability of permitting a sufficiently healthy industry to function and the absolute need to attune its place and its function to the requirements of public health.

In closing this book, we return to our summary of recommendations from Chapter 1. As we have intimated throughout, there is no simple solution or single bit of magic that can be worked to address the range of problems confronting the field of medicines. This field is as complex as the human condition. But giving serious attention to a few key issues will certainly help.

First, the system for promoting innovation worldwide must be refocused on the development of new therapeutic classes, with the lesser emphasis on extending product lines through minor modifications. There are various ways to address this objective by retooling the patent system (including the introduction of quasi-patents to protect minor modifications), by extending and improving subsidy programs, by the use of targeted prizes and others.

Second, additional transparency must be introduced into the system by which medicines are assessed and approved.

Third, the marketing of prescription pharmaceutical products directly to consumers introduces both direct costs of promotion, and indirect costs from elevated demand. The heavy promotion of new prescription products increases risks that unforeseen injurious effects will be spread more widely. There is good reason to curtail the trend towards direct to consumer advertising of these products.

Fourth, private civil litigants play an important role in increasing transparency and identifying pharmaceutical product risks, in addition to redressing injury. Courts should be very wary of curtailing the role of private litigation (for example, US state causes of action should not be pre-empted by federal law). If the US Supreme Court ever moves in this direction, Congress should step in to correct the situation.

Fifth, there is a great deal of regulatory cost imposed by country-to-country assessment of pharmaceutical products. While some degree of regulatory heterogeneity is necessary and appropriate to take into account matters such as differences in climate and disease patterns, it is not necessary that every country review and approve every drug. In light of the current state of global political affairs, we recommend increased efforts on a regional basis to cooperate on and coordinate medicines regulatory policy and implementation.

Sixth, it is important that low-income developing countries maintain focus on 'essential drugs' policies that seek to assure wide access to the most needed treatments. This is particularly important as the 2009 global economic climate threatens to reduce even modest levels of support from developed countries. It remains vitally important that developed countries continue to provide support for medicines purchases for countries and populations that are not viable participants in the global pharmaceuticals market.

NOTES

1. MSF, Oxfam, TAC (2001), 'Drug companies in South Africa capitulate under barrage of public pressure', Press Release, Médécins sans Frontières, Geneva, 19 April.
2. H. Sjöström and R. Nilsson (1972), *Thalidomide and the Power of the Drug Companies*, Penguin Books, Harmondsworth, Middlesex.
3. M.N.G. Dukes (1973), 'Personal view', *BMJ*, 1 September, 496.
4. WHO (1976), *The World Health Organization – Constitution*, Adopted 1946; Amendments by the 26th World Health Assembly in force from 3 February 1977.
5. WHO (1988), *How to Develop and Implement a National Drug Policy*, 2nd edn, World Health Organization, Geneva.
6. WHO/EURO (2003), *Drugs and Money: Prices, Affordability and Cost Containment*, 7th edn, ISO Press and World Health Organization, Regional Office for Europe, Copenhagen.
7. W. Rudowski (1980), 'World Health Organization Biomedical Research Guidelines and the conduct of clinical trials', *J Med Ethics*, 6, 58–60.
8. WHO/EURO (1993), *Clinical Pharmacological Evaluation in Drug Control*, EUR/ICP/DSE 173, World Health Organization, Regional Office for Europe, Copenhagen.
9. WHO (2004), 'The WHO prequalification project', Fact Sheet No. 278, May, World Health Organization, Geneva.
10. I.R. Edwards (1997), 'Adverse reactions: finding the needle in the haystack', *BMJ*, 315, 500.
11. WHO (2006), 'International clinical trial registry platform', Press Release, 16 March World Health Organization, Geneva.
12. WHO (2008), *WHO Medicines Strategy 2008–2013, Eighth Draft*, 13 June, World Health Organization, Geneva.
13. M. Huff-Rousselle and F. Burnett (1998), 'Cost containment through pharmaceutical

procurement: a Caribbean case study', *Int J Hlth Planning & Management*, **11** (2), 135–57.

14. T. Chalermpalanupap (1999), 'ASEAN 10: meeting the challenges', ASEAN Secretariat official website (accessed 31 July 2008).

15. J. Abraham and G. Lewis (2003), 'Europeanization of medicines regulation', in J. Abraham and H. Lawton Smith (eds), *Regulation of the Pharmaceutical Industry*, Palgrave Macmillan, Basingstoke, Hampshire.

16. Editorial (2008), 'Clean hands, please', *Nature*, 7 August, 454.

17. ICH (1997), *Revised ICH Terms of Reference*, International Conference on Harmonization of Technical Requirements for Registration of Pharmaceuticals for Human Use, Geneva.

18. On occasion even technically advanced agencies in other parts of the world have criticized the propagation by ICH of so-called 'international' standards on which they have not been consulted and that have been developed in a manner lacking transparency and accountability. See report of an International Conference on National Medicinal Drug Policies, *Australian Prescriber* (1997), 20, 14.

19. This section reflects discussions at the US Pharmacopeia Annual Scientific Meeting, Kansas City, MO, September 2008.

20. DT (2008), 'Denmark aims for 1.5 percent GNP aid level', *Development Today*, 1 January.

21. K. Outterson (2006), 'Patent buy-outs for global disease innovations for low- and middle-income countries', *Am J Law Med*, 32.

22. TRIPS Agreement, Article 66.2, provides that 'Developed country Members shall provide incentives to enterprises and institutions in their territories for the purpose of promoting and encouraging technology transfer to least-developed country Members in order to enable them to create a sound and viable technological base.'

23. See proposed US-Colombia Trade Promotion Agreement, at Art. 16.12.

24. GAO (2006), 'US Government Accountability Office: new drug development. Science, business, regulatory and intellectual property issues', Cited as Hampering Drug Development Efforts, GAO-07-49, November.

25. Claudia Ines Chamas (2005), *Developing Innovative Capacity in Brazil to Meet Health Needs*, MHIR Report to CIPIH, April 2005; WHO Ref. CIPIH study, 10d (DGR).

26. R. Nader and J. Love (1993), 'Looting the medicine chest: how Bristol-Myers Squibb made off with the public's cancer research', *The Progressive*, February (accessed website March 2008).

27. T. Neal (2008), '*Pharmaceutical Lobby Spent Big in 2008*', MedPage Today (website, accessed 4 July 2008).

28. WB (1993), *World Development Report 1993: Investing in Health*, The World Bank, Washington, DC.

29. M. Suhrcke, M. McKee and R.S. Arce (2005), *The Contribution of Health to the Economy in the European Union*, Directorate-General for Health and Consumer Protection, European Union, Brussels.

30. M.D. Vickers (1995), 'Monographs in the Drug and Therapeutics Bulletin', *BMJ*, 310, 663.

31. M. Brettingham (2006), 'Department of Health ends contract with drugs bulletin', *BMJ*, **332**, 1109.

32. A. Huxley (1932), *Brave New World*, Harper Collins, London.

33. 30.9 million prescriptions were issued in that year under the National Health Service; the number issued in private practice is not known. The population of the United Kingdom in 1979 was 56.2 million.

34. C. Medawar (1992), *Power and Dependence*, Social Audit, London, 1992, p. 85.

35. HOC (2005), *House of Commons: Select Committee on Health (Fourth Report): Summary*, London, April.

Index